LA JOLLA
AJIJIC
SANTA BARBARA
LA JOLLA
VENICE
ROME
MUNICH
PARIS
VILLARS
ATHENS
ANKARA
CYPRUS
ISRAEL
CAIRO
SUDAN
PAKISTAN
INDIA
BURMA
LAOS
CAMBODIA
VIETNAM

Enamored
with Place

As Woman + As Architect

Enamored with Place

As Woman + As Architect

Wendy Bertrand

eyeonplace press
SAN FRANCISCO

M ost of us grow, with our struggles and (hopefully) triumphs. Wendy Bertrand tells us how she grew to be firm, outspoken, hard-hitting, and confident. Her story is most certainly a woman's tale, but it will touch all readers. It will invigorate anyone who seeks to remedy the ills and imperfections of our society, our environment, and our professions.

I admire the skill with which Wendy invites us into her heart, her mind, and her senses. We learn about the care with which she as an architect has approached every job. We learn how she develops the will and ability to tackle the difficult aspects of life. We enjoy, with her, the various successes she has achieved.

Enamored with Place deserves more than reading; it deserves emulating, both in the efforts that women undertake and in the examples they provide for one another. Let us hope, too, that it enlightens the actions and views of men who work with women in all professions.

Ellen Perry Berkeley, architectural writer;
volume editor of *Architecture: A Place for Women*;
formerly a senior editor of the *Architectural Forum*

To my daughter and all daughters

First Edition 2012

Designed by Irene Rietschel, Studio Italics
Printed by Arizona Lithographers, with vegetable-based inks on FSC-certified
paper, using 100% wind power energy
Manufactured in the United States of America

Library of Congress Control Number: 2011944996
ISBN: 978-0-9837834-6-6

eyeonplace press, San Francisco, California
www.wendybertrand.com

Facing the title page: With École des Beaux-Arts classmates, 1965

Table of Contents

Preface

It should be no surprise that this hands-on historical and critical perspective of the architectural profession emerges from San Francisco, an architecturally vibrant city that for years has been a place of choice for architects to work and live. Yet, in spite of our shared profession, as individuals we experience our common work culture and historical period with significant differences. As a woman who graduated from architecture school in 1971, a time when it was rare to even hear of a practicing female architect in most of the United States, I detail some of my experiences, values, and concerns—both then and now.

Enamored with Place introduces readers to some of the inside processes of becoming and being an architect during my lifelong feminine journey, and I hope that by the end of this book you will look at spaces, buildings, and places with a concerned and critical eye.

When I was a university student as well as a mother, I became aware of how my personal life and my school life had to mesh daily, and that awareness held as I worked and experienced the enormous expectations for women to manage work so publicly, and to manage family and social conditions so privately. Professional men appeared to dismiss this social duality that remains a top priority for workingwomen. You will read here about both the personal and the professional threads of my life twisting, tangling, and wrapping around each other—as woman + as architect.

Concern for the social components impacting women in the workplace, in the home, and in most of the spaces and places being built has been underrepresented—I might even go so far as to say almost avoided—for decades. Perhaps witnessing my trials, errors, and joys in the role of architect will provide you with a wider screen and a broader outlook on your own work adventures, and motivate you to find lots of little (and big) ways of discussing, incorporating, and encouraging more attention to the profound and complex cultural values dwelling in the physical places you observe, use, arrange, own, design, or build.

WSB
San Francisco

Introduction

Here, sipping a glass of hibiscus tea in the petite Victorian cottage I remodeled 25 years ago, I pause and look up, immersed in my unfettered desire to translate my memories, thoughts, and intentions into words. Handmade curtains decorate the double-hung windows above my desk. Beyond the thin window glass, caterpillar-shaped cones cling to birch limbs, and an urban tapestry of San Francisco rooftops and back porches scrolls down to the bay. This is my tenth writing season. I frame my ideas about being an architect to build these pages during the morning hours, word by word, from the brief days of November until the Mirabelle plum's spring leafing.

At the beginning of this book project, my main objective was to record my professional experiences in the field of architecture. I wanted more of women's history to be known—only one biography in ten is of a woman's life, and less than 4 percent of architects were female when I finished my graduate architectural studies in 1972. Mary Catherine Bateson's book *Composing a Life* (Plume, 1990) helped me to recognize an inner urge to make the invisible more visible, to provide myself as one more mirror of woman—one more female architect in our social history.

I still plan to send my archive to the International Archive of Women Architects, housed at the Virginia Polytechnic Institute and

State University, in Blacksburg, Virginia, so that my experience will be documented alongside those of other women architects. Being part of a women-focused collection is important for visibility—if the accounts of women architects are only sprinkled here and there, much in the way we have worked, our stories could get lost in history. My hope is that a sizable collection will encourage scholars to dissect the evidence, discover details in our experiences, and acknowledge our values—not just our buildings.

But I also wanted to share my love of architecture and place with those less familiar with the profession. After several drafts and a critical review, I realized that the whole quilt of my life—or as Bateson would say, the "artistic rendering of my life composition"—would provide the decorative textures, colors, and style of my particular cloth. Thus, I have written these memoirs as if creating a quilt, sewing together square patches from different bolts of my life fabric—my architectural projects, professional promotions, and organizational dramas. Often, I have hand-stitched the emotional drape into my feminist folds. Some of the real names of people have been changed. Personal relationships (especially with my daughter and lovers) border management decisions, and social ideas about architecture. Patterns of private challenge and professional development line up next to lessons learned about place, gathered from my world travels and the towns I have lived in. Here and there, I contrast the glossy freedom of practicing architecture on my own homes with the hidden fears of the cultural limits attached to being female in the work world.

Architecture has traditionally been recorded as the culmination of monumental structures and their heroic creators; yet, as we are also many *everyday architects*, I think it's important also to write about the everyday career trek tangled with daily events—the way it is, especially for workingwomen. In these pages, I highlight my zeal for beauty and my belief that the conception of buildings must include appropriateness, fairness, and integrity, all of which have keenly influenced—sometimes blissfully and other times under hail—my journey as an architect.

Not so long ago, I sat in awe of author Alice Walker, who was being interviewed in a San Francisco lecture series titled "Extraordinary Women." She made an impressive pitch for each woman to know herself, to wonder. "I even wonder about these chandeliers," Walker said, and we all looked up at the silly drops of glass tied together into giant bouquets of light. Her call *to wonder* opens my winter writing season with the dramatic swish of velvet. I have approached the telling of my professional trek from 1959 to 2011 with the elevated senses of a story-teller, to embolden the reader's perception of what she might translate into her own world of work, and to arouse sharpness in her views of the everyday built environment we all depend on for so much.

My professional destination was never to design multi-million-dollar mansions, but rather to ensure the integrity and value of our public trust: government buildings. Although I did design many buildings, I primarily influenced the look, shape, and program of buildings by administrating projects and managing other architects in my role as the public's representative and steward of federal facilities.

Studying the character, traits, and attributes of structures is one of the most fascinating aspects of being an architect. Buildings can be as wacky, dull, innovative, complicated, or practical as people. Clare Cooper Marcus, professor emeritus in the Department of Architecture and Landscape Architecture at the University of California, Berkeley and author of *The House As a Mirror of Self* (Conari Press, 1997), can match up people with their homes without speaking to the residents; she proved this on *The Oprah Winfrey Show* by matching three houses with three couples. I can't do that, but I often *wonder* why some people choose the house they inhabit.

I am just back from France, and as I sit at my writing desk, my mind's eye lingers on images of my niece's odd-shaped house in the town of Nîmes. We had not been face to face since she was a child, when I lived in France with my then-husband, who is a Frenchman. My niece, a former world judo champion, seemed fascinated by the fact that I'd had a successful career as an architect. I *wonder* about the choices she and I have made in our lives: choices that got us to where we are today, choices chiseled by our core concerns, made within the changing landscape of our cultures.

I have been extremely fortunate. Looking back, I've come to realize just how much my essence as a person and a woman has found expression in the art and practice of architecture. My passion for place made the challenging process of obtaining the title *architect* both meaningful and pleasurable; I loved every day in architecture school and most days at my job.

"I need to retrain," my niece told me. Her open reflection prompted my analytical mind to evaluate her situation—clearly, she felt herself to be at a major crossroads in life. But while she focused on her need for a more satisfying job, I zeroed in on the heaviness of her awkward house. This strong, intense, and handsome 47-year-old woman hadn't made space for herself, not even her own desk, yet she had made with her own hands the unfortunate alterations that hindered her efficiency, like not leaving enough space on each side of the sink to pile dishes. The misfit between the house's personality and her family's needs troubled me. My niece sat on a short stool next to her three small children and her mother, eating breakfast at a low table in her contorted and contrived, cluttered kitchen. "If I had it to do over," she said, "I would have studied architecture. I think it is a wonderful career." After spending a weekend together, I concluded that my niece liked the actual putting together of the pieces of her house; however, the planning and practicality of the design phase was incomplete. I couldn't bring myself to tell her the reasons why her house was actually hindering her activities when it should have been a nest that supports life—there was just too much going on at the time and she didn't exactly ask me. Even if she had asked, I wouldn't have been ready to define all the problems. Not one was easily remedied. For instance, most of the windows were also unnecessarily tall glass doors that were constantly opening and closing, so that no one could ever sit near daylight to read, work, play, or eat. This troubled me, because I want the built world to be all it can be.

The word *Victorian* usually conjures up images of grand spaces and royalty; but some of the homes built in the 1870s—like mine—consisted of only four small but tall rooms and were called *worker's Victorians*. I bought my Noe Valley lot-and-a-half in 1975; over the course of ten years, I slowly converted the cottage into a duplex. As I write, Tada Kogiso, my long-time friend and carpenter, stands outside on a 24-foot ladder, his graying, frizzy hair spilling out of a rubber band, his keen eyes narrowed as he concentrates on the tapping of his chisel. Tada is repairing the "L"-shaped custom-made window I designed and he installed to catch the downtown vista 25 years ago. I adore working with Tada because he hangs my drawings on the wall, studies them, and asks questions that show he understands my intent. He is the artisan and I am the architect. No matter how complicated or untraditional, my designs continue to evolve during construction, as I see opportunities or he suggests improvements. It takes time, but it is so rewarding to work closely with the builder, unlike my experience as a government architect, where designs went to the lowest bidder and were managed by another division. Today, I have earned more value from the investment in my Victorian duplex than from my regular salary of 21 years working as an architect for the federal government.

As well as being an excellent carpenter, Tada is also keenly interested in people; he listens well and builds relationships by following the anecdotes of his clients' lives. For several summers during the '90s, Tada brought his tent to my property in the country, eight hours north of San Francisco. I'd fallen in love with the forest settlement of Gasquet near the Smith River in Del Norte County, and Tada came to work on the cabin I bought with my then-boyfriend, Greg. We cantilevered a kitchen nook to catch the sun, added a large covered porch to transition to the orchard, raised the roof to add more daylight space to the bedroom, and shoehorned a tiny sleeping area for guests off the already solid staircase. I appreciated the way Greg respected my role as architect, but that didn't mean I blindly dictated my ideas; his practical suggestions filtered into the layers of my design concerns.

The word *architect* doesn't always bring up positive connotations, as the client-architect relationship can and does sometimes go haywire. But I've found it interesting that many people over the years have expressed a fond desire to be part of a profession whose workings they know so little about. My niece isn't the only one. One of my female high school classmates, who had listed "architecture" as a career goal in our senior high school annual of 1959, told me a few years ago, "A counselor at Stanford discouraged me." After she read an early draft of this book, a young editor wrote, "I almost majored in architecture, until I found out how hard it was!" Last fall, a glib French gentleman at a dinner party shared his regret at not becoming an architect. "Oh, to build great buildings," he said, swinging his left arm grandly in a swift gesture between bites.

Aesthetics are rooted in my ancestry. My clear-witted boundless mother collected inexpensive ethnic folk art. No surface of her vintage cottage was without a handmade basket, a clever instrument, a pair of Peruvian multicolored knit socks, a tin Mexican mask, or a darling miniature box from Thailand. Her Finnish-born mother was an exhibiting painter. My father, who separated from my mother when I was two, painted scenes of marshland habitat and won the Maryland Duck Stamp Award in 1982, seven years before his death.

As a girl, I created my own clothes. In college, I cut and folded paper into lamps. Envisioning, planning, designing, finding the materials, following the rules, and constructing things have always come naturally. However, my discovery of architecture as a career did not come easily, nor did the shift from working with the pliant structures of yarns, fabrics, and papers to working within the structures of a profession that created functional works of art from timber, concrete, and steel.

When I walk with my birder friend in the National Forest, he distinguishes birdsongs and notices hidden (to me) wildfowl, while I look at the structure of flower petals, the shape of fern leaves, the texture and shades of tree bark. Another friend remembers the names of his elementary schoolteachers, while I remember the classroom layout. When I return to San Francisco, my nose savors the bakery smells, while my eyes are aroused by the changes to the *buildingscape*—how new fences, gates, and trellises have appeared in my neighborhood, and how occupants use their porches, driveways, and yards.

Research on the brain shows that the link between the left and right sides of the brain is larger in women than in men, which allows women to multitask more easily than men. This is just one of the many reasons I believe that women are especially suited to architecture, which is multidimensional—not linear. For example, when you design a window, you must balance the need for day lighting; energy conservation; views; costs; window type and material, how it will open, how it will lock, and how to get to the glass on the outside for cleaning it—all at once and in no particular order.

At the end of this winter writing season, I will drive my black 1972 Citroën north to my country cabin, where I have resided during summer seasons since leaving my government position. When the once-abandoned Gasquet cabin had been renovated and revived, my field of vision expanded to include local environmental land use issues, community concerns, and visual impact questions. In parallel, I knitted, spun yarn, and wove woolen rugs. I published the *Rug Retrospective: Eight Weaving Seasons 1999–2007*, a coffee-table book depicting photos of the 23 rugs I use and exhibited in the summer of 2008 in Bandon Oregon.

The book in your hand is not a how-to book (although I do reflect on the direction of architecture and women's future role in making place in the epilogue), nor a coffee-table book of fantastic built art objects. Rather, it is a memoir from the life of an everyday short-skirted architect interested in social issues. I share my working adventures and concerns to encourage you to slip into low high heels and experience the less tangible circumstances of making architecture and the places we depend on.

For most of my watch, I have been intensely concerned with the quality of work environments and buildings—both are gnawingly undervalued, like the air we breathe and the water we drink. Yet, we can't live without place, air, or water. My hope is that you, my reader, will enjoy reading about the human-made world as seen through the eyes of one architect, enamored with molding it.

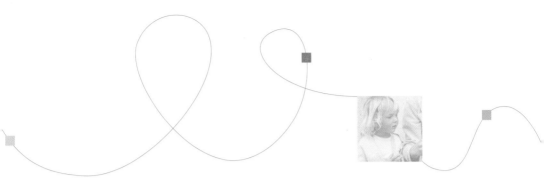

Double Lot

Childhood to 1959: La Jolla and Mexico

Where we sleep is often of special interest to children, family members, and tax collectors. The first time I lived in France, I was surprised to find that whenever I met anyone new, one of the top three questions they'd ask was about my sleeping arrangements—*where was the bed and was anyone else in it?* Today I realize that where and how I have slept over the years has been a shaping reference to my character; it was the turtle's shell to memories of my happy childhood and, later on, the girding of my adult life. Maybe, because I lacked the structure of a traditional nuclear family, I attached my existence in the world to the physicality of built spaces—to the double lot where I grew up; the leafy shelter of my mother's garden; the main house, little house, attic, alley, and garage—rather than to any particular branch of my family tree.

The only time I saw my mother under the covers with a man was during a family trip to Mexico, where she knew an Englishman named Bushy who was flying around the world in a hot air balloon. Every summer, Mother would give notice at her engineering job so she could take my younger sister and me on a trip during school break. Mother liked the less touristy parts of central Mexico; so she jumped at the chance when she discovered (in one of the many magazines she subscribed to) an opportunity to work in the colony of English-speakers living in the lakeside village of Ajijic. I believe it was the group's desire to open an English library and teach the Mexicans English that caught my mother's attention. She always enjoyed dabbling in other languages and loved to volunteer in teaching programs for foreigners.

The drive to Ajijic, only 30 miles from Guadalajara, seemed to take all day, the rickety bus stopping at every village on the way. Those summer adventures—whether we traveled away from home or remained in La Jolla to enjoy the lush privacy of my mother's gardens—are interwoven with my recollection of the secure, if somewhat unconventional, rhythm of life she provided us.

Attractive and brainy, my mother was raised in the suburban farming community of Brewster, which was on a train line north from New York City. She married my father soon after she graduated from Cornell University, when she was only 20, and discovered the Pacific Coast beach town of La Jolla during the time he was stationed in the San Diego area. A naval officer since 1943, my father was usually away at sea, leaving my mother, my younger sister, and me in a ground floor apartment with the letter "I" on the door at La Jolla's Beach and Tennis Club. My sister, Susan, and I slept on cots in the alcove between the bedroom and combined living room/dining room/kitchen. Since our unit was small and somber, we spent most of our time outdoors.

I was a naturally gregarious and friendly child. My mother, on the other hand, carefully limited her social gatherings. Even so, Mother was never one to limit her children—by age four I could step out the door any time of day and go around the corner to the central garden off the tennis courts. There, among the lounge chairs and palm trees, I could always socialize with an interesting assortment of neighbors and strangers.

Me, *left*, with my mother and sister

Mother once told me she chose to settle in San Diego County because she valued the beauty of the West Coast, the practicality of being able to walk everywhere, the snowless climate, and the long distance from her parents. As soon as she and my father divorced, Mother looked in the paper for small houses within blocks of our elementary school. In 1947, she borrowed the down payment for the property from her friend Wheeler, who lived near the Beach and Tennis Club in a spacious adobe-style house with large Persian rugs. Wheeler was never around much, but I remember Mother telling me that his boxer dog had saved his life by leading the neighbors to him when he became trapped in a collapsed cave on the beach below his house. Since a military couple was still renting our new house when Mother bought it, we had to wait almost a year until the couple was transferred before we could move in. Mother was 28, I was 6, and my sister was 4.

The summer of 1947, after visiting my newly widowed grandmother in the New York countryside, we moved into the vintage 1918 cottage my mother lived in until her death in 2010. The simple wooden, brown-shingled home sits near a corner of Herschel Avenue, bordering residential blocks in central La Jolla, and across the street from commercial properties including the Mercedes dealership and garage. Mother slept alone in the living room, the largest room of our colorful snuggery. The hardcover books from her mail-order Great Books reading club filled floor-to-ceiling shelves on either side of her double bed— always made, before we girls got up, with a zucchini-green bedspread and bolsters to lean against when we listened to the radio. The bolsters were home upholstered, crafted on the Viking sewing machine I later learned to sew on. Mother was a competent seamstress; when she and my father first separated, she made and sold slipcovers to bring in a little extra cash.

Susan slept in the lower bunk, but neither one of us spent much time in our thimble of a room, darkened by the shade of a flowering jacaranda tree. Most indoor activities occurred within the deep green, red, and mushroom-gray hues of our lively living room. Mother read from her mounds of magazines, while my sister ironed and I laid out my sewing pattern pieces on the carpet-less crimson floor, kept shiny by my mother's biannual repainting. On special winter nights, the three of us sat facing a wood fire, spooning sticky tapioca pudding from hand-painted Mexican bowls as we listened to holiday records.

My mother's interest in folk art was humanistic rather than historical. A tin mask with punctured holes for eyes decorated the corner near her bed, stamps and paper-clips were stored on her desk in delicate boxes covered with Japanese silk-screened paper, and we drank from her favorite hand-blown rippling blue glasses (also made in Mexico) until they broke. Her passion for clever, useful, and simple handmade objects brought my mother to her lifelong love affair with folk art. I often heard her praise these objects with the fondness of an elder musician raving about primitive foreign instruments. Family museum visits were always to folk art exhibits, and she instilled in us a respect for the art as daily culture. During my adulthood, Mother's collectibles grew to include a mirror-dotted camel's saddle she tried to give me and the knee-high Peruvian hand-knit socks she hung near the stairs to her sewing nook, where dozens of rustic baskets were herded into a corner. All were bargains from her thrift-shopping safaris and subsequent adventures to locations around the globe where local cultures still made most of their wares by hand.

While I was growing up in La Jolla, the neighborhood around us transitioned from individual cottages and cottage complexes to larger two-story apartment buildings and commercial businesses. A few years after we moved to Herschel Avenue (Herschel being the last name of the great British brother-and-sister astronomers, 1750–1848), Mother saw the opportunity to have one of the cottages that was scheduled for demolition moved to our property. I watched with great interest as the tiny one-room house glided down the alley to the back of our double lot on a flatbed truck. We called it the Little House, and it became the home away from home for my grandmother Lydia when she came to visit us and get away from East Coast blizzards. On weekends, Lydia helped my mother garden, and during the week, she took pottery classes from the nearby art store. Before moving to the country, Lydia had been a salesperson in a large department store, and she'd retained a certain fashionable flair in her dress and style.

Lydia Rahlson, my mother's mother

My sister and I flocked to the kitchen when our grandmother prepared dinner or baked. She did not tell us any family stories, a trait my mother seemed to have inherited. Instead, my grandmother entertained us by preparing paper-thin oatmeal cookies or Finnish coffee bread (*pulla*). Her husband, Kurt, a dark-haired German immigrant 14 years her senior, had been a successful business manager in New York City. Although I can't remember what he was like, I am told my grandfather adored the performing arts and was a serious fan of opera—even writing reviews about what he had seen. Lydia preferred the visual arts; her haven was the Metropolitan Museum of Art.

Sadly, during the financial crash of 1929, my grandparents had to give up their city house and move to their country house in Brewster. After her husband's early death, Lydia never moved or remarried. Her exhibits of abstract and still life paintings, depicting her garden's seasonal cornucopias of rosy melons and contorted rough-skinned squashes, were considered local news and reported in the Brewster newspaper. Maggie, my classy outspoken aunt, who was older and taller than my mother, stayed on the East Coast and only visited California once. She wrote rarely and had two husbands, a succession of Siamese cats, and no children.

Jeannie became my pal early in life, as her naptime cot at our childcare center neighbored mine. In a town of upper-middle-class families and old money, Jeannie and I had the rare distinction of being the daughters of slightly unconventional, working single mothers. Jeannie's mother rode a red scooter to her job as telephone company receptionist, and my mother rode her bike to do her Saturday errands. Weekdays, Mother took an early city bus to her job in downtown San Diego, where she designed the curvature of commercial airplane wings. Mother liked the technical, unemotional, problem-solving aspect of engineering. She was not actually trained as an engineer—her undergraduate major at Cornell was philosophy—but a friend got her the job as an engineering aide. She loved the technical edge of reason and did so well that they kept her on, and she advanced to calculating the curve of airplane wings.

In elementary school, Jeannie and I danced together in ballet class and performed onstage as smiling poinsettias or toy jack-in-the-boxes. As we got older, she liked to stop by for a snack on her way home from Catholic middle school a few blocks from my house, claiming she didn't get enough to eat at home, now that her mother had married a mean man. When it was sunny, we carried our peach milkshakes out to the garden chairs to sunbathe and gossip. Jeannie seemed superficially cheerful and a little reckless, but in those days she didn't tell me much about what was on her mind. Mostly, she talked about the boys at the Wind and Sea Beach, where she hung out with the surfers.

Looking back, I realize that my family's extended summer visit to Mexico initiated an unfolding of my worldview. I was only nine years old when we lived in Ajijic, but even then, the town layout made an impression on me. There, I stepped from our front door directly onto the sidewalk, while in La Jolla I had to cross our humble front lawn. Houses in La Jolla were dotted on rectangles of land with random patches of vegetation. In Ajijic, houses were hidden behind adult-height whitewashed walls topped with sharp broken glass to discourage intruders from climbing over; every so often, a dark pink splash of flowering bougainvillea or branches from a tree I'd never seen before would soften the walls' flat glare. Sidewalks bordered the continuous walls next to dirt roads that all seemed to lead to a paved, open parklike setting called La Plaza. This small town's public square was traditionally designed with benches, streetlamps, plants, and a bandstand pavilion at one end. Modest storefronts opened onto the Plaza.

Mother worked at La Posada, a restaurant in a walled compound on the shore of Lake Chapala, only a few blocks from our rented casa. I often swam in Lake Chapala, Mexico's largest lake, while my sister—who was less interested in swimming—talked the neighbor into letting her ride his donkey up and down the beach. When I wasn't cooling myself in the lake's vast waters, I liked to climb high into one of the mango trees at La Posada—not to read on a tree branch, as my mother said she had done as a child, but to pick mangos I then gave away to tourists and other children.

Pipsqueak and Juanita, our two Mexican dogs, loved to play and slide on the smooth ceramic tile walkway of our casa. This walkway served as a transition from the walled dirt courtyard—filled with five colors of oleander trees—to the outhouse, and to all the rooms of the house, including the one Susan and I slept in. Every evening, after our tour around La Plaza to listen to the lively musical performance and to indulge in people-watching, Susan and I returned to our sparse bedroom for our bedtime routine. Before slipping between the sheets, we had to use a flashlight to check the unpainted mud walls and under the covers of our metal-framed beds for scorpions, since the only electric lightbulb in the house hung from the kitchen ceiling.

Our Mexican residency stretched into the fall months. Most of the time, Mother dressed us in shorts, ignoring the opinions of religious locals who did not consider this appropriate attire for girls. On school days, Susan and I wore the required blue jumper and white shirt uniform to the Mexican school we attended. That year, I sat at the back of my class in one of those chair/desktop all-in-one seats, sharpening my pencils with a double-sided razor blade. Unfortunately, the flood of Spanish stuck in my ears without trickling to my tongue; it felt like being in a play where I liked the stage set but didn't have a speaking part.

When we returned to La Jolla in January 1951, Mother's boss rehired her, as he did every year. Curly-headed Mr. Traylor, my first male teacher, taught my fifth-grade class. I liked him very much because when it was time for arithmetic, he'd come over to where I sat with the others—at the poor reading table—and move me to the advanced math table. When we ran races on the playground at recess, I discovered that I could run short distances better than most of the other boys and girls. On my first report card he noted, "Wendy has just been elected our class president, she shows remarkable leadership and fairness in her judgment." Even then, I intuitively appreciated Mr. Traylor for appointing me as team captain and for gently and specifically introducing me to the concept of personal weakness and strength.

Mother agreed to let me move from the bunk bed I shared with my sister to my own room in the attic. Moving upstairs became possible because Mother had stairs built on the back of the house; before then, the only access to the attic was through a hole in the hallway ceiling. It was well worth climbing the outside stairs to the narrow platform, where I had to pull open an accordion window/door and stoop down in order to step up into my neat tree-house-like nest. At nine-and-a-half, I could stand up straight under the roof peak, but there was barely room for me to sit up reading in bed without my hair catching on the roof's rough rafters where the slope lowered. Dinnertime found me up in my room, sitting at my drop-leaf desk finishing up my long-division problems, the aroma of fried eggplant, baked brownies, or tuna-rice casserole drifting into my nostrils from the space in the attic left open above the stove.

In winter months, when Mother unpacked our woolens, the odor of mothballs seeped out from the storage area behind my sleeping space. A few years later, when I could no longer comfortably stand in the attic, I asked to have my bed moved to our detached garage, and once

I help my mother frame the windows so I may sleep in the garage

windows were added, we carried my bed down to my new room.

We always called it *the garage*. Mother got permission from the city to close it in, and together we framed in windows and a door to replace the garage door. The one-car converted structure was stationed next to the house on the lot much the way a drinking glass is positioned next to a dinner plate on a placemat—at the back edge and to the right. Walking outside to get to my room was again part of the fun that came with having my own private space, while my sister remained in the only bedroom of our house. When I got home from school, I'd enter my bedroom from the front garden; if Mother needed to fetch a screwdriver or pair of pliers, she'd use the garage's back door. There was nothing separating my mother's toolbench and home repair supplies from my sleeping space. One time, a glass jug of turpentine exploded on a high shelf and splashed on me. I awoke, shocked by the bang and stupefying stench, but I wasn't cut. Immediately, I went to the main house and told my mother what had happened. Her tensed eyes and reddened cheeks expressed her concern, but no word consoled me. Emotions rarely emerged as language. Instead, she came out to the garage, swept up the mess, opened the windows to rid the room of the reeking turpentine, and moved my bed away from the chaos.

If the winter wind whistled, I could hear my mother's bamboo poles rattling and rustling in the garden. Mother worked tirelessly to groom her prized bamboo into a visual wall between the main house and the Little House; the bamboo wall formed an impressive tropical backdrop for the white flowering oleander, wild rose vines, arbor-spilling false grape tendrils, and rust-colored chrysanthemums circling the back lawn. When it was my turn to rake up the bamboo husks, I often ended up with sharp, painful splinters in my palms. Although I enjoyed being outside, gardening was a chore I did only for my weekly allowance.

Made-in-Japan bamboo curtains, cut by my mother in café style, covered the bottom half of my bedroom window. No doubt bought for a bargain at the thrift store near her bus stop, my bamboo curtains provided semi-privacy from the street, and because the garage walls were so thin, they wavered sympathetically with their natural *unmanufactured* cousins in the windy garden outside. Yet, I was never afraid of man or nature in my detached bedroom—unlike the fear I experienced sleeping in my grandmother's barn, where horrendous lightning and thunder blasts kept me up all night. (And yet, those visits to my grandmother in the country were my first introduction to the possibility and pleasure of rural living; from her I learned about the advantages of changing houses with the seasons. Lydia lived in a remodeled red cow barn during the summer. During the rest of the year, because the barn was too cold, she lived in her white classically New England Colonial house across the road.)

Mother also used part of the garage to store her *New Yorker* magazine collection and mucho other stuff she was saving. I wanted to hide all that and to have a place to hang my clothes. She agreed with my idea to cover her well-labeled storage bins with five narrow closet doors. When I told her I wanted to paint the doors bright colors (the natural unfinished wall surfaces were rough and dark), she let me ride my bike to Meanly's Hardware to select the paint colors myself. I thought purple and pink a fabulous combination during that year, and my preteen room reflected my unusual taste in décor.

The three doors to our main house were always unlocked. I was perfectly comfortable walking from my room through the garden to the main house. I found the mild climate, familiar ground, and flat distance made the change from outside spaces to inside spaces feel natural, as if our whole property were the living unit, not just the house. At night, if less than half the moon smiled, I pressed my flashlight button; otherwise, I knew the route by heart, and the suburban wildlife—raccoons, moles, and skunks—instinctively avoided my path.

We probably spent more time in the back garden—set between the garage, main house, and Little House—than anywhere else on our double lot. (Actually, it was years later that I recognized we did, indeed, live on a double lot, in surveyor's terms—two city parcels. It never felt like two narrow lots, probably because other lots on the block varied so much that lot size didn't appear standard.) In spring and summer, my sister or a girlfriend and I often pitched a tent to sleep out on the back lawn, and we always hung our laundry to dry on the wooden racks back there. But mostly, the garden was our own very private, very green park, and our primary eating room. No matter what meal, if the sun was shining, my mother would insist we eat in the garden. We were glad to help her lift the outside table and walk it to wherever the sun had alighted. After serving our food in the kitchen, my sister and I would carry our meals through the living room, past the bathroom and bedroom, to the French glass double doors that opened into the garden. On weekends, even if only one sunray lit the concrete landing near the lawn, the three of us carried our plates of French toast or bowls of Wheatena outside for breakfast. I didn't mind making several trips back to the kitchen for forgotten salt, spoons, or sugar. We all savored the daylight, the greenness, and the company of the familiar plants Mother pampered with the zeal of a hummingbird mending her nest.

After Saturday chores, my sister and I liked to stretch out on Mother's bed and listen to the Top 30 popular songs or a mystery on the radio.

Mother with her rakes

When the program ended, Mother played her classical records loudly, not because she didn't hear well, but because she wanted to walk around the house doing things at the same time. Afternoons, she would be up in the Chinese elm tree fastidiously pruning away any branches that showed signs of caterpillars, moving the hose around on the front or back lawn, or repairing her collection of bamboo rakes.

My sister tended to engage in interests different than mine. Susan liked horseback riding, while I walked or rode my bike to the community tennis courts and chatted with other players sitting on the bench as I waited for my turn. Being the only girl on the courts didn't matter; the men, usually much older than I, included me in their doubles games and cheered me on as I earned my status as a regular.

Besides working full-time during the school year and gardening, Mother tried the guitar, flamenco dancing, and several boyfriends, but never remarried. She said she didn't want to have to make decisions with someone else. My mother's eccentrically independent, self-propelling character both singed and strengthened my sister and me. We were three independent peas in a pod, and that didn't cause conflict. Anger was rare; we lived in an amazing cocoon of harmony.

On occasion, Mother took us on the city bus to the zoo, ballet, or circus, but the rhythm of my childhood bounced between solitude and sociability. During the week, Mother had to leave the house before we were awake in order to get to work on time, so my narrow-waisted sister and I jumped out of our beds, made our own breakfast and bag lunches, and walked to school, several residential blocks away. I depended on school functions for social interactions, exposure to life, approval, and nourishment for my outgoing nature. In my teens, I walked a few blocks to the local ballroom dances or to the movie theater. Home seemed less social, as we were on our own, without supervision, until Mother stepped off the city bus from work just before dinnertime. Susan and I often had supper started by the time she got there. Some year-ends, Mother would invite friends over for an open house breakfast, but dinner parties were unknown; she kept up with her friends and family by typing letters and newsletters—a routine she told me started with her father when she left home. I was a contented child; there was structure to the day, security in my mother's reliability and cheerful mood, and a consistent atmosphere of order and liberty.

The German ladies who owned the yarn store near my ballet class taught me to knit when I was 16. Although I sometimes made errors—knitting a stitch backwards, forgetting the order of stitches, or using needles that were too big or too small—I persevered and completed my projects. My first hand-knit sweater fit snugly, but I wore the cabled cardigan for a few years.

In seventh grade, while the boys were taking woodshop, the girls learned "homemaking." Sewing produced the pleasure of accomplishment I needed in order to thrive, and I loved the feel of fabrics on the face of my fingers. At a recent Green Festival in San Francisco, Alice Walker said, "This would be a better world if you all created something artful with your hands. Get out your embroidery." Thread for thought!

My school grades were high enough to include me in the Girls Honor Club, where I served as president one year. When speaking, I could be persuasive and dramatic. My weaknesses were reading and writing. Luckily for me, English teachers gave two grades: one for content and one for grammar and spelling. Ironically, my best subject was physical education. Not because I played the games with great skill, but because my gym clothes were always clean, I followed the rules, and I loved the sportsmanship and socialization of team sports. Winning was not essential. Here, again, the teacher often assigned me as team captain, which I didn't mind or crave.

Living in a town full of millionaires didn't faze me. We didn't have a TV, dishwasher, washer, or dryer, but I didn't feel deprived or envious of my classmates. When Mother gave me permission to take my sweater sets to the cleaners instead of handwashing them, I felt I had reached the peak of luxury. In high school, I worked my way up from dishwasher, via salad maker, to waitress in the German restaurant three blocks from our house. Most of my girlfriends joined sororities, but I didn't take to their exclusiveness. Jeannie moved to Berkeley for high school; I visited her once and we exchanged short letters at the holidays, but for the most part, we temporarily lost touch.

Maybe my lifetime fondness for elegant odd cars came from spending my younger years sleeping in a garage. My appetite was triggered when a fellow high school cheerleader asked me if I wanted to buy his 1931 Model A Ford. I did. The car intrigued me, more as a designed object than as transportation. The wheels had spokes like a bike's. Two spare tires were standard equipment; one rode in the driver's side fender well, the other on the fanny of the car. The horn's "Ah-ugga" sound had sex appeal and the body was classy, but I didn't know much about taking care of a car. Our family had never owned one, perhaps because men were missing at home—no father, brother, uncle, or grandfather came to see us. Since the garage was my bed's domain, the Ford lived at the curb in front of our house, parked among the newer Fords in need of repair that the Ford dealership (later to become a Mercedes dealer) kept on our side of Herschel Avenue.

With my Ford in front of the house on Herschel Avenue

One foggy morning, my favorite mechanic noticed me leaning down to see why my car wouldn't start. "What are you looking for?" he asked in his warm Latin voice.

"I'm going to be late to school," I said, glad he'd arrived to work early.

"Don't worry," Francesco smiled. "This won't take long. Where's the crank?"

Once I found and handed him the crank I'd never even thought of using, he cranked the car calmly and I made it on time to school. Over the next few months, Francesco gladly showed me the basic ins and outs of car maintenance, and I caught on quickly. I so thoroughly enjoyed the minor tinkering with my car, as well as meeting other car enthusiasts, that I joined the San Diego Model A Club.

When my sedan's radiator ruptured, the car club fellows encouraged me to fix it myself, so I had the car towed back to Herschel Avenue. The new radiator and a pair of men's overalls arrived promptly from Sears. Excited, I confidently shopped at the local auto supply store for wrenches—open-ended, box, and socket sets—repair manuals, tiny lightbulbs, windshield-wiper blades, and motor oil.

Before pulling out the radiator, I sat on the curb, contemplating the instructional diagram to remind myself of how easy the surgery looked. Toeing each leg into my new white overalls, I pulled the zipper from crotch to neck and slipped on my greasy gloves. Mother wasn't far away,

I am changing the Ford's radiator

crouched down with her dull screwdriver in front of the house, wedging up crabgrass as she preened her precious dichondra. Later in life, she admitted she liked the idea of my taking control of the car; she called my period of Ford ownership "pivotal," claiming it was the first non-social activity to hold my attention. I think she was secretly happy to see me able to work for hours alone, focused on the mechanical steps required to fix my cherished car. The logistics looked straightforward: I disconnected some hoses, drained the water, unbolted the leaky radiator, bolted in the new, reconnected the hoses, added water, and started the car. When no leaks spouted, my heart flooded with the pleasure of fixing something technical. The concreteness of car repair fanned my fancy. There was no gray area to fumble around in; it worked or it didn't—like electricity or algebra.

Mother was always too busy and active for dialogue, partly because of her temperament and partly because being a working single mother is darn demanding. Sitting to eat was okay, but sitting and only talking was an unspoken waste of time. One afternoon, on return from an elementary school playmate's house, I announced, "Wow, their house is so different! Their living room is pie-shaped and you enter from the kitchen. Jana showed me how the piano area could be closed off like a wall by a thick pink curtain. Her bedroom and the living room wrap around their garden…"

"Sure, her father is an *architect!*" my mother responded in a defensive tone. Maybe she felt I was being critical of our house or of her.

The word *architect* was not part of my vocabulary, and I was left with a word I didn't really understand. My mother moved toward the garden, deflecting any further discussion, so I let my thoughts move on to other things—like playing tennis—rather than seeking her out to drill her for the meaning of this new word, which settled with a good feeling into my unconscious. The word *architect* certainly wasn't used when Mother and I stopped at houses under construction to investigate and analyze the framing to see if we agreed on the location of the kitchen and placement of windows. Mother noticed what was going on around town but never threw out any ideas for what I might explore as a career.

Once, I asked my grandmother Lydia if she thought a future in fashion would suit me, since I liked making my own clothes and was named best-dressed girl of my class. She offered to contact a friend at Bloomingdale's, but I didn't follow up, both because I didn't feel I could draw well enough and because I thought becoming a buyer seemed too far-fetched. Besides, New York City was 3,000 miles away. A recent viewing of Yves Saint Laurent's life collection at the de Young Museum reminded me how much I love fashion and made me wonder what I would have brought to the *runway* if I had followed the fashion career track.

The carriage of a working life comes early and quickly to some. However, as my high school graduation approached, I felt embarrassingly uncharted; I was counting on college to set me on my development course.

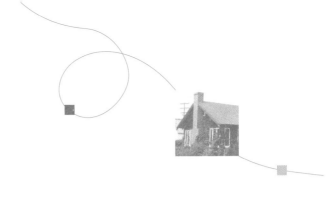

Leaving Home

August 1959: La Jolla

I was 18 and ready to leave my postage-stamp shelter, my security blanket, and the incubator of my childhood. A glance around the garage assured me there was nothing else I needed to pack for college besides my tight-fitting shoes, sweater sets, and handmade garments. Satisfied that I hadn't left out anything important, I unplugged my small radio, folded the alarm clock, and stuffed them into the cloth suitcases my father had sent money for when I requested some for my 13th birthday.

Mother had encouraged us to write to our father for special items. Other than that, his influence on my upbringing was imperceptible. I can remember visiting him only twice as a child, but if you saw us together, the resemblance would have been striking—we had the same broad forehead, wide-apart nut eyes, and generous freckles. I'm sure some of my artistic drive and determination, as well as my love of nature, came to me via his genes. He had another family in Pennsylvania, yet I never felt fatherliness, even when I was visiting. My tall father's life seemed so different from my mother's: he drank cocktails, smoked cigarettes, and lived in big houses with swimming pools on enough land to train his hunting retriever champions. His dogs dominated his days. Along with training, he dedicated much of his time to painting portraits of the spaniels and the wild lands they roamed. In 2002, when I broke decades of distance by visiting my half-brother in Martha's Vineyard, he told

My father, Arthur
Rutherford Eakin

me that in the months before he died my father felt sad about not spending more time with his girls. He did pay my mother child support for 21 years, but his affection didn't reach me.

Before leaving the bedroom of my youth, I set the suitcases down on the straw mat covering the concrete floor and leaned over to smooth the disturbance they'd left on my tailored linen bedspread. I'd sewn the bedspread the year before to dress up my room but decided at the last minute to leave it on the bed for my later visits home. That done, I threw back my shoulders the way my mother often reminded me to do, lifted my two bags, and proceeded out past the jacaranda tree, across the short grass to the sidewalk where my faithful Model A Ford sat waiting at the curb. Caroll, who was riding with me, arrived with her boyfriend just as I was tucking my baggage onto the Ford's backseat, next to my two tennis rackets and a bag of car tools. While my friend and her beau took too long kissing good-bye, I walked back to the main house.

"Mom, where are you?" I called. "Are you going to watch us leave?"

Smiling, she peeked out from her standing-room-only kitchenette, a teabag dangling from her fingers. A whiff of cardamom from reheated *pulla* mingled with my impatience.

"We don't have time for tea," I told her, wondering why in the world my mother was choosing to make tea at this moment. Because *it is time for tea,* I told myself, realizing it was not because she wanted to relate any last-minute intimate thoughts. Mother wasn't like that; I never expected heart-throbbing conversations or tears. "Caroll's waiting," I said, so my mother fetched her Brownie camera and followed me outside. Over the years, I have often felt that my mother's taking or asking for photos has been one of her indirect ways of trying to show affection without letting her emotions experience outward lovingness. Her photo-taking that leaving-home day punctuated our separation, acknowledged a rite of passage, and allowed us both to keep smiling.

Caroll and I were enthusiastic about leaving La Jolla together. We had tied paper signs announcing "University of California" to the front of the car and "Santa Barbara or Bust" on the rump.

"Have a grand adventure," Mother said as I stretched my arms around her for a good-bye hug. I kissed her cheek, tanned by hours of gardening, and stepped up onto the Ford's running board. "Thanks for making this possible," I said quickly, surprising myself; we didn't use expressions like *Thank you for caring, I'm sorry,* and *I love you.* I was, however, deeply appreciative and confident that she was pleased to see me on my way to college. In the past, she hadn't shown any signs of worry or sadness. In fact, I only saw her cry once in my life, and when I asked her why, she said it was because her boyfriend had said something that upset her. Writing this now, it occurs to me that perhaps my mother was stalling with her cup of tea so she could swallow her feelings.

The springs under the driver's seat squeaked as I settled down on the red sailcloth slipcovers I'd sewn for the bucket seats. I engaged the clutch, tightened my right hand over the black knob of the floor shift rod, and signaled with my left hand out the window (no blinkers existed then) as I nosed my Ford toward the edge of adulthood. The August morning sky was overcast, as usual.

Caroll and I casually cruised the first stretch of Highway 1 along the Pacific Coast, our short blond hair fluttering in the sea breeze. The passing scenery seemed to symbolize a curtain closing on one act of our lives.

A vague curiosity replaced certainty. After some silence, I said, "Do you know what classes you'll take?"

"The teacher's program is pretty cut and dried," Caroll answered, checking her lipstick in her compact mirror. She had known for some time that she wanted to be a teacher—in fact, our college campus had been a teachers' college before the University of California added Santa Barbara to its roster.

I, on the other hand, was still unsure as to what profession I would choose. What I did know was that I didn't want to be a teacher—or a secretary or a nurse. Since I also had no clue about how to choose a college, I'd merely followed Caroll, who had made her choice by following her sister.

"Photography and psychology, maybe sculpture … even geography sounds neat." My carefree mind never for a moment doubted that a workingwoman I would be; however, my mother's hands-off style of parenting had left me on my own to figure out exactly what kind of workingwoman.

Traffic thundered past us, people waving and honking from all sorts of vehicles. Even in 1959, a Model A seemed ancient. The encouragement helped us believe we could make the trip, but it also indicated a frequency of danger. I knew the distance would press the Ford far beyond any journey I'd attempted since purchasing the antique only a year before. But for all the risks, motoring into the future felt exhilarating, and our goal of attending college had been approved by both family and society.

Entering the concrete jungle of Long Beach, Caroll and I couldn't help but be amused at the sight of young waitresses zipping around on roller skates, serving hamburgers to noisy patrons in their cars. The dingy drive-in restaurants were plentiful, scattered among smelly gas stations crowding the billboard-cluttered main drag.

"Ever been to a drive in-movie?" Caroll asked.

"Uh-huh. Last summer I drove two boys to see that Alfred Hitchcock movie, *Vertigo*, at the drive-in theater in Mission Beach."

"Your mother let you?"

"Sure, but on the way home, the Ford broke down and the police picked us up for hitchhiking." Caroll looked shocked as I told her the story. "The door handles in the back of the police car were missing and there was a dirty urinal in the corner of the jail cell. I'd never seen a urinal before, and figured the cell was only for boys, but the officer made me go in, too. I was locked in there behind bars, just like in the movies."

"Weren't you scared?"

"Oh no, I was too surprised to be afraid." The boys' parents didn't say anything when they came to pick up their precious sons, but I could see in their eyes they blamed me. Rightfully so, I guess. I was the driver.

"I bet your mother was mad, then."

"Nope. She just signed me out and then walked me the three blocks home."

"I would have preferred to have my boyfriend pick me up," Caroll said.

As Caroll rambled on about how happy she was with her boyfriend, I reflected on Curt, who had been my main boyfriend in high school. Curt combed his stallion-black hair in a mean wave but kept his demeanor easygoing. Instinctively, he avoided saying too much. Knotted-up emotions lingered under his pale skin when he was with me, but surfaced in the sketches he drew of his brother beating up any other boy who might show interest in me. Yet, he was never violent with me; he respected my preferences and never forced me to do anything. His watercolor harbor scenes won awards.

Curt usually drove me home after school in his sleek 1957 Ranchero truck and taught me to drive in his red TR3 sports car. His mother was a fashion model, and his father owned a large plumbing shop, where Curt worked after school.

Everyone took his/her shoes off before stepping onto the white wall-to-wall carpet in the nondescript magazine interior of Curt's parents' elegant house. I didn't go there often because Curt preferred to come and see me so he wouldn't be yelled at for making housework for his mother. My house was on a flat street in the center of town, while theirs was high enough on the hill to claim a higher status, but that didn't matter to Curt; we'd go out to football games, school dances, and even to Tijuana to see the bullfights. Lanky, handsome Curt would sometimes sneak into my bed in the garage, but since I refused to go all the way, he finally took up with a girl who would. When I found out, that was the end of wearing his school ring around my neck.

The Ford's speed suddenly sagged as the valiant car approached the long steep grade between Los Angeles and Ventura. Within seconds, a motorcycle policeman pulled up next to us—"Follow me." Caroll and I giggled nervously as we painfully realized the vulnerability of our situation. The motorcycle officer became an unlikely midwife for a slow spot on our journey to college. He accompanied us as the Ford labored up the hill until we reached the descent, and then we were on our own again toward the flat strawberry fields of Oxnard.

"These buildings really seem like they fit together," I said as we sailed down State Street, the main artery in the heart of Santa Barbara.

"What do you mean?"

"The planted courtyards, the roofs … the wrought iron ornamentation on the windows." I sighed fondly. "They remind me of Mexico." I had no way of knowing then that the town's Spanish-Mediterranean theme, with its red-tiled roofs, arched facades, central courtyards, and muted plaster exteriors, was the result of Pearl Chase's pioneering work in the fields of conservation, preservation, and civic planning. Later, investigating the works of women architects, I learned from the still very active Pearl Chase Society just how much she had influenced Santa Barbara. Although she wasn't an architect, she worked tirelessly all her adult life establishing civic organizations, using her position as chair of Santa Barbara County's Plans and Planting Committee, and applying her personal power of persuasion on civic leaders to save natural parks, preserve historic character, and build only attractive buildings. Even the gas stations matched the early California theme. In 1952, Pearl Chase was named Woman of the Year by the *Los Angeles Times* for keeping Santa Barbara to an architectural theme that is still recognizable today and that gives the city much of its integrity and appeal.

"You were in Mexico?" Caroll was impressed.

"Just for half a year ... I really do like it when the buildings look like they are in the same family." Although I couldn't have explained it at the time, I had instinctively identified the harmonious results of urban development synchronized by design guidelines—and perhaps by a womanly hand.

"Yeah, glad we will be close to this place," agreed Caroll.

"Instead of Long Beach's main street," I added. Even though I judged what I saw, I accepted the built world as a given.

Continuing a dozen miles or so into Goleta, we passed long stretches of orange groves accented with fieldworkers' modest houses, until we saw a stand of larger buildings rising up beyond the lagoon in Isla Vista. Fields of tall brown wild grasses, scored by a worn narrow path, gave the university campus a rural and restful feel, and I was happy to call it *my college.*

"We've arrived without busting!" I shouted, spinning the thin steering wheel as the Ford rolled onto UCSB's main road.

We easily found our way to the dorms, where we unloaded Caroll's bulging bags, the scent of eucalyptus alerting me to the nearby groves. The campus atmosphere felt friendly, and I wanted to explore, but my bones bowed from the day's drive. I doubled back to Santa Barbara, where I was to live my first semester in a boardinghouse for 12 girls on Prospect Street.

The two-story, shingled, flat-faced house was perched high above the street on a ledge, so one had to climb a long outside staircase to reach the front door. Plaid suitcases in hand, I began my ascent, my slow-motion steps lifting on the steep weathered staircase with the conviction of a sailor reaching shore. Wrought with the sweetness of being 18 and launched, I paused at the top landing, breathed to my center, and smiled down on a patchwork of red-tile roofs.

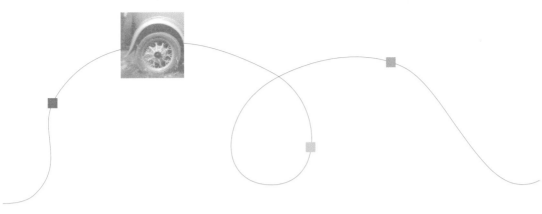

College Threshold

Scholastic Year 1959 to 1960: Santa Barbara

I was standing on a chair, measuring for curtains in my boardinghouse room, when Sandy knocked on the open glass door. My roommate's bed was neatly made, while mine was strewn with half-full suitcases, novelty red shoes, a Fannie Farmer cookbook, and a hardcover college dictionary. The disarray was temporary; I'd rearranged my bed to add a worktable, made with an old door I'd found in the backyard.

"I know a great fabric shop where you can find material for your curtains," Sandy said with a perky smile. Her parents had been coming to Santa Barbara every winter for years, so she knew her way around town better than any of us.

Although I had signed up too late to move into the dorms on campus, my name showed up on the list for spring semester, so my time in the boardinghouse would be short. Nevertheless, that didn't hinder my intent to become fully acquainted with my new four walls. Immediately, I took charge the way a hermit crab approaches her shell—not as somewhere to live forever, but as a shelter whose qualities I sought to understand and embellish during my stay.

"I was wondering if I could be your roommate," Sandy asked.

I recognized Sandy as the redheaded Canadian who'd said my Ford was a jazzy car. "I thought you moved in downstairs already," I said, scooting the chair over so I could measure the second window.

"Yes, but your roommate told me she doesn't mind switching with me."

That night Sandy and I sat elbow-to-elbow, as we would throughout the semester, looking out over Santa Barbara's cityscape while eating dinner with our ten boardinghouse sisters.

"I haven't ever had *fresh* green beans." I stared at the beans' brightness. "At home we had frozen or canned vegetables to save time."

"Fresh vegetables are better for you," said Sandy. The youngest and bossiest of three children, Sandy was in her second year of home economics at Santa Barbara's City College.

"Wow. This is the third homemade pie in a week." I breathed in the fragrance of cinnamon as I pressed my fork into a slice of squashy apple, remembering my first pie-making disaster—the beaten eggwhites looked more like icebergs on a sea of lemon pudding than a snowy peaked meringue blanket.

Sandy had no doubt about her future, which reassured me that I would find my way. Both of us had one Scottish grandparent, made each other laugh, and were fast becoming best friends. One time, Sandy locked me out the back door naked. No other houses looked down on the laundry room, isolated in the backyard full of eucalyptus trees, so I'd decided to add what I was wearing to the washer and run inside—but due to Sandy's quick thinking, I was instead caught *outside* on the plank that ramped to the laundry room like the gangway on a pirate ship. Pranks and jokes grew to be common fun at the boardinghouse, while my academic life remained seamless and blurred.

I enjoyed roaming the formal paths crisscrossing the spreading campus, random field trails, and groves between the older wooden structures and tan modern block buildings, all the while instinctively registering the areas of recent growth. Yet, I hadn't located the signposts, instruction booklets, or detailed maps to guide me toward the trailhead of my scholarly interests.

Besides being so much fun, Sandy had a thoughtful listening style that triggered a comfortable feeling I came to rely on. Soon I confided my disappointments. "I just found out I have to take Basic English and California History."

"What did you want to take?" Sandy tuned in to my concerns as she lounged on her bed, arms behind her head.

"I wanted to take photography, geography, and psychology. But, I didn't know what major to take, so I just checked the 'undecided' box." I gazed up at the stucco blankness of the ceiling.

I moved into a campus dormitory the following semester, but I'd lost track of my friend Caroll. My new roommate, Betty from Tarzana, rolled her hair in large curlers at night and ratted it with a comb in the mornings. She was only 16, had movie-star blue eyes, and even smoked cigarettes, though not in our room. The furniture in the dorm room was built-in, so personalizing it became impossible. Apparently, many students liked to study on their beds, but I preferred the long tables of the largest room of the campus library, with its high ceilings, focused students, and open floor plan. Even though I tried my best to study, my poor reading and writing skills skewed my ability to comprehend the subject matter of my homework and scuffed my motivation. I continued trudging along with my library routine until an English teacher suggested I attend a reading clinic. I wanted to read better, and went, but the clinic provided little satisfaction, and the downward sliding of my test grades continued.

Because of advancements in brain research, we now know that lesions on the brain from birth can hinder certain direct communication circuits. Apparently, lesions can interrupt the most direct word-sounds channel. This is called *dyslexia*, a condition that has long been misunderstood, as I recently learned when I discovered—by chance, on the new-books shelf at our local library—Dr. Sally E. Shaywitz's *Overcoming Dyslexia* (Knopf Publishing Group, 2005). Lesions do not affect one's intelligence but do impact people to different degrees; one in five people is thought to have some lesions or signs of dyslexia. So now I understand why my spelling has been (and still is) so poor, why I read slowly, and how I pocket concepts over individual words. Knowing this has dispelled the shame of not spelling well, which has haunted me since my elementary school report cards, and explained away the pain of my difficulties.

Betty headed to one of the round tables spaciously arranged in the new cafeteria. I handed over my meal ticket and waited for her previous roommate, Naomi, who was studying education like Betty and most of the girls I met. As we approached Betty's table, we both noticed she had that telltale grin that could mean only one thing.

"Did you see that cute boy in the black T-shirt?" Betty said, taking her dishes off her tray while staring across the room goggle-eyed.

"The one with the butch haircut?" I questioned, wondering what she could possibly see in him.

"I wish I could meet him," Betty gushed.

"What happened to the last guy you picked out?" Naomi sat down, blocking Betty's view.

"Butch is leaving," Betty said, staring past her.

But I didn't look in his direction. I was more interested in the seating pattern filling the chairs; students who knew one another clustered together, while strangers spaced themselves somewhat evenly in the emptiest locations, from the windows inward.

Sandy, still living at the boardinghouse, came out to campus for evening lectures given by such greats as Margaret Mead, the cultural anthropologist who walked onstage with her forked walking stick and talked about her fieldwork in Samoa. I thought her style of living with the natives was what made her a unique anthropologist but later realized it was the sexual attitudes she was recording. We also heard Ashley Montague, author of *The Natural Superiority of Women* (Macmillan, 1952), speak about women being stronger biological organisms than men. The gist of his lecture didn't exactly set off a domino run on my awareness board, but it stuck in my memory bank, on deposit for later use.

After a full year at UCSB—my threshold to college—I still hadn't found one intellectual passion more engrossing than my trusty car, but a car dealer or mechanic was not what I wanted to be. Maybe the academic anatomy before me—the muscles, bones, and sinews I needed to identify and build on for a life's work—was unrecognized because of my ignorance and my lack of maturity and know-how. Where were the obvious hands to shake, seductive subjects to court, and intriguing voices to heed? How could I find those meaningful pursuits? Not that I spent hours defining *meaningful*, but if there had been a design school with graphic design, interior design, and architecture departments, I might have felt the attraction.

Frankly, the working world wasn't even on my radar, and no classes offered an understanding of the various vocations and how they were structured. And so, I merely coasted in the newness of my status as a college student. I didn't expect family to visit me, and I don't remember a phone call from my mother or sister. I wasn't sad, but without much perspective on life and no habit of asking my mother for advice, I just went with the flow, adjusting to a vacuum I couldn't define. Up until this point, musicals and western movies had been my main picture window onto adult life. Although I thought Doris Day and David Niven were delightful, nothing but their cheerfulness transferred from the screen to where I was sitting in the dark.

I was back in the morning coastal drab of La Jolla for the summer, still feeling slightly empty and raking leaves, when the mailman delivered a letter from my ballet buddy, Jeannie. I found my mother in the backyard, searching for her faithful pruning saw. "Look, Mom, Jeannie wants me to go to Europe." I doubt my mother knew that Jeannie had been to England for an abortion since I'd seen her last and wanted to get back to see more of Europe. Now that she had received a lump sum from her mother's second divorce, Jeannie was ready to see the world, and she was insisting I go with her.

The possibility of an open-ended trip to Europe brought up images of exotic flaky pastry, paling the white sliced bread of college. As Mother took the letter in her garden-gloved hand, I crossed my fingers, feeling I had a 50-50 chance. After all, she had not said no often; her liberal values rated travel to be as educational as college, and I certainly wasn't absorbing the academic lessons of the university.

Tuesday morning, Francesco crossed the street to see why I was tinkering under the Ford. *"Buenos dias, senorita."*

I rolled out, saying, "You won't believe this: I'm going to Europe."

I felt relieved to hear that Francesco was willing to watch over and drive my car occasionally, make sure nobody broke anything, and even wash it so it didn't appear abandoned. Everything seemed to be going my way. My father and his family even agreed to see Jeannie and me depart for Europe from New York Harbor on August 23, 1960.

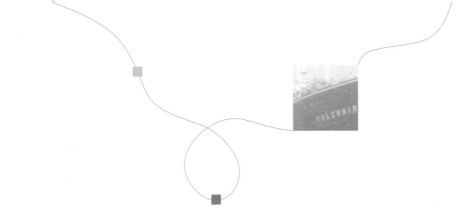

Ship to Shore

August to October 1960: New York, Venice, Florence, Munich

"That felt like concrete," I said to Jeannie once our heads popped back up above the lukewarm surface. We were both smiling but slightly shocked at the realization that we could have seriously hurt ourselves jumping four stories down from the ship's railing into the glassy mint of the Adriatic Sea.

Jeannie agreed. "Being relaxed must have saved us."

Most days aboard ship, I wore my not-so-itsy-bitsy, teeny-weenie beige bikini. My feet-first plunge into unknown deep water had just happened spontaneously, and then Jeannie and a Yugoslavian girl splashed in after me.

We gently bobbed alongside the ship, spitting out salty Latin water and laughing at the stupidity of the knee-jerk jump I'd initiated. This sudden urge to leap alarmed me; my swift decision-making style could be daring but had never included such a dangerous physical act. The cruise ship's rectangular pool had suddenly appeared overly puny, even though we'd dipped into it every day so far on the two-week Atlantic crossing. The sun blazed, but still I wondered what impulse propelled me overboard from the *Vulcania*'s deck as she anchored off Greece to unload cargo before reaching Venice, our final destination.

Jeannie and I swam well. Maybe we would have enjoyed the life of olive collectors on a tiny Greek island, but it would have been a

The *Vulcania*, 1960

long crawl to shore. The consequences of washing onto Greek sand—without money, clothes, or passports—didn't have time to sink into our silliness. As soon as we swam around the ship's hulk, several weathered crewmembers on the ship's loading area extended their burly rope-pulling arms toward us, without any questions, to pull us back onto the Italian ocean liner.

Maybe they remembered us. Although we bunked below water level in the women's dormitory, we went upstairs for activities. At the Masquerade Ball, Jeannie had dolled up as "Tragedy," her dark curly hair piled atop a Sophia Loren stare, while I stood beside her with my sleek blond ducktail, my clown-blushed cheeks, and a wholesome innocent smile as "Comedy." Our costumes reflected our differences—her younger life was darker and cloudy next to my clear calm sky. Jeannie had broken her front tooth one drunken day in middle school, and she suffered from the tight hold of an alcoholic stepfather and a Pollyanna mother.

Jotting down ideas, events, or feelings hadn't been one of my girlhood pastimes. No secret diaries with a lost key hid under my pillow in the attic or garage—not even scribbles about the cherished Ford's history. Maybe it was because I wanted to avoid the friction of tripping over spelling errors or because writing didn't feel productive enough for my activities-oriented mind-set. Instead, I had hit a tennis ball, ridden a wave, or sewn a vest. But on this trip, within one week, I began writing my first enthusiastic account of ship travel. I launched into weekly letters home and wrote notes in small Japanese fan-folded notebooks. I labeled them *The Tones of Life, Volume I and Volume II*. My journal began:

> This book is a special record of the new experiences that come with traveling. The windows that open with travel let in an amazing quality of light that makes one see more and grow faster.

Not even a fortnight into my journey, I understood that travel would influence my person, but how was unclear. I now believe that the viewing of foreign places can give to architects what reading books gives to writers: exposure to rich architectural variety, knowledge, and a broader realm of possibilities.

During our crossing of the Atlantic, Jeannie and I often stood on the deck, fascinated by the sheer scale of the cloud formations, sky dome, and textured ocean. "Look how the gray-marines of yesterday are now purple-blues," I said, panning the horizon as a couple of seagulls screeched overhead and the wind blew fresh expressions onto our faces.

"I love to travel," said Jeannie, arching her back into the wind.

"It's the vastness," I said, absorbing the endlessness and colors of this place called ocean. The skyline extended the real and symbolic potential beyond childhood, home, and college. Surely, my calling would call, my passion would ripen, or my destiny would tickle one ear. The cool expanse, void of other landforms, stretched my sense of space into forever, uplifting the vernal shoot of my soul.

Before reaching our jumping-off place, the *Vulcania* had made several ports-of-call. We'd arrived in the British colony of Gibraltar well after sunset. Not many passengers left the ship, but Jeannie and I tromped into the city center. We could feel the three-mile-long, 1,400-foot-high Rock of Gibraltar to our right because of its darkness in the mist. I peered downward at the coarseness of cobblestone streets, lit by decorative metal lanterns attached high on tile façades. The fist-sized stones were roughly fitted together, unlike the poured smooth concrete I had known on Herschel Avenue or the dirt and pebbles of Mexican roads. "This is amazing," I murmured.

Jeannie and I didn't say much to each other; our attention followed our eyes with the pull of a yo-yo on a string. Hers went into the taverns with guitar music, while mine lingered in the spaces between buildings, where the same lantern shapes at the top of lampposts created a nocturnal beauty that imprinted indelibly on my sheltered psyche. Earlier Spanish, Portuguese, and Moorish cultures had built delicate arches supporting surfaces intricately carved, rounder and tighter, than the massive New York skyscrapers we had seen in our port of departure. Late-night restaurant odors of saffron, olive oil, paprika, and paella slipped into the air around us. My taste buds stiffened and I glanced at my wristwatch. "We better head back."

"I could walk all night," answered Jeannie as we made an about-face. Jeannie didn't pay much attention to time and schedule when she was by herself, but she never resisted my … attitude when we were together. No one ever mistook us for sisters, even though we were both thin, about the same height, and with similar flat chests. They did, however, recognize a comfortable togetherness, blended from our childhood history, our perky Southern California demeanors, and our parallel curiosity for place. We didn't lean on each other, but we were tight.

The *Vulcania* anchored for a limited cargo drop in Palermo, Sicily, but passengers were not allowed to leave the ship. During such lulls, I often played chess or bridge with other journeyers, while Jeannie sunbathed. Before reaching Venice, we were able to disembark one more time (after our jump overboard) in the port of Dubrovnik, a walled city situated on the Adriatic coast of what was then called Yugoslavia. It rained slightly, but Jeannie and I left the ship anyway, exploring the city in our red-white-and-blue skirts and cotton tops. We joined up with Frances from Pennsylvania and her much older uncle Jack, my friendly chess teacher and opponent. Jack and I became such good chess buddies that a year later he sent me a glass chessboard he'd made, but it arrived in a million useless pieces.

"Going over this bridge feels like we are entering a castle," commented Frances as we passed under a colossal stone city gate.

I tried to imagine how many people standing on one another's shoulders it would take to reach the top of the high walls.

"Imagine, this has been here since the 16th century," said Jack as he glided his hand on the ancient wall's surface.

We ambled in wonderment on the limestone pavement, polished from generations of use and shining because of the rain. The idea of a place that was still alive after three centuries of history radically extended my concept of the age of buildings. With so much time to grow, I figured the expansion of the buildingscape was part of a natural process, slowly and organically adjusting, like sand on dunes, to the shape and character of the buildings that were there before them. This trip differed from any I'd ever experienced; on summer vacations with my mother, we camped, visited relatives in Oregon and New York, or lived in Mexico, while on this tour, the wonder of site seeing saturated the hours of our days.

Walking without cars in the streets was kind of like swimming without a bathing suit—wonderfully unencumbered. With no cars, I had the option of being with the other pedestrians in the center of the street or peering into storefronts. We didn't buy anything, not even a honey-smelling snack from an inviting open window. "The men are handsome," I said to Jeannie in an astonished voice, as if they shouldn't be. I couldn't imagine the streets in downtown La Jolla being closed off to traffic, but here, the narrow car-less streets lined with buildings felt appropriate; they were built before cars were invented.

I wrote home, not about the tall-dark-and-handsome hunks of the Adriatic, but about the stone shapes of the walled city, articulated with semicircular and rectangular towers, decorative fountains, and church profiles, all huddled together for security, crowning the rocky coast of the Adriatic Sea. The personality of place opened a new folder in my mind that I thought my mother would enjoy much more than hearing about the food on the ship or the social acquaintances I was making. Although she didn't ask questions, her letters encouraged me to write about the concrete corners and predicaments of our travel: "I like all the details rather than just writing that you are having a great time, like most people would do."

At noon the next day, the *Vulcania* docked in the "City of Water," ending our voyage and beginning our vagrant roving. We trotted down the ramp into Venice, headed for the lodging desk of the almighty American Express office. Jeannie looked for distractions and I scanned the street names. Carrying one suitcase each, our purses around our necks, we wandered the pedestrian alleys behind the famous St. Mark's Square in search of an affordable *pensione*. Our shapely legs marched up and down over stairs and bridges, some covered, some open to the sinuous canals where placid gondolas lulled like taxis. Continuous walls of buildings slipped around the canals like sleeves over slender arms. Decorative balconies popped out or pulled into the façades randomly, with columns and florid friezes. When we left our *pensione* to explore the city, I tried to memorize the flower-tumbling window boxes, carved wooden doors, and colorful shutters, so we could find our way back. But these were not just a few blocks, clung to for historical reference, like special districts in American cities; this was an entire city, where long alleys, buildings, canals, and squares had lived for centuries, remaining workable and lively, resembling one another in the way words of a language do. Desiring to understand the visual grammar of Venice, I had to pay attention to the decorative punctuation. Not that all canals looked exactly alike, but here there were no rectangular blocks with lettered streets in one direction and numbers in the other, as in San Diego. The ancient physical language of Gibraltar, Dubrovnik, and now Venice affected us with the warmth of a wise hand, holding us with the same care reserved for rare books or hummingbird eggs. Was it the artistic culture, the randomness of chance, or the wisdom of living over a long period of time that made these European cities so intricately textured and humanistic in scale, compared with the sprawling grids we recognized in Southern California?

St. Mark's Square and other open spaces extended the buildings as public living rooms, patios, hallways, playgrounds, and church entries. We didn't have enough money to sit at the tiny circular café tables that spread out into public spaces from the arcaded shops and restaurants like water on unlevel ground. So, we moseyed in between the tables and sniffed in deeply the fragrances of fish dressed with onions, spiced vinegar, pine nuts, and raisins, or big black cups of cappuccino—depending on the time of day. In 1960, *sidewalk cafés* were not part of the American urban vocabulary; and, thank goodness, there was not a Starbucks on *any* corner.

Jeannie and I spent three magical nights at our modest *pensione*, which, even at a half-dollar a night, cost more than our budget could support for very long. We slept on two narrow beds in a closet-less room: a converted boudoir darkened by a shuttered window and decorated with Italian colors, curtains, miniature paintings, and mirrors. I had never stayed in a hotel before, nor had I filled my head with magazine images of European boudoirs before arriving. But it didn't matter; we didn't have any expectations and didn't need a reference. Scents of citrus and bergamot lingered from previous occupants. We sensed directly and fully the *Italian-ness*—the atmosphere and layout for guests: sleeping rooms off the canal, bathrooms down the hall, and stairs to the foyer. The unusual luxury of the interiors gilded our fantasies; however, the moment we opened our window, the smell of the saltwater lagoon reminded us that this was the City of Water.

The second day, Jeannie and I walked to the centrally located train station and bought tickets to Rome. The 1960 Summer Olympics were being held there, and we planned to meet up with Curt, my exboyfriend from high school. We knew about the event because he had bought his tickets for the Olympics earlier in the summer, before leaving for Europe with his brother and parents. I left a note for Curt in Rome at the reliable American Express mail desk. In our day, the American Express office was available as travel agency, bank, and message center. It worked out well for us because Curt's family had returned home and Curt was traveling with a new friend, John, a short, blond fellow from Nebraska.

We all joined up for opening day. High in the open-air stadium, Curt, John, Jeannie, and I observed Abebe Bikila, an unknown Ethiopian marathon runner who sprinted the entire race until he made his break in the last 1,000 meters. When he glided like a gazelle into the stadium, running in his bare feet, he not only won the first Gold Medal for Ethiopia, he set a world record. Spontaneously, each person in the audience stood up and lit a piece of paper, symbolic of the Olympic torch. I gasped as the stadium glowed with fire, but we followed the crowd and lit a paper, too. What seemed to me a dangerous and unruly act happened quickly and without trauma; the fire died as naturally as it was ignited, and the smell of smoke faded. In Tijuana, the behavior of the bullfight crowd had been sweaty, loud, and rowdy; yet here was another way of clapping, participating, and expressing collective admiration.

Most of the travelers in Rome's large hostel were young Germans or Australians, but we ran into Americans, too, usually male. The inexpensive communal lodging of youth hostels suited us. We exchanged information and shared stories in the central communal kitchens, as we sliced easily prepared one-dish meals. Jeannie and I had not mapped out our itinerary before leaving home, but we used a map of Western Europe to plan our trip as we went along. We could easily flex the next day's direction to whatever sounded exciting when coming from the lips of other travelers the night before. For that reason, after throwing coins in the fountain at the Spanish Steps—a tourist's tradition—we left the huge hostel in Rome for Florence, where we took up residence at a smaller hostel in a lovely converted villa with a walled courtyard entrance.

The elegant design and decorative architectural features of commercial Florence awakened an aesthetic appreciation I had barely known growing up. I raved over church façades patterned with white, red, and green marble; the Gothic second floors of residences that cantilevered out over the street; and the enticing variety of small-scale shopping opportunities. My department store shopping experience in San Diego was so different from Florence, where one-room boutiques, street carts, and booths artistically displayed handmade accessories, leather gloves, and jewelry. The snappy smartness of our college-girl outfits dimmed compared with the cosmopolitan luster in Florence.

One of these fabulous boutiques was next to the Arno River, which is crossed by the famous Ponte Vecchio covered bridge. Standing in front of the boutique's window, Jeannie and I were discussing the glitz of the garments when the owner opened the door and said in clear English, "Please come in." We were surprised that she would invite us in, as we were obviously window-shopping students. The owner must have noticed me drooling over a hand-painted pair of purple cotton pedal pushers, matched with a long-sleeved, brown, hand-woven wool top embroidered with small bunches of grapes in pink and purple yarns.

We thought of ourselves as *poor* students, but the stylishly dressed store owner seemed to know that we were *rich* Americans. "Would you like to try something on?" she asked kindly in her best saleswoman English.

Why not? I thought, and headed for the one-person curtained dressing area at the back of her thimble-sized boutique.

"These are so special," I said, stepping out in front of the mirror, dazzled at how the clothing changed my appearance from traveling student to young artistic knockout. It took half a month's budget, but after 45 years, I still enjoy wearing the top, so in retrospect it was a sound investment. And the quality of Italian design raised the bar on my own aspirations for making things.

Florentine proportions, building materials, and details were as rich

Jeannie and me in front of the youth hostel in Florence

as in Venice, but here, hundreds of cute scooters buzzed in the streets, a marked change from the rippling sound of gondolas. Since we had little baggage and the weather was mild, I decided without much deliberation to buy a used Vespa and a couple of helmets. I wanted to get around as the locals did; mostly men were on the scooters, but I saw women riding, too. We figured the Vespa would give us more flexibility and be fun, and I calculated that it would be cheaper than paying for two train tickets to Germany and France.

Autumn crept up on us. Early one cold morning, we bundled up, pulling on our helmets, sweaters, and jackets over our skirts with black tights. Mounting the reliable white Vespa, we left the colonnaded hostel villa—which claimed to have housed Mussolini's mistresses—scooting northward for the Oktoberfest in Munich, 300 miles away. En route, we rested in the Italian hostels in Bologna and Verona, before continuing on to the winding mountain road up the 4,700-foot-high Brenner Pass between Italy and Austria. The long climb reminded me of driving my Model A Ford, because it was slow going on the upgrades. Jeannie wrapped her arms around my waist as I guided the little Vespa on the two-lane road, exposed to the mountain air, verdure, and long vistas, cars passing us by.

Just beyond the top of the pass, on a short part of the road that crosses Austria, we stopped at a Tyrolean chalet rest stop to buy fresh buns and sweet butter. The scenery couldn't have been more picturesque, and nothing at home tasted so good. But my ability to register my surroundings was still developing; the layers of history, politics, social constraints, and the web of traditions hadn't yet broken the surface of my understanding beyond museum exhibits, tastes on my tongue, and random conversations with other travelers.

We simply pushed on toward Munich because we wanted to find two American Olympians we had met in Rome. Like the Olympics, the Oktoberfest was billed as a must-experience event. Gigantic temporary white fabric tents nestled among the permanent structures, so it was easy to find the action. No rules limited the drinking age. At 18 and 19, Jeannie and I found a place at one of the hundreds of picnic tables arranged around the bandstands, and we prepared to start drinking. A waitress wearing a red and blue dirndl dress with a lace-trimmed white apron took our order and returned carrying a heavy-looking tray of dark and light beers. Jeannie and I drank from gray steins and sang our own words with the rollicking crowd, scanning the merry-makers for Peter and Matt, who had played for the US water polo team in Rome. We didn't see them right off, but after a while they walked by our table. We bounced up and I said, "Hi, remember us from Rome?"

"Oh yes," said Peter, who kept on walking. He was the one my heart irrationally beat for. Matt liked Jeannie and he handed her his phone number, but they were older than we were by a few years and didn't pay us any more attention. After that brush-off, I was happy to run into Curt and John, whom we knew would be there, too. It all felt so urban, so communal, and so well managed, but I didn't like the smell of hops. The layout, the people, and the crowd's behavior piqued my attention.

People were getting loud and boisterous, but the tents closed at nine o'clock—thank goodness, as Jeannie was plastered and we had to weave our way on the Vespa back to the hostel through thick traffic. This time she clutched my waist for her life, leaning heavily and unsteadily against my back as I managed to steer the little scooter home. Curt and John found our hostel and climbed in bed with us—their idea of getting a free place to sleep. Curt and I kept it friendly and cozy, but Jeannie wasn't going for John's advances, and the two men had to leave. I supported Jeannie's decision not to share her bed with John just because he was with Curt. We were all traveling on a shoestring, but their laces were shorter than ours. They often tried to keep from spending their coins whenever they saw the opportunity to avoid paying, but it didn't work out for them that cold October night.

In Munich, Jeannie and I were invited to dinner at the home of one of my married cousins, who was stationed with the Army. She and her husband were scheduled to ski in the French-speaking part of Switzerland over the Christmas holiday. "You might enjoy that, too," my cousin said at the wonderful meal, much more copious than we were used to, in her formal dining room.

"That sounds fun," I answered, "but a budget buster."

On the back page of my mind, I contemplated the oddity of Americans living in Germany, eating butter imported from Finland and skiing in French-speaking Switzerland. Nevertheless, Jeannie and I immediately wrote to our mothers about skiing in the Alps as the only gift we wanted for Christmas.

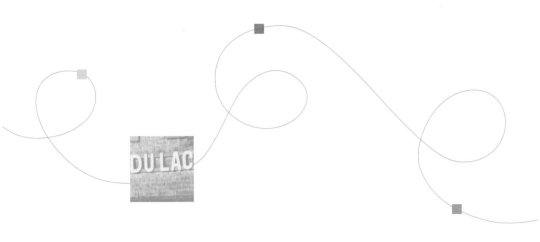

City to City

October 1960 to March 1961: Paris to Athens

Jeannie and I crested the edge of Paris on the saddle of our Vespa expecting to see the Eiffel Tower—and the Arc de Triomphe—or at least
Notre Dame. Instead, we found ourselves winding down urban canyons
of multistory buildings, grayed by the ash of pollution. (Decades later,
Paris took to cleaning façades, and this dramatically lightened the city's
complexion.) We both wanted to stay in Paris longer than the hostels
would allow, so after a short hostel stay, we rented a furnished room
with two narrow beds. Situated directly beneath a mansard roof, the
room was designed centuries earlier to house servants, five floors above
their bourgeois employers' luxury apartments. Our high new home
afforded us long views, ample light, and many stairs to climb with our
string bags of groceries. I wrote in a letter from 7 rue Andrieux, Paris
8ème Arrondissement:

October 18, 1960

Our metro stop is Villiers. We live in an apartment owned by Madame
Petite, her other room is smaller and rented, but we haven't seen the person yet. She speaks only French and is very pleasant, never losing her tem-
per, always smiling, and never snooping. We live as if we were alone. We
have use of her living room, bathroom, and kitchen—all are very tiny.

Very primitive cooking utensils, but that is Europe. The bathroom is just a sink and tin tub, which is fun; you sit on a little hump on the floor of the tub. Then wash with shower-like hose. You don't get too cold because your knees are against your chest and then if you spray your back and chest the hot water runs down and keeps you warm.

Our room is not tiny or primitive. In America, we would call it colonial, with a few antiques like the large maple closet (armoire) in very good shape and acting as decoration as well as a place to hang clothes. I'm writing from my bed; straight in front of me is a long door window. Through the balcony rail, I see another gray, shutter-trimmed building, so it doesn't seem like I'm six stories above the ground. The French don't count the ground floor. They call this the fifth floor. To my left is the fireplace, I don't know if it works but fortunately, I haven't needed to try it. An electric heater sits in front of it. There is also a small Persian rug and two wooden chairs with red print cushions.

Today I have a few chrysanthemums in my HofBrau mug from Munich and a 4-piece band played on the street. It was loud and clear from our floor. We don't miss a thing. I couldn't be happier.

In Paris, street became stage. Jeannie and I carried ourselves with intentional grace, gliding along the wide sidewalks of the grand tree-lined boulevards as if we were in ballet class with well-dressed French citizens. Afternoons, we'd rest on the park benches of the city's orderly public gardens, sitting with as much arch in our backs as we could muster, our legs elegantly crossed as we discussed the events of our day with nonchalant sophistication.

We mingled with artists, travelers, and students on the sidewalks of the Latin Quarter—so named because, in the past, Latin was the practiced language of this school-studded neighborhood. Colleges in Paris are not the isolated campuses they are in the United States; rather, school buildings are integrated into the fabric of the neighborhood. I was intrigued by the lively bohemian buzz in the streets, filled with young people in berets carrying books in their hands, intensely engaged in conversation as they walked briskly to and from cafés and class-rooms—but the lively scene also made me feel slightly unequipped for the intellectual level of the "big city."

Traveling close to the ground, we didn't read guidebooks. France wasn't yet organized into the friendly tourist economy it is now, with its fabulous network of tourist offices, cluttered with flyers on every imaginable subject in several languages. Instead, Jeannie and I depended on the information we could breathe like air. Our wandering style blended the ease of visual survey with the superficial bounce of a cocktail party and the trial-and-error survival tactics of explorers.

We were outside most of the day, partly because of our need to shop for food, partly because of our desire to experience the elements of Paris—and partly because walking didn't cost anything. The city's well-designed urban features pleased our intellect, while delicate women's items in shop windows aroused our femininity—the colorful lace lingerie symbolized the ultimate evolution from our white cotton background.

Beauty was common. Vintage art deco metal signs marked the entrances to parks and Metros, while monumental wooden doors decorated with robust moldings and flowery carvings limited access to private courtyards. Over the years, I have come to value the richness of decoration as a means of expressing humanity in buildings, and I credit Paris for introducing me to this layer of character, so underused in American places. Fortunately, our student status entitled us to enter many grand historic places cheaply, or free. I would often pause where the staircase to the public library or museum widened—the radius of its curved railing following the first three low steps—to enjoy the pull of grandeur, ready to tow me toward a pair of giant entrance doors. Experiencing Paris was intense and fulfilling—no program of events was required; the urban shapes, textures, and energy of Paris enlivened and sustained my awareness of how genuinely exciting a place could be.

Of course, Paris is better known now that Americans have been traveling and bringing back their tales and slides. But in 1960, no one I knew had been to Paris.

My hometown was tucked into the undulating coastline of beaches, cliffs, and caves along the rugged Pacific. I grew up thinking in terms of beaches rather than neighborhoods: beaches for shell collecting, beaches for swimming, beaches to scuba dive, beaches where the macho expert surfers rode waves without hitting rocks. Below the newer expensive houses on the hill, the town's original vacation cottages bordered and blended into the grid of a dozen commercial blocks of businesses and sophisticated shops; yet there was no magic at the entrances and no welcoming public spaces in between them.

In Paris, thin city streets tangled like savage dense roots—well watered—adjusting into distinct, livable urban patches between bold boulevards. But for some reason, neither the city's structure nor the buildings' designs grabbed me as a source of study. Neither did Paris inspire me to write poetry, become a food wizard (as Julia Child did when her husband had a job in Paris), or paint romantic scenes from the quays of the Seine. But I did want to learn French (as did Julia), and on the second Monday in October, Jeannie and I enrolled in the Alliance Française for intensive French lessons: two hours, five mornings a week.

Remnants of history came to us in odd ways; I learned about a city planner named Haussmann from a lesson in my French language class. Haussmann was ordered by Napoleon III to design a connecting matrix of wide boulevards across the medieval texture of Paris's tightly meshed buildings and narrow winding lanes. This enabled Napoleon to better move his army through the great city and prevented rebels from building barricades, but it also improved the city's muddy unsanitary conditions. Once the urban 1850s surgery healed, Paris became the stunning, lively public stage of generations—and our current theater.

Until I came to Paris, I'd never before thought of art as a way of life. In Paris, when walking to school or shopping for food, we were eye-to-eye with art gallery windows, painters behind their easels, and mobile bookstalls selling prints and posters. Jeannie and I were closer to art than ever before in our young lives, and in my own way, I wanted to delve into the fine arts to see what I could do.

I found an art teacher from the Alliance Française bulletin board. André saw something artistic in me, in spite of my weak drawing skills; rather than have me sketch, he encouraged me to make collages by tearing up and arranging colored paper on the wall of an attic studio. Painting eventually became Jeannie's passion, although she never made much money from her exhibits; she couldn't tolerate the marketing. Years later, Jeannie told me that most of the art gallery curators had insisted she name her paintings, but she never felt a need to do so. In fact, the idea was strangely uncomfortable, so she asked others to name her paintings for her.

As always, I was fascinated by fashion. My constant "Oh, look what she's wearing" at every gorgeously dressed Parisian we passed must have unnerved Jeannie, who didn't spend money on clothes. Jeannie's field of view focused more on men's faces.

"Look at these women," I said. "They don't wait for a Saturday night dance to dress up."

I immediately wrote home, asking my mother to send my favorite long-sleeved dress, my plaid woolen suit, and my dressy black high heels.

Jeannie kept herself well groomed but continued to make do with what she had. We didn't share clothes, just as we didn't share money.

While Jeannie successfully attracted men and was invited out often, I anguished over my struggle with the *dictées* and spelling in my French lessons. An entry in my journal indicated my frustration:

> … the ugly part is that I know what knowledge is and want it but my arms just can't reach it. If I knew not the pleasures of intelligence, I could be happy with my pea brain. But I stand knowing I lack and feel it as if I were in a caste system.

Our life as Parisian students ended when our mothers generously responded to our desire for a week ski package in Villars, Switzerland. In rereading letters written to my mother, I was surprised by how much I relied on her for support. Besides sending money regularly, she followed our adventure closely and responded favorably to my needs and whims, more so than Jeannie's mother.

Jeannie surprised me by leaving for England to visit Matt, the Olympian she'd kept up with since Munich, before meeting up with me in Villars. Feeling increasingly abandoned, I was ready now to leave Paris and glad to go skiing. I arranged to sell the Vespa and make the day trip to Villars on my own, finding a ride on the American Express bulletin board as far as Geneva. Jim, a Stanford graduate who gave me a ride in his VW bug, had been disappointed with his education in architecture. In an extremely bitter tone, he announced to me his decision not to be an architect. Unfortunately, at the time, I wasn't in the habit of asking questions (now I would do so boldly), so I missed a chance to find out more about why he was quitting architecture. To this day, I wonder if that missed conversation might have provided me with useful information for navigating the challenging currents in the profession that lay ahead.

When Jeannie arrived in Villars, we strolled the freshly snow-cleared streets of the town center, marveling at the clustered weather-worn chalet hotels, intimate ground-level shops, and picturesque homes trimmed with green or red shutters, wondering what it would be like to spend time here in a mountain village. The following day, Jeannie and I decided to go ice-skating. Next to the old rink, we discovered the construction site of a new skating rink. In this sleepy alpine village, we didn't expect to see a huge crane poking up into the sky like a ladder for a giant. We camped it up for the town photographer, who promoted his business by taking photos of ice-skaters and posting them in the front of his shop. This was fortunate for Curt and John; after seeing our photos in the window, they were able to track us down to enjoy Christmas with us before heading to Israel. Needless to say, I was happy to see them.

With Jeannie, *right*, in Villars, Switzerland

The holiday package included ski lessons, our hotel room, and all meals. Evenings were unplanned. Jeannie went out every night with others from our hotel to drink, disco, and diddle, while I went to our room and took advantage of room service with a warm glass of milk and a few cookies. I wrote in my journal about going from city to city and turned off the light early.

Jeannie and her party-loving friends couldn't understand why I would choose to spend time in a room all by myself, but I thought the varnished smooth wood walls delightful. The lampshades were made of printed fabric and the first down comforter I had ever set eyes on covered my bed. I felt wonderfully lavish, enjoying the cozy warmth of a Swiss chalet hotel in this winter wonderland. Although I didn't talk about it then, I now know how much I still enjoy periods of solitude.

Not surprisingly, Jeannie and I liked the area and wanted to stay longer. In our wobbly French, we started asking around about finding work. We eventually got jobs at Alpina, a girls' boarding school, where we traded labor for room and board, taking young girls ice-skating and skiing. In our single week of skiing, we had not learned much more than how to snowplow and stop, but we were not asked to demonstrate competence and felt we could handle little kids. Our bedroom at Alpina lacked the decorative touch of the hotel, but it was spacious, with a sloped ceiling, and best of all, we could see the spiked peaks and snow-laden pine forests of the Alps from our windows.

Without consciously knowing what I was doing, in my letters home, I started to diagnose the approach, feeling, and urban design features of our ski resort—the shape, signage, and land use—as I experienced them:

January 4, 1961

We have a special shortcut through the forest from Alpina to town. This is where you can walk into a room of forest atmosphere, for the sky is hidden by the treetops and the silence of winter is protected. Very few animals are to be seen, all hibernating, I suppose. The silence is so amazingly stimulating, that whenever I'm alone I stop and listen to enjoy this non-sound, which I so rarely experience.

I like to call Villars my home, even though my postal address is Chesières. Both towns are small with only a bridge to separate them. I really see no reason for two post offices so close together. There is a bright modern royal blue sign as you cross the bridge. On one side, it reads *Villars*, on the other *Chesières* – both in equally large white letters.

A sharp turn divides the town into sections. This gives an excuse for two pharmacies, four souvenir shops and almost double of everything tourists will use. I don't see a hardware store, thrift store, lumberyard, fix-it shop, cleaner, car garage, or telephone company, etc. The shops are close together, making pedestrian shopping easy for skiers.

I enjoyed Villars; yet, after a while I yearned, with goal-oriented determination, for a reason or destination to curb my creeping restlessness. Jeannie had been having affairs with men here and there, yet neither of us spoke about wanting husbands to support us. We both knew that marriage was what was expected of girls, but I was more at the *having a crush—let's dance* stage. Marriage seemed distant and I certainly didn't want to become pregnant— perhaps because my mother was single or I wanted to be self-sufficient, or maybe just because I wasn't in love. Not one white-horse-riding Prince Charming had crossed my path, and even if I had seen one, lassoing his attention was still far beyond my *savoir-faire*.

I knew that child support from my father would stop soon, and I thought I

Learning to ski in Villars

should be self-sufficient by then. In the movies, I had seen young ladies hang their nylon stockings to dry in their New York boardinghouses between job interviews; it looked like fun, but I didn't perceive green dollar bills bulging from their purses. Gradually, the idea of returning to college, with its planned learning and diploma, emerged in my journal as the best blueprint for my future.

In spite of all the skiing, skating, and walking to and from the village, after two months of gorging on rum babas, lemon tarts, and croissants, my face puffed into chubbiness. I'd gained 15 pounds, and our routine at Villars was losing its zest. Without much discussion, Jeannie and I agreed that our adventurous life was being stalled by our easy job of taking kids out to play. During a freezing day in February 1961, we wrote home about our decision to leave our *au pair* job, informing our mothers that instead of returning directly west from Europe, we would return home going east. We wanted more excitement, I suppose, but going around the world also seemed to fit my pressing need for a measurable goal. This decision was not as spontaneous as my impulse to jump into deep Greek water, but it had the same elements of ignoring risks and upstaging reason with ignorance and bravado. As soon as our mothers had acquiesced to our new plan, we gave notice to the director of Alpina; her eyebrows shot up, but her expression remained positive in the face of our youthful resolve.

On our day off, we bused to Geneva. "We are looking for knapsacks," I said to the luggage shopkeeper.

"Right over here," he motioned.

"We'll be going around the world back to California."

"You girls are courageous," he said with warm conviction.

"We have been traveling six months already; we don't need anything too big," I said, looking directly into his curious calm eyes.

"I'll take 10 percent off these," he offered after we had picked out two of his smallest cotton knapsacks.

With this one gesture of generosity, my virginal concept of *fixed* prices ended. Up until this point, the idea that prices could shift was as radical to me as cracking a watermelon to let a baby chick out. Money suddenly dropped from the category of something consistent and immovable into something far more human and far less tangible. To this day, I try to remember that almost everything is *negotiable*.

During our last week at Alpina, the director lent us her maps to study. In spite of our enthusiasm, we didn't have a clue about the geography of our route. Early the next Sunday, we boarded the train for Belgrade (in what was Yugoslavia at the time), bringing with us only our tiny gray backpacks and a keen appetite for moving forward.

The trip from Belgrade to Athens required avoiding communist Albania via a combination of automobile and train rides. Jeannie and I had never hitchhiked before, but others treated it as a normal means of travel, so we tried it when we found no public means of transportation. In Greece, we hitchhiked from Solonis to Athens, and I described the adventure for my mother and sister:

February 25, 1961

These two ordinary men let us off on the main road at a large Mobil Station where most of the traffic gets its gas and coffee. Thick Turkish coffee without cream served in the company of a tall glass of water. The attendant was full of smiles and immediately asked around for cars to Athens. We found a ride with the average Greek man of the road, knowing only a few words in English and French. This man who had given us papered sweets, suddenly left us high in the mountains five hours from Athens and three kilometers from the nearest town for no obvious reason. We tramped toward town. Soon a local girl carrying sticks of firewood walked with us.

When we arrived in Athens, we sensed the closeness of the Middle East in the lower buildings, the longer fuller clothes, the sticky honey pastry, the dangling jewelry, and the covered heads of some women.

These were the years when the local Greek population produced most of the items found in the open-air market. Jeannie and I bought woven woolen bags, one of the few exports still seen on the shoulders of American college students today. Like me, my mother enjoyed wearing unusual earrings; but in Europe, we hadn't seen them for sale. It was in Athens, the exotic gate to the East, that I bought the first pair of earrings for my mother as a souvenir to bring home and to thank her for this trip. My idea was to buy her a pair in each country now that I was circling the globe.

As our distance from chic Paris grew, Jeannie and I became more concerned about staying warm rather than looking fashionable. Bundled up in low-zippered shoes, black tights, skirts, and sweaters, with the hoods up on our jackets, we climbed to the Acropolis. The frigid March wind blew from the Mediterranean Sea, numbing our cheeks and our concentration. It was well worth the hike; the enormous Doric-columned temple of the Parthenon, dedicated to the wisdom and sacred character of the goddess Athena, awakened my appreciation for public monuments to the feminine. Except for the Statue of Liberty, I had never heard of nor seen any statues dedicated to women.

Before exploring the site, we sat down to rest on the steps overlooking the whiteness of the city spreading below. I was lost in my thoughts, contemplating the sheer size of the 6-foot-wide and 40-foot-high Doric columns. They were seven times as tall as a human, built to house the towering wood, gold, and ivory statue of the goddess Athena, unfortunately destroyed by the Crusades in the year 1203. The columns appeared so tall next to the marble female figures, only slightly larger than humans. The figures were used as supporting columns (known as *caryatids*) for another structure nearby. The caryatids we saw were actually replicas, placed there to protect the originals from man and nature, but that didn't make any difference to us. What struck me was that the caryatids could only be appreciated when viewed at close range, while the Doric columns could be seen for miles; unconsciously, I was observing the symbolism of scale and gender.

Jeannie broke the silence. "I have decided to go meet Matt in Majorca next week." Her voice rang unflinchingly.

"What do you mean?" I snapped. She had left me alone from time to time for her lusty affairs—I'd even slept in the same bed with her and one lover in a hotel room on the Yugoslavian coast. But this felt different.

"I'm not going to continue around the world with you." She narrowed the lids around her convincing eyes and shifted to a softer tone. "I am sorry, but you can catch up with Curt and travel with him, can't you?"

Jeannie's words reminded me, once again, of how strong the pull of men was for her. Clearly, finishing what she started wasn't as important to her as it was for me. But it wasn't in my nature to argue or try to change Jeannie's mind. Not that I wouldn't defend my ideas, but trying to keep someone from doing what she wanted to do didn't motivate a debate in either one of us. Although her shallow love affairs irked me, I was glad I was now free to hook up with Curt, who was in Israel with

John. Curt had witnessed other parts of my trip—in Rome, Munich, and Villars—and I'd heard that John was considering returning directly home. Besides, Curt knew my quirks, and I intuitively understood that his tallness, strength, and masculinity would be valuable assets while traveling the Middle East and Africa.

I wrote to my mother about Jeannie turning back and my new plan to continue around the world with Curt and still be back in time for fall semester at the university in Santa Barbara. She agreed to enroll me and to keep sending a monthly allowance, via the American Express international banking services. I now think my mother vicariously savored my chance to experience exotic places.

Curt's parents wouldn't have recognized my mother if they saw her in the Safeway—and I'm sure he hadn't yet mentioned it—so I doubt they'd heard the plan. In reality, Curt hadn't yet fully agreed to go with me, but I didn't let that get in the way. Once I earnestly decided to go around the world—even without Jeannie—it felt edgy and expanding. Any doubt or fear I had was canceled out by my reserve of self-confidence and staying power; I was a long way from home, with the whole world before me.

Country by Country

March to April 1961: Greece to Sudan

Sadly smiling, Jeannie left Athens on the first day of March 1961. My future remained vague, but my direction was clearly eastward. With Europe at my back, I now faced territories that would require cholera and yellow fever shots—and malaria pills. My immediate destination was Israel via Turkey; I planned to link up with Curt and John, who were staying at the Beit Hashitta Kibbutz. It was a long shot, but Curt had mentioned wanting to go to Africa and John would soon be returning to Nebraska, so I optimistically presumed that my once high school steady would ultimately agree to continue traveling with me—at least in Africa.

For the first leg of the trip, I found a ride at the American Express office with Grady, an American soldier on his way back to Ankara after a recreational leave in Athens. Although there was land between Turkey and Israel, I learned that I couldn't take a train or bus straight from Ankara to Tel Aviv because of political reasons—Arab neighbors didn't allow travel directly to Jewish Israel. So I took the train south to the harbor of Adada, where travel to Israel was possible by water via the large island of Cyprus, freshly independent from Britain. Had I known the political geography or done more research, I would have traveled directly from Athens to Cyprus.

Traveling alone became tricky for me, in that the police, hotel owners, ticket sellers, waiters, harbormasters, and ship captains all were men, who naturally took notice of a young blond woman. I was careful to make sure my hand waving, eye gymnastics, and facial dicta were coordinated to clearly say, "I am a serious, purposeful traveler," as opposed to a woman looking for male company—and it worked.

In the harbor town of Famagusta, Cyprus, I awakened each day to warm yeasty scents rising up from the bakery below my rented room. First thing in the morning, I spoke with the harbormaster—a kind, middle-aged, mustached man, who quickly gained my trust as he focused on helping me get to Israel. Thanks to him, after ten dragging days of hot whole-wheat buns and juicy Cypriot oranges, I became the only passenger on a cargo ship carrying fuel and flying a Norwegian flag. Soon after we anchored in the Tel Aviv harbor, a customs officer rowed out into the murky water to greet our ship. He cheerfully checked my passport, allowing me to disembark onto Israeli soil from his rowboat.

No cell phones existed then to check with Curt. At the busy open-air bus station, I held up Curt's letter so the ticket seller could read the name of my destination—Beit Hashitta Kibbutz—fearful that my pronunciation might otherwise land me somewhere that was not where I wanted to be. The bus dropped me off at a rural intersection near well-cultivated flat farmlands, in front of a long driveway leading into the kibbutz.

"We were just about to leave, but since you made it, we can stay a little longer," Curt told me, looking down into my tired, stunned dusty face. I set down my backpack and gave myself over to the sheer pleasure of not having to search for anything else; being with familiar company after ten days alone felt wonderful, too.

We three slept in our own guesthouse but ate all our meals alongside the large kibbutz community. Breakfast was at eight, after we'd first spent two peaceful hours picking grapefruit—the kibbutz's crop. To beat the heat one day, we joined a few others for a swim in an oasis not far from the kibbutz. We were all getting along well, which probably contributed to Curt's being willing to go to Egypt with me before making a decision to go the whole way around the world. Years later, Curt shared a letter he'd written from the kibbutz:

Wendy wants me to go around the world with her. I still haven't made up my mind yet. I want to go but I don't think I like her and maybe I might begin to, even though I don't want to, because five months is a long time to be together. She sure has changed in that she is easier to get along with, not so critical. One thing, she's the only girl I know that I could travel around the world with, she gets $120 a month.

After a few restful, grapefruit-picking days, we were ready to continue traveling as a trio. Again, travel between Israel and Egypt was not allowed, so we booked passage on a ferryboat from Israel back to the port of Famagusta, Cyprus, the pivotal harbor in the region. During the crossing, we met a fellow from Denver who had just been traveling in India. When he heard we were heading east, he made a list of places for us not to miss. Decades later, when I asked Curt about it, he said, "The specific places on that list helped me to visualize the trip home; that is how I decided to continue around the world with you."

The harbormaster was clearly happy to see me again. "There is a schooner hauling oranges to Port Said," he offered. "I can ask the captain for you."

We waited in suspense on the dock while the harbormaster talked to the captain. We envisioned a sunny trip across the water while we ate our fill of fresh oranges.

"He said yes," the harbormaster told us. "He only asks for a docking fee of $10."

John had to wait in Cyprus for his parents to send some money. We headed out without him but planned to meet up with him in Cairo.

The voyage was to last two days, but four hours out, the choppy Mediterranean was so rough that the captain had to anchor for 24 hours while we waited for the waves to calm. When the first evening fell, the captain pointed to the second bed in his cabin. Curt and I tried to share the narrow one-and-a-half-foot-wide bed, bruising our hips, while the captain slept in the second similar bed, but after a few hours, Curt felt so cramped that he got up and slept outside on the crates labeled "The Doctor Oranges." The voyage stretched into three days and four nights.

Fortunately, the eight crew members, in their torn tan robes and painted toenails, were respectful. The captain was equally gracious; sporting a gold watch and blue

The boat on which Curt and I crossed the Mediterranean

baggy pants that looked like pajamas, he made sure we had plenty of oranges to eat, but they didn't make the Arab bread less dry or more memorable. Although I enjoyed the one time he played *The Nutcracker Suite* on the loudspeaker, the blaring Arab music, blasting day and night, soon became too much for me.

In Port Said, the city port for Cairo at the northern tip of the Suez Canal, the customs officers gave our passports to a skinny fellow who led us up an indoor staircase to a small room with nothing but a desk. He left us to stand while he sat down behind the desk and asked us for money in exchange for our passports. When neither English words nor crumbs of French worked to convince him that we were not rich, I grabbed the passports off the desk and ran down the stairs. Curt ran right behind me, and we got away without having to pay.

After checking into the primitive Cairo hostel, Curt and I went to see the *Family of Man* photo exhibition, on display in a business high-rise as part of the International Agricultural Show. The black-and-white photos were artistic and compelling: children playing with stones in Mexico, Peruvian mothers with felt hats carrying children on their hips, and peasant men toiling behind oxen in Southeast Asia. The idea behind the collection, presented by the Museum of Modern Art in New York, was that humans around the world belonged to the same family and needed peace. Viewing these handsome images validated the way we were traveling because we were seeing and experiencing similar vignettes of life, country by country, weaving among humanity, close to the ground.

Camel guides on each side of me in Cairo

John had arrived from Cyprus via Alexandria. He was waiting at our hostel when we returned, and the three of us made plans to see the pyramids the next day. I had imagined the pyramids way off in the desert, but instead we rode a local bus to the edge of the pyramids' parking lot—complete with postcard stands, boys selling Coca-Cola, and white-turbaned men renting camels and horses. After climbing the pyramids, we rented camels, along with their owners, to guide us into the desert, so we could visit other architectural sites. We were so fascinated with the desert that we then rented horses and rode even deeper into the dunes, leaving our guide behind for several hours as we explored the broken architectural elements protruding from the unending sand. It was a good thing the golden sand didn't start blowing, because there were no roads or signs. Now, this was an *adventure*. My definition of that word kept expanding.

I could tell that Curt was sorry to see John leave for the States, but much later, he shared this note to his parents:

> Wendy was sick one day this week, so every day she eats in the Nile Hilton Hotel, which costs her about one dollar. While she's in there I use the bathroom with all the luxuries: hot water, soap, toilets you can sit on, soft paper and then a man brushes you off when you leave—to get his tip. From the hotel, I go across the street and I eat for six or seven cents. She is on my back about not spending any money, not like John who thought I was spending too much.

In one of Cairo's open-air markets, Curt and I posed in front of a big box camera draped with a black cloth to take the required photos for our Sudanese visas. My face was tanner and thinner than when I left New York, and a red

Curt and me—1958 in La Jolla, 1960 in Cairo

scarf held back my stringy blond hair. Curt had let his beard grow, but he'd gotten me to cut his hair in the courtyard of our hostel while the locals looked on in amazement.

On the last day of our week in Cairo, I bought a pair of Egyptian earrings for my mother, and then we visited the International Agricultural Show, which had exhibits from the United States, Soviet Union, both Germanys, China, Spain, Ghana, Indonesia, England, and Italy. We went to the Russian Building to see a movie about the new Russian-designed Aswan High Dam, in construction 600 miles away. This was our first chance to see the so-called Cold War Russian enemy in person, but they didn't throw us any "ugly American" stares. We watched the documentary in a long room filled with hundreds of interested African men. Although I was probably the only female in the room, what impressed me at the time was that Curt and I were the only non–Africans. Thinking we might be investors, a few of the men came up to speak with us after the film.

"Can you imagine, it will be 375 feet high," said Curt as we walked toward the hostel.

"But … 60,000 people are going to be displaced." I was thinking of the social impact.

"They're building the dam to prevent flooding," Curt reminded me. "To generate electricity and provide water for agriculture."

I said no more, but quietly continued to mull over the social design dimensions that seemed to be overlooked. The truth was, there were also many archeological sites that had to be moved, not to mention environmental dimensions that I hadn't even thought of.

Policeman and me outside of Cairo in sandstorm

We hitchhiked out of Cairo. When I realized I had left my passport under my pillow at the hostel, Curt went back and got it while I waited with a policeman in the middle of a sandstorm. Another hitchhiking adventure on the back of a truck got us to Luxor, where we boarded a multi-level Sudanese riverboat servicing the Nile, the world's longest river.

Curt and I were the only non-Egyptians among the passengers in third class; the other European travelers were on the first- and second-class levels of the boat above us. We slept on the same deck, at water level, with the farm animals, whose odors drifted our way over the rope between them and us. The quiet river water flowed between ancient desert shores without exotic wild animals, vegetation, or glamour.

Just before the Egyptian-Sudanese border, the riverboat stopped at the Nubian Abu Simbel temples, one of the sites we'd heard about in the documentary on the Aswan High Dam project. As ambitious and grand as the project seemed to be, it genuinely troubled me that this ancient site would soon be under water.

Our boat pulled up along the muddy shore without fanfare, under a blanket of harsh light and heat. No one collected admission money; only a few boys sold Coca-Cola in bottles. We walked toward the two temples, built between 1279 and 1212 BC to impress Egypt's southern neighbors and to reinforce the status of Egyptian religion, luxury, and power. Four colossal statues of Ramses II peered down on us from the 60-foot-high rock at the entrance. Inside the temple, we wandered the relatively thin but cool spaces between giant columns, glad for respite from the heat. The second smaller temple was dedicated to Hathor, the Egyptian goddess of love and beauty. As we were leaving, I turned around to take in once more the incredible proportions of the temple site, clearly reflective of an ancient desire to leave an immortal reputation at great expense. We were not in Egypt long, but this idea of marking a civilization's presence with so much architectural boldness topped Athens and was sinking into my consciousness.

The rare photos I snapped were usually of buildings or places. I took one of the temples, but I also took one, not far away from our Nile riverboat, of mud block shapes clustered into a village. Offshore, anchored fishing boats dangled from long ropes, their sails rolled up and simple pole masts pointing upward like antennas.

Scene of the Nile

The riverboat didn't stop often. Passengers were packed in with the closeness of silver sardines, but we respected one another's personal space. The mood was calm and warm.

Several hours later, our riverboat docked at Wahti Halfa. I tied my red bandana around my face to avoid the flies and gnats buzzing in clouds as we fled into the dusty Sudanese border town. Icy fruit drinks of lime and banana, concocted in an electric blender by street vendors, relieved the hot and bother of waiting seven hours for our train. But we got through it and finally boarded the fourth-class compartment of the train to Khartoum, capital of Sudan, another country newly independent, in 1956, from the British. In Khartoum, which means "meeting of two rivers," we went to see the amazing juxtaposition of colors as the Blue and White Niles converged unevenly, leaving a distinct edge where the dark blue color touched but didn't immediately blend with the chalky white color. The Nile we had traveled from Cairo was the confluence of the Blue Nile flowing west from Lake Tana in Ethiopia and the White Nile flowing north from Uganda.

In the center of town, we found handsome large government buildings and embassies surrounded by lacy garden walls, through which we could see the lush vegetation and tropical flowering trees so unexpected in the middle of a flat desert landscape. At the open market, we bought bananas to snack on, and I bought earrings made of ivory. (Today elephants are protected from being killed for their tusks, and I wouldn't buy ivory; in those days, this was not a known issue.) After inquiring about transportation to Ethiopia, we went to the outskirts of Khartoum, where travelers could pay for a lift on cargo trucks caravanning across the desert.

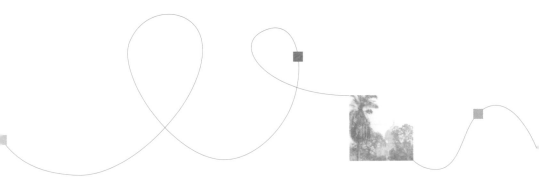

The Elegant Experience

April to May 1961: Africa to India

Curt and I headed east into the Sudanese desert, standing up with ten Muslim men in the back of an open truck. When the six-truck caravan stopped for a rest, a humble man with an expressive face appeared from behind the dunes and walked toward me. Dressed in a long musty robe, he carried a tea-filled tin cup in one hand, a glass in the other, and he gestured that the glass of tea was for me. The humanity of his gesture read easily; we sat together drinking the fragrant amber liquid, speaking with our presence rather than with words. No wonder Curt thought I was getting special treatment, but I didn't mind.

It was another thing during the night hours of the crossing; Curt had to push one man away when he tried to snuggle up to my backside as we attempted to sleep on top of the truck's cargo—cartons of cigarettes piled six feet high. I'm not sure what I would have done if Curt hadn't been there; I probably would have turned toward the encroacher with a back-off stare, which wouldn't have worked well in the dark. Maybe I would have screamed. I don't think I would have hit him. To this day, the only person I ever tried to hit was a woman in Berkeley who grabbed my purse off my bicycle, and then I chased her and caught her sleeve, ripping it enough that she dropped my purse and kept running. Regardless, I was never one to worry much about crime.

For 24 hours, the trucks' droning motors mixed with Arabic murmurings as we passed an uninterrupted vista of sand dunes. Finally, Curt and I climbed down from the truck bed into the trade center of Kassala, Sudan. Hungry, stiff, and tired, we wondered about the bus schedule; there might not be more than one bus leaving per day, and we did not want to just miss one. I kept a firm grip on my backpack (because I'd almost forgotten it on one truck) and stayed close to Curt, ignoring the soft stares as we walked toward the swarming open market.

"May I help you?" a Western-dressed fellow in his 20s asked.

"We want to go to Asmara," I told him.

He led the way to the bus station, where we discovered that the bus for Ethiopia (now Eritrea) didn't leave until the next afternoon. Smiling, he said, "I am a Seventh-day Adventist preacher. Please stay with me and my family." Five of us slept on low cots set out on a paved area in front of his simple abode—that's what the Sudanese did during the hot months.

We made sure to be at the bus stop for Asmara early the next day. Bus drivers rarely turned away any passengers, so the aisle filled quickly, and late arrivals had to cling to the top of the bus or to the outside ladder with all their bundles.

Constructed under Mussolini, Asmara's town center was a blend of Italian neo-Romanesque, modern, and even art deco buildings—a dominant, dramatic, and surprising sight next to the traditional huts we had just passed, their cylindrical walls topped by conical roofs.

The next day, we descended from 8,000 feet to the sea-level port of Massawa, Ethiopia. Once I recovered from 60 miles of swirling hairpin turns in a smoke-spewing, speeding truck that made me vomit, I was in a better position to take in the sights. I relaxed a little, noting the Italian influence in the buildings, inhaling the coffee aromas that drifted from sidewalk cafés, and relishing the resort atmosphere. At the time, I thought coffee was in Ethiopia because of the Italian population, but I now know that Ethiopia gave birth to the coffee bean. Turkish-Egyptian-styled buildings—a testament to three centuries of Ottoman and Egyptian rule—enriched the urban texture. As much as we were intrigued by the multicultural surroundings, we were equally grateful for the American hospitality of the US military. There were few American tourists here, so we were an oddity in this part of the world; the American sailors insisted on arranging for us to stay in their recreation housing and fed us sorely missed American food. The doctor on

My mother was pleased to get letters from my world travels

board the Navy ship that was docked in the deep-water port gave us the shots he said we needed against tropical diseases.

Beyond the Gulf of Zula are the 200 islands that form the Dahlak Archipelago. We visited some of these islands, where we were able to swim a long way out into the shallows of the Red Sea—fun because it was so expansive, but not cooling, because the reddish water was almost as warm as the air. In my journal, I wrote about how sincerely Curt and I marveled at life, alert to the simplest details of our days: the robustness of the desert sun, fragrant finger bananas, and half a moon in an Ethiopian sky. And yet, when somebody stole Curt's German jackknife, he said he felt like going straight home and began to resist stopping for too long in one place.

If we hadn't been in such a hurry—and Curt hadn't lost his knife—we might have stayed longer than the six days we waited for a ship to take us another segment on our circle. But ship arrivals and departures were rare and unpredictable, so we decided to board the local rusty bus, which was bruised and dented by overuse. The natives often ignored us; they were busy enough trying to keep track of odd-shaped baggage and numerous well-minding children. We gazed out the open bus window as monkeys scattered into the jungle and indigenous people without much clothing stepped aside to let the bus pass. At the end of the day, long, lanky Curt squeezed himself into the overhead baggage rack, giving me his sleeping bag so I could sleep on the seat and would agree to continue traveling through the night.

The next day, we boarded a train for Djibouti, Somalia. Before reaching Dire Dawa, a major train stop in Ethiopia, our train broke down in a mountain village. It was cold enough for me to have my hood up and not want to move around much for the few hours we had to wait until the train was repaired. Curious children collected around me—not to beg, but to keep me company and watch me sitting on a rock writing in my journal. Maybe they had never seen a woman write in a book. Curt took a photo.

The men decorated themselves with animal skins and beads, but for comfort, they wore modern loafers on their feet and didn't appear fierce. I knew I was the odd bird, far from my natural habitat, yet I innately assumed a positive acceptance of my surroundings, feeling it was okay to drop spontaneously into other cultures. The friendliness of strangers seemed normal.

With Ethiopian children

Because of its strategic location at the juncture of the Red Sea and the Gulf of Aden, the French established the port city of Djibouti in the 1800s, both for commercial interests and as a coal station. The long stay of the French is reflected in the neighborhood grid of two-story arcaded classical French buildings, con-structed to provide shade for pedestrians in the desert sun of Somalia, a dry coun-try of nomadic herders.

The pirating of ships was not as common then as it is today, so we didn't worry about that, but we were stagger-ingly disappointed when we learned that a ship headed for Bombay had left the day before. It may be difficult to imagine, but in those days, ships went about their business without a central place like the Internet to register schedules. I was wishing we had left Massawa after five days instead of six; but, as with spilt milk, running out of gas, or being in a car wreck, there was no going back. Djibouti was expensive and crowded because of an international event taking place there, so we slept one night on the beach and then decided to fly to Aden, where we thought we could find a ship to Bombay. It took weeks for mail to travel home, so we had already written to our parents announcing that Bombay would be our first city in India, and where they should send letters and funds.

A sense of urgency drove us to keep moving so we would be home in four months for the beginning of the school year. Even so, we enjoyed adapting to the adventurous spirit and to setbacks, as in the movie *Around the World in Eighty Days*, which I had loved.

At the Aden airport we were stopped by immigration officers, because of a rule that entering foreigners needed to have 100 English pounds (about $300) to prove they would not burden the country by running out of funds. We each had only about $100 in traveler's checks. The American Consul was called in and wanted to send us back to Djibouti, but we vigorously argued against that move and were given 18 hours to find a way to Pakistan or India. That is why on May 6, 1961, we found ourselves aboard the Italian Ocean Liner *Asia* for four days of expensive luxury living, en route to Karachi, Pakistan. We were so frazzled by the set of events leading up to the voyage that we hardly knew how to mix with all the wealthy travelers. We also didn't have the clothes to fit in. However, the tropical mixed drinks were a new draw for us both and loosened our tongues as we basked in the temporary luxury of our adventure thus far.

"I'm glad we didn't turn back," opened Curt at one of our happy-hour drinking sessions.

"It never occurred to me to turn back," I said, sipping through a straw.

The daily task of living within a wider context of humanity than my native Southern Californian homeland nourished a part of my personality that I couldn't pinpoint but dearly valued. I wrote home, "The entire event seems worthwhile, even if I have to work a hundred years to pay it off." I felt enriched and privileged as I toured. At the same time, I was bothered by the arduous task that others faced—and survived—with less food and resources than I knew at home. I even thought I didn't need to eat so much. American life seemed so extravagant next to what we witnessed from the worn edges of vivifying local streets.

Most of the time, my attention beamed outward, but here and there, the logistics of travel rudely impacted my inner emotions, as I wrote in my journal:

May 13, 1961

On this trip, I have felt extreme emotions: love, hate, anger, disappointment, luck, joy, success, failure, and sadness. Today is sad and as depressive as they come. Karachi, with no mail or money and today is hot, sticky, and humid. My hair is hanging and my body itching, pale and exhausted from restless sleep and mosquito bites. I have nine on my right inside wrist alone. Tonight will be my first experience sleeping under mosquito netting.

Seeing so many places, even with my internal ailments, sad moments, and itching insect bites, still registered as rewarding and real. We didn't talk about it then, but Curt later told me that he had made up his mind to pursue a career in architecture when he was in Spain with his parents, before he linked up with me. At the time, I had no thoughts about becoming an architect, but as I look back on it, we both developed a common interest in buildings and structures, appreciating their character, beauty, historical origins, and response to wealth, climate, and culture—essential ingredients of architecture.

The bus from Delhi ejected us into a dusty Agra street, bustling with early-day activity. We were there to see the Taj Mahal and wandered in its direction through Agra, where turbaned men pulled carts of onions; filthy barefoot children with matted hair and missing teeth waved sticks or begged for coins; and women in colorful saris sat in front of piles of melons, potatoes, or bags of red and yellow lentils for sale. The scent of curried spices pooled around street vendors, while pedestrians moved in currents, doing their best to avoid unruly monkeys and horned stray cows.

Soon Curt and I were moseying along the wide sandy banks of the Yamuna River, weathered by centuries of use. The sun seemed to lift slowly until we saw the red sandstone protective walls appear in the distance. Simultaneously, Curt and I simply and silently veered toward the informal park grounds marking the entrance of the famous Taj Mahal mausoleum.

Engrossed in the present and without a whiff of sophistication, we crossed the threshold of the red sandstone gate. We turned slightly. The Taj Mahal stood, silhouetted in full splendor through a delicate tall archway, stunning the extremity of our imaginations. The white marble geometry glittered with patterns of pastel gems. Skilled artists had chiseled Persian calligraphy and formed delicate jeweled flowers into the surfaces of the mausoleum. The boldness and beauty halted our stride in front of lotus bulb roofs, the glowing façade, and thin minarets—all in double, for the grandeur was perfectly reflected in a long narrow pool of water, bordered by cool green cypresses dotting the formal paths. We, in our raggedy traveling clothes and young careless hairdos, looked at each other, awestruck.

Slowly we made our way through the arch into the welcoming courtyard, ample with lawns and accent trees. So few people, and no postcard salesmen, Coca-Cola stands, beggars, or guides barking at us here. We paused respectfully; the passion for place crouched below our lips. Harmony, sacredness, and intensity of design created an elegant experience elevating aesthetics to its quintessence. Here was an enduring place, created from 1630 to 1653 for a woman, Mumtaz I-Mahal, by her husband, Shah Jehan, Emperor of Mughal India, designed by an imported Persian

Taj Mahal, India, 1961

architect, Ustad Ahmed Isa, and built by many craftsmen of the Islamic tradition. However, neither the devotion of a husband to his wife nor the building of such an extravagant memorial to that love held particular importance for us. What sunk to the bottom of our intellects, like gold in water, was the beauty and power of the architecture—to have lasted for so long, in such good condition, and to be standing there, so softly colored and irrevocably majestic.

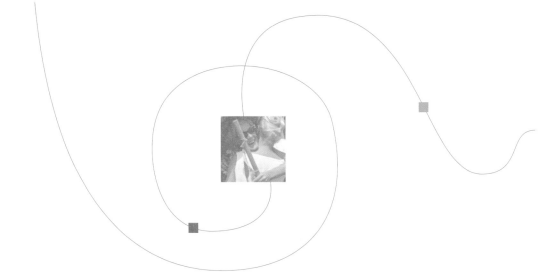

Closing Circles

May to August 1961: India to California

Slowly, my usually ample and reliable reserve of energy drained to an unbearable low point. I couldn't get out of bed and felt listless and weary. At a New Delhi hospital, I was diagnosed with a strange African hepatitis and given six brown jars of pills to take with me. We had already bought our train tickets for Calcutta and were not about to stop and rest for the six weeks prescribed.

Curt and I had traveled from Karachi to New Delhi, visiting Lahore, Agra, Banaras, Patna, and Katmandu. Our sleeping arrangements during those ten nights varied, from cubbyholes in the YWCA for me and YMCA for Curt to Salvation Army dormitories to a rope bed with a straw mattress in a rented room of nothing but mud walls. Thank goodness we could take showers, for a reasonable fee, in train station stalls resembling one-person closets.

One major task was to balance our budget with our circumstances. Scanning the open markets, we searched for affordable nourishment that either didn't require cooking or was cooked by street vendors in front of our eyes. We were attracted by the sizzling ripe smells and low prices of peanuts, vegetable balls, deep-fried pastry, cut fresh pineapple, and shaved-ice drinks. Gradually, I got better.

Fifty miles outside of Rangoon, Pegu was home to a giant reclining Buddha, built in 994 A.D. and restored many times since: another impressive example of monumental architecture. Green hanging tropical vines and thick rain streamed from a tin roof sheltering the Buddha and us. The statue rested 177 feet long and 50 feet high, smiling down at us with strongly arched black eyebrows, his right oversized ear resting on cushion-like blocks. His feet were turned so we could see the decorations on the soles.

"This was built so long ago, I wonder why people still keep it up," I said, gazing into the gray dilapidated village and muddy lanes between sheets of warm monsoon rain. Bony, barefooted people squatted under overhangs or in doorways of dingy, thin mismatched walls, some broken—none decorated—waiting for the downpour to stop. Both men and women wrapped their heads and their bodies in pieces of cloth. The opulence of Buddha next to the lightly dressed, undernourished, and betel-nut-chewing Burmese seemed so discordant.

Bangkok was equally alien and exotic. Hundreds of golden Thai Buddhist temples dominated the narrow, primarily carless town of two million. People dressed more simply and shabbily than in the scenes of the popular 1956 movie *The King and I*—my only reference to this part of the world. We spent a few hours wandering around the low, robust white-walled compounds, which sported semi-layered roofs with corners turned upward and were trimmed with metal hooks resembling animal horns. These were working temples with monks and believers; here, the mysterious religion and sovereign royalty were alive, unlike Egypt and Greece, which felt ancient. I couldn't imagine being born into a culture saturated in religion and royalty.

Recently, good friends back from a trip to Bangkok told me they enjoyed themselves so much that I went online and saw photos of the now world-class modern city of eight million people, modern buildings, and highways. As in so many of the places I passed through in the 1960s, massive development has overlaid what I saw, greatly changing the proportions, character, and lifestyle.

Curt and I rode in a passenger-filled taxi—the most common form of transportation in these parts—to Laos. Military men stopped our taxi at seven checkpoints set up to catch gun smugglers. This was the spring of 1961—tension from the Communists' violent struggle to conquer South Vietnam added a hostile dimension to the atmosphere, along with the humidity and the heat. From the border of Laos and Cambodia, we took a bus to Vietnam. The US military had been in Vietnam since 1945 but was on the brink of increasing troops under President Kennedy.

The conflict expanded radically in late October, after we left. While we were there, we saw guns but smelled no smoke and heard no shooting.

Saigon (now Ho Chi Minh City) was appropriately called the Paris of the Orient. Graceful women, dressed in high-necked, long pastel tunics slit to the knee on each side over loose-fitting flowing trousers, walked the tree-lined boulevards and formal public gardens. Many of the city's modest two-story houses had French arches and shutters, along with Vietnamese railings, colors, and decoration.

Equally evident was the widespread desire of colonialists to construct buildings like those in their homeland. Handsome structures and, often, whole neighborhoods of European-style buildings had survived for decades. Vibrant Vietnamese pagodas towered next to pastel French neo-classical train stations and post offices. Roman and Greek arches, columns, and pilasters topped with balustrade railings—typical elements of the Beaux Arts School—existed (and still exist) from the French colonial years of 1861–1954. Naturally, I wanted to stay in Saigon longer, but after one short week in June, we took the first boat to Hong Kong.

Sailing between the low Kowloon Peninsula and the mountainous Hong Kong Island, Curt and I were delighted by the sculptural composition of Victoria Harbor. The shape of the land formed a natural round harbor fringed with patches of white buildings clinging to the slopes among bushy dark vegetation. Shadows from an afternoon sun underlined the bustling boats: Chinese junks with poetic delicate sails, long British destroyers, Pearl River sampan silhouettes, merchant vessels, and enormous international cruise ships.

We made the usual first stop at the American Express office to check for mail, and then boarded a ferry crowded with workers for Kowloon. Once in Kowloon, we melted into the high-rise packed streets in search of an affordable hotel. The signs were all in Chinese except for the Lung Hoa Hotel, where we could at least read "Hotel," although the manager didn't speak English (or French). We were glad to find it; the room was clean and just big enough for the double bed, but the sober windowless space remained hot and muggy, even when we were naked with the ceiling fan on high. After I had depended on Curt for money for 18 days, my funds from home finally arrived—an event worth celebrating with a divine Chinese meal.

After lunch, I wanted to check out the local custom-made-shoe-and-clothing industry in the "tax-free port," widely advertised for its incredibly high quality and low prices. My backpack of clothing

In my custom-made dress,
Hong Kong, 1961

was showing wear, and the lively city inspired me to spruce up. In a small dress shop, I chose a royal-blue printed cotton fabric for a Chinese-style dress I saw most of the women wearing. My measurements were taken, and in three days I was wearing my custom-made dress. Although the temperature was in the 90s, I also bought a red cashmere cardigan with embroidered silk trim, fearful that I would never have another chance to purchase such extravagant luxury.

Curt and I had traveled successfully for four months, sleeping in the same bed, affectionately and carefully. Curt's parents never asked the details of our togetherness, but they sure didn't want him arriving back in La Jolla with me with the two of us looking like a sinful couple. So, they flew to Hong Kong, first class, to fetch him. We were surprised, but we had no choice. Curt went to visit with them in their hotel as soon as they landed, and they made him stay and sleep in their hotel room.

Two days later, on July 3, 1961, Curt went with me to the harbor to make sure I got off as I continued alone from Hong Kong to Osaka, Japan, by ship. He seemed slightly embarrassed by his parents' actions, but I didn't feel angry with him. We said good-bye in the harbor without any tears, probably because we were practical partners rather than inseparable lovers.

Decades later, when I asked Curt to share his thoughts about our travels together, he said, "I liked it because we did so much, instead of just hanging around in our room as I might have done alone." Not the emotional revelation I was digging for, but he was right. We had penetrated our surroundings by swimming in the Ganges and renting a rickshaw without the driver in Katmandu's center. In Burma we rode with the locals and barrels of live fish in the back of a mini-truck taking passengers to the jungle community of Pegu.

In Osaka, I ended up lost at the end of the extensive Japanese train system: I couldn't remember the long station names, even when the signs were written in the International Phonetic Alphabet, looking like

English, next to the Japanese characters. Getting directions was difficult, too, as all I had was a map to the hostel. I asked one man for directions and followed him, thinking he was showing me the way, but instead he led me into a small house without the familiar Youth Hostel sign outside. The moment I realized it was his house, rather than removing my shoes as he had done, I turned around and headed back to the station, red-faced.

In Tokyo, I settled into a Japanese-style hostel with tatami mats where we slept on the floor. Sliding shoji panels with translucent paper separated one room for males from one room for females. Hostelers used the neighborhood public bathhouse; women went to one hot pool and men to another. The Japanese women took an extra look at my bathing suit tan lines, but out of politeness, they didn't say anything; my skin shade matched theirs, except for the white skin my bathing suit usually covered. After several visits, the bathers began to acknowledge me with a slight bow of their heads, and I courteously bowed back.

Being in one place for a month meant I saw some of the same faces and could even do odd jobs. Two European fellows who had been at the hostel over a year helped me to find work and suggested places to visit. I substituted as an English teacher for one of them and worked a few days as an extra in a Japanese film.

One of my mother's friends had read some of my letters, and she sent me a gift of money. I used the gift to celebrate my July birthday on Mt. Fuji, the famous volcano crater, 12,395 feet high. A fellow hosteler and I rode the local bus to the timberline, intent on climbing the last 4,000 feet. Along the path, we passed small shelters deliberately located after a series of steep switchbacks. The relationship of the tiny wooden stations to the nature they served struck me as artistic, humble, and appropriate. Attendants served us tea and burned the stations' numbers into my wooden climbing stick. Most of my trip had been city to city, with nature in between, but this outing was like going to a National Forest.

The dozen or so climbers staying in the traditional mountaintop refuge slept in a single line on the floor under cotton quilts. We all awoke at dawn to see the orange sunrise and to get an early start back, hiking straight down the volcanic gravel slope. I turned 20 years old on Mount Fuji.

In Tokyo, American tourists visited the Imperial Hotel because it was luxurious, had withstood a 1923 earthquake, and was designed by architect Frank Lloyd Wright. I went because it was close by, didn't cost anything to visit, and was strongly suggested by a hostel mate. Without any preconceptions, I felt a gracious sense of welcome as I passed under the low concrete ceiling of the very wide, semi-open lobby. The architectural elements had been designed to create layers of surprise, and I certainly felt the magic. Although I wasn't at all familiar with Wright's history at the time, I later learned that he designed the hotel with the intention of building mutual respect between the West and Japan by using local carvers, shapes, and materials. During that visit, I did register that the designer of this internationally renowned hotel was a living architect—unlike the architects of the buildings I had been seeing—and the character and success of the hotel were being attributed to the architect, with strong praise.

People on the ship to Honolulu spoke English, and I unexpectedly enjoyed long conversations about travel and life with fellow passengers. I was beginning to feel the underpinnings of accomplishment that my trip had anchored. Honolulu was my last stop. However, hotel prices were such a shock that on the first night, I ended up waiting for morning on a hotel couch.

At daybreak, I found breakfast and the earliest bus to a UCSB classmate's address. Naomi lived on the backside of the island of Oahu, away from the rows of beach hotels, where the water was too rough for tourists to swim. Her family welcomed me for a few days; we made flower leis, they served me Hawaiian food, and I bought the last pair of earrings for my mother. My plan was to mount them on a board with the names of their countries of origin for her to match up; she adores puzzles.

My mother and my sister meeting me at the airport

On August 17, 1961, the movable stairs were pushed up to the nose of my airplane at the (then) open-air San Diego airport. I paused at the curved, shiny open door to breathe as deeply as I could in my fitted Chinese dress, slit on each side to mid-thigh. My blond hair was carefully back-combed into a puffy pile. I held a sand-pan hat in one hand and my Mt. Fuji walking stick in the other. Not far away, I saw my sister and mother madly waving and grinning from behind a low chain link fence. Curt, too, had come to see me arrive. My 90 pounds of bones straightened to their tallest as I descended, relishing the sound of each step on the metal treads, closing circles—a full year's cycle and my circling of the world.

My French Digression

August 1961 to September 1962: California to France

When I left for Europe, my mother folded her approval right along with her expectations. Her exact words were: "I will treat your trip like one of your years of college."

After the year around the world, my vision of the earth's geography had been recalibrated. My concept of public transportation was considerably now more vast and varied than the San Diego bus line. Having seen so many manmade structures—created for man's many reasons—had enriched my vocabulary of place. I realized that the ways people had fun, slept, washed, collected water, and went to the bathroom were not uniform. During my travels, I had slept in bunks and cots, next to a captain and farm animals, on riverboat decks and tatami mat floors, under electric fans and mosquito net tents. In my mind, these experiences were not isolated from the cultural activities, climatic influences, political pressures, and religious traditions of the many countries I'd visited. The physical appearance and impact of all I'd seen had seduced me; I had fallen in love with rooms and buildings, the shapes and spaces of cities, the grain of urban and rural textures—the very concept of place—but not yet with the profession of architecture. And so, I'd landed home, motivated to study with a ruthless determination, but without a main subject.

During my freshman year at the University of California, Santa Barbara (UCSB), my poor academic performance had resulted in probationary status. My grades included three Ds, four Cs, a pass in English 1A, two Bs—one in design and color and one in tennis—and an A in elementary fencing. But, freshly armed with my confident after-the-trip attitude, I didn't let my poor grades bother me.

Betty, *rear left*, me, *front right*, and roommates, 1962

I contacted my pretty former UCSB roommate Betty, who invited me to be the fourth roommate in her off-campus pad. We lived on the second floor of a substandard apartment complex in the newly developing student enclave of Isla Vista. The complex had exterior metal stairs serving several apartments, including ours; any time of the night or day, we could see and hear anyone using the stairs. Our front door opened within six feet of our neighbor's; when both doors were open, we could smell whatever was cooking, see the couch, and hear what records were playing.

My three fair-haired roommates were education majors. They liked having company for smoking, drinking coffee, and playing bridge (I played bridge). Each morning, I'd listen as the two Midwesterners fretted over whether to have ham or bacon with their breakfast. I was repulsed by their drive to eat so abundantly, and I reacted by buying meals in a can to get my nourishment; I even went so far as to leave the apartment so I wouldn't have to watch them prepare the food and pile their plates with it. How much food we needed to eat each day wasn't clear to me, but my compassion lingered for those in the world who had much less than I.

Not able to continue with an *undecided* major, I selected history as my major and took the History of Europe both semesters. My history grades were average, but I did very well in French, Cultural Geography, Anthropology, and Modern Dance, earning As and getting myself off probation.

However, circling the world was a hard act to follow. Even my Cultural Geography teacher, who knew of my travels and whom I liked, couldn't convert me to cultural geography. I stood before the world, overwhelmed as though looking at a library filled with fascinating books or a pantry well stocked in preserves but lacking a framework for deciding what to read or what to taste. I tried to visualize a rewarding career based on what I'd seen and experienced of the world so far, but the vision was as blurred as an unwashed jar of marmalade.

If there had been a major at UCSB with the word *international* in it, the way there is today in many universities, that might have helped. Instead, the advent of jet planes and the expanding opportunities in air travel drew my attention as a way to engage with the world and still make a living. Without many apparent options, I had listed "stewardess" as a career in my senior high 1959 yearbook. The difference now was that I wanted to fly with an international company and use my French. I knew one girl from high school who was making good money working for Southwest Airlines. Those stewardesses wore hot pink and orange swishy outfits, designed to be as short and sexy as possible to keep the male passengers flying. My long legs were shapely, and at five feet, six inches tall, I qualified for the rigid height limits of the day. It occurred to me much later that I could have selected to become a *pilot*; I would have been very disappointed—even angry—if, as a stewardess, I woke up serving coffee, tea, or milk and realized that I could have been in the cockpit. But in 1962, that didn't come to mind. I needed to speak a foreign language to work as an international stewardess, so I got right down to learning more French as the spring semester ended.

Cheerful and charming Arnaud turned around from the row in front of me and passed me his handheld blackboard. It was the second week of language lab—French flowed in my earphones, Mandarin in his.

Would you like to go for a walk? Arnaud had written the question in light blue chalk on the slate he used to practice Chinese characters.

Sure, I chalked back.

We were both attending the ten-week intensive summer language program at The Monterey Institute of Foreign Languages (now The Monterey Institute of International Studies) in Monterey, California. At the end of my trip, I'd written in my journal that I preferred France for the language and India for the handsome men. But now this real Frenchman, with his poetic choice of words, sunny Gallic face, and black turtleneck shirt, indisputably aroused my interest.

The institute was within walking distance of Monterey Bay's curving beaches. Over the next week, Arnaud and I took several after-class strolls near the rolling Pacific waves. In excellent English, he told me he had come to this country via Virginia, where he'd visited the family of a young lady who had boarded at his parents' Paris apartment. He told me how he had skied in Yosemite and wanted to tour the West, and how he had studied Mandarin in Paris and had wanted to attend one of the language schools in Monterey, famous for its Mandarin program. I was swept off balance by Arnaud's direct manner, his concentrated attention when I spoke, his raw curiosity, and his way of wanting to include me instantly in his life.

"Wendy, why don't you move in with me and Steve?" Arnaud held my hand as we ambled along the foamy edge of the icy waves. This was our third walk.

We had kissed a few times. And he knew I was on a low budget. But this was so sudden. Infatuated, yet unsure, I said aloud, "I guess I could." The practicality of his proposal blended perfectly with my love-sick thoughts. "My rent in Pacific Grove is month to month."

"Steve's wife lives in Berkeley," Arnaud added. "He sleeps on the sofa anyway. We have only one bedroom … the bed is big."

Our eyes embraced.

"I want to think about it," I said, looking away as I tried to absorb, sort, and tabulate the consequences of my decision. The commotion of feelings climaxed with the thought that he would expect me to do more than sleep in the same bed. Curt and I had cuddled and kissed in the same bed during our travels, but here was a man from the country of love, and I was now a 21-year-old adult. So, I figured this *being in the same bed* would also mean indulging in the complete sexual act.

He must have detected my hesitation.

"You like me, don't you?" Arnaud questioned in his delicious French accent. Emotional insistence was second nature to him and slightly disarming to me, as I had grown up automatically employing reason. Our family was so uncomplicated—feelings were rare, drama unknown.

"I'll tell you tomorrow," I muttered impulsively.

Without much deliberate thought, I pushed the idea under my pillow for the night. Who knows what a woman's heart, body, and synapses do during sleep, but somehow, by morning, a clear yes had filtered to the fore. The outward reasons seemed logical; there were only seven weeks left of the program, so it seemed the most economical, practical, and fun thing to do. I'd had other boyfriends, but this was different; Arnaud was five years older and from France, and I wanted to learn French. My mother hadn't expressed an opinion on romance, but the repetition of *happily ever after* at the end of the musical movies I'd seen as a child had unconsciously confirmed for me that happiness was the obvious and conventional ending to all romantic journeys. The romantic glow was strong and my feelings wonderfully present.

That first morning, Arnaud gently smiled and pulled me toward his chest. Loving feelings pumped through my heart, and I returned his smile, relieved to have crossed the maiden bridge between lovers the night before. Everything seemed to fall in place in my heart and body. I was floating on the clouds of romance at high speed, in contrast to our simple stucco residence with an old-fashioned washing machine and a clothesline that moved on a pulley. Both were like luxury to me because in La Jolla, my sister and I had hauled the family's dirty laundry in a wagon or on our bikes to the local laundromat. Now I could wash any time, an unexpected luxury I indulged in often.

Happiness upstaged everything. Arnaud's playful nature shows in a photo where he is supporting me in a backbend; I have a daisy between my teeth, as if we are ending a long, exotic tango. Living with a new lover was not like dating or traveling. Every moment, even doing routine housework, held an aura of romance. We kissed after making the bed in the morning, held hands walking to school, ate by candlelight, and went to bed early. Everything was fun, and I was so willing to be in love, my first fully physical love; it felt so natural and carefree. At the end of the summer, our roommate Steve returned to Berkeley, and Arnaud announced his return to Paris. To his surprise and my amazement, I dropped the airline idea and spontaneously said, "I'll go to France with you." It was as if I had been dabbing short strokes of earthy greens and browns for a year, when with one wild swift gesture I grabbed a wider, bigger brush and poked it into a valentine red spot of color. Not because I was thinking of marriage, family, or taking care of my future. It was more like the impulsive decision style of my traveling days. I knew I liked France, and this French man-flower had caught my fancy with the same delight that a dragonfly must feel in discovering the eyelashes at the center of a nasturtium.

"Sure," Arnaud replied with a honeyed glint.

So, at 21, I changed my course to follow my darling Frenchman. I invited Arnaud to meet my mother, as I needed to return home to La Jolla to sell my Model A. After owning my treasured Ford for four years, I sold it to a man in a pink Cadillac for three times what I'd paid for it. With the cash, I bought a ticket to leave with Arnaud on a French cruise ship, departing at the end of August 1962 from New York City to Le Havre, France. Arnaud had charmed my open-minded mother, who accepted my French digression without any pleas that I finish college.

And I understood that I was on my own, without the security of the educational monthly allowance I had relied on for the past three years.

Arnaud and I joined Otto, a German fellow with a muddy, used Chevrolet, who was looking for paying passengers to take the three-week trip to New York City while seeing some of the United States. Arnaud suggested we take the southern route. Otto did most of the driving, while Arnaud and I used any excuse to make love under a blanket in the backseat. The two men had their ideas of what they wanted to see, and so far, their suggestions were okay with me—I was in love and on my way to France with my Frenchman.

Their suggestions were okay, except when Arnaud and Otto made a beeline for the closest restaurant on reaching a Louisiana border town. "Hey, wait a minute," I said. "See that little white sign in the window that says 'No colored'? It means if you are Negro, they won't serve you. I don't want to go there."

"Okay, so we'll look for a restaurant without that sign," said Arnaud, thinking this an easy snag to dislodge.

We spent more time than a load of laundry trying to find restaurants owned by nondiscriminators in the neighborhoods where traveling students like us ended up. However, we were determined, and happily entered the first one we found. Fine fig jam, new to me, was served with breakfast—a lifelong reward for our persistence.

In New Orleans, we toured the French Quarter, heard people in one grocery store speaking Cajun French, and marveled at the decorative character of the wrought iron balconies. "France doesn't look like this," Arnaud said. Otto and I laughed, not knowing what exactly he wanted us to know, without asking for any explanations.

Arnaud and Otto especially wanted to hear gospel music. "We'll start walking, and when we see a church, we can listen from the sidewalk," Arnaud suggested. Sunday morning, about 10 a.m., we walked where there were plenty of down-home-looking churches. At the fifth church, we heard singing. Arnaud and Otto both looked at me. "What shall we do?"

"We'll just go sit in the back very quietly," I said. I had no church experience, but it seemed like a good idea.

We *gently* pulled open one of two oversized wooden doors, then slid between the back pews as discreetly as possible.

Nevertheless, we were noticed. At the end of the service, a family gathered around us and a middle-aged woman said, "How nice of you to visit our church. Where are you from? Would you like to come home with my family for the gumbo lunch we are having in our backyard?"

We traversed the length of their long house to enter the backyard. The two-story neighboring buildings bordered three sides of the dirt yard, making an open-air box. Arnaud and Otto helped unfold two long tables while I arranged the dozen chairs and stools brought from corners of the house by family members. We were delighted when the after-church gumbo arrived, steaming and smelling heavenly of fish and Cajun spices. But for some reason, the backyard's sad emptiness made a deeper impression on me than the kind animated faces of our hosts.

During the comfortable conversation, between bites of cornbread, I asked, "Where would be the best place to listen to jazz?"

"Bourbon Street," one fellow volunteered. "Look for open basement doors." I imagined jazz played in fancy nightclubs that required men to wear ties and women to dress up. But no, we found one of those basement doors and went down a few concrete steps into an undecorated room humming with horns and strings played by elderly black men in full swing. This was what we came to New Orleans for; we landed on three wooden chairs with the swiftness of a trio of swallows to a warm wire.

In Georgia, we rented a metal boat and rowed into a mossy swamp, startling the local birds into flight and attracting alligators from the mangrove-rooted waters—the finale to our three-week journey. From Georgia, we sprinted to New York City to catch our ships. Otto dropped us at the harbor, as he planned to visit the city before returning to Germany. I was remembering how Jeannie and I had departed from the same harbor two years earlier as Arnaud and I boarded the cruise ship for our open-ended destination: France.

Test Results

Fall 1962 to 1964: Paris to French Alps

Arnaud and I went directly to Auteuil, in the 16th Arrondissement of Paris, to stay with his parents. We entered the vintage six-story apartment building at the back of an inner courtyard at 3 Villa George Sand. The bare cobblestone courtyard provided access and daylight to the rear apartments, but sculpture, landscaping, and benches, so common in public spaces, were regrettably absent.

"What does *villa* mean?" I asked Arnaud as we passed the glass front door of the concierge's apartment. I ignored the *George Sand* part of the street name—the pen name of a well-published woman of literature. The concierge watched us with hawklike attention, as she observed all who passed the entryway. French concierges have gained a reputation for being a special interface between buildings and their residents. Author Muriel Barbery breaks the gossipy outgoing stereotype of the uneducated concierge in her bestselling novel *L'Elégance du Hérisson* (Gallimard, 2007) by having the main character be an intellectual concierge with elegance who also keeps the building clean and the tenants happy.

"*Villa*, in this case, means a dead-end street, not a big house in the country," Arnaud replied. He squeezed my hand, evidently pleased to be bringing me home to meet his parents.

We took the elevator up to the fifth-floor apartment. The door opened and there stood Arnaud's mother, wearing a full apron over her slacks and smiling from an intelligent face that never saw makeup.

"*Entrez*," she said, and immediately gave me a tour of her Parisian home. Each tall, tiny room had a large window, opening inward to accommodate the metal shutters behind long, heavy curtains that were both closed at night without fail. In each room, the space between antique furniture restricted our circulation to one person at a time, so unlike my home in La Jolla, where there was more space than furniture. In contrast to the richly colored decor in most of the house, the kitchen, including the tile surfaces, was a sterile white, except for grime and stray bits of food missed during weeks of overly speedy sponge strokes.

"Looks like this kitchen gets a lot of use," I said cautiously.

Noting the absence of a refrigerator, I raised my eyebrows. But before I could say anything else, Arnaud's mother darted ahead. Arnaud took her absence as an opportunity to compliment me on my handling of her dirty kitchen. We caught up to her as she opened a screened cupboard protruding into a shaded lightwell outside the dining room—her cool food storage area.

When the church bells rang ten, Arnaud's mother, Hélène—whom everyone called *Moucha*—lifted her apron and excused herself to go shopping for lunch items. A stout, big-boned woman with a great French nose and intense hazel eyes, Moucha had wavy gray hair that was brushed straight back and hung without fuss. We liked each other right off.

Like most French women, Moucha went out to shop every morning while her husband, Jacques—like most French men—was out of the house working. Arnaud's father was a cocky man with a hungry need to hold an audience. He didn't talk about himself or his past, but during meals he'd drop nasty comments about his wife's cooking, which to me seemed uncalled for, as she did her best. Jacques sold concentrated fruit syrups; a can of grapefruit concentrate was always on the table to mix with our drinking water as an alternative to the label-less red wine served at lunch and dinner. The job didn't pay much, which was why Moucha often took in a student boarder.

On Sunday mornings, Jacques usually brought home a large bouquet of cut flowers; I thought it odd at the time but now understand that he was probably returning from the house of his young mistress. Exuding a mild fleur fragrance, the tall bunch dominated the small salon from a round table: a shield for his unfaithfulness that his wife never saw past.

Arnaud's younger sister, France, was studying medicine; she lived in the servants' room, on the floor above, with her working husband and their two-year-old daughter. They usually had meals with us, and Arnaud's father liked to use his blond ticklish granddaughter to call attention to himself by setting her on the table in front of him. I frowned on this, but the family tolerated it. Arnaud's sister, Chantal, older by five years, and her husband lived outside of Paris with their growing brood of eight children.

I immediately enrolled at the Alliance Française on the Boulevard Raspail, where Jeannie and I had begun learning French during our days in Paris. French became my focus because I thought I would be living the rest of my life in France. I soaked in everything French, expecting that my new community would then absorb me. I didn't know that even if I wore French clothes, cooked French food, spoke French words, and washed with French soap, I would always be considered an American. My country of origin trumped my individuality.

"Where are you from? What kind of work did your father do? Where do you sleep? And what do you think of your president?" the French usually asked on meeting me.

Although Arnaud and I lived with his parents, we were running low on money. In December, Arnaud found a job for the two-week Christmas holiday as a ski instructor at a Club Med ski resort in the Alps. Luxury accommodations and fancy meals were included for both of us. In our unsettled state, the paid sojourn provided a short diversion, but the resortlike atmosphere, overabundance of food, and festive nightly activities attracted a crowd the French would call bourgeois. Arnaud, like his mother and older sister, was an active French Communist, and the Club Med lifestyle didn't fit the program. They attended monthly Communist Party meetings. I didn't, but I did attend a theater production about a populist revolution: *The Paris Commune of 1871.* I liked the way it highlighted, among other communist themes, the participatory democracy of the workers and feminist reforms during the few months when the Communists successfully managed Paris before being overtaken by Republican forces.

There were usually more than six people at meals, and I bubbled with questions amid the big family feel. "How many people are there in the Communist Party?" I asked at one dinner conversation.

Moucha responded quickly and fervently, "More every day." And that is about all I learned about their meetings. Maybe they thought I wouldn't understand, being an American. I left it at that and started to clear the table. Arnaud and I often helped set the table and wash the dishes, but his mother did the clockwork activities of shopping and cooking.

Arnaud and I slept in the back bedroom, the one Moucha rented out when it was not in use by family members. The only way into the room was through a bathroom with a tub and sink. My French family may have been behind in owning a refrigerator, but an on-demand water heater served the tub and sink. Forty years later, energy-savvy Americans are just now buying these heaters for their efficiency.

There were two single beds in the narrow room, placed end-to-end, but we adapted. Soon after returning from our stay in the Alps, Arnaud and I sat together on one of the beds. I snuggled up to him and said, "I think we should move to a place of our own." The extended family was a great asset for the transition from California, but we had been leaning on Arnaud's parents for room and board too long for my comfort.

He lifted my hair to unlatch my necklace. "If you think so." His voice casually faded to let me know he didn't think independence so important, as he brushed the warmth of his breath into my ear. We kissed with the kind of affection I took to mean agreement on the previous question. Within the week, I was looking for a room on bulletin boards at the Alliance, the American Express office, and UNESCO.

One cold but lovely Paris evening, Arnaud and I strolled toward the Metro after seeing an evocative Japanese film. *Naked Island*, made in 1959, used only music and images to convey beautifully how precious water is to life.

"That was so good," I said, trying to remember if I'd ever seen a foreign film before.

"You know, I studied filmmaking and made a few movies," Arnaud uncorked.

"Really, what kind?" Somewhat intrigued, I instinctively braced myself, knowing Arnaud's uncanny way of dropping new information about himself or what he wanted to do during moments that were already so sweet that their glaze would coat his message.

"Short movies for advertising products on TV, but I want to make full-length documentaries."

"I don't see how you would have time. You're already studying Chinese *and* skiing," I said, turning to observe his optimism squarely.

Undaunted, he answered, "Sure, I could." His palm tightened on mine.

"You are doing so many things," I said weakly. Then my thoughts deflected to my situation and perked up with, "What do you think I could do?"

"Maybe you could take a test to help you decide."

"Good idea," I said, feeling enough muscle in my French language skills to search for a career in France. I was glad I had asked and touched that he had suggested something significant.

Within the week, Arnaud scheduled me for a counseling test, administered at no cost by the Ministère de l'Éducation Nationale Service d'Orientation Scolaire & Universitaire. I arrived decked out in my homemade purple and green plaid skirt, and took a seat among a dozen others. The testing was not exactly what I'd expected. After I'd checked all the multiple-choice questions and written an essay—in French—about my family, the test-giver said. "Now, draw your family." Obediently, I drew my sister, my mother, and myself, as if posing for a photo—not very original, specific, or inspired. "Here is another paper," the test-giver said. "Please draw three trees." Again, following his instructions, in a style considerably less than artistic, I drew one resembling a palm tree, similar to the graceful palms that lined the streets of our San Diego suburb. Next, I drew a leafy broad tree, cousin to the enormous rubber tree my mother liked to point out every time we went to the zoo in Balboa Park. The last was a Christmas-tree-shaped fir with a couple of squiggles to represent birds flying in the sky.

"How did it go?" asked Arnaud, looking up from his Chinese reading as I entered the living room.

"Fine," I said, feeling satisfied I'd understood all the questions but drained from eight hours of testing. "I go back in a month for the results."

Arnaud was keen to find ski instructor work. In France, ski instructors teach for the ski association of a resort town, or for Club Med, or for the UCPA (Union Nationale des Centres Sportifs de Plein Air), federally subsidized centers providing sport lessons to French citizens. At the beginning of 1963, when Arnaud was away substitute teaching,

I decided to find a temporary way to support myself, even without a work permit. I moved out of his parents' apartment to take care of the six-year-old son of an American couple working for UNESCO, in exchange for cash and the use of their furnished basement studio south of Paris in Meudon.

Arnaud was still away in March when my vocational test results were ready. Fortunately, Sandy, my Canadian college roommate from Santa Barbara, was visiting me in Meudon. She came with me to the interview, which I insisted on referring to as a "blind date"—a hopeful chancy event. As we waited in the lobby, we chatted cheerfully. A middle-aged woman finally announced my name and led me into an office with gold velvet curtains and a vase of daffodils. From behind her desk and spectacles, and without any small talk, she started, "I have reviewed your test results and firmly recommend you consider architecture as a profession."

Architecture—the word held the mystery and power of a Chinese proverb. How had the counselor leapt from my drawing of a tall palm, a rubber tree, and a fir to a career in architecture? It certainly was not my drawing ability. Vision, boldness, color, context, composition, proportion, and choice of materials—not lines on paper—had always been my artistic suits.

"Well, if I didn't pursue architecture, what else could I do?" I asked, trying to regain my composure and hush the shock of her radical suggestion.

"I think architecture is for you," she insisted. "It stood high above anything else. Why not consider it?"

"I never imagined being an architect, but it sounds interesting." I studied the daffodils as if pausing at an intersection, slowly acclimating to a new sense of direction that seemed both clear and confusing. I had no idea what it would take to become an architect; my mind raced to find remnants from my past to substantiate the plausibility of her counsel.

In retrospect, I had enrolled one summer in a drafting class at Point Loma High School, a long bus ride from home. As the lone seventh-grade girl among eleventh- and twelfth-grade boys, I'd felt I was in the wrong league. They treated me like the class mascot rather than as a sister student. And then I flashed back to Curt, who was attending drafting classes at San Diego Junior College and would soon go to architecture school at San Luis Obispo. Was the invisible dimension of gender blocking my vision of becoming an architect? Guys like Curt, yes; girls like me, no?

"Thank you so much," I told the counselor, with the naïve euphoria of someone accepting a perfect gift. I stood up to shake her hand and floated out of her office on the wave of possibility that had just crested into my awareness.

Sandy and I immediately bought a liter of red wine to celebrate. The career counselor had freed me from indecision. The next day, I began looking into where I could go to school. Soon, I learned about the École des Beaux-Arts, where the architecture faculty was distributed in ateliers across France as part of a public federal school system for the arts. Here, location was the choice, not the quality of the school, as they all taught the same federal program. In between visiting museums with Sandy, going to French language school, working in Meudon, and writing letters to Arnaud, I found out that I qualified to attend the École, even with my American education. All I needed was proof of my two years of university work.

At the end of skiing season, Arnaud came to live with me in my studio in Meudon. We were happy to be together again, and I was feeling upbeat about the future. Just before dinner, I showed him my certificate for finishing the fifth level in French.

"Good timing," Arnaud said, as we started shelling peas for dinner. By now, we conversed only in French. "I found a full-time job as a ski instructor for next season at the UCPA in Les Contamines, and you can live with me." His expression concentrated on my face without any sign of the fear of rejection. "Les Contamines is in Haut-Savoie," he continued to explain, glancing up from the piles of peas and pods. "Just a short train ride to the National Ski School in Chamonix, where I need to take my ski exams."

"Exams?" I didn't think of skiing as a career. I had skied in California, and the guys who hung out in the mountains teaching were called *ski bums*. My eyes were within blinking distance of his, but his were looking inward.

"To be certified in France, the National Ski School requires written and skiing performance tests over five years. I'm lucky to have landed a job just one valley from the school."

"Wow," I said, feeling my shock and the radiation of his satisfaction.

"You will see how magnificent the Alps are, and you can ski every day." Arnaud put the peas in a pot, cupped my chin with his right hand, and leaned his lips into mine for a *sealing-my-desires*-type kiss.

Although Arnaud had been pleased when he heard about my decision to become an architect, skiing was obviously *his* serious career direction, and he deemed this job offer pivotal. So, I shifted my objectives, entrusting my life to our zigzagging course as a couple, while my vision of being an architect sank to the bottom drawer of our priority chest. We needed to make a living, and the immediate plan unfolded automatically around Arnaud's career goals, not mine. Still, I ordered my transcripts, seeing them as the key to my impending, yet unscheduled, architectural education.

Life at the UCPA was communal, which fit in perfectly with Arnaud's political philosophy, and I was being introduced to and liked. The UCPA was a newly formed, semi-governmental body, set up after the war by the Ministère de la Santé to sponsor sports camps for skiing winters and mountain-climbing summers. (Since its inception, the UCPA has expanded to include other sports and other countries.) Young coal miners and factory workers won a ski week for good performance, while students and other groups with few means came on scholarships. The equipment, all-day lessons, and lift fees were provided, along with room and board. We all ate at the same hour in the common dining hall. The young people, called *stagiaires*, would set the tables and bus the dishes.

Les Contamines-Montjoie village (population under 1,000) huddled at the end of a valley with all the picturesque details of a winter postcard, sending a friendly snowy welcome. Neither of us knew anyone when we arrived, but I started to build friendships with the ski instructors and their wives, in spite of the fact that I was being constantly teased and ridiculed for no reason about small comments I made or the way I did things a little bit differently than they did. I learned much later that tacky teasing was a French way of showing affection, even though it hurt. (Since then, I have run into American men doing the same thing. I just don't get it.)

Skiing in Les Contamines, 1963

On the first day of one ski session, each *stagiaire*—I among them—skied down a short slope so the instructors could screen us by skill level. "Wendy, over here," said Mini, indicating that my technique was above average. As soon as the class was formed, we were off behind

Mini, our instructor for this level. Late in the day, I hit a mound and fell, but my ski binding didn't release! I looked down at my left foot; it was going the wrong way on my leg, but somehow it hit the packed snow and turned back in the right direction.

"Are you okay?" asked the fellow right behind me. Then everybody rushed up.

"I heard my leg crack," I whispered, lying crumpled on the chilling slope. Soon the ski patrol arrived.

Arnaud was waiting when I reached the bottom of the mountain in the rescue basket. I looked up into his face. "We are taking you to the nearest hospital in Chamonix," Arnaud assured me, looking frightfully concerned as he caressed my cheek with the back of his always-warm hand. "They have good surgeons there because of all the ski races. Don't worry, my love."

During surgery, three metal rings were placed around my left fibula to clamp the splintered bone together. I was confined to a hospital bed in Chamonix for two weeks and then grounded in Les Contamines in a full leg cast. The season was only half over. I don't think Arnaud had any idea that I now saw myself as a trapeze artist who had just missed a bar and was carried further away from architecture—not for lack of desire to be an architect but because of the reality of my accidental broken leg.

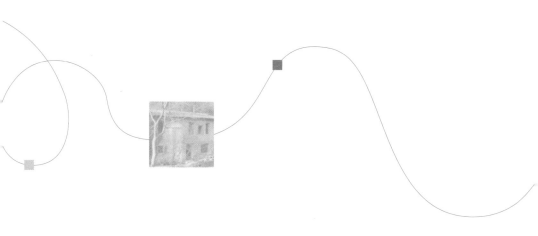

Thinking Like a Couple

April 1964 to July 1965: France

We returned to Paris in early April. Arnaud accompanied me to the hospital, where I was scheduled to replace my full cast with a shorter, below-the-knee cast. A black curtain divided the windowless room so that two patients could be worked on at the same time. Within moments after the technician began sawing off my cast—*click-rumble-buzz*—I tried to stop him.

"You're cutting my leg."

"Don't worry, that's not possible," he insisted and continued. "This saw just vibrates."

Tears trickled, motor clattered, and plaster splintered, while Arnaud looked on helplessly. After what seemed like enough time and noise to fell a giant sequoia, the technician pulled opened my cast to reveal a straight bleeding line of wet red.

"Oh, I never saw that before," the technician said sheepishly.

My emotions seesawed between being angry that he hadn't believed me and feeling validated that my complaint had been substantiated. I limped out of there with my walking cast, perplexed and pensive. Could I have expressed myself differently so that the French male technician would not have dismissed this complaint—from a female American patient?

We were temporarily living at Villa George Sand again. The concierge delivered the mail to his parents' apartment daily. When my college transcript arrived, I told Arnaud right away.

"Oh good," he said, looking up from the Chinese volume of Lao Tzu that he sat reading in his favorite Louis XIII replica chair. Then, as if pulled by a magnet, his attention returned to the page.

Later that evening, while Arnaud and I relaxed in our bedroom, I decided to tell him about the town I was considering for my studies in architecture. When I first began looking into how the École des Beaux-Arts was organized, Arnaud and I had talked about several towns in the southern part of France so I would be close to his mother's summerhouse near Nice. "I've decided to apply to the atelier in Aix-en-Provence," I threw out matter-of-factly.

"Good choice. Aix is a beautiful old Roman town," Arnaud said, rubbing a clear ointment on the last of his psoriasis spots that flared up periodically.

"The school sounds so different from college in the States," I said. "Did you know that the final exams are all held in Paris after five years?"

"That's how it is here," Arnaud answered without shifting a muscle, not even his eyelids. He moved to the bed to practice Chinese characters on his hand-held slate, an activity he fit into any crack of spare time.

"That's scary, I mean, that's a lot of time before you know how well you're doing. I'm used to semester grades." My thoughts reached deeper into the mirror as I brushed my long, fine Finnish hair, envisioning my school days ahead.

Arnaud put down his slate. "I was going to wait until I had the exact date, but perhaps now is a good time to tell you—I found this great opportunity to go to China in June."

The brush stopped in mid-air and I faced him directly.

He continued cheerily, "The Chinese government wants to increase foreign language skills by importing native speakers."

I understood why he was applying. His passion for Chinese and his leftist leaning made Peking (now Beijing) an attractive destination. There was no talk of my joining him; I would be pursuing my architecture. We had been apart before, I reasoned speechlessly; he would only be away for one year. On the other hand, he knew my plans, while I felt his were hidden; we were not yet thinking like a couple. My focused determination to start school must have cushioned the blow, because I rebounded, thinking about my destination, "I will enroll in the architecture atelier tomorrow." I had goals, too, so I simply read his behavior as being similar to mine; the authority often wielded by men because of their self-perceived superiority wasn't yet on my radar. However, for a fleeting moment that I still remember today, I wondered if Arnaud believed in my commitment to architecture school. In hindsight, I know that he was always pursuing his goals, no matter what I did.

"I will write you lots of letters, *ma chérie*," he grinned, and turned out the light as if this were all very ordinary.

At the end of April, Arnaud and I took the night train to Nice; we planned to stay with his mother in her summer place while we waited for the Chinese government's response to his teaching application. I was waiting, too—waiting for the École to start in the fall. We were both excited about our own plans; how our lives would join back together was taken for granted with the same certitude of animals that separate but always return as mates for life.

I slept through most of the Rhone Valley scenery, until the train reached the coastal towns along the Mediterranean Sea. A bearded passenger across from me took out his pocketknife and started the spiral peeling of an orange; the tangy smell reached me as I looked past him out the window, where pink oleanders, palms, and drought-resistant flowering plants reminded me of Southern California. The train stations were attractive stucco structures in the center of town, painted soft cantaloupe colors, often furnished with outdoor benches and decorative plants, and marked with tastefully crafted signs naming the stops. At the next melon-colored station, we gathered up our luggage to get off at the following stop: Cagnes-sur-Mer.

Every spring and summer, Moucha left Paris to live in her beloved stone house, once a water mill, which we called Le Moulin, situated on the outskirts of the artistic town of Vence, just north of Cagnes-sur-Mer. Her property was the last one at the south end of *le vallon*, below the village of St. Jeannet, perched hundreds of meters above. Arnaud spent much of his time there piling river rocks in wire structures to dam up the year-round running creek, thus creating a

Le Moulin in Vence, France

refreshing pool for us to dip into. Each day, the sun of the *midi* warmed our spirits, and we ate our meals with his mother under a serene bamboo arbor close to the house.

Le cabanon

A narrow footbridge crossed the flowing *riverlette* from Le Moulin to *le cabanon*, the one-room hut without electricity or plumbing that was our private home when we stayed there. Although I was still in my walking cast, Arnaud and I reveled in the atmosphere of Provençal May; we were not thinking about our careers or our future.

We'd sleep in *le cabanon* after lunch and read after dinner until the sun sank beyond the cliffs of *le vallon* (the little valley).

My broken leg was not mending as quickly as predicted. "You must wait another month to take the cast off," the doctor in Nice had said. But as soon as we were out of reach of the doctor's ears, Arnaud suggested that he remove the cast. As we gazed out at the inviting waters off the stony beach at Cagnes-sur-Mer, Arnaud's loving authority seemed natural to me, even when it countered the doctor's. I was glad to get the itchy cast off and swim, but I limped for a year.

On May 30, 1964, the day before Arnaud left for China, we exhibited true tenderness in a black-and-white photo taken in front of *le cabanon*. We would be going our separate directions once again, but, overall, I felt secure and content in our relationship as a couple.

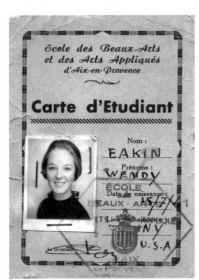
My École des Beaux-Arts
student card, 1964

The École des Beaux-Arts didn't start until the fall of 1964.

I left *le vallon* to rent a bed in a residence in Nice for working young women, where I earned my stay preparing the breakfasts. In the evenings, I made money babysitting for an agency that paid well and gave us white smocks to wear so we looked like nurses to the American clients. Image pays.

Arnaud was a prolific letter writer. He wrote long pages about learning Chinese with his tutor, teaching

French, traveling to the countryside, and loneliness; he said how much he loved me and thought of me; and he asked about my schoolwork. His social life was drastically limited by the firm reluctance of the Chinese to mix with foreigners. Our regular and energetic connection by mail lightened the strain of our geographical distance.

From Aix, I wrote to my Arnaud:

We are five architectural students; four are men. We are learning to draw Doric, Ionic, and Corinthian columns and using black ink wash to shade the curved forms. It seems unnecessary to me. Solid geometry, figure drawing, and architectural history are the other subjects. I am having a hard time with *théorèmes, corollaires* and *réciproques*. When I draw the assignments as accurately as I can and I reach the last line, it misses the first line by half a centimeter. Not good.

The accumulation of lines drawn with inaccurate degrees showed at the end of my work and is very frustrating. Yet, I go to the atelier all day five days a week and feel engaged. One fellow, Alain J., is very helpful in showing me stuff. I told him about you and he respects our relationship as a couple. He watches over me like a big brother, which I like. The school is in the center of Aix. This town is a joy to be in.

My first lodging was alongside a decrepit orchard outside of Aix-en-Provence. I rode my motorbike in Cézanne's countryside to town, where major fountains gracefully divided the wide main street. The French rural aesthetic and scale suited me, and I settled in like a cricket in a prairie of red poppies. Then, at midyear, my classmate Alain J. decided to transfer to the École in the bigger town of Montpellier, as his parents were moving back to Montpellier. He persuaded me to change ateliers, too—Alain J. felt the larger atelier would be more satisfying, and I agreed. Plus, by then I was glad to leave my second room, a lovely villa outside of town, rented from an eccentric angry woman. Here I was, following a man's lead again; but this time for my career, not for travel or love.

From Montpellier, I wrote to my Arnaud:

Recently, I drew a Herringbone pattern for the stonework façade, which was fun to draw, but somehow I felt I was re-creating historical buildings rather than meeting the needs of a modern culture.

The 11 French male students accept me rather well and we have espresso every morning and afternoon at the local café. Our atelier is in a funny narrow building, built into the ramparts of a public garden. We take drawing classes in a classical old building off the garden. I work hard to keep up, but I am definitely the weakest student. My classmates help me but also tease me. I don't know why I am teased so, because I am female, because I am American, or just because I am so gullible. Some of us have dinner together at the student mess hall with very cheap food, brain was ok, but intestines I couldn't stomach the taste.

With my drafting board at the École
in Montpellier, France

Three years had passed since I'd left California, and I was happy when my mother said she would visit. Mother arrived in Montpellier in the early spring of 1965. She was a good sport about staying with me in my matchbox on the second floor of an ancient, poorly remodeled apartment building, and didn't say anything when I showed her how the primitive shower worked in combination with the stand-up Turkish toilet in the hall outside my door. With only a hand-sink in my room, we had to make do with ready-to-eat foods, like canned tuna that happened to be bad and made us both sick and vomit. She only stayed a few days, but her visit helped me to recognize how focused I was on my school life and how content I was in Montpellier, despite the meager living conditions. Student life required little money; Arnaud had given me some, I had saved money from my odd jobs, and my mother added money to the pot when she saw how little I had to live on. Architecture was for me, and Mother was witness. Even with the topography of the architectural profession beyond my periphery, my course appeared to be on solid ground. Near the end of the scholastic year, the École arranged a bus trip to view the rural Roman architecture to the west of Montpellier. Most of my classmates and I signed up, along with students from other faculties: law, fine arts, and economics. The presence of the other students added an interesting dynamic—on this trip, my atelier mates stopped teasing me and instead became attentive and protective. My status changed from American female to fellow architectural student, which felt wonderfully inclusive. Plus, I bunked with the other females on the trip and met Jacqueline, a law student, who to this day remains a lifetime friend.

While I was in Montpellier falling in love with architecture, Arnaud was becoming even more attached to his Chinese studies, and he elected to stay in China another year. He wrote, "Dear love, I want you to come and live with me in Peking. I like it here and I am learning so much."

École classmates in Montpellier

"How would that work?" I wrote back, open to the possibility of living in China to be with Arnaud, but feeling a little behind the decision-making curve. And what about my education? Even so, I think I entertained the idea of going to Peking partially because I didn't feel at home with the French method of teaching architecture. I had never even noticed a column before traveling in Europe, and now I was spending hours becoming adept in drawing and shading the acanthus leaves of a Corinthian capital. Where was I going to use this skill? Making places suited my idealism, but not with Corinthian capitals.

To Arnaud's surprise, the Chinese government was not willing to pay a loved one to accompany her man to Peking; he would have to return and marry me if he wanted me to join him. I also needed a French passport, as the United States didn't want Americans going to China in 1965. My full attention went to getting all the paperwork in order before he arrived. This decision was indisputably a pivotal one. In thinking about it later, I can see how the dangling of two loves—travel and my man—outweighed my new love of architecture, two to one. My thinking was that career could be added to marriage—there wasn't any prescribed order or conflict between them.

Arnaud and I married on July 17, 1965. It drizzled that day in Paris, but I still wore the backless red, yellow, and orange striped sundress from the local Super-U for the civil ceremony at the mayor's office. The actual wedding day was not a big deal for either of us. We had been a happy couple for three years—albeit not a traditional couple. We had been apart and together in extraordinarily beautiful places: Paris, the Alps, and the south of France. Arnaud and I took our wedding lunch alone in a restaurant, rather out of character for us but probably suggested by a family member. Later that afternoon, a few of Arnaud's friends and close family members came to his parents' apartment for sparkling wine and a piece of our wedding cake: a mountain of golden, golf-ball-sized creampuffs that I took photos of to send to my mother and sister.

Now a married couple with French passports, we were off to China. However, architecture was not forsaken; during my months at the École, the budding stem of architecture had been solidly grafted onto the stalk of my identity—I could feel it.

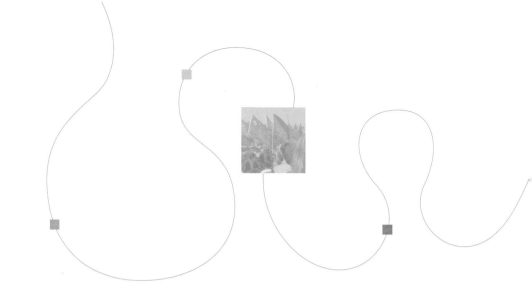

There Is Time

August 1965 to November 1966: China

At the Moscow airport, a midnight tray of cold but tasty food was served to hold us until our final destination. We stepped from the Russian airplane onto the dusty tarmac in Peking, both of us glad for the warm morning. It was easy for the Chinese government to keep close track of the foreigners working for them; most foreigners needed to be escorted everywhere since they didn't speak Chinese. Arnaud, however, spoke fluent Mandarin, and he quickly marshaled a taxi to get us to the Institute of Foreign Languages, on the outskirts of Peking. Our taxi was one of few cars on the two-lane paved road crowded with buses, bicycles, and animal-drawn carts. Peasants sold yellow and red watermelons from parked trucks on the side of the road, but we didn't stop. Arnaud chatted with the driver. I observed contently—my travels around the world had well prepared me for touching down in the foreign landscape of a still-rural Peking.

The taxi dropped us at the austere campus compound. Surrounded by agricultural fields, the campus consisted of concrete-block, ash-colored buildings grouped in rows at hard right angles, softened only slightly by the leafy limbs of an occasional tree. Crossing an empty quad of yellowish dirt, we carried our few bags to Arnaud's room, located in the middle of the second floor of an undecorated college dorm. There were no kitchen facilities, as everyone ate in the communal dining room. We used the toilets, sinks, and showers at the far end of the hall intended for anyone on the floor—although we were the only ones using them. A smiling male Iraqi teacher and an older spry Australian woman occupied two rooms downstairs, while the other 30 sleeping rooms in the dorm were vacant. Most of the teachers preferred to live in the comparatively luxurious Peking Friendship Hotel in town, reserved for foreigners. We also could have stayed there, as lodging was part of the payment for work, but Arnaud wanted maximum access to the students. I bought a young potted palm and a few oranges from the only grocery store within walking distance. They weren't much, but they helped to make our monastic quarters homier.

At scheduled times each day, students and teachers poured out of the classrooms into the open dusty areas between buildings. I watched as they performed exercises to a recorded voice on a loudspeaker barking instructions over the music. And I joined in once or twice.

By the end of our first week in Peking, I could not help but be aware of all the time on my hands. One evening in our somber room, Arnaud and I sat on the bed talking about an interesting conversation he'd had with a teacher who missed his village terribly. Arnaud loved to teach and was impressed with how quickly his students were learning French. I could see he was genuinely happy in China, and I felt good about coming, but I had also been thinking about how I could be productive during our stay.

I reached over to touch his hand and said, "I think this would be a good time to have a child"—as if I'd been programmed that children came with marriage.

"You do?" Arnaud couldn't have looked more surprised if a baby had dropped from between my legs right then.

The air between us filled with intense reflection. We had never discussed having children before, so I understood his stunned searching expression.

"I have a whole year free to get pregnant," I continued calmly, caressing his forearm. "There is time to have a baby ... what do you think?" I was the one practicing birth control, but I wanted his concurrence.

"I guess it's a good idea," Arnaud said, adjusting quickly. "Everything is paid for here." He seemed to be settling in with the concept, focusing on the practical first. It was almost as if it had never occurred to him that we would at some point decide to have or not to have a child or children.

Then he smiled and added, "A little girl would be nice," as if I could just dial in the desired gender.

Within that brief conversation, we took on one of the biggest decisions of our lives. One month later, I was pregnant. We were very pleased; life seemed to be reeling in our *happily ever after*.

Except for occasional sightseeing, we rarely left the institute; everything we needed was provided. Arnaud and I ate with the other foreign teachers, relegated to the corner closest to the kitchen in the vast, stark dining hall. We would rather have mingled with the students and local teachers, but mixing was iron-handedly discouraged and we respected this code; we didn't want others to get into trouble. Strict peer pressure compelled people not to stray—including us. Although relationships were not easy to build, one cheery cook—who had previously cooked in an embassy—made us European dishes like mashed potatoes and gravy. He was an older, chubby-cheeked man, and when he realized I was pregnant, he made me special dishes with more meat in them, initiating a heartwarming friendship, in spite of the rules not to do so. Soon I felt comfortable enough to venture into the kitchen and thank him personally in my budding basic Mandarin.

I mainly spoke French with Arnaud, but when it became known that I was American, a school administrator asked him if I would become a paid part-time teacher. Within days, I was given a textbook and told to stand in front of an advanced class, reading English aloud so the students could hear a native speaker. Only 24 and uneducated in communist doctrine, I showed a lack of political correctness when students asked me questions about life in the United States. For example, when one curious boy asked me, "How do you find a job?" I responded by saying, "We can apply to work anywhere we want to, even travel to another city. We don't need permission from the government like you do here." I was slightly out of line. I had been told to just read the lesson—easy enough and I made an effort—except that rote teaching wasn't my thing.

We didn't need much money in China, so I insisted we send what we made back to France. Arnaud agreed and asked his father to bank it for us.

In December, all the students left the institute for winter holiday recess. Arnaud wanted to ice skate, so he arranged for us to stay at the Friendship Hotel. Designed for foreign residents, the six-story hotel towered above Peking's traditional one-story structures, built over the course of seven centuries. Besides being high, it was bulky and plain, like so many of the newer buildings—not adding any delight to the city's historic profile. Just two decades before, the Imperial Buildings, with ribbed, glazed, golden-tiled roofs and large upward curving corners, had dominated elegantly the flat cityscape.

With an onlooker at the
Summer Palace, 1965

Arnaud couldn't dance, but on the ice he glided with the grace of a crane in flight. We'd brought our ice skates from France, and after a restful night in our hotel room with its modest but clean private bath, we took the local bus to the Summer Palace, about six miles away. We had visited the Summer Palace when we first arrived in China, and enjoyed walking the long corridor joining octagonal pavilions, temples, and decorative bridges. I was enchanted then with the palace's long history, going back to the Chin Dynasty (1153). Burned by allied Anglo-French forces in 1860, the Summer Palace was rebuilt in 1888 and 1900 when the fearless and powerful Empress Dowager ordered the site to be her playground. In fact, her continued summer visits gave this imperial palace its name. *Summer Palace* was the common name, but I liked the more formal name—*Yi He Yuan*—"Garden of Nurtured Harmony," one of several translations, because it caught the image of man working to be in harmony with nature.

The Summer Palace in December was a sight to behold. Silver and glassy ice replaced the lotus plants and rowboats of summer, and fewer people visited. Skates in hand, Arnaud and I advanced toward the frozen lake, strolling along the exquisite 2,000-foot-long covered walkway, even more colorful and whimsical against the season's muted grays.

Every built surface on the grounds was painted—posts and lattice railings were often bright red or green, while beams were decorated in blues and gold. We found a bench close to the ice and sat down.

"Lace up, *chérie*," said Arnaud, reaching to tie his first skate.

My being three months pregnant might have worried some couples, but not us. "This is magical," I answered, overawed by the wintry splendor as we ventured out onto more ice than I had ever seen.

"Easy does it to start with." Arnaud took my elbow.

After a few minutes of skating hand in hand, I said, "You go ahead. I need to get used to it."

"Okay." Arnaud smiled and squeezed my hand before unclasping his hand to push off into an endless glide.

Bundled up in my padded indigo blue jacket and peasant pants, I remained cautious, and Arnaud wasn't pushing me to try new turns the way he liked to. While Arnaud skated, joyfully and obsessively

Pregnant in Peking, 1966

forming figure eights, I marveled at the scale and charm of this planned park, now open to anyone all year 'round, thanks to the communist government; in the past, the palaces were forbidden territory to ordinary people. There was no fee to pay at the entrance gate and no rental stands or snack concessions.

There were 14,000 different paintings on the beams, kept up every 12 years by painting crews. I skated less than Arnaud, giving me time to linger and view many of the paintings in detail, discovering and delighting in the variety of flowers, architecture, landscapes, and scenes from classical literature wrapping around the park's splendid structural elements.

Just before we were to return to the institute from our two-week holiday, a school administrator told Arnaud that I was not to teach anymore. We thought spies had reported that I was saying too many good things about my homeland: I had said positive things about freedom instead of critical things about capitalism. Their reason for banning me from the classroom went unexplained, but Arnaud was outraged and we didn't move back to the campus. He commuted to the institute.

My Chinese communication skills were improving, and the Friendship Hotel was a direct bus ride from anywhere in town, so I felt confident enough to take the bus by myself to shop. Walking the crowded streets of Peking, I got used to seeing people wearing white surgical masks to keep from spreading colds and to avoid dust. I'm sure I was noticed, even though I wore the traditional black cotton shoes and blue peasant outfit, but I was never approached in kindness or malice; I felt safe. The special corner stand, with its tasty yogurt in a glass pot, became a favorite destination, as did the large home goods store where I bought blue and white rice bowls with matching plates and cups. The cashier returned everyone's change with tongs, so as not to touch the money. I didn't buy much.

Any discretionary income the Chinese people gained was used for extra food, household items, or special events. Tourism was nonexistent, and the politics required that anything old or bourgeois be destroyed or hidden, so there were no antiques stores, clothing boutiques, souvenir stalls, or gift shops, as there probably are now. One department-like store for foreign workers sold luxury goods; I bought two yards of emerald green brocade and had a skirt and top made. I didn't wear the outfit much, but I still treasure it today as a souvenir.

Peking, like many cities in China, was designed as a series of rectangular walled courtyards. The city's layout was particularly intriguing: the Forbidden City lay at the center of the Imperial City, which was itself within the Inner City, all gated by the Outer City wall. From the gate at the southern main entrance, a wide road ran straight into the very center of the Forbidden City, forming a grid with the main streets it crossed along the way. In between these larger streets huddled the *hutung*, a labyrinth of walled lanes hiding modest houses. Arnaud took his private lessons in one of these traditional neighborhoods, and I would sometimes accompany him to the Huas' house. Stepping from the wide noisy street where the buses ran, we'd enter the *hutung*. All the houses were built to look into their own courtyards rather than out into the lanes. Unlike Europe's round-shaped castles, the Chinese system of square spaces was followed in most plan layouts and house design, including the Huas' home.

In earlier days, the Chinese thought the European practice of building into the air showed that they were so poor, they didn't have enough land to stay near the ground. But that changed in Peking during the 15 years before our arrival. The state built awkward, monumental, multistory architecture, even opposite the gate of the Imperial Palace, the obvious and aesthetically unfortunate result of political pangs. Chinese architects didn't have time to decide between traditional Chinese elements from the Ming Dynasty—a major influence on the city's character—and the institutional drab enforced by the Soviet Union's recent occupation. Clearly, defining a new state that included everyone took priority over urban design considerations. A radical physical change hit Peking, much as it had Paris a century earlier; however, in Paris, the pleasure of the everyday use of the street was amplified by rows of trees, parks, and paths. Here, size seemed to be the overriding criterion of new museums and "halls to the people," each a quarter-mile long.

Peking, May 1, 1966

We visited Tiananmen Square, the largest open square in the world. Chang'an Boulevard runs along the Square, lined with lampposts topped with an inverted bunch of grape-shaped globes. The expansive street was designed to accommodate political processions, particularly on Workers' Day (our Labor Day), when all six lanes were filled with marching people. On May 1, 1966, Arnaud and I sat in amazement with the large orderly crowd gathered to watch the event from temporary bleachers.

I made friends at the hotel and started to hand-sew a maternity dress and clothes for my baby, due in early June, only to find out later that the proportions were all wrong—her baby arm couldn't fit in the tiny sleeve. I wrote letters home and to friends, even though letters from Peking were noticed at the post office, according to my mother, but not stopped. Feeling particularly energetic in the eighth month of my pregnancy, I went with Arnaud to hike in the foothills and visit the compact, red-walled Ming Tombs.

One of my new friends, an Englishwoman who knew about the Lamaze natural birth method, gave me Erna Wright's book from the National Childbirth Trust in London. Being so isolated, I appreciated her guidance and read about what to expect during childbirth. Arnaud and I practiced the breathing exercises together; there were three levels of breathing to learn, and Arnaud's job was to help me determine when to shift from one to the other. Early on June 2, 1966, I said to Arnaud, "My water broke; I think that means we're to go to the hospital."

"Wonderful, I'll get a taxi to the old American Hospital."

Letter from China to my mother

The moment we arrived, I was whisked onto the only bed in the middle of an inglorious and otherwise bare room. Arnaud stood holding my hand. No papers to fill out, no payments, and no hassle—everything was simple and taken care of.

A woman doctor in a white coat checked my progress and said, "Oh, you are just starting. Go home and come back when contractions are one minute apart."

After a long night of timing my ever-closer contractions, we returned to the hospital. Again, the same dull, no-frills room awaited us. I was prepped, and then Arnaud and I were taken into the birth room. I think the doctors were as glad as I was that Arnaud spoke Mandarin so well; he stayed in the room for the entire birth event.

Our daughter, Chanette, was born at one o'clock in the afternoon on June 3, 1966, weeks before my 25th birthday. Arnaud and I were both exhausted, but he joked that if Chanette had waited until June 6, it would have been a fitting D-Day.

Looking rested the next morning, Arnaud said, "I brought you strawberries, dearest one."

"They smell good." I popped a red berry into my mouth. "Find the nurse to bring Chanette." No buttons to call the nurse here.

"She can't miss Shuang Shuang, the only blond baby among the dark-haired ones," he answered, and we both laughed.

Arnaud's last name was translated as "white" in Mandarin, so Arnaud and his tutor came up with the name Shuang Shuang—"White Snow Falling"—for Chanette. The name *Chanette* was inspired from

Chamonix, one of our homes in the Alps. I had friends named Linette, Josette, and Henriette, and I wanted to use the *ette*, a common French ending to female names. Since Chanette is not the name of a saint, the French thought it was an American name, while the Americans thought it was French. (I found out decades later that Chanette is a girl's name in Denmark.)

On June 21, 1966, I wrote in my journal:

> Now that Chanette is here, I can't help feeling a bit resentful sometimes, being left with all the little problems and duties of parenthood, while Arnaud continues to do everything he did before. He has a great fear of wasting time with the baby. He always said, "I want a wife who has a profession, not a femme au foyer (housewife)." But I have the feeling of doing all the work and making all the decisions. This is difficult for me because I too am struggling to have my place as a mother, but also as an architect. It is always the mother sacrificed for the child in our society while I want very much to participate in the evolution of man and not retire at 25 years old to parenthood and nothing else. Of course, I am only into the first 18 days of motherhood, and can't even study my architecture here, but I fear a bad habit setting in and I am disappointed in him. But maybe it is just because I'm tired, things are new, and I see things blacker than they are and Arnaud will later divide the responsibilities of the baby.

Arnaud continued his Chinese lessons with Mr. Hua. Sometimes, Madame Hua, the tutor's wife, opened the courtyard gate for him to enter from the lane. On his first visit after Chanette's birth, she told him, "Don't take the baby out until one month after birth."

"Why is that?" Arnaud asked.

"This is tradition. After one month, you dress her in red and take her out to meet the world." She emphasized, "This is an important life-passage."

Arnaud told me about the ritual, and we agreed to follow it. I bought a baby red silk jacket for Chanette to wear; when the day arrived, Arnaud suddenly became interested in showing off his daughter.

Since Chanette was ready to meet the world, I started going with Arnaud to the Huas' house more regularly. To pass the time, Madame Hua decided to teach me the order of brushstrokes to form characters. Even without understanding their meaning, I enjoyed the calligraphy and practiced between lessons in a thin notebook with squares instead of lines—one box for each character. Madame Hua and I grew closer, and one day I asked her in my shaky Mandarin, "May I measure your house?"

"Why does she do that?" Madame Hua looked to Arnaud.

"She wants to be an architect," Arnaud explained. "Since your house is a typical one, she would like to draw it up as an exercise and a souvenir."

On our next visit, I came armed with pencil, tape measure, and paper. Madame Hua held one end of the tape as I walked the length of the gray brick outer wall. Then we measured the wood partition between the house and the courtyard. The attractive partition consisted of a decorative wood lattice frame, backed with white rice paper on the upper portion, and with lower glass windows that opened like an awning into the courtyard. This was my first attempt to record an existing building to scale in plan and elevation, as I had learned at the École des Beaux-Arts. I drew it up at home and made note of any measurements I needed to get on future visits.

Oh, I was proud of my efforts; I put in the dimensions and labeled the uses of each part of the house, even applying the wash technique I'd learned to show 45-degree shadows. The architectural exercise engaged me—I was also quietly highlighting for Arnaud my enduring intent to become an architect.

Only one restaurant in Peking served European-style meals. Arnaud and I rarely went out to eat, so several times I joined my European friends for dinner. We routinely ate Chinese food, which was good, but I was homesick for pork roast, salad Niçoise with olives, and croissants with butter and jam. At the institute, our daily eating situations were communal—we all ate the same things—but at the restaurant, I liked being able to order individually. Our one-year mark in China was approaching, and I had begun looking forward to once again savoring French food.

Chanette Lea Bertrand came with me everywhere, although Chinese aunties (babysitters) were available and commonly used. I took naturally to motherhood, and carried her or pushed the baby buggy to the dining room or on the bus to the tutor's, park, or market.

By November 1966, the Cultural Revolution was in full swing; foreigners were considered out of place, and we were required to leave China. We had already been there longer than a year, and while Arnaud might have lobbied to stay much longer, now he couldn't. As we left Peking, Cultural Revolution posters lined the streets and tense crowds filled the new train station. The Red Guards clutched their Red Books. Our flight to Paris departed from Shanghai, where the buildings were taller and closer together than in Peking. From our fancy Shanghai hotel room with stuffed lounge chairs and plush carpet, we observed the nightlife that didn't exist in Peking—where peasants rose and turned out the lights early. Arnaud had traveled during his two years in China, but I hadn't, so I enjoyed being on the move. My detour from architecture appeared to be over. Chanette was six months old.

When we got home to Paris, I avoided telling people I had been in China, even though I had been happy in Peking. It was very safe, theft was unheard of, and the culture was rich and practical. The food was tasty, and the people were friendly, considering the social pressure not to mix with foreigners. However, I was rather subdued by the frugal quality of life, the Communist political thrust, and the required conformity in behavior and clothing. The foreigners who were in Peking radiated an air of superiority that I felt was unjustified. I came back feeling humbled by the experience and in no way wanted to bring attention to myself because of it. I lacked the social intelligence to explain the context of my experiences and was afraid to misrepresent life in China. I couldn't imagine people in Paris understanding one-horse carts collecting sewage, flour ground by an ox turning a stone in a circle, swarms of bicycles in wide streets with few cars, or crowded parks with everybody wearing the same unfashionable blue caps and jackets, blurring class and style. The French considered China exotic, and the Americans saw China as out of reach, but my recent stay had been down to earth and enjoyable. Still, instinctively and consciously, I kept silent about my time in China, turning my attention instead to my marriage, my daughter, and getting back to architecture.

Ignoring the Knot

December 1966 to May 1968: French Alps to Berkeley

Somehow, Jacques, Arnaud's father, had spent the thousands of yuan we'd sent home from our Peking paychecks. When we asked about our bank account, he said the money was gone. Angry and disgusted, I felt we had both been bitterly betrayed. It was more than I had ever saved, and I'd been counting on financing my studies with a portion of the tidy sum. Arnaud was upset too but never asked his father to say what he'd used it for—or to pay us back.

"What about us?" I asked, already tightening my grip on our vulnerable purse strings.

"He must have needed it," Arnaud responded, and that was the end of it.

We reported in early December for the 1966–67 ski season at the UCPA in Chamonix. High in the French Alps, Chamonix had been a historic mountaineering destination for centuries, as it was located near a major glacier (La Mer de Glace) and Europe's highest mountain— Mont Blanc.

I thought I was happily married. Along with the monthly salary my husband received, we enjoyed our rustic sleeping chalet, nestled in a spectacular valley. At mealtimes, we'd amble the few crunchy steps on the snow to the main UCPA chalet, where communal tables were set for 60 people to eat breakfast and dinner. France's famed reputation for fresh food held true, even in communal living. Each evening, after a delicious dinner, we'd join the others at the huge rock fireplace next to the dining room. There, we'd warm ourselves listening to our friend Joe play songs from his Romanian gypsy origins on the flamenco guitar.

While Arnaud and Joe were teaching skiing, Joe's wife, Linette, and I spent time in each other's neighboring chalets, usually hand-sewing and taking care of our young ones; her son, Vanco, was one year older than Chanette. We knew Joe from Les Contamines. Two summers before, Joe and Linette had come to Le Moulin to spend their honeymoon in Vence with us. I took a snapshot of radiant Linette peeking from under a full-brimmed white hat, her beautiful straight brown hair hanging well below her shoulders; but then I drank too much champagne and misplaced the roll of film, never to be found. How could that have happened?

On New Year's Day, before we crossed the snowy grounds to the main chalet for a celebration, I announced my New Year's resolution to Arnaud. "This year I want us to go back to California so I can resume my architectural studies." I was giving him plenty of lead time for the following fall.

He smiled his easy smile and playfully picked up Chanette. "Okay, I like California, and, sure, I want you to be an architect."

"You can teach skiing there, too," I said to seal the deal. He laughed, and I planted an especially loving kiss first on my daughter's cheek and then on my husband's lips.

Arnaud and I had a routine worked out. Late in the morning, I carried Chanette to the babysitter's house, then went to my part-time job selling ski clothes at a nearby sporting goods store, which was run by two broadminded middle-aged sisters. I earmarked my earnings for my architectural education in California and rejoiced when the news reached me that the only architecture school in the UC system—at

Berkeley—had accepted my credits from the École des Beaux-Arts, UCSB, and the Monterey Institute for Foreign Languages.

Late in the afternoon, Arnaud, who was gaining interest in his daughter by the day, picked up Chanette after ski lessons. He basked in the attention he received from showing her off to his students—a little too much, for my liking—and reminded me of the way his father had played with his grandchild in Paris. Arnaud liked to practice Chinese on Chanette, who didn't speak any language yet, and he used only her Chinese name: Shuang Shuang.

The French commercial workday ended just before our much-welcomed dinner hour at seven. Strolling home from the sporting goods store, I mused at how wonderfully my career and family life were entwining. At last, advancement toward my career had moved to the top of our priorities and had been placed on our family calendar.

We owned a used Deux Chevaux *camionnette*, which literally translated meant, "two horses of little truck." The classic, inexpensive gray Citroën was made of corrugated metal, shaped in a half-cylinder like a mini Quonset hut. There was ample room in the back for our belongings and a sleeping basket for Chanette—just an arm's length away, behind the canvas garden seats. The engine huffed with the whine of an over-weight lawnmower, but the wavy metal car proved reliable and sturdy—which was why half the population in France drove some version of the Deux Chevaux, and many still do today.

Arnaud loved teaching and passed his final national ski test. At the end of April, the snowy carpet on the lower ski slopes melted, closing the UCPA season. We left Chamonix in our *camionnette*, rolling down through the sprouting valleys into warmer and greener landscapes as the little car carried us toward the Mediterranean Sea. My scholastic year in California was to start in August, and we planned to spend the summer at Le Moulin, my mother-in-law's country place in Vence, a good day's drive south from Mont Blanc.

Springtime glowing, the little engine humming, I pondered the details of our trip to California. "I am ready to buy our tickets," I said, shifting my gaze and sense of urgency toward Arnaud. "We need to be there in three months."

His eyes and hands held firmly to the road. "I'm not going with you," he said, without an ounce of dramatic intention.

My mood melted, my breath choked, my mind raced red. "I am going anyway," I fired back.

My bullet of conviction silenced the air. We didn't say any more about it. Stunned by this sudden turn of events and stunted by our unhealthy pattern of not resolving conflict, I felt myself shut down. Neither of us spoke during the next six hours of winding through mountain passes, pastures, and villages.

The windshield helped me reflect on my thoughts about our togetherness. For the last five years, I had followed Arnaud to France and China. I thought it fair that it was now his turn to follow me. He had lived in the United States before, spoke English, and had a green card to work. His coming with me was very doable, and he had no job to go to in France. Why wasn't he willing to come? I did not know the word *sexism*, but I recognized that I was bearing the brunt of unfair treatment; the word *chauvinism* might also have explained it. Knowing these concepts may have helped me to understand the situation and challenge his unwillingness to support me in my career, but at the time, my emotions were too immature to untangle this nasty knot. My husband's refusal to explain his sudden decision not to accompany his family was too outrageous and mysterious for me to tackle.

Chanette and me
in Vence, 1967

At dusk, we veered right at the narrow Roman bridge onto the unpaved road down to Le Moulin. The subject of my architectural education remained submerged for now, but I was going to architecture school in California with my daughter. I would buy the tickets as soon as possible.

The summer days ticked by … Arnaud seemed content, freed from following his wife and child, yet expressing loving words as if no thorny conflict existed. His rosy manner seemed mildly insane, but being so fixed on going my own way, I ignored the deeper meaning of his behavior. We had been apart before, but this was not just one more time. Being together didn't seem an important part of marriage to him, while the idea of our being apart was too much for me.

We celebrated Chanette's first birthday, hung out by the creek, took day trips to the Mediterranean Sea, and munched celery root salads under the grape arbor. Arnaud tried to dam up part of the river with rocks to make a swimming pool. Moucha and I pitted golden Mirabelle plums for annual gallon batches of jam; we got along well because of our activities, not because of long conversations where we discussed life and love. When I used the good china to prettify the table, she was delighted, as her two daughters were not interested in domestic tasks and aesthetics the way I was.

By mid-August 1967, Chanette and I were on a plane leaving Paris with two worn suitcases. No one said not to go, but I knew Moucha wondered and worried.

After being away for five years, I first visited my mother, who found me unusually introverted. Again, I didn't talk about my trip to China for fear of being misunderstood. This silence was rather out of character for me, as in the past I had been quick—probably too quick—to say what was on my mind. We visited Jeannie, now married to a man 20 years her senior. A girlfriend from La Jolla was going to France, and I suggested she visit my French family.

Jeannie and Robert in Point Loma, California

In Berkeley, Chanette and I settled into a one-bedroom apartment on Derby Street, a few blocks south of campus. I slept in the living room, as my mother had during my childhood. To help with the pronunciation of my daughter's name, I began to use "S" instead of "C," so that in English the "Sh" in her name "Shanette" sounded like "Shannon."

Child care dictated our routine. Each weekday morning, I snuggled 16-month-old Shanette into the child-seat of my bike for the ride to

Mrs. Howe's home, only a flat mile from Derby Street. Then I'd pedal up newly planted, tree-lined Telegraph Avenue to reach my first class of the day by eight in the morning.

During calculus class, every quiz seemed to be over before I could read the questions. I just couldn't gear up for the quiz rhythm and failed each one. Right after getting my grade, I would arrange to meet with the professor during his office hours to learn what I didn't know. I was learning the material, but too late—*after* each quiz. These first failures roused anxieties and gave me cause for reflection about my abilities. After the third calculus flop, I visited the makeshift counseling office trailer, wondering if architecture was for me. A counselor asked me to take a test of multiple-choice questions and return the following week for the results.

"Yes, architecture seems to be your area of interest," said the confident counselor, looking down at the page he held in both hands. "Architecture isn't listed as one of our subjects, but you rate high in psychology and engineering, so I think that is as close as you can get to architecture." His eyes, filled with kindness, lifted lightly off the page.

That was all I needed to hear. I stood and said, "Okay, I'm going to stick with it." It was as if a faucet dripping self-doubt had been repaired with a new washer; I felt fixed. My technique of learning, even after each quiz, must have worked because, miraculously, I passed the class with a B. Funny thing, though—calculus was more of a hurdle than a skill I ever used in my career.

Wurster Hall, UC Berkeley

The majority of my day was spent in architecture classes, taught in Wurster Hall, the College of Environmental Design. Wurster Hall was named after William Wilson Wurster, a distinguished architect and the first dean of the college. By chance, his wife, Catherine Bauer Wurster, was a professor of city and regional planning and a leader in the field of public housing. Wurster Hall's controversial concrete tower had been built with exposed utility systems so that students could see the pipes, wires, ducts, insulation, and structure usually hidden behind a building's walled surfaces. Unlike many, I liked Wurster Hall. Three architecture faculty members, Joseph Esherick, Vernon DeMars, and Donald Olsen—all of whom I knew by sight—had designed the building, built in 1964.

Once, while washing my hands in Wurster's women's restroom, I asked a sister student, "What time does the library open today?"

"What country are you from?" she inquired, studying me as if I'd dropped in from another planet. Apparently, I spoke English with a French accent and didn't even realize it.

"I'm American, but I have been out of the US a while," I answered, not prepared for this sort of culture shock. The liquid hand soap smelled harsh; I quickly dried my hands and left, still not knowing what time the library would open.

Little new things were awkward. For example, when I opened my first checking account, the clerk thought it strange that I didn't know how to write a check and conferred with the manager about my request. In France and China, we used only cash. The Admissions Office also gave me the "foreigner" treatment because I was married to a Frenchman. I had to pay out-of-state fees, resulting in an unexpected need to borrow a lot of money from the Student Loan Office and from my mother, who fortunately liked to play banker at a mutually beneficial interest rate. I had saved money from my job at the sporting goods store, and Arnaud had given me a few hundred dollars, but that didn't begin to cover this unplanned and significant financial outlay.

From the day I left France, I considered myself a married single mother without regrets. I wore short skirts and wrote long letters to my husband and his mother, both tenacious correspondents. Among the details of daily life, their letters lobbied for my return. I thought they were discounting the importance of my education, and I countered with, "Come be with us."

The letters turned ugly when Arnaud wrote to me how much he cared for the girlfriend I had sent for him to show around, while emphasizing that he still loved me, of course. His mother saw me as the guilty one. "This wouldn't have happened if he hadn't been left alone," she wrote, while I faulted my husband. The devastating news eroded my trust in our marriage. My so-called girlfriend reckoned with the problem by returning to the United States and marrying as quickly as possible; our relationship healed but remained strained for years.

Weekdays, promptly at five, I pedaled to Mrs. Howe's house to pick up Shanette, who spent the day with four other youngsters, all under two years old. My scholastic focus adjusted around my daughter's needs; evenings were tightly scheduled to be with her for dinner, playtime, bath time, and the story before her early bedtime. While she slept, I found another couple of hours to continue preparing for my History of Environmental Design course; I made presentation boards of the Temple of Hera, the Paestum, and La Maison Carrée in Nîmes, using colored paper, ink drawings, and text to compare approach, columns, interiors, and massing of space. I welcomed this method of studying historical architecture much more than I had drawing columns at the École. Calculus and physics didn't require any graphics, so I could do most of that homework between classes at school. I reached for the light switch about ten, feeling fulfilled.

My hanging lamp creations

Traveling the world on a shoestring had taught me how to live cheaply, so I didn't think twice about my money being limited. On Saturdays or Sundays, we'd look for furniture at the Alameda Flea Market, or I'd make hanging lamps with cardboard and colored paper or tie-dyed fabric. The few lamps I didn't use to dress up the apartment, I'd give to friends. Shanette often played until naptime on the porch stairs with the tall brown dog living in the apartment below. While she napped, I studied my calculus or did the problems for the physics lab I hadn't been able to complete during the week. No movies, no theater, no dancing the Twist to Ray Charles, and no dinner parties. No matter—I was enjoying the number-one rated architecture school in the country.

The daily student practice of architecture pleased and satisfied my sense of effective learning, while at home I was dedicated to my gentle blond daughter. As the French would say, "I felt good in my skin."

Hold the Rope

June 1968 to June 1971: Berkeley

After living close to campus on Derby Street for a scholastic year, Shanette and I qualified to move into one of the university's married housing units. Albany Village, as it was named, consisted of rows of remodeled asbestos-sided army barracks. Our ground-level address, 1139 F Ninth Street, amounted to nothing fancy: no garage, bathtub, dishwasher, or washing machine; no patio or deck; and only one weensy closet. But it suited us fine. Once again, I slept in a corner of the front room, as my mother had done before me. Shanette and her guinea pig stayed in one of the pocket-sized bedrooms, and the other became my student office.

UC married student housing in Albany Village

My sociable two-year-old daughter only had to step out the kitchen door to find playmates, and my neighbors were like extra parents. When Shanette caught the chicken pox, a neighbor watched her while I went to class. In the evenings, when Quinton, the boy upstairs, needed a baby sitter, he stayed with us, while his parents, both PhD candidates in chemistry, went to see a movie. I don't know how I could have managed without Albany Village's watch-out-for-one-another's-children community culture.

Weekday mornings, Shanette and I crossed the street, her sweet hand in my big one, to a well-managed childcare center. This gave me

My student desk in the bedroom

an eight-hour block of time to study; and I did, with the rigor of a job and the pleasure of creating art. Knowing Shanette was safe and happy, I wove my bike through the residential five miles uphill to campus, even in the rain, until I bought an old Nash to make the trip in bad weather. The library, photo lab, and wood shop were my refuges between lectures, physics labs, and art studios. A couple of afternoons a month, I made time to arrive at the child-care center an hour or two early to play with the kids. Shanette liked that, and I did, too.

"Mommy, hold the rope," she'd shout, incorporating me into her game and providing precious motherly moments.

During the winter quarter of 1968, I took Elements of Sculpture, a required course for bachelor of architecture students. The mustached visiting sculpture professor had straight sandy bangs and wore cow-boy boots. The first day, he announced in a deep Southern voice, "It doesn't matter what you do. I can tell how much time you've spent on your projects, and the more time you spend, the better the grade." Per my sculpture professor's suggestion, I checked out the wood shop in Wurster Hall's south wing, as yet unexplored. I was excited at the sight of table saws, sanders, drills, and flat work areas in the well-lit, oblong shop; but the hands-on smell of sawdust sold me. For my first assign-ment, I glued 16 short redwood pieces together in one plane, leav-ing the unevenness between the blocks to create a surface of texture and shadow. A second plane, less than half the height, intersected at a 90-degree angle. Satisfied with this first object of art, I envisioned, for my final, a redwood object with two planes intersecting a triangle. The first cuts were easy; however, I soon struggled with the compounded angles required to fit the components together.

"Could I help you get that to fit?" The workshop manager—a master carpenter—had observed that I still wasn't making much headway after several serious attempts.

"Sure," I mumbled, relieved to get some help, even though I hadn't thought to ask for any.

He adjusted the saw blade, then brought over clamps and showed me how to use them, all without any condescending comments, which I appreciated. I would have loved to construct my piece ten times larger, but the 25-inch size kept construction manageable. After sanding and sealing the warm natural color of the redwood, I stepped back and

One of my class sculptures

walked around my sculpture, feeling artistically pleased with the angles and planes from every direction.

It was like an affectionate pat on the back when, at the end of the quarter, my sculptural works were included in the display case in Kroeber Hall, where we had our class. I also learned how the making of unusual things could complicate the building process, but that didn't discourage me from continuing to explore unique shapes. During the next quarter, I designed and built a collapsible stool, two connected cubes, and two tetrahedrons. Still, as much as I loved wood, there was no chance of defection from architecture to carpentry.

No one could ignore the student activities against the Vietnam war; in fact, one of my classmates in sculpture was a troubled veteran. The year 1968 saw Huey Newton, leader of the Black Panther Party, convicted of voluntary manslaughter; Eldridge Cleaver banned from lecturing at Berkeley; and Angela Davis sent to jail. Even without watching TV or reading the newspaper, I was well aware of the potent political climate.

My architectural classmates spent long hours in the design studios located in the eight-floor tower of Wurster Hall. But I didn't; I worked alone at home on my design projects when Shanette slept. My architectural tools covered a makeshift desk, made from a door. A wooden drawing board, rolls of tracing paper, plastic triangles, a T-square, an engineering scale (divided into tenths), an architectural scale (divided into twelfths), pink and gum erasers, a metal eraser shield, a fine compass set bought in Switzerland, a slide rule, a bottle of India ink, pages

Kern compass set

of rub-on black alphabets, and drafting-pencil holders—all hand-held tools—were condensed years later by computer design into a single hand-held mouse.

I inserted graphic components into most assignments. My heavily illustrated History of the Environment assignment came back with a note from the professor: "An excellent paper! Also an effective presentation, you've gotten at the essence of Ronchamp and its subtle relations to the Renaissance." I interpreted her comments as validating my talent for architecture, and that offset the tug of letters from France, urging me to return.

My drawing of Ronchamps for report

Summer quarter, I enrolled in Construction Systems and Production, devoted to keeping a field diary of a building under construction. Like most people, I didn't realize how many architectural decisions had to be made during the construction management phase. I chose the Material Engineering Laboratory, conveniently on campus, for the topic of my case study. The architect came to visit the construction site every Wednesday, but I went more often, during the lunch hour, when I could talk with journeymen and laborers. They knew I was an architectural student and expected my odd questions, such as, "Why is the concrete floor so wavy?"

"Finishing lightweight concrete is more difficult than normal concrete," the superintendent told me, lifting a white bread sandwich to his nose before taking a bite. "It tends to roll on you because there are no stones to hold it flat."

I asked and noted the meaning of terms that were new to me, like *holiday*, which referred to a spot missed by a painter; *make like a tree*, meaning leave; or *wedding band*, meaning the circular patching to connect pipe ends. I instinctively understood that I needed to learn these pet words as part of the building-site language, and I did actually hear and use them later in my career.

One long lunch hour, I mentioned a few miscellaneous items to the prime superintendent on his rounds and then dared, "I notice you have a male secretary."

"I wouldn't mind a female secretary," he replied, leading me into his on-site office trailer. "In fact, I would like it. A woman might add a note of charm."

"Is that the only reason?" I followed along, carefully stepping around the construction materials scattered about.

"Well, no, but it might be too complicated from a human relations point of view. There is no other office staff, and the workers are used to treating each other in a rough, perhaps even a coarse, masculine way." He chuckled. "Do you want a cup of coffee?"

"Okay, a short one." The whiff of old coffee didn't stop me from sipping some as I thought, *If I were the architect, he would have to deal with me.*

I left the trailer, glad for the rapport and frank talk but concerned about opportunities for myself and for my sisters in the construction industry.

I asked the lead inspector about what I perceived as a lack of non-whites and women on the project. It was his job to watch the contract for compliance, so I knew it was a hot question, but someone needed to let the steam out.

"They just don't exist," he answered without much concern. "I might have seen one or two laborers but never a plumber, steamfitter, or elevator installer. And certainly no females: in fact, you are the first girl student I have seen out here."

"About 30 percent of my class is female," I replied, pulling an apple out of my brown bag as the workers' conversations drifted to other subjects—like ballgame scores.

Another day, I asked the architect who was the contract's enforcer, "What about affirmative action?" We had just put on our hardhats and were headed out to look at some electrical wiring in conflict with a door location not yet framed.

"Our firm, Skidmore, Owings & Merrill, doesn't have any Negro architects," he told me. "There are only a handful of Negro inspectors or architects practicing today in the whole country."

Hostile and discouraging remarks, reported to be one of the main reasons women couldn't work in the field, didn't reach my ears during that assignment. If I had been a worker, I might have been treated differently; however, as a female student, I wasn't taking anybody's job. The dynamic, cooperative, and positive feel of being around a building under construction set well with me; I could easily see myself being part of this productive activity.

I took the 1969 winter quarter off because my husband had joined us; he'd found a job teaching skiing at the lodge in China Peak, east of Merced, in the Sierra foothills. Once again, in addition to Arnaud's salary, room and board would be provided for us, which was wonderful— no first and last month's rent, no deposits, no utility bills, and no grocery shopping or cooking. The lodge owners raised their eyebrows appreciatively when I offered to work part time as a lodge maid; I think they were surprised I was willing to wash toilets, but I wanted the money for my education as an architect.

Shanette took two private ski lessons a day with her father. Arnaud thrived in the father-teacher role, even when Shanette was only three.

Shanette during a ski lesson

I didn't fight it, because Shanette enjoyed the attention and wanted to please. At the end of the short season, Arnaud returned to France. Shanette and I returned to my apartment, which I'd sublet in our absence.

The fact that Arnaud wanted to return to France displeased me, but he claimed he had a movie job to work on. This was unexpected. Skiing and teaching had been his primary occupations up to this point, although I knew he dreamed of making documentaries. Yet, while we were together, he was fully attentive to our little family. He proposed that Shanette and I come to France for the summer and then he would find work skiing in California the next winter. He said he was working and making money, but I didn't see much of the money and remained cautious; the letters flew back and forth.

In comparison with the architectural curriculum taught for decades in France, my Berkeley classes seemed avant-garde, exciting, and hands-on—which suited me. For my Social Determinants in Architectural Design course, I drove to Richmond, California, to observe and interview tenants living in Easter Hill, a successful low-income public housing project. After scouting the layout, I knocked on one of the doors. "How do you like living here?"

"I like that public transportation is close," a woman in house slippers said from her half-open door.

"Have you lived here long?" I questioned, sincerely interested. "Do you know your neighbors?"

"Yes, I know most people. A lot of the men work on their cars in the parking lot."

A curious fellow with grease on his hands walked up, wiping a car part with a rag. "We get to know each other," he interjected.

"Thank you," I said, and continued questioning the woman. "Do you hear your next-door neighbors when you are inside?"

"Sometimes, but I like to know someone is there. If I need help, I can bang on the wall."

This was *all* interesting to me. I learned to ask questions and listen to "the users'" answers, which was a big thing at Berkeley. Clients who pay for the design may not be the users or even consider the users' perspectives, putting the architect at a disadvantage in conceiving the project. While architectural design classes held more prestige for other students, the interface between architecture and the social aspect of life increasingly intrigued me.

Design wasn't taught in my high school, but it could have been, even with a simple object like a cup. Introducing the variables involved in designing a cup could help to broaden a person's understanding of what goes into making things and places. The life of a cup can range for centuries—as in the case of a ceremonial teacup—to less than an hour for a throwaway paper cup. The designer's job is to recognize that lifespan, among many other criteria, when conceiving a cup's design. Designers may also consider other criteria, such as what other dishes the cup is to complement, what it would cost to manufacture, and how to stack the cups for shipping. Designers imagine how to hold the cup—with a handle or not. They predict the temperature of the contents and determine how the cup should feel in a person's hands. They may decide whether it is easy to wash, whether a top is desired, what decorations are appropriate, and so on. Because less and less is handmade in our culture, people often forget the many variables a designer must consider.

Architectural design is similar in that there are a great many aspects and criteria for buildings. When our class assignment was for a real project on a real site, the class started with a site visit to understand the physical determinants, including slope, vegetation, climate, orientation, and character of the neighborhood. Site visitations were sometimes out of town, which presented a slight problem for me. In one class, we designed a new educational building at the University of California, Santa Cruz, a couple of hours' drive south. Most of the students had no family issues to deal with, so taking a Saturday to visit a site was no problem for them; but, as a single mother, I usually brought Shanette with me.

Each quarter, we had a different kind of building to design or analyze: public housing, swimming pool changing facility, restaurant, residential college, prison, or art gallery. The design phase offers architects

Site model for design class with architect Bill Turnbull

tremendous creative freedom and personal satisfaction, and each student came up with a unique yet valid solution to the same *program*. The *program* outlines the sizes and types of spaces desired by the client; the relationships of the spaces; and special needs for orientation, access, and utilities. We made drawings, built models with sugar cubes or cardboard, and documented our progress with photos. The presentations were elaborate, yet the professor's feedback seemed vague. This is the artistic, talent-driven, glamorous side of architecture, which typically gets most of the publicity. However, I took notice in my administration class when Professor Howard Friedman said, "Less than 10 percent of all people working in architecture are involved in the design phase of the project." I remember thinking that those were poor odds, and a gambling woman I didn't want to be.

At the same time, the majority of our professors were principals in their own architectural firms and controlled the design of their projects. There was no question, the design phase was vitally important to the synthesis of all the factors that go into envisioning, planning, and building structures. Yet I later thought it unfortunate that we studied with so few of the other 90 percent of the architectural profession who were supporting the design: the writers of specifications, drawers of plans and details, estimators, researchers, administrators, and construction managers. Although I appreciated all the time spent on design—design definitely wasn't taught on the job—once I actually became a working architect, I realized we could have benefited from learning about the more practical, and equally demanding, necessities of the occupation. Fortunately, for the most part, these skills *were* part of my on-the-job training.

Our Design Theories and Methods class focused on getting pertinent information for design decisions. For example, when an architect is leading a meeting of people who will use the building, instead of only listening to what the boss says he or she wants, we were taught to ask all the attendees to *write down* their considerations or concerns. An example of a question asked might be, "Which of the four streets do you feel the entrance should be located on and why?" We were then to collect the answers and organize the comments so that we could lead the discussion to include the concerns of many, rather than just the one authorized person. I embraced this democratic approach.

In parallel, I also took classes about structural systems, environmental control systems, and the use of materials. Related fields, such as city planning, landscape architecture, and urban design, also captured my interest.

I held a firm grip on my career, as well as the rope for my daughter. To free up my winters so I could focus on my family when Arnaud came to teach skiing, I attended school for several summer sessions. Before the winter solstice in 1970, I sublet my apartment while Arnaud and I rented a rustic flat under towering conifers, not far from the Alpine Meadows Ski Area, halfway to Tahoe City. Arnaud hitched a ride to his job up in Alpine each morning so that Shanette and I would have the car. We skied every day, and I took photos of ski classes and of Arnaud racing or jumping. Our bathroom served as my makeshift darkroom, where I developed the black-and-white shots—a skill I had learned in the Wurster Hall photo lab.

It was up to me to make sure that Shanette was on the slopes and ready for her ski lesson with Arnaud after her nap. One late afternoon, she broke her leg. It wasn't a bad break, but at four years old, she walked in a cast for a month. I was upset because I'd told Arnaud that I thought he was pushing her too much, and here was proof. Why had I let his desires override my intuition?

Arnaud was getting weekly letters from France in Chinese; he said they were from his Chinese teacher. After the ski season, he returned to Paris, as he had the year before. I returned to architecture school and found work-study jobs: first as a teaching assistant, then as an engineering aide in the Department of City Planning in Richmond. Among other easy tasks, I colored maps to help planners and engineers with a coastline environmental study of the San Francisco Bay that showed the bay was now half the size it had been a hundred years before, because part of it had been filled by developers. I learned that action was severely threatening the bay's ecology.

This was my first experience in an office with a timecard, a boss, and the use of a government car. I felt fortunate that 3 of the 11 professional staff were women, even though the most senior female architect committed suicide soon after my quarter ended. I never learned why. My immediate supervisor was female and I liked that.

My boss, Lois, invited me to a women's awareness meeting soon after she sized me up. That evening, I was one of more than 50 females standing in her colleague Ruth's poorly lit living room in south Berkeley.

Ruth (who now calls herself Spring), a tall sturdy woman with a relaxed and compelling ability to explain issues clearly, launched into her pitch. "We, the Bay Area Women Planners, are a newly formed group." She advocated women meeting and making themselves aware of the not-so-obvious but different ways that society treated workingmen and workingwomen. She pointed out examples of how the work world was unnecessarily entwined around the man's role as the breadwinner with a wife in the home to do many of life's everyday chores. Workingwomen didn't have wives (or husbands) at home, so how was this going to play out? Her speech filled us with enthusiasm for equity.

"Ruth," I said from behind the long couch, "I see what you mean, but I don't want to meet with a bunch of women just because they are women."

"What do you do?" she asked me.

"I'm an architectural student."

"Well, then," she bellowed back, without missing the beat of her mantra to organize, "start a group of women in architecture."

Immediately I became more observant of women's issues in general and particularly in architecture. As one class ended, I overheard a male student informally ask the professor, "Why are the women's projects so good?"

"Because they have to work harder," the professor answered.

I thought his response perceptive. In one way, I was glad my professor noticed that women worked hard and did good work, but in another way, I didn't think it was fair. I could feel in myself an awakening sensitivity to inequality based on my being female. I couldn't understand this inequality, but I started to fear it. This was not the fear of success or the fear of failure that women's magazines talked about, but rather the fear of not getting a fair chance.

Facts began beaming onto my mental screen: "Less than 3 percent of licensed architects in California are women; the 630-member Northern California Chapter of the American Institute of Architects includes only nine women," reported the November 16, 1971, *San Francisco Chronicle*. The fact that a woman earned 59 cents for every $1.00 per hour that a man earned on a national average was a solid statistic, if not common knowledge. Of the 60 architectural faculty members at UCB in the early 1970s, only two were female: one a licensed architect, the other an architectural historian. What was making these numbers so female unfriendly? We assumed that the jobs men held paid more because most women were secretaries, while men were hired for the high-paying professional jobs. In the 1950 movie *Annie Get Your Gun*, it seemed a woman just had to be very good—shoot as well as a man shot—to succeed. It followed that accomplished women would get the high-paying jobs, too. But the evidence before me now created doubt, I began to believe that skill was not enough; things were not so simple.

At the same time, I was married and feeling I wanted to incorporate more family life back into daily living. Even with time apart and an untraditional marriage arrangement, I planned to return to my conjugal French life after graduation. I wrote to my husband in the spring of 1971 that I would be finishing school in the summer and coming home. He wrote back, "Please come and live with us [meaning himself and the author of those Chinese letters]. I love you and Shuang Shuang so much." He enclosed photos of his mistress and her daughter.

My mother-in-law was the first to condemn her son. She wrote several pages to me about his unacceptable behavior. She believed he would come to his senses and we would be back together as a happy family soon. All I needed to do, in her view, was to return to France and claim my rightful place.

In June 1971, I graduated with a bachelor of architecture (with honors) and an urgent need to recompose my life.

Hold the Rope

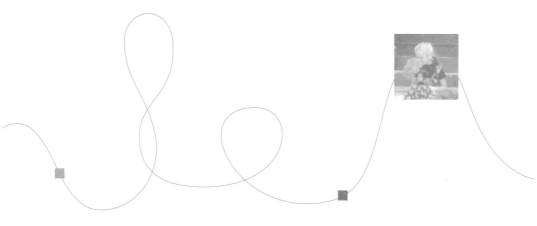

The Feminine Dimension

Fall 1971 to Fall 1972: Berkeley and Oakland

My devotion to my marriage unraveled after my husband's proposal to live with him and his mistress. Even though it was the 1970s, the French *ménage à trois* held no appeal; I believed in linear romance, one man at a time. I relinquished my marriage without profound regret. Knowing Arnaud, I don't think he anticipated my move toward divorce.

I graduated in September 1971. By November I had filled out the Nolo Press Do-It-Yourself Divorce Kit and submitted the necessary documents to Alameda County. Any clamor from Arnaud seemed unlikely, and he did, indeed, agree to all the terms. I didn't feel victimized or bruised; I was just at the end of my rope. Impulsively, I enrolled in graduate school to offset the outside-a-couple feeling I had become accustomed to over the last nine years.

Although I was not looking for a new man in my life, I took a folk-dance class to dilute my loneliness for male companionship. Sheng, a sweet math student from Taiwan, and I had fun attempting new dance steps together. Before long, he was coming to the house. His delicate attention and manner with Shanette and me brought heartfelt companionship and social pleasures. Even so, both Sheng and I felt things were temporary. I was at the tail end of a marriage, and he, in his last year of a PhD program, would be leaving Berkeley at the end of the year. But

Shanette adores Sheng

we enjoyed our time. I took a Chinese cooking class, so Sheng and I cooked Chinese dishes regularly.

Soon Sheng left to work in Indiana as planned. After a worldly and maturing year, he stopped to see us on his way back to Taiwan, but as far as I was concerned, our relationship as lovers had ended when he left for the Midwest. The last I heard from Sheng was seven years later, when he sent me a color photo of his bride in a wedding snapshot signed, "To our dear friend." Good for him. But for me, a traditional wedding seemed out of context. The women's movement was blooming all around me, and I wanted to be part of the bouquet.

In 1971, when one of my teaching assistants was ready to return to England, he and his wife offered me their apartment close to Berkeley. Between March rain showers, Shanette and I moved into the lovely flat on Hillegass Street in North Oakland. Our new home was on the second floor of a brown-shingled house that could have been a

Shanette in front of Hillegass House, 1971

wealthier cousin to my mother's cottage in La Jolla. The Oakland block, one house from the Berkeley city line, was peppered with other brown-shingled residences, all gracious and serenely middle-aged. The house's lush front lawns were unencumbered by hedges or fences, and the flowering plum branches on both sides of the tree-lined street almost touched. We were especially fortunate, as the redwood tree towering above our roof's peak shaded our flat from the afternoon sun. Fridays, residents sat on their steps after work to share a glass of red wine with neighbors. We had block parties, too, during summer and fall. An added bonus to the apartment was inheriting Shaderack, a mellow black cat whom Shanette befriended and cared for.

When my daughter started first grade, I agreed to serve as a board member for the before and after school program she attended at St. James Community Center. This innovative program included a rich collection of performing arts activities, which may have kindled the spark for Shanette's teaching dance in later years. I confidently dropped her off before seven, knowing that she enjoyed the creative childcare staff.

I worked at efficient planning and rigorous scheduling, but the margin of risk for things going wrong seemed thinner than the Queen of Hearts; one late task or unexpected expense triggered the barely controllable fear that my house of single-mother cards would collapse around me.

Being happy and healthy myself also helped me focus on my growing passion for feminist issues, which certainly swayed me to select Social and Behavioral Factors in Architectural and Urban Design as the major for my master's in architecture degree. Otherwise, I might have selected one of the other areas of emphasis: Design Problems, Environmental Control Systems, Structure and Production, Design Theories and Methods, Administration and Related Professional Studies, or History of the Environment.

Just as I was becoming imbued with the belief that women could— and should—be treated with equality in society, I began to believe that architecture could better consider the concerns of women. Some of my classmates were interested in children's environments: the size of doors, the height of light switches and drinking fountains. Others were concerned with wheelchair users: ramps, low mirrors in the bathroom, turnaround space in elevators. Specific social issues, such as affordable housing, farm lodging, or homelessness, had caught the sympathy of other classmates. Our professors lectured about numerous determinants that needed to be synthesized in order to conceive effective building; yet the concerns of women had not been mentioned.

I thought buildings should reflect equality and uniquely feminine dimensions. At that time, the lack of a women's restroom in a public building was often held up as a logical and acceptable reason for not hiring a woman. This is no longer the case, but to this day, if you are female, you have probably noticed that the lines at women's restrooms are still longer than for men; the number of toilets needed for women continues to be underestimated, especially in airports and theaters. Other small items that architects could specify in women's restrooms are often missing, too, such as dry places to put a purse or briefcase; ample hooks to hang a coat; and wide shelves for backpacks, shopping bags, or books. As a student, I didn't yet have ideas about what equality in the built world would look like, but I did know that the feminine dimension in architecture should translate into physical elements that went far beyond the number of toilets.

One of my graduation requirements was the completion of a Comprehensive Examination Report. To meet this requirement and to satisfy my growing awareness of femaleness and maleness (the word *gender* entered my vocabulary later), I wanted to study an aspect of architecture that I deemed particularly sensitive to women's concerns. As a mother and budding feminist, I set out to explore the birthing environment primarily from the mother's perspective, in contrast to other users, including nurses, doctors, and administrators. Early on, I surveyed the literature and found pockets of emotional concern from the nursing and midwifery community for mothers during birth. However, mothers-to-be were not at the planning table. One of my advisors, Roslyn Lindheim—the only female architect on the faculty— paid particular attention to the interface between medical issues and architecture. She agreed with me that childbirth should not be treated like a disease and encouraged my exploration.

The majority of births in the United States had by this time moved from homes to hospitals, due to the safety improvements offered by modern medical technology. However, I was convinced that hospital births deserved to be viewed closely, and not just in terms of medi- cal safety. Childbirth was a rite of passage; yet considerations for the social, creative, and physiological ramifications of birthing were being ignored in the rush to stress modern technology's ability to minimize health risks. Couldn't the design criteria for the birthing ward respect— *even highlight*—the significance of childbirth and still be safe? Architects could then envision a space that created an enriching birthing experi- ence for mother and family, as well as embodying a social statement that reflected the dignity of women as the *givers of children*.

To reinforce my understanding of childbirth, I enrolled in various classes, including Women's Studies in the sociology department, along with a child-mother relationship class and a hospital administration class in the public health administration department.

Alta Bates Hospital, in Berkeley, agreed to let me observe their procedures. Starting at the hospital front desk, I diagrammed the path a pregnant woman followed to the admitting office, labor room, child delivery room, and recovery room, and finally to a private room where guests were allowed to visit. Each room had three nurses, one for each shift of the day, so that the mother-to-be was interacting with a changing staff at the same time that family visiting hours were being arbitrarily limited. Surgical suites in the hospital basement, designed for people under anesthesia for their operations, were also being used for delivering babies. But during childbirth, many women are awake, without family, lying on medical furniture and staring upward at giant ugly light fixtures. Clearly, the design of rooms and their sequence had been dictated by the administration of the hospital and the hierarchy within the staff, not by the experience of the woman or family. This all seemed unnecessarily complicated compared with my experience in China, where I was in one room before and after delivery, and my husband held my hand most of the time. In my report, *A User in Need: Women During Childbirth*, I argued for the inclusion of mothers' voices in design:

No matter how short the stay, psychologists, sociologists, and anthropologists agree that the childbearing experience has major influences on a woman's personal and social life. If the childbirth experience is going to be more joyful and satisfying to the women involved, we designers are going to have to evaluate more critically the specifications given to us by the Bureau of Hospitals, State Departments of Public Health and/or client/doctors or client/administrators. We must understand better women in general and mothers-to-be in specific so that alternatives to the existing monopoly may be proposed. I acknowledge that women are not the only users, but they are the ones lacking a voice that needs to be heard by architects.

I proposed a separate new building—the Family Birth Center. I didn't design one, but I did suggest program and scope items that addressed the social, aesthetic, and psychological attributes of this rite of passage for the entire family—not lessening medical safety but shifting it to the background.

For example, I said:

> When women give birth at home, they are not moved from room to room
> for different stages in the birth process. From the mother to-be perspective
> there is no reason to move from labor room, to delivery, to recovery area,
> to hospital room. Therefore, the Birth Center would be designed so that
> she goes to only one room.

Today, I see online that there is an American Association of Birth
Centers offering a list of centers by state. Websites give the pros and
cons of birth centers in general, including the fact that the costs are
usually significantly less than in the hospital. Alta Bates has operated an
exemplary birth center for decades, which features *one room for labor and
delivery.* Maybe my report had some influence; as I heard Alice Walker
say recently, "You never know who is watching."

My vision of feminist influence in the built world was very broad.
In retrospect, it doesn't surprise me that my research into the childbirth environment didn't automatically key me into a professional life
designing birth centers. With graduation only two months ahead of
me, I needed to think about earning a living, and began to hunt down
one of those hard-to-find entry points. Jobs in 1972 were as sparse as
beauty in the tract houses that were steadily rolling out into the suburbs.
Even so, I ignored the first federal job announcement that arrived by
mail from the military. In fact, I threw the announcement away before
I'd even read the last line. When I received a second invitation to apply
for a job opening at the Western Division Naval Facilities Engineering
Command (WestDiv), my vantage point must have expanded—or perhaps I was becoming more realistic about job scarcity—because I paid
more attention and investigated to find out more. I learned that I was
receiving these official announcements because I had filled out a federal
service application at the suggestion of a well-rounded male classmate
whom I admired. None of my professors worked for the government.
But I'd had a satisfying experience with the City of Richmond during
my work-study job, although I had never considered working for the
military, one of many agencies in the federal service system. What were
they building? Would the buildings all be gray?

On a crisp spring day, I drove my steel-green Nash west across the
Bay Bridge, passing San Francisco on Highway 280 to San Bruno's
Sneath Lane exit. A uniformed security guard waved me into the chain-
linked compound at the end of Commodore Drive. I parked near the

shoebox-shaped World War II barracks lined up in a "U" formation, then walked past the grand flagpole flying three flags: the American flag, the California flag, and a WestDiv navy flag to identify when the admiral was on base. The place seemed peaceful enough. Most people dressed in civilian clothes, only a few wore navy uniforms, and no one I noticed carried a gun. My father had been a proud naval officer when I was a baby. I'd had no personal negative experiences with the navy and the conflict with Vietnam was virtually over, so I didn't see myself as helping a war effort.

The personnel director eagerly shook my hand, and her enthusiastic introduction indicated that she wanted to increase the number of professional women in the navy's engineering department. "We are an equal opportunity employer," she said, her eyes sparkling. The government was flying the banner of "Model Employer" in those days, and that meant consistent fair hiring and treatment of employees. "Once you become a federal employee, you can transfer within federal service and keep all your benefits." She made the situation sound forward-moving and comprehensive. "And you qualify to be in our training program."

"Training program?" I echoed, particularly interested in this unforeseen job benefit. I was aware it would be difficult to get experience in all ten of the topics that the Architectural Licensing Board required, particularly construction management. Sending a young man to a construction site was common; sending a woman was unlikely.

"Construction management could be worked out with the architectural branch head," she told me when I inquired; her tone remained encouraging.

I wrote *construction* in my notebook. "I like the idea of engineers and architects working together in the same organization."

The marketing continued, "You would be automatically promoted to the next level, GS-11, assuming you've successfully finished the training program. You would immediately start earning sick leave and annual leave [vacation] and have good retirement and health plans."

That sounded handy; I wouldn't have to wait a year to take days off. However, I hadn't done my homework and was naive about the job variables one should consider. UC Berkeley didn't offer any programs to prepare graduates for their job search. (I heard later that Cal Poly's architecture school did.) This juncture between school and work still seems to be a vacant terrain in need of attention, but at the time I muddled through without specific guidance.

The personnel director sent me to meet with the architectural branch head. Mr. Scamell, a balding middle-aged man, quickly put me at ease by telling me his wife had studied architecture and now worked as an interior designer—his way of disassociating himself from prejudice against women, I guessed. He explained, "WestDiv is responsible for the planning, design, construction, and administration of new facilities and large repair projects to support the navy, marine, and air force bases in the nine western states." The bases were essentially mini-towns full of office buildings, stores, recreation facilities, clubs, auto hobby shops, handball courts, childcare facilities, medical clinics, maintenance shops, laboratories, fire stations, dining facilities, and housing for officers and enlisted personnel.

Mr. Scamell didn't ask me any common awkward questions like, "How could you travel, being a single parent?" or "Do you think a woman can lead a meeting?" His smoke-tinted, friendly voice made me feel I would be welcome. After a calm comfortable conversation, we stood for a tour of the workspaces. I walked behind him from his private office at the front of the narrow building, through the boring reception area, into a long room with rows of desks and drafting tables where more than 40 males sat with their heads down, looking busy.

It looked as if I would be the first female architectural graduate to sit among these men. Being the only female didn't strike me as earthshaking or inevitable. I liked the large engineering command, and the military presence appeared to be minor. This was a civilian operation, led by an admiral with engineering credentials and a few officers in management positions; no target practice was required.

I knew it was more difficult for women to get jobs, but I wasn't fully aware of how volatile architectural jobs were in the private sector. However, the job security aspects of civil service—an important attribute for a single wage-earner—didn't consciously influence my decision. At 31 years old, I was anxious to get started and this was my best offer. I filled out the additional paperwork with no idea how long the wait would be.

By September 1972, I graduated with a master's of architecture; that same month, a landmark article reported that the field of architecture was a grim one for women. Ellen Perry Berkeley was the author of the article "Women in Architecture," published in the *Architectural Forum* (see the Epilogue). Berkeley, a senior editor at the *Forum*, was well positioned to collect and share many alarming anecdotes from credible women practicing in the top design offices in the country.

She wasn't intimidated by the establishment's cries that there were no hard data substantiating her examples of discrimination. One story was about the dean of an Ivy League school of art and architecture who was approached at a party. "I'm one of your students," said the young female student. He tried to place her. "In graphics?" he asked. "No, architecture," she responded, probably with naïve confidence. To which he swiftly replied, "Women shouldn't be in architecture." Surely, this was an awkward encounter for the young female student. It rang an undeserving tone, as if letting female hands use T-squares was like sharing sacred secret tools that with the wrong people might lead to an epidemic of some communicative deadly disease.

At that time, only about 6 percent of architectural students in the nation were female. Even if you managed to find a job, became experienced, and achieved licensing, the cold currents of non-acceptance mysteriously shipwrecked many women's success. Berkeley reported the irrefutable evidence:

> A woman who recently graduated from Yale and had almost a year's office experience, was hired at $1 an hour less than a man who had no experience. She asked him to speak to their employer but he declined, afraid he'd lose the dollar. At her insistence, the employer "remedied" the situation raising her salary by 50¢. (Another woman, registered for years, was doing the same work as men earning considerably more; when she asked for a raise she was told, "What are you complaining about? You're the highest paid woman in the office.")

Not all the stories were about salary; an amazing array of incidents illustrated how female participation was being deflected, belittled, or dismissed. Berkeley quoted from a report by the National Institute of Child Health and Human Development: "The women architects reported considerable discrimination in admission to the profession, acceptance by peers, evaluation by professors, acceptance by clients, promotion practices, and hiring."

Her words shuffled around in my brain, settling into the crevices of my consciousness, but they didn't dilute my determination to land a job. At this point, even though I'd had no news from my interview with the navy, I decided not to interview with any traditional architectural firms. I thought it wiser to search for jobs among the less obvious sectors and even applied half-heartedly to teach. The proof of job scarcity (not just for women) hit me hard when one of the star *male* graduates in my architectural year returned home to Kansas, despite his preference for living and working in the Bay Area.

But I resisted worry. I had obtained my educational credentials in architecture, my status as a happy mother was officially single, and—even with only one promising interview during a recession—I blindly believed that the conditions exposed by Berkeley's article could be surmounted by those of us riding the wave of feminism.

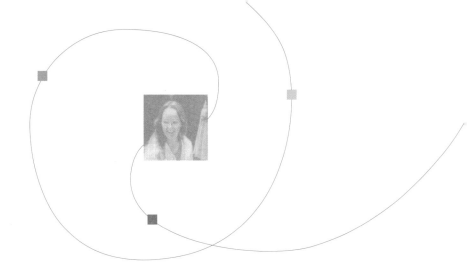

Feminist Sunshine

1972 to 1973: Oakland

Boston's Women Architects, Landscape Architects, and Planners (WALAP) had recently organized to combat discriminating behaviors and attitudes on the East Coast—a feminist agenda I could identify with. "The Case for Flexible Work Schedules," a compelling article by WALAP about the swelling need for serious part-time work, followed Ellen Perry Berkeley's article in the September 1972 issue of the *Architectural Forum*.

My thoughts plowed the fertile soil of these readings, as seeds planted earlier in the year at the "consciousness raising" evening in Ruth's living room began to sprout. Knowing others were organizing and feeling ready, I brought up the subject with Danica, an architectural acquaintance from Slovakia, who knew Mary, an architect from Bulgaria, and Mui, a graduate and working architect originally from Hong Kong.

Danica recognized our common interest in women's issues and invited us to a tasty lunch in her Nob Hill studio apartment. Even though we didn't know one another, the subject was so dear to each of us that the conversation quickly and naturally synchronized. While our hostess concurred that women in architecture should meet, her idea was to create an informal group based on the European tradition of salons for writers and thinkers. However, that was not our direction: Mary, Mui, and I wanted to join forces on a platform of fair treatment and feminism. The three of us agreed to explore organizing a group dedicated to enhancing the position of women in architecture.

Less than three weeks later, we scheduled a meeting. We invited as many working females linked to architecture as we could find by word of mouth. Late in November 1972, on a Thursday evening, 11 women climbed the outside staircase to my flat in Oakland. Most were foreign born.

"Women make up 50 percent of the architects in Bulgaria," said Mary, standing proudly to make her point; she was wearing sturdy dark shoes and her right arm waved with conviction.

The rest of us remained seated as we went around our circle, each one speaking about her working situation and concerns.

"I'm the only woman working in my office," Ruth B. told us in her crisp German accent.

"During an interview, what do you say when asked about your children?" wondered a mother of two.

"What do you say when your boss won't let you travel to the job site?" a planner asked in a faint tone, her leg kicking nervously.

"When I have questions about work, I feel more comfortable asking other women," offered Gloria, a petite woman from the Philippines whose dark hair extended to her waistline. "But I don't know any other women."

"I think we should share how much money we are making because it is so hard to know what salaries are being paid to women," I added.

"A group like this would be great," Mui agreed, ending our meeting on an upnote.

All these statements made sense to me. Just being part of a likeminded group changed the wind direction from against us to with us. Talking to other women helped us to sort out the impact of being female from other concerns about work; our discussions brought to the forefront the idea that one's work life and personal life were interdependent. At the end of the round robin, we decided to reach out to other women for a second meeting. The benefits of forming a supportive, resourceful community became salient to us. Although at the time we wouldn't have described it in these words, we were a *new kind of professional group*. Everyone was excited, and many of us were extremely dedicated to developing the group.

Even though it seemed odd to us, it became increasingly obvious that one's personal traits, including being female or nonwhite, influenced one's ability to find work—much more than acknowledged by the American Institute of Architects (AIA), a national professional organization representing architects. AIA defined itself with the values and concerns of its members, but 98 percent of the AIA membership *and* the entire profession were male. Since men didn't need to think about gender discrimination, they acted as if it had nothing to do with practicing architecture. Women just needed to adapt.

Common advice was, "Be good at what you do." Clearly, men's and women's values and personal lives differed, but what annoyed us no end was how that *difference* supported men and hindered women. The slippery slope of inequality was just beginning to be explored and exposed, and we were anxious to find the underlying cause and change it. We had no idea how deep one would have to go, and 35 years later, the digging continues.

I wanted to bring my concerns, many of which were about gender, into the everyday world of architecture. Some of our members disagreed, preferring avoidance or denial—*If I don't mention the word "female," I won't be rejected.* This silent mantra has been part of women's history in architecture for a long time and still exists. Gender is still a sensitive issue for women architects because it calls up so much resistance to our participation in the field. In 2001, Maggie Toy, editor of *The Architect: Women in Contemporary Architecture* (Watson-Guptill Publications, 2001), addressed the subject of gender controversy among the architects featured in her book. In the first paragraph of her introduction, she explains that *The Female Architect* was rejected as a title because it highlighted the fact that the architects were women. That has never been my stand; I *wanted* to discuss women's issues—from a feminine *and* feminist point of view. Intuitively, I believed women could contribute greatly to architecture and to the world. Being female is a good thing.

However, selecting the name for our group triggered an explosive debate, particularly because of the word *women*—should it or should it not be included in the name of our organization? Most of us didn't know any history of women architects; we were reacting from our own experience. "*Women* should not be included in the title, as men do not say *men* in their organization's names, and the group should stay open for men who would like to join," Kathleen said. I backed her. Ruth K. and most of the others were of the opposite opinion. "If we do not specify that it is primarily a women's organization, it will be misleading."

Mary wasn't as worried about the word *women* as she was about the word *architect*. "We must use *architect* because that is the term only licensed professionals may use." Most of us were not yet licensed, but

Mary, as one able to use the term, argued, "That doesn't matter; you will be in the future." And she was right.

The majority vote, of more than 22 of us at the February 1973 meeting, was for the name *Organization of Women Architects* (OWA). Shortly afterward, the name was officially changed to *Organization of Women Architects and Design Professionals*.

While Shanette attended elementary school, I worked at home on administrative and conceptual tasks for upcoming OWA meetings. My first inclination was to create a survey to learn more about the women interested in organizing. Survey questions included years of work experience, salary, education, marital status, and number of children. We discussed the results at an OWA meeting, and when members learned what other women were earning, a few asked their bosses for a raise and got it. Hallelujah! But the secrecy around salary still exists, for both men and women, although women suffer more because we usually earn less. OWA is a good place to try to find out about payment and benefit issues because at work, one may be the target of reprisal for crossing boundaries that employers want hidden. *Working Woman* magazine covered this persistent and delicate problem 20 years later, and I would wager that knowing what salary figure to target is still a sore spot for women.

By June 1973, OWA had a full steering committee of five coordinators and five alternates. Mui was the coordinator of newsletters, Bobbie Sue was coordinator of public relations; and Mary coordinated education, Lucia employment, and Rosie finance. I was the alternate for finance, along with the other four alternates. The alternates were to take over after a six-month overlap. The concept was to have a high percentage of the members involved and to spread out the tasks. Every member was expected to take on a task when she could schedule it. At that time, 10 out of 40 members gave a strong representation of the group. This was a membership organization where all attendees had a voice at any meeting. You walked into the room knowing that your voice counted. We called it a horizontal structure because we wanted to be inclusive and democratic.

The term *affirmative action* was being thrown around as if it were understandable. I had no idea what it meant, but I guessed that becoming informed would help dilute discrimination. I drilled into the Federal Registrar and read that the word *underutilization* was defined as having fewer minorities or women in a particular job category than would reasonably be expected by their *availability*. Just saying "This isn't fair" or "You are discriminating for no good reason" wasn't going to get anyone anywhere; I wanted to know the law and be able to state it clearly. Then one had to prove *availability*. The worldview was that there were just no women or nonwhite males in the field, and the thicket of decoy jargon was mind-boggling. Employers would say, "There are so few women available." Yet, many of the attendees at our meetings were looking for work. During this time, we counted the jobs wanted posted on the AIA bulletin boards and found that 25 percent of the names sounded female. Granted, the San Francisco Bay Area had a concentration of women in architecture, greater than the national average of 4 percent, but certainly not 25 percent. Women were available—disproportionately so.

Luckily, while waiting for a response from my interview with the navy, I found a short-term job with my city planning professor. Donald Appleyard had obtained a grant from the Institute of Urban and Regional Development to study the impact of the Bay Area Rapid Transit (BART), and it was my job to help him compile data.

Each evening after work, I picked up my cheerful Shanette from her after-school childcare program, and we walked home to make dinner together. One Monday a month, I would take Shanette next door to play with my neighbor's daughters while I attended the monthly OWA meeting. Meetings were invigorating; I didn't want to miss one. I felt they were essential to my success in the field, and these were very interesting people to befriend. More than three decades later, many of these architects remain my closest friends.

Interestingly, not all women working in architecture wanted to join our budding group. Women had been practicing architecture in California for 75 years, slowly, one by one. Established female architects often seemed to feel that if they were good enough, they would be valued and treated fairly, in spite of the professional filter straining against diversity.

Professor Howard Friedman

About this time, Mary and I arranged to have lunch with Howard Friedman (Howard Friedman and Associates), one of my professors and the president of the San Francisco chapter of the American Institute of Architects. We agreed to meet at an Italian bistro close to Mary's office.

"Howard, why don't you have any women working in your firm?" I asked as the waiter filled the water glasses at our cozy table.

"Well, I don't know. I guess I could." He looked up from his menu, tickled by my directness. "None have applied."

"We have members in our new organization who are looking for work," Mary said, a glint in her serious dark eyes.

Howard answered cautiously. "I've never had experience with women in my office."

"Would you be willing to interview one?" I set down my menu, more intent on persuading him to say yes than on ordering my lunch.

ORGANIZATION OF WOMEN ARCHITECTS

OWA title on 1973
brochure cover

"I guess with you two on my case, I'll have to," Howard laughed. He genuinely liked us and clearly thought we were onto something deserving his attention.

We sent him Lucia, whom he did hire. And then he did more: Howard arranged for a booth to be donated to our new organization at the 1973 AIA National Convention. Held in San Francisco, this convention is where OWA made its formal debut into the architectural community.

Now that we had an event to rally around, our members worked hard to develop a brochure with several articles to hand out at our booth. The brochure's cover featured a black-and-white photo by Bragstad, taken on the rooftop of the San Francisco Art Institute. Shanette, the only child in the photo, stands with me in the front row. A life-sized copy of this photo served as the backdrop to our booth. The *San Francisco Chronicle* published a big splash about our presence at the

AIA Convention. Among others, I was quoted as saying, "There is an obvious need."

The *Chronicle* also quoted Beverly Willis—the rare prominent female architect who owned a large successful firm—as stating, "Women often don't know how to sell themselves." This comment stunned me

Photo on the back of 1973 OWA brochure

and other OWA activists, so we invited her to speak at an OWA meeting on "How to Look for Employment." Soon after the meeting, a few listeners applied to work at her office and got jobs, which indicated to me that speaking up paid and that meetings were good places to learn about the profession.

The variety of meeting topics was as broad as life; we didn't limit ourselves to technical trade topics. For the convenience of our members, we alternated our meetings between the East Bay and San Francisco, and several meetings were held in the South Bay. At one meeting, we invited the affirmative action officer at Stanford to speak. That was where I finally understood that *affirmative action* meant to take action to counter *underutilization*—or, some would say, past discrimination. A consultant in childcare and education spoke at another meeting, sparking several women to reevaluate their husband's role in childcare, while a presentation about the health benefits of running inspired many of us to start jogging.

We used our OWA newsletter to share our interests with one another: book reviews, reprints from the *Californian*, and information from the California Commission on the Status of Women. We reviewed films, such as *Cities for People* and *Portrait Photography,* and printed summaries from members who attended the St. Louis Women in Architecture Program or the Oregon West Coast Design Conference.

During our monthly OWA meetings, we enthusiastically gathered steam. Feminist values were integrated into every aspect of the procedures, methods, and structure. For example, unlike the AIA meetings of the day, where attendees sat in rows of chairs while being lectured to as an audience, we mingled over a homemade buffet dinner in a private home of one of the members or in an office where a member worked. After eating, we'd form a circle and open the meetings with self-introductions that were often more than just a name; we added new information each time—relative to the current program topic, for example. The open forum took time, but it helped members to become acquainted and provided the opportunity for anyone to voice her ideas and trigger dialogue, both pillars of our philosophy to network. Policy and organizational business were discussed and voted on by all present, usually by a raise of hands. It felt right. We were no longer the odd minority; we were building our own professional community, where women were the norm.

One of the strengths in OWA's collaborative leadership style was the frequent rotation of duties, such as leading meetings, organizing food, and editing monthly newsletters. We stretched the interpretation of our by-laws and practiced a flat leadership style proudly. Any member could initiate her (or his) own special projects and bring them to the group—and there were many, including house tours, high school outreach, competitions for the letterhead design for OWA stationery, employee surveys, and membership directories.

Gender issues weren't important to the few men who joined early on, but these men were sensitive to our issues, were progressive in their thinking, and wanted to be part of a professional group that was personal and democratic.

The holistic prism of the OWA meetings during these early days stimulated my thinking so much that ideas continued to churn and keep me awake long after I'd picked up Shanette from next door and kissed her goodnight in her bed. There was so much to do, but I was hopeful that we were going to design ourselves out of the paper bag of discrimination.

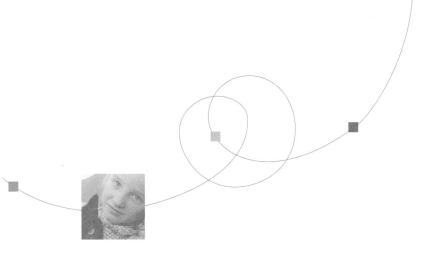

Merged

1972 to 1973: Oakland

The Bay Area Rapid Transit (BART) system opened its station doors, above and below ground, on September 11, 1972. For ten maiden weeks, I stood close to the agent's booth—watching intently as travelers arrived. My observation was part of a pilot research project being conducted in various BART stations during scheduled periods. Whenever a traveler couldn't figure out how to use the ticket machines, the agent would glide out of his or her glass booth. I moved, too, discreetly as a noon shadow, listening to the traveler's questions and jotting down notes.

The architects' challenge had been to design the path from entrance to platform clearly enough for travelers to find their way without help or hassle, ensuring that a person new to a station could find his or her destination as easily as a drop of water flowing through the architecture of a riverbed. We thought the questions travelers asked might reflect the station's configuration. For example, in some stations, including Civic Center and Ashby, the train platform is sandwiched by the inbound and outbound tracks, while in other stations, like Oakland West, there are two staircases, one for each direction.

"How do I get change?" "Which station is for 73rd Avenue?" "Can I use the restrooms?" "Which platform is for San Francisco?" "How do I transfer?" "What time will the train come?" Soon we realized that there were too many variables to determine how station design impacted the questions asked, but we did learn things about the interface of travelers with the stations.

Rather than restricting our note taking to the physical elements of the stations' architecture, we collected all the questions. Professor Appleyard told us that our work in recording and grouping questions, although only a short-term effort, had yielded results that were unexpectedly interesting. Other data collecting, which I was not involved in, took more time and apparently produced fewer immediate results. One study was about the number of lights turned on when the sun set in neighborhoods around some of the stations.

Each element of the large research project was published separately for future comparison. However, we saw many signs, ashtrays, and maps appear within days of our draft report. To this day, I wonder if our study has ever been dusted off and used as the virgin benchmark it was intended to be.

Over the last four decades, I have ridden BART on and off, observing the changes. Just this week, at the Embarcadero Station, I was handed my first survey. "Please fill this out on your trip and drop it at your destination," said a young woman with a clipboard. Most of the questions were about transportation links outside the stations, not about the interface between the user and the station. I particularly favor the latter slice of architecture, as opposed to complying with codes, making sure the roof doesn't leak, and calculating the space needed for pipes and mechanical equipment. On the few lines of the survey designated for comments, I suggested that more benches be added and bathrooms be improved for travelers.

I wish I had thought to write a comment expressing my alarm at the overflowing billboard advertisements in the stations. They've invaded unlikely corners of our public space, wrapping the bottoms of columns and using the stair risers for photos, subjecting travelers to an unending blast of commercial visual megaphones, and upstaging the neutrality of our urban places. In 1972, there were no advertisements. They increase yearly, as if they are a natural result of station age, like rings in the trunk of a tree. But age and making money should have nothing to do with it: limits need to be set, not just because so much advertisement dulls the space and becomes confusing, but because it is ugly and silently oppressive.

Just before I took the job conducting the study of BART stations, I'd read an article in the *Architectural Forum* about Bostonian architects exploring flexible work schedules. The article gave me the idea to negotiate a special 32-hour workweek. Professor Appleyard allowed me to leave at two o'clock on Tuesday and Thursday to pick up Shanette. The first few afternoons, when I left right on time, my fellow and sister employees looked up in disbelief—not because of the schedule, but because I stuck to it! Once, during a lively meeting, I stood as one presenter finished and then left before the next presenter started. Fortunately, my boss and everyone else soon respected my unique new schedule as normal. Success with this tiny feminist gesture initiated a ripple of belief inside me that one could alter how work was tradition-ally organized.

Befittingly, as our BART report was readying to go to press—and after more than six months of a federal hiring freeze—I received the official notice to report to the Western Division Naval Facilities Engineering Command (WestDiv) in San Bruno. At the next Friday neighborhood-on-the-steps wine-social-hour, a retired neighbor heard me mention that I needed a car (the Nash had been sold in Albany Village). I adored his Peugeot 404 sedan, which was parked right across the street. The sale was completed in less than 30 minutes, giv-ing me transportation and launching me into a nonstop love affair with Peugeots. Passion holds: I am currently on my sixth Peugeot.

On my first day of work in February 1973, Shanette and I rose early to get ready. "Mommy, what do you think Shaderack does all day?" Shanette asked, looking over at the cat as I helped her on with her coat.

"Oh, he probably sleeps," I replied, wondering if she was feeling as anxious as I was.

"He sure sleeps lots," said Shanette. She expertly sidestepped the cuddly cat rub-bing against her leg as we made our way down the outside stairs.

Shaderack and Shanette

The majestic redwood at the curb marked our passage from home to work in the predawn sky. After a very short drive, I kissed my daugh-ter's sweet cheek, savoring my maternal joy. Still not fully awake, she ambled toward the attractive St. James Community Building to start her full day.

Commuting 12 miles in each direction extended my workday well beyond the elementary school hours. By seven in the morning, my compact four-door French sedan ramped up the freeway entrance, as I happily thought about how lucky I was to have this coordinated arrangement of public school and childcare. Childcare was a rare social resource that could not be taken for granted at any price, even in Berkeley. There seemed to be a cultural gatekeeper limiting innovative childcare services. I mentally underlined childcare on my ever-growing list of feminist issues impacting working mothers. The few choices for childcare made me painfully aware of how mothers, who wanted to work, felt caged at home. To this day, the structure of work needs to be expanded and remodeled to honor good parenting, another feminist list item.

The slight rise in the Bay Bridge afforded spectacular views of the bayscape as the pale morning light stirred my thoughts into the present. We were in a recession, and I was going to a secure job. If I'd had someone to tell, I would have relished a conversation about my excitement. It wasn't the same excitement as roaming the desert on the back of a camel or viewing the elaborate elegance of the Taj Mahal. And it wasn't the excitement of the unknown, but rather the excitement shaped by the potential to participate—to try my hand, alongside others, at designing buildings.

Arriving at work, I entered a cloud of vague social confusion. Mr. Scamell, the architectural branch head who had interviewed me, was out of the office and no one knew where I was to sit. Deskless, I was given a tour. Welcoming remarks from my new coworkers often referred indirectly to my femaleness: "Who will take care of your daughter?" and "There were no women in my architecture classes." After the tour, I was given navy manuals to read in the interior design office. It was almost as if, since the interior designers were female, it was expected that this was where I should be penned in with other females.

The awkwardness waned by day two. My first boss, Joel, escorted me with sweet patriarchal flair to an empty desk in the center row on the ground floor. I deposited my things next to Dong, a considerate and dedicated recent graduate of UC Berkeley's architectural school, and a member of the navy's Professional Development Program that I was about to begin.

Joel invited me into his undecorated cubicle, where he showed me the Naval Facilities Engineering Command organizational chart as an overview of the agency. Reaching over his desk, he pointed his chubby index finger to the top of the chart, to the admiral headquartered in Alexandria, Virginia. From there, Joel worked his finger down to our engineering field divisions, our department, our division within the department, our architectural branch, our section (one of four), and finally to me. Each designation had codes; for instance, the architectural branch was code 401.

The size of the organization didn't scare me; on the contrary, I radiated the confidence of a baby bird succeeding at her first flight. My destination was to obtain the experience and knowledge necessary to become a licensed architect. To complicate things a bit further, individuals fell into a series. The "engineering series" was 800; the "architectural series" was 808. Everything had a number, but I didn't let that inhibit my actions or my ambition.

Like each state, California gives tests to applicants who want to hold the title of architect. Technically, the federal government was out of line calling all 808-series employees architects, as there were no licensing requirements to work in this series when I started with the navy. Professionally speaking, I was a *graduate architect* or an *intern architect*. However, within the navy, I was called an architect even before I was licensed by the State of California—which took a minimum of three years of experience and a set of tests on a wide variety of topics in architectural practice. I'll admit I experienced a bit of internal conflict about the specific legal meaning of the tag *architect*, but after years of wearing student rags, the term glowed. I now sported a designer label.

When our big boss, an architect and the engineering design director, announced his decision to require professional licensing of the engineering and architectural journeyman (GS-12 level) employees, I thought management should follow up by encouraging and helping employees to obtain licenses. As a GS-9, with only two weeks into the job, I requested by memo that an extra half-hour be allowed at lunchtime for study, once a week. Several architectural graduates needed to study before the Licensing Board exam came up in 14 weeks. I invited speakers like Vartan, an in-house structural engineer who willingly came to our building to help us shore up our structural engineering knowledge. Colleagues joined me. Licensing seemed a high bar; many don't realize that the architectural license requires much more, both in the number of hours of testing and years of work experience, than the engineering license. I knew from feminist literature that many women graduating in architecture had not obtained their licenses, thus limiting their options and their perceived seriousness. This awareness cinched my determination to study, practice, and take the training for jumping over the licensing hurdle.

Of course, I studied outside of the office, too. At OWA meetings, we were thinking of ways to prepare ourselves for the architectural licensing exams. We figured that studying and practicing together in a friendly atmosphere would help us. No study groups of this sort had previously existed. A committee within OWA developed a ten-hour mock design exam for OWA members and friends, led by the now very successful Oakland architect Rosemary Muller. I was one of more than a dozen who took the first OWA mock exam, which I believe helped me to know what to expect. After several successful years, AIA joined in giving the mock exam, and after several more years, it was out of the mock-exam business.

Our cozy Oakland apartment was a delightful place to spend time. Shanette and I could see trees through all the tiny paned windows. Sloping ceilings from two dormers carved dynamic volumes into a peaked roof. One was over our rectangular table—good for eating, sewing, and art projects like egg decorating. Architect-white walls matched the wall-to-wall white carpet, rather than typical "property-owner-off-white" walls with beige rugs. Getting to the backyard was awkward and no window overlooked it, so we spent most of our home time in the chic, uncluttered apartment. Shanette's room was nicely proportioned and twice the size of her room in Albany Village. I felt the adjacency of the rooms had been thought out for the best use of the occupants, not lined up to save a few feet of water and sewer pipe, like so many cookie-cutter remodels that attach the bathroom to the back of the kitchen— no matter what—as if there were a cultural taboo not to.

Unlike my mother, who didn't want to waste time cooking, I had taken to the art of preparing food in France and wanted to share kitchen activities with my seven-year-old daughter. We were in the kitchen for projects, as well as meal-making; we let milk ferment into yogurt in a cardboard box outfitted with a light bulb, and whenever we needed an egg in the spring, we didn't break it open and throw the shell away. Instead, we followed a set ritual.

"Mommy, put a hole in this one so I can blow on it," Shanette would say. She'd fetch a glass bowl to catch the insides of the eggs so we could keep the shells intact to decorate for Easter.

With a sewing needle, I lightly punched pinholes into each end of the common white eggs. Shanette would sit the bowl down on the kitchen table and proceed to do the honors while I worked at the sink washing dishes.

"Look, Mommy, it is coming out!" She'd carefully blow hard into the tiny hole, rest, and then blow again until she'd forced the runny contents to exit through the pinhole at the other end.

"Good job!" I always patted her back below her blond ponytail.

When Shanette had finished emptying the eggshells of their innards, she'd beat them for baked custard or for scrambled eggs. My daughter and I were doing things together essentially every minute outside my work schedule.

The transition into the architectural aspects of work came gradually. Reading navy manuals evolved into drafting simple working drawings from sketches provided by senior staff. Coffee breaks in the compound's cafeteria became an informative workday punctuation. At 9:30 a.m. and 2:30 p.m., I entered the cafeteria to make friends and tune in to the informal network. My coworkers tended to sit together at long narrow tables generally by engineering discipline, not by race or by gender. On one such coffee break, the chatter was about the supervisors' plan to change our office-seating layout.

Intrigued, I checked with Joel right after coffee. "I hear the supervisors are doing some planning that might impact all of us."

"We are in the process," Joel said matter-of-factly, not expecting any response.

"Maybe you could use some information on what the nonsupervisors would like to see in a new layout," I offered in my best helpful voice.

He pushed a few stray graying locks from his crinkled forehead. "What do you mean?"

"I could take a survey to find out preferences about a new office layout."

"I will talk to Mr. Scamell," Joel responded gingerly. He stood; I took this as a cue to return to my desk and get back to work.

A few days later, the secretary asked me to come up front to the architectural branch head's office. Within minutes, Mr. Scamell gave me the go-ahead, so I got busy making my one-page survey. Respondents could answer "I agree," "I'm neutral," or "I disagree" to 11 questions. The questionnaire was anonymous except for an "S" for supervisors and an "NS" for nonsupervisors. I cheerfully handed out surveys to everybody; within a couple of days, 27 were returned. All 4 supervisors and 23 nonsupervisors responded; 3 didn't. I promptly tallied up the scores, analyzed them, and posted the results:

It can be deduced from Questions #3, #8, and #9 that the nonsupervisors feel that this branch should work as a team, they would not like to be completely isolated and would like to work in clusters of 3 or 4 architects—1 being a junior person. The supervisors are split on question #6, "The spatial arrangement should symbolize the administrative hierarchy of the office."

"I see they are teaching new things in architecture school since I attended," one extroverted senior architect said.

"I would never think to do a survey," said the reserved blond fellow sitting two desks from me.

Asking employees their opinion seemed new to them, and posting the results for everyone to see was outright revolutionary. But I just continued doing what I had learned in school as if it obviously needed to be done.

A few days after the posting, Mr. Scamell called me into his office again. "Wendy, I like what you found out," he said calmly. "Would you take some time to work up a seating arrangement based on the survey results?"

Delighted to accept this challenge, I designed a clustered seating arrangement—pods of four workspaces with one young person sitting with three seasoned employees. In my simple layout, each supervisor's office bordered the clusters of a dozen or so employees he was responsible for—in contrast to the supervisors' being huddled together near the front of the building. I hadn't been given criteria. These were elementary layout decisions, but they were based on my coworkers' desires.

The supervisors didn't post their final design, but when changes started to happen, I recognized how the major elements of my plan had been merged into the official plan. For example, fabric-covered freestanding panels were installed to divide pods of four-person cubicles, redistributing the three open long rows of desks that existed when I arrived. However, I had not been included during the final design process, so I missed the discussion about the seating of junior members, the location of supervisors, and other considerations. I would have preferred to witness the entire process, but I still felt mild twinges of satisfaction because I had found a way to insert my skills, and my coworkers' concerns, into our workspace changes.

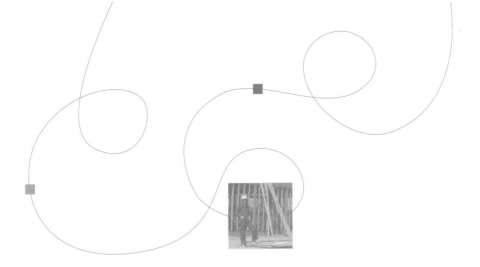

Hippity-Hop

1973 to 1974: Oakland

Even without a map for short-skirted, high-heeled adventurers, I felt fully capable of navigating the training rotations within the navy. The same vim and optimism that had propelled me around the world a decade earlier now continued to energize me. I approached my work with an alert, critical eye, through a lens of trust, wonder, and idealism. The organizational order and ranked authority provided a clear framework, yet for unknown reasons I didn't feel restricted; on the contrary, I came to envision the potential for change and creativity all around me.

Nothing was even remotely glamorous about the navy's work environment. Not a stick of designer furniture to be found anywhere, no hardwood floors with colorful rugs or large, artfully arranged bouquets in the lobby, as I'd seen in the big downtown firms during OWA meetings. But in spite of the lackluster décor, our office space had its pleasant points. It was quiet, the scale felt roomy because of the high ceilings, and the windows opened, allowing fresh air and daylight to enhance our drafting tables. Even so, the overall atmosphere barely rated a C; it sorely lacked character, color, and drama.

My thoughts doubled back to my work-study position for the Richmond Planning Department. I'd given those offices a B+ rating, partly because of the generous landscaping I passed as I entered the recently built civic complex from the parking area, and partly because of the animated space I worked in. Oodles of graphic equipment, art posters, and giant central layout tables covered with in-progress projects created an atmosphere of working artisans. As much as I valued the visual character of the places where I lived and worked, and despite the disappointment of this plummeting trend in office appearance, I firmly believed that the professional opportunities offered me by the navy far outweighed the dullness of my daily desk location.

After an inaugural month in the Architectural Branch, I began the hippity-hop phase of my training year. Soon I sat among engineers in the Acquisition Department on the second floor of a parallel shoebox-shaped building. Male project managers, desked in drab cubicles, mothered projects to keep them on schedule and within budget. One of the key reasons this job attracted me was the navy's policy of rotating fledgling architects to other disciplines, and it was playing out as marketed. With incredible reliability, my rotations followed the schedule set at the beginning of the year.

After the first month, I hopped one more building down the row to the Master Planning Branch, where the staff included almost as many women as men. They were younger than the architects, more colorful, and more hip—half of them were new arrivals—sparking an obvious camaraderie that was absent in the Architectural Branch. The planners decorated their floor with large potted plants arranged to soften the odd spaces between desks. Although city and county zoning and building codes didn't apply to navy real estate, the navy had a well-deserved reputation for creating reams of planning and design manuals. During my rotation in the early 1970s, the drawing boards were covered with 20 new master plans—some already bound into soft-covered books—for bases in the nine western states.

Planning is an envisioning art, one that comes to life over decades, project by project—if it survives the influences of interpretation and weathers political debate. A planner may see only the first phase of a plan actually built in his or her work life. Master planning is what has made some navy bases so impressive upon arrival—akin to walking into a graduation ceremony and feeling the years of work it took to get to this point. On the other hand, the architectural hodgepodge of bases built without good planning is reminiscent of a kitchen catchall-drawer and can make one feel lost.

For the entire summer of 1973, my corporate wardrobe changed from skirts and heels to pants and low laced shoes that I tied in double knots.

Each morning, I drove from Oakland to the Construction Management Office on Treasure Island, at the mid-span of the Bay Bridge between Alameda County and San Francisco. Often I would pause outside my office, gazing toward the Golden Gate Bridge, tickled by an inner appreciation for the geography and the moment. This was work—real,

In the field for construction management on Treasure Island

rosy, and at the navel of a 360-degree view of the San Francisco Bay. How lucky could a girl get?

First thing, I'd walk to the farthest corner of a cavernous warehouse, a leftover from the San Francisco World's Fair of 1939, where I would pick up my assigned hardhat (my name was written on it) and the keys to one of the gray trucks. One particular morning, I slowed the truck to study San Francisco's urban composition in the distance. Mindfully and academically, I evaluated the city's profile and texture: pale-colored buildings stretched unevenly over the steep hills, taller in the city's center and gradually lowering toward the shore. Only the Bank of America's black tower blatantly deviated—was this an accent or an urban scar?

My construction management supervisor, Navy Lieutenant Futch, junior grade, was about my age and had completed the first part of the test for his civil engineering license (EIT). He could have been the poster child for "an officer and a gentleman," his solid, square-shouldered stance and thick brown hair offsetting a milky complexion. We worked with two longtime civilian inspectors whose job was to observe and then report to the lieutenant any deviations from ongoing contracts.

"Wendy," said the chief inspector from the desk next to mine, "go have a look at the road repair at the top of the hill."

"I don't know how roads should be built," I said with alarm and hesitation, but I stood up to show him I was willing to go.

"Oh, that doesn't matter," he replied. "Just go stand around. That will keep the contractor honest."

And so I did.

Within days, the alert lieutenant decided I was capable of administering a large painting contract for more than 100 housing units for officers and enlisted men, assembled into 26 buildings. At the pre-construction conference, the contractor asked the government representative to indicate paint colors for a few areas he'd found on the drawings where the color was undesignated. The preferred method for making design decisions during construction was to ask the designer. In this case, the Navy Public Works Center gave permission for the construction managers to select the missing colors—which left that decision up to "fresh-out-the-gate" me.

It would have been fun to select the colors according to my own design vision; however, from my experience, I knew to check the master plan for the selected colors before proceeding. Sure enough, the Treasure Island Master Plan called for olive green, mustard, and cream.

Overall, the painters and the tenants respected my choices of where to put cream, mustard, and olive green if it was not specified on the drawings. But, unexpectedly, when I arrived at Treasure Island one beautiful middle-of-the-bay morning, the office staff seemed uncommonly agitated. The conscientious lieutenant broke the news, "A captain's wife on Yerba Buena has complained about the color of her house." (Yerba Buena is the natural island attached to the man-made Treasure Island.)

"Did she say why?" I asked.

"She is *very* upset."

"I selected the colors from the master plan," I said nonchalantly.

"She is very, very upset. The captain called my boss." He looked directly into my eyes to be sure I understood the full ramifications of this undesirable situation.

Fortunately, I knew enough about the navy's ranking system to know that when a captain, ranked just below admiral, called a lower-ranking officer about something under his control, action was the only response. "I could go to her house and explain how I selected the color," I suggested, without giving my response any thought. I wonder now what had triggered my behavior. What other options might I have had—how would another in my hardhat have reacted?

Lieutenant Futch's frown faded as he dialed the number to arrange for an appointment. The dynamics of a junior lieutenant talking to a captain's wife had now shifted to a woman (architect) going to talk to another woman (captain's wife). He clearly thought it worth a try.

Later that day, I knocked at the door of the freshly painted, mustard-colored house, sunk low in a grove of lanky eucalyptus trees.

"I don't like this color," the captain's wife said, clutching her doorknob. She was ready for me. "It looks like I live in a slum."

"I'm sorry you feel that way. You see, this house was a little darker than the others, so I selected the master planning color golden-mustard, as I thought it would cover the existing color better than the cream color of your neighbors."

Her irritated expression and explosive red lipstick were louder than her voice. "This color is not fit for *officers'* housing," she cringed.

"Do you think we should repaint your house another color?"

"Well, it is really upsetting." She opened the door wide enough for me to enter and motioned me in.

"If I had known your concern, I could have selected a different color," I assured her. "But now that the work has been completed, we would have to pay the contractor to repaint it."

She sighed. I sensed tensions uncoiling.

"Well … we *will* be moving in a few months … I guess it isn't absolutely necessary."

"Thanks for understanding," I said, looking around at the plush furnishings we hadn't even had the time to sit on.

She mustered a weak but sincere smile as she guided me out the front door. "Yes, well, I appreciate your coming up here to speak with me."

Driving down the steep hill toward the construction office, I considered how to avoid unnecessarily annoying navy personnel in the future with colors that triggered such negative emotions. When I pulled up next to the office, it was almost time to go home. The forestalled and anxious lieutenant relaxed after hearing about my visit with the upset captain's wife. Visibly relieved, he put on his khaki garrison cap and stopped for the day.

Since I went to work so early, I was able to pick up Shanette earlier from childcare. The summer days were wonderfully long for outings with my dear daughter, and I treasured these opportunities to give her my full attention. One of our favorite things to do was to ride the merry-go-round in Tilden Regional Park, on the ridge in the Berkeley Hills, not far from where we lived.

"Mommy, can we go see the farm animals, too?" Shanette asked from the backseat of the Peugeot.

"Of course."

Shanette liked the baby goats, rabbits, and baby deer in the park's petting farm. "Could we get a bunny?" she dreamed aloud as I pulled into the parking area.

"Not now, we don't have a place for it in the apartment."

A warm breeze riffled through the tall stands of trees on the side of the road, infusing the air with refreshing eucalyptus. Shanette ran in front of me as we headed across the grass for the tiny park farm.

"I would really, *really* like a bunny," Shanette repeated delicately as she sat cross-legged in the sawdust petting a soft brown rabbit.

Tucking that thought away, I suggested we take a ride on the merry-go-round.

I truly loved being a mother. Each night, I felt the tightly focused concentration of work dissolve into the comprehensiveness of mothering, like butterscotch pudding mix in warming milk. Luckily, Shanette was oblivious to the mounting barrage of multi-page letters I was receiving from her father and grandmother, arguing for me to come and live my life in France. I felt less vulnerable than in the past, believing that a healthy awareness of my own goals and needs would protect me from their coercion.

Mind you, I had been divorced for over a year—with full custody of my daughter—yet child support only dribbled in and debt payments never arrived. Even though I loved France, it seemed normal for me to want to live in my own country. Looking back, I realize that the stress of negotiating this geographic and psychological distance with my French family put me in a constant state of running from their demands. I coped by clinging to the reliable reins of my independence. Regardless, I didn't have any objection to Shanette's spending time with her dad; the previous Christmas holiday, he had come from France and she'd spent her school vacation at Alpine Meadows, where he worked.

Finally, the last of the housing units on Treasure Island had been painted, everything on the "punch list" (the inspector's final list of items missed by the contractor) had been rectified, and the as-built drawings (working drawings updated with the changes made during construction) had been noted.

I approached the lieutenant. "Could I devise a questionnaire to get feedback from the tenants on the painting contract?"

"What kind of questions?" he asked, firming his attention.

"Questions about the colors. The results might influence color choices in the future."

Soon I set out on foot to deliver my questionnaire to the tenants. The doors opened in most units. "Could you please fill this out now and leave it outside?" I requested with a sense of urgency. "I will return within the hour to pick it up." The first paragraph announced my motive:

It is often argued that you can't please everybody, and this is true. However, it is the spirit of this survey to find out what you, the tenants, think about the newly painted exterior colors of your housing. Your thoughts will help give meaning to future color choices.

The positive responses to the survey reinforced the premise that navy families liked being asked their opinion. I deemed the results interesting enough to write them up in the Housing Office Newsletter for the tenants to read. I titled the article, "Color Color on the Wall, Which Is the Best Liked of Us All," and signed it W. Bertrand, rather than Wendy Bertrand, to avoid being automatically dismissed by male readers. (I had just learned that many female authors used this tactic.)

I shared this work experience at the next OWA meeting and was genuinely curious about hearing what others were doing at their jobs. Soon I began advocating that members, instead of just outside guests, present the program after the business portion of the meeting. Most of us needed opportunities to practice our public speaking anyway, and the work we accomplished was so varied. Why not highlight our own members, as well as feature outside speakers? But, to my astonishment, OWA members were unexpectedly shy about public speaking. Even in our friendly forum, they resisted bringing attention to their projects, their jobs, or their person. Fortunately, that changed in later years, when many members gladly became featured OWA meeting speakers.

These short stints in branches of WestDiv's Acquisition, Planning, and Construction departments effectively introduced me to how government buildings were administered from conception through birth, groundbreaking, construction, and readiness for occupancy. During my rotations, I also paid attention to my coworkers' views and behaviors, as much as to their skills, because how the organization functioned intrigued me as much as how buildings were designed and constructed. Early on, I sensed the delicate play between the individual's priorities and the organization's motor.

At the end of each of my on-the-job training rotations, I was rated using eight evaluation items, none of which addressed "architectural quality," but all of which contributed to making a solid all-around architect—or any other worker, for that matter. The evaluation items—ability to complete assignments, effectiveness in dealing with people, ease in written communication, ability to follow supervision, excellence of judgment, adaptation to teamwork, potential for promotion, and rank in overall performance—were the only formal feedback I received from the organization for my performance. My job was not like a sales job, where one works for a commission, or like that of a waitress, where one sees immediate results countable in dollars. We weren't on TV, so there were no public ratings; building users, architectural critics, and contractors were not asked for their evaluations. However, like most employees, I wanted to know how I was doing. Ratings were not usually discussed among peers, but a copy of the evaluation went into my personnel folder and could be used for awards, promotions, or position changes.

The lieutenant rated me highly; all eight accounts were glowing, with "Outstanding" or "Very good," followed by, "She was highly resourceful. A go-getter." At the end, he wrote, "This form should be revised from the masculine to the neuter tense to better reflect Equal Employment Opportunity policies," and he checked the 'Prefer *Him* to Most' box. This pleased me; but I already liked the lieutenant because he had continued to increase my responsibilities with the keen eye of a successful sports trainer.

In the fall of 1973, the *Navy Civil Engineer* published a profile of naval facility engineering personnel, revealing the depth of the ocean I was swimming in. Worldwide, the number of engineers (800 series) totaled 1,140, with only 11 percent of those being architects (808 series). Although the article advocated the recruitment of young graduates, it did not mention reaching out to the obviously missing worker pools of females, nonwhites, and disabled people. Of the 118 navy architects worldwide, the number of females was not spelled out. I, myself, knew only one other female architect in the navy; she became an OWA friend and worked in our Planning Department. But soon, thank goodness, more females arrived.

During November, I hippity-hopped again, from Treasure Island back to San Bruno for a rotation in two branches within the Design Division of the Acquisition Department. In the Specifications Branch, I learned that the information written in the specifications should never duplicate what is noted on the drawings because each complements the other. My month in the Estimating Branch introduced me to how estimates were calculated using rules-of-thumb and price guidelines in books, depending on the locality of the job site.

For self-improvement, I joined the Toastmasters' Club (rather than the Toastmistresses' Club), probably because I knew some of the men in the club. I titled my icebreaker speech "Self as a Painting."

At the end of my first working year, I graduated from the training program and was promoted, as promised. Back in the Architectural

Branch, I had a new supervisor, Ray, a good-natured architect who wore striped shirts and more browns than grays. Athletic and younger than Joel, Ray was an even-tempered, mild-mannered boss who liked to play tennis at lunchtime; I played doubles with him a few times.

I sat in Ray's section between Ted and Dixson. Both were married and close to my age. Ted, fair-haired and about my height, was contained, careful, conservative, and considerate. Ted and I lunched on occasion. Quiet, arty Dixson had young children and had just bought an old house to fix up in the San Francisco neighborhood of Noe Valley. He came from Texas and described his 180-degree turnabout when he arrived in California by saying, "I used to be a *redneck*." As desk neighbors, we observed each other's style in dealing with projects, overheard telephone conversations, and could ask each other questions about following procedures or finding information.

Dixson would say on his way to coffee, "Wendy, do you want to go for a break?"

With one year under my belt, I had earned two weeks of vacation and had enough money to start paying back bigger chunks on my loans from my mother and the university. Even with those payments, I felt financially flush. I had been a penny-pinching student for so long that my lifestyle was still relatively inexpensive, and I didn't use a credit card.

My ex-husband increased the lobbying in his letters, urging me to bring Shanette to France. "You have few friends and I am the adult most intimate to you.... I know you have tenderness for me, my daughter needs me." Fearing that I might not uproot my life or do whatever he wanted, he upped the bait. "I will pay the tickets for both of you to visit this summer."

Of course, I resisted. The scars of divorce were deep and still too painful, but, more than that, I could see no reason to uproot my daughter or myself. Meanwhile, Arnaud's behavior remained charming and controlling, not loving and responsible. He didn't send child support, or gifts for Shanette's birthday and other holidays. With everything he wrote in his letters, the painful difficulties for children of divorce went unacknowledged. Arnaud didn't seem to be able to distinguish right from wrong.

Lacking the emotional skills to back him off, I fumbled, confused by his mixed messages. The hopscotch rotations at work continued satisfactorily, yet the legacy of my marriage that I so wanted to dismantle weighed me down with the outrageous impediment of a prisoner's ball and chain.

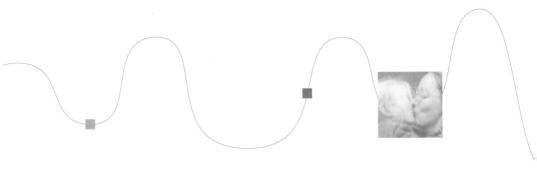

Heartskipping and Soft Spots

1974: Oakland

The navy revered organizational intelligence, orderly processing, and timely project completion. I took to the paperwork the way a child learns to use a spoon and fork—so practiced that it soon becomes effortless. Although the actual design decisions of my early projects were minor, the navy process and format needed to be mastered. One of my first assignments was to prepare the drawings for a contract to paint and replace the floor tile in the interior of a building at the Naval Reserve Training Center in Ogden, Utah. So that all contractors would bid on the same scope of work, the navy required a detailed map of the center's exact location, including the building's cross street, what level of preparation was required, how many coats of which color paint, where to paint, what kind of tile—those sorts of things. The navy hired the lowest bidder and wanted to be sure that bids were comparable.

Another early project was for Treasure Island's naval station staff civil engineer, who wanted to transform an unused patch of weeds between two buildings into an outside sitting area. I designed and prepared construction drawings to add that landscaping.

Each project varied in scope, location, and responsibility, which suited me fine. Soon I was assigned to design the architectural portion of a gas station for a navy exchange. The exchange consistently relied on a *typical* service station design, which could be site-adapted to any location in the world. My project was at the Naval Air Station on Whidbey Island in Washington State. After some study, I concluded that their *typical* floor plan was unnecessarily sexist, so I went about changing a few doors and walls to eliminate the subtle discrimination. The women's restroom door was off the gas station's sales showroom, where tires, hubcaps, and other products for cars were displayed (this was before mini-markets), while the men's restroom was off the service garage. This visibly implied that the inside workers were female and the mechanics were men. Also, it surprised me that only the men had a locker room and lunchroom. With little effort and at no cost to the project, I relocated the doors so that both restrooms were off a hallway between the service garage and the sales area. This way, men and women enjoyed equal access to both activities. I also added a women's locker room and enlarged the lunchroom to serve men and women.

The shape of the building didn't change, and I didn't offer to defend my few changes. Once the architectural drawings were complete, the mechanical and electrical drawings followed my design. It was just that easy; I had quietly integrated my ideas about gender and equity into Whidbey Island's gas station. We everyday architects have values, personalities, and priorities that color our work—lightly or dramatically—like other workers, professionals, and artists.

Most WestDiv architectural contracts went to private firms; the gas station, however, was an in-house design project and one of few exceptions. Some of the firms—referred to in the industry as "A/Es" (architects and engineers)—targeted government work. The person within the navy who was assigned responsibility for the project design was called the *engineer-in-charge*, or EIC. Architects were also called *engineers*-in-charge, the same as engineers. I thought architects should be called *architects*-in-charge, or AIC.

"Don't get worked up, Wendy," one of my coffee-break buddies said as he stirred an inordinate amount of sugar into his Styrofoam cup. "The engineers *are* in charge here. That's just the way it is."

"They may be in charge of the organization, but aren't we in charge of the buildings' design?"

I was still trying to arrange the logic of my thinking as I walked back to my desk, a couple of buildings away. Before I had a chance to sit down, my supervisor, Ray, asked me to come into his office.

"Mr. Scamell suggested I assign this to you," he said as he slid a freshly labeled file folder in my direction. His tone implied that he

personally thought it might be too soon to assign me such a substantial and complex project.

"Great, what is it?" I asked.

"It's the first step of a large project in San Diego." He said it like a good soldier, not blinking.

"I'm sure I can do it," I said, as casually as possible, considering my heartskipping excitement.

"Congress is in the process of allocating design funding for the Recruit-in-Processing Facility in San Diego. You will be the engineer-in-charge, so you need to provide the necessary documents for their decision."

Some of my colleagues clearly had to swallow their surprise when they heard that their feminist colleague had been assigned such a paramount project. But I paid them no mind, remaining focused on my mission.

The next afternoon coffee-break, I resurfaced my concern about where architects fit into the building industry. "*Arch* is a prefix meaning 'chief' or 'main,' and *tekton* means 'worker,'" I told my coffee-break mates. I had looked up *architect* in several dictionaries, and found that it was from the Greek, literally meaning "master builder." "We are the chief workers to design buildings," I followed, "to draw up plans and to generally supervise the construction—*including* all the engineering functions."

"We know that," said a senior architect, hoping to steer me to another topic. "But architects are still only involved in 5 percent of what is built."

For the time being, I dropped the subject, but it continued to weigh on me. Although *everyday* engineers seemed to enjoy a positive reputation in my office and with the public, *everyday* architects were called engineers-in-charge and somehow didn't even show up on the public's radar screen. The title *EIC* just didn't ring true, sort of like calling a woman *he*. But to my dismay, it wasn't bothering anyone else.

At home, letters from Shanette's father in France bombarded my mailbox, demanding that she attend the French-American School in San Francisco. And still, as the moon rose every month, no child support arrived. I was fine with Shanette's becoming bilingual, but I couldn't pay for the private school. In my reply letters, I held my ground, insisting on Arnaud's financial backing before I could agree to a school transfer.

A call from NavFac Headquarters went out to design divisions worldwide, asking us to give our input for guidelines to improve the appearance of naval facilities. At WestDiv, the assignment was passed from the Design Division director to the Architectural Branch head, to my supervisor, to me. I quickly prepared a report with photos of what I referred to as "mechanisms for getting the most appearance value out of every project."

A month later, Mr. Scamell called me into his office. "Wendy, I asked you to come in because I just received a call from Headquarters on the *Appearance of the Shore Enhancement* booklet. I don't usually get calls thanking me for a good job. I thought you deserved to know."

"That's great. Thanks," I responded, wishing he had made the kudos during a meeting in front of my colleagues. Organizational behavior was in the hands of managers, who could help you cross the organizational street, get training, and move up the promotional ladder, so I was paying close attention to any and all organizational gestures.

My job satisfaction and morale had been bolstered by the good rapport with my supervisors and my stellar record of successfully completing assignments. However, as a young female in architecture who didn't know as much as she thought she should, I felt my insecurity quiver when my competitive male colleagues challenged me with, "You don't know that?!" Luckily, OWA shored the keystone of my professional confidence. I was doing well with the work, but my confidence was still being challenged as a female architect.

Perhaps this attitude was a sign of the times. According to one of the current high-class billboards bordering a San Francisco freeway, "You can't know it all, but you can fake it …" It never occurred to me to *fake it*. On the contrary, I slowly came to understand that there would always be things I didn't know, and that was *okay*. Yet, when I couldn't answer a question, self-doubt tugged at my composure. Men didn't seem to worry. Maybe they just hid their feelings, while I wavered before this kind of scrutiny and strove to handle it with the grace of an aikido student. OWA became a good forum for evaluating these minor moments of despair because other ambitious women openly and willingly discussed how to tackle the tricky verbal holds and footwork.

By May 1974, the *OWA Newsletter* had expanded to a record ten pages. The calendar listed lecture series, pertinent seminars, art shows by women, and available jobs and scholarships. There was an excerpt from *Viva* titled "Women in the Professions," an article about federal laws against discrimination, and a letter to the editor challenging Mr. Longstreth's presentation in the Heritage Lecture Series for insinuating that Julia Morgan was indifferent to feminism. We young professionals needed to evaluate the steep terrain of our trek, and every word provided much-appreciated information for navigating the uneven ground.

Shanette's father had written about his plans to take her to France for the summer. "I will arrive by her eighth birthday on June 3rd. I will have her flown back with friends on whatever date you give me, since you know my policy all along has been to remain in agreeable agreement with you concerning Shuang Shuang." He made it sound friendly; he wanted to stay on my good side as he was still trying to influence me to enroll Shanette in the French-American Bilingual School.

Somehow, Arnaud convinced me that everything had been arranged for his friends to bring her back from France. Just the same, I wanted assurances that she'd be back a week before school started so she'd be rested and ready. Knowing Arnaud's demanding personal style, low funds, and lack of permanent lodging, as well as his record of moving around to find work, I was skeptical as to how this trip would play out.

When he came to Berkeley in June, Arnaud acted in many ways as if I were still his wife. He wanted to use my car, which was startling and unnerving because he had another life; he would have moved into my apartment and jumped into my bed; he had no boundaries of his own, and I was always raising the height of mine to hold him off. To Arnaud's surprise, he had to arrange for another place to stay and take the bus to get around. Regardless, he remained concentrated on his objective.

"It is very important for Shanette to learn French," he repeated with the insistence of a broken record, a TV commercial, or a woodpecker circling the trunk of a tree.

"I have no quarrel with that," I reiterated, "but the school is very expensive."

"I will get a grant from the French government."

"How will she get to school in San Francisco?"

"I will find her a ride; I have already talked to some of the teachers."

Unconvinced, I gritted my teeth and kept to the logistics of the summer vacation. I felt obliged by the divorce agreement to arrange for Shanette to see her father, but France was far away and she was only in the fourth grade. Further, I abhorred Arnaud's hardsell and manipulative manner. Since we had been together for nine years, he knew most of my soft spots, while I was just beginning to learn how to shield them. Nevertheless, I gave him the benefit of the doubt.

Reluctantly, I packed Shanette's bag, assuring her that I would have a good summer and would be happy to see her when she returned. She was looking forward to a summer of outdoor fun. I wanted her to know her French family and culture, but I was also slightly fearful of Arnaud's knightly charm. He was a royal recreation daddy, and he treated her more like a fairytale princess than a delicate daughter. I drove them to the airport as if everything would be fine. Watching with dread as the plane lifted off from the runway, I could only hope for the best.

While Shanette was in France, I dated a fellow I'd met at a gourmet wild mushroom dinner that my neighbor had dragged me to. Tom was an outdoorsy Japanese-American, 12 years older than I, who worked for the California courts. He loved art and dreamed of becoming a stone-carver. We went to art museum openings and camped in Yosemite, where he introduced me to mountain-climbing techniques. Having fun with Tom was a delightful diversion, but it didn't keep me from pining for my daughter, so far away.

The French letters continued to arrive, from my mother-in-law and Arnaud, filled with anecdotes of how happy Shanette was and how pleased everyone was to be with her. "This is where she should be. Why don't you come and live in France?" One letter was written in English, as if Shanette had written it, "I went to the sandy beach and I jumped with a parachute." And, at the end, in her hand, "I am having so much fun. I love you. XOXOXOXO." The Xs and Os continued up the page, wrenching my heart; I could see my daughter's concentrative way of filling each hand-plaited X and O with care. Otherwise, the overflow of letters from Arnaud was laced with the usual emotional bullying. He and his mother acknowledged my role as mother; in fact, they dwelled on it, while ignoring my origins, feelings, and goals. I felt targeted, yet dismissed.

Arnaud wrote that his friends would escort Shanette home on September 2. However, on August 27, he telegrammed, "Friends could not bring her back as I had hoped and she will fly alone."

I was horrified and angry with him for taking such a risk. Although flight attendants took Shanette through customs in Los Angeles, my motherly rage mounted at the idea of my young daughter enduring the 11-hour flight alone. She arrived depleted, her blond hair scattered in wild directions, mirroring the out-of-control tangle of my mood.

"Mommy, my ears hurt," she said as we hugged. Her embrace and sincere kisses melted my heart. All I could do was comfort her as I told myself that we would quickly get back to our routine and she would soon settle into her schoolgirl status.

Shanette didn't talk about her summer. But for the next few weeks, she kissed me unexpectedly and repeatedly, her face beaming. Her loving manner exhibited a youthful relief to be back to mother, home, and cat. She didn't like to travel; and when she was older, she told me so, confirming my instinct that she was too young to have traveled so far by herself. Arnaud wasn't visiting her as most fathers visited their

Shanette coming home from France

young children back then. I felt he was forcing a visit from her to happen and only on his terms, thousands of miles away. His disregard for distance was unnecessarily stressful on our Shanette during those skip-roping years, and I truly regretted surrendering to his insistence. Even though the motive of seeing his daughter was acceptable, the impact of his decisions on *her* reality deserved more respect.

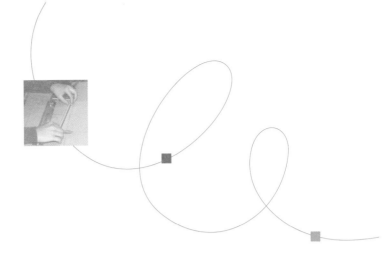

High Jump

1975: Oakland

Life settled into a routine. I joined a carpool with several interesting men and women—not all architects. The minute the doors slammed, we launched into continuous conversation, ranging from why more women than men in architecture were single or childless to how to arrange shopping bags of groceries in the car trunk so they wouldn't fall over on the way home from the supermarket.

Although I didn't think about my projects beyond the office walls, the lively half-hour of car chat was a welcome warm-up to sitting down in front of my drafting table—when my work thoughts took off running. Still green by most standards, only three years out of graduate school, and not very far along in passing the many parts of the architectural licensing exam, I felt fortunate when the Recruit-in-Processing Facility was funded from the booklet I had prepared for Congress. I was now the EIC of a multimillion-dollar facility; it would be the third of its type in the navy. Of course, I now realize that this project moved me a quantum leap forward on the intangible *take-charge* scale, but at the time I just held my breath and made the high jump. Fortunately, there was lots of work in our department—all of the men and two of the new young women had plenty to do—which fostered an upbeat, busy work climate. From the small talk I'd overheard, I gathered that my co-workers were curious about how an outspoken feminist would fare.

Without any detectable malice, they took note that I had been put in charge of the design of this plum project. The size and status of project assignments seemed to indicate the organization's confidence in one's skills, and I can't help but think that my handling of this assignment strengthened the respect given to me by my boss and co-workers.

I came to rely on OWA as an *expectations gauge.* "How is your work going?" I asked one experienced member at the next meeting. "Are you still working on laboratories?"

"Well, Wendy, I am *now* an expert on laboratory built-ins, but I'm tired of it and want to do something else. I'm even thinking I might have to change firms." Unfortunately, she seemed to be suffering from a lack of variety in her projects. Her comment underscored the advantage I was enjoying in my large office, where my drawer was filling up with different types of projects, buoying my job satisfaction.

Shanette and my mother at the La Jolla Cove

Since I planned my own business trips, I arranged for Shanette to travel with me to San Diego when I went for my first meeting with the users at the Recruit-in-Processing Facility. My mother still lived in La Jolla, in the same brown-shingled cottage where I'd grown up, so this was a wonderful opportunity to combine business with family.

Shanette played and gardened with my mother on Thursday and Friday, while I interviewed one uniformed officer after another: the medical captain, dental captain, supply officer, testing and classification officer, records officer, navy training officer, and exchange officer in charge of the barbershop.

"We need an assembly area near the entrance that can accommodate 70 recruits," said the senior medical captain.

I wrote symbols before each comment: M-101 for *medical–first floor–first room.* "Where do the recruits go from there?" I asked.

"I need counter space for five to eight corpsmen to check health records, examine hearing, and give eye tests." I scribbled M-102 and beside it, his description. "Then the recruits go to the inoculation area for blood tests," he continued. "And I need a skin-testing area."

"Do you need privacy for giving shots?" I questioned.

"Oh, no, we just go right down the line," he responded, as if they were all men. (I didn't catch that at the time.) I noted M-103 with this information, and so on. After jotting down the functions, along with the extent of privacy needed, and the doors, windows, and equipment needed (from audio-testing units to toilets and sinks), I drew a flow diagram with arrows depicting the order in which recruits were intended to visit each receiving station.

After the medical captain and I had completed our interview, he telephoned the dental captain. "The architect is here. Are you available?" I noticed he didn't give away my gender or age; navy respect for rank and role included my standing as an architect. In another situation it could have been, "A pretty young woman is here to interview you. Are you available?" I appreciated the respect of naval officers. The organization's manners mattered; like wax on surfboards, they reduced friction and increased efficiency.

That weekend, Shanette, my mother, and I walked to the Cove Beach, only four blocks from my mother's house. An intense peacefulness seeped into my often-overstuffed thoughts as I watched my mother show my daughter how to explore the tide pools, while I let the waves take me with them, back and forth.

Back to work Monday morning in San Bruno, I transformed my messy notes into a 22-page document, which I copied for each user representative to review and comment on. In my role as owner's representative for the navy, my task was to understand and coordinate the users' needs and to arrive at a building design that was useful to them. But I also wanted to make sure that the building was an attractive investment for the navy and that it was a positive addition to the portfolio

Drafting at my WestDiv desk, 1975

of the public trust, used the land well, and respected the character of its location. Essentially, my function was to ensure that we were developing first-rate buildings, good government architecture. As you may imagine, the comment *good enough for government work,* meaning *it doesn't have to be that good,* still hurts my everyday architect's pride.

During a quick trip back to San Diego a few weeks later, I held a group meeting with all the user representatives to talk about the desired character of the building. After not too much discussion, they reached a consensus about the facility they envisioned and described it using the following words: motivational, orderly, new, welcoming, manageable, high standards, sturdy, pleasant, and comprehensible.

At the end of the meeting, the dental captain took me aside. "Wendy, I noticed you added a women's restroom for dental officers, but we don't need that. We don't have any female dentists."

My lips curled upward as I savored my response, "Well, you may have some in the future. I think it best to design for both male and female dental officers."

"Okay, I was only thinking of saving money," he replied respectfully.

Another decision I made was to uphold the recent Disabilities Act, which required access, in our case to the second floor, for wheelchair users.

"Recruits aren't in wheelchairs," said one officer.

"Staff or visitors may need to use a wheelchair," I reminded him. He let it pass.

I condensed the program into a matrix chart, lining up the activity, square footage, number of people, acoustic needs, types of windows, and stray concerns. Condensing and integrating the data into charts was something I particularly liked to do. All this information helped form the program and scope of work to go to the A/E (architect and engineer) firm; it was accompanied by other contractual requirements, such as the budget, the number of submittals, and the length of time allowed to complete the work. Working independently was wonderful; my boss Ray never hovered over my shoulder.

The next step was to select an A/E firm to design the Recruit-in-Processing Facility. A/E firms interested in designing the project had sent in their qualifications to the A/E Services Branch. Three navy professionals, including the Architectural Branch head, were asked to review the applications received and select five firms for the project's short list. Later, a panel of three professionals interviewed each short-listed firm for exactly 45 minutes. The restricted interview time was to ensure that we were fair to all applicants.

Mathew Lapota and Associates, a Los Angeles firm that had completed many navy projects, was selected to prepare the design contract for construction of the Recruit-in-Processing Facility. I met Mr. Lapota for the first time several months later during the negotiating meeting to determine fees and schedules. I embraced this first assignment as EIC with the authority of a well-bred lioness guiding her cubs.

Mr. Lapota's experience and calm temperament complemented my fresh Berkeley-graduate enthusiasm. He was a pleasant man in his 60s, who held his well-tanned jaw with unusual seriousness. I thought we forged a dynamic team. For example, he took the wheelchair access requirement I insisted on and designed a handsome ramp to be a major architectural feature at the front of the facility. Long lines of recruits could easily access the second floor; and the platform, where the ramp turned, could be used for speeches and instructions to those standing in the staging area below. Mr. Lapota determined the shape of the facility, considering my spatial requirements while still embedding the appropriate character traits outlined by the users in the program (*orderliness, motivational, high standards, sturdy, pleasant,* and so on). This conceptual design phase is where an experienced designer can creatively integrate the physical, aesthetic, and program requirements into a fine original building that is more than the sum of its parts. Mr. Lapota did this expertly, while I enthusiastically applauded and approved.

Of course, I had other projects at differing stages in their development to attend to in between the Recruit-in-Processing Facility's three design approvals. The design phase took about a year to develop; in the final set of construction drawings, each of the 157 sheets was dated and signed by me, the Architectural Branch head, the fire chief, and, lastly, the Engineering Division director. An artist's conception, called a rendering, was part of the final submittal. Mr. Lapota's rendering showed

Rendering of Recruit-in-Processing Facility

only men located around the building, so I asked him to add female figures. He graciously did so, both in civilian dress and navy uniforms.

Evenings, I wrote letters to France: to my friend Linette, who was still living in Chamonix, where Joe taught mountain climbing and skiing; to Alain J., my architectural schoolmate living in Montpellier; and to Jacqueline, then a law student, with whom I am still friends. Then, there were letters to my French family: to my mother-in-law and occasionally to Chantal, Arnaud's oldest sister, who was very supportive of me and equally concerned about Shanette's well-being. Over the summer, Shanette's father sent me 28 pages (in six letters) about why the French-American Bilingual School in San Francisco would be good for her and how I could arrange my life to accommodate her attendance there. He pointed out that I could afford the school since I was working and he had to use the little money he had on himself, among other sad stories.

At the beginning of the 1975 scholastic year, after much negotiating and an agreement that *all* costs would be accounted for by the French government, Shanette was enrolled in the French-American Bilingual School—meaning she would have to go to San Francisco five days a week. Waking to a ringing alarm clock at 5:30 in the morning and remembering all the stuff we each had to take for the day was trying enough for me, but I felt it was asking too much of a fifth-grader. Shanette didn't complain, but her sleepy sweet face said it all as we headed—our arms full of book bags, lunch bags, and my leather briefcase—for our separate carpools. Her 30-minute commute, often before dawn over a major bridge in heavy traffic, made me anxious.

One morning after several exhausting weeks of this routine, I looked into my daughter's dreamy gray eyes, her good-bye kiss still fresh on my cheek, and decided to move us to San Francisco. I'd been considering the move for several weeks, but I somehow awoke that morning confident about what I needed to do. I was able to make this radical decision in part because my job had proved to be so rewarding and stable. Being in San Francisco would bring many benefits. And when she got older, she could take the bus. Yes, with a deep inhale, I decided it was time to start looking for a place to live in the big, beautiful city on the other side of the bay.

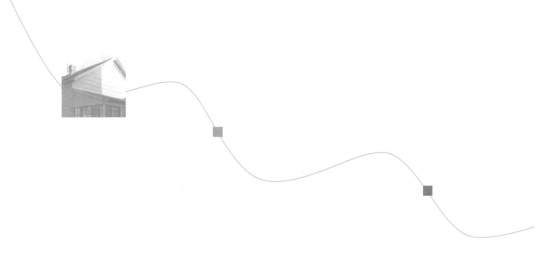

San Francisco Landing

1975 to 1976: San Francisco

Our carpool passed San Francisco's stunning panorama five days a week, but now I needed to learn about the residential terrain sprawling from the skyline's ankle. In short, I had no clue where to begin looking for housing. My reference points inside the city clustered in the civic and commercial centers. I knew the Museum of Modern Art near the Civic Center, where I'd attended art openings with Tom, and I had purchased a stainless steel wok from a little shop in Chinatown. I'd shopped for remnants of Marimekko fabrics at the Design Store in Embarcadero Center, and I had picked up friends at the Greyhound station on Seventh Street below Market. But there ended my previous explorations, and residential living in these areas was dense and too tall—not what I had in mind. Tom's small apartment was on Russian Hill, in the northern part of the city. I'd been there a few times.

Tom and I had continued to see each other after Shanette returned from France, but I was not entirely comfortable with the relationship. He was not legally separated from his wife. Although they had lived apart for years, they hadn't divorced because of their teenage children. He would have liked us to be close by, but moving in with him near the crooked block of Lombard Street was definitely unworkable.

The French-American Bilingual School was in a corner building of the Steiner Street block featured on a popular postcard, depicting a row of colorful Queen Anne–style houses. However, it was not my intention to live right next to the school, which was near a shabby area well known for criminal activity. My search for a rental began in the sunny southern neighborhoods between Shanette's school and the freeway entrance I would take to work.

For lack of time, rather than walking *all* the hilly streets hoping to find "For Rent" signs, I responded to want ads in the *San Francisco Chronicle*. After several refusals on the phone, and two in person, I raised the dilemma to my OWA friends. One gave me an article from the *Chronicle* about rent discrimination against families with children; another suggested I buy rather than continue my disheartening search.

Coincidentally, buying houses was a hot coffee-break topic at work. The next day, I joined several fellows who were all ears with envy while Dixson, who usually only listened, told a story about his fixer-upper. It wasn't long before I seriously began to consider the option of buying— a gargantuan stretch that my mother helped me reach by lending me the money for a down payment. I set myself a few requirements for the purchase: the house must stand in a sunny part of the city and have a garden, a city view, and a price tag of less than two-thirds of the going rate. People rightfully called me overly optimistic when they heard my heady criteria—but I got lucky.

Dixson was happily living with his family in a southern neighborhood of San Francisco called Noe Valley, and he set me up with the realtor he'd used to find his place a couple of years before. Short, round, and redheaded, the realtor reminded me of a fortune-teller. Over the next few Saturdays, she showed me a number of houses in Noe Valley, which is lodged between the foggy panorama of Twin Peaks and the flat warmth of the bustling Mission district.

I rejected one place on a busy street and another for being too big. On the third weekend, my crystal-ball-reading realtor picked me up in her cluttered Datsun and drove me to a heedlessly weathered Victorian cottage, perched high enough on Noe Hill for several windows to open onto views of the valley below. Tenants had recently vacated the place because the owner wanted to tear it down. The word *Victorian* usually conjures up images of grand spaces and royalty, but some of the homes built in the 1870s—like this one, which consisted of only four small tall rooms—were called "workers' Victorians." The building had been sorely neglected, and most of the unique exterior moldings of the period had been removed. Yet, the vintage cottage, with its ten-foot-high ceilings and country character, pulled at my imagination with the force of a scenic photo on the front of a puzzle-box. One window caught the city center profile; another faced east toward the bay's water and hills beyond; to the west, one could envision the crab-grass-filled yard becoming a wonderland of wildflowers. Call it love at first sight. Of course, I immediately recognized the long vistas and garden views as added visual

My workers' cottage, 1975

square footage that highlighted the personality of the house. It felt right.

The previous owner of the odd-shaped property had planned to demolish this aging two-story structure at the back of the lot so he could build five apartment units with parking below. He was a contractor with plans to create yet another oversized, boxy, and tacky apartment building—until City Hall denied him a permit. I put in a low offer, although it was still a challenge to my budget. Buyers had not lined up to purchase the offbeat property on Twenty-Seventh Street because of several daunting quirks, the most glaring being that the utilities for my house were connected to the house on the property in front. But I knew I could change that, so the fortune-teller and her crusty, cigarette-smoking husband acted quickly to close the deal.

Shanette and I took possession of our worker's cottage on November 15, 1975. We easily moved everything from our classy white apartment on a level street in Oakland to our new abode, sited on a street that would have had a good slalom race slope—if San Francisco had been in ski country.

The cottage, which I like to call my *maisonette* and where I still reside during fall and winter, sits in the rear corner of its L-shaped lot, as a postage stamp sits in the corner of an envelope. Tall Siamese-twin redwood trees mark the western boundary, and a mature plum tree huddles up to the backyard's northern property line. Although humble during November, this Mirabelle plum tree has bloomed with perky white petals every March for the past three decades and has produced more delicate, golden, teaspoon-sized plums than half a dozen preserve lovers can pluck in a season. These plums taste sweet when promptly harvested but are rather tart in jelly and jam.

When I bought my *maisonette*, the very steep stairs to the front door entered directly into a leftover slice of an indoor porch that became Shanette's library. She arranged her French and English storybooks on a low wooden shelf balanced on concrete blocks. Her small bedroom was just off the living room, with ample views of the garden, but she spent most of her time on a purple velvet cushion in her library reading, cutting out magazine photos of wild animals, and drawing.

I placed my bed in the tiny eastern room off the square kitchen. A back door opened to a landing that connected to exterior stairs leading down to the unfinished lower level of the house, while another door opened to a lean-to bathroom packed with personality and potential. As a first-time owner, I dared to paint the bathroom's sloping ceiling an uncommon salmon color. But I got my own lesson in the power of color as I watched the salmon-colored gloss become brighter and brighter with each minute of drying. I quickly repainted it with coats of soft yellow flat paint, remembering how the captain's wife on Treasure Island had felt about the mustard paint on her house—not because it reminded me of a lower class of occupants, but because it was oppressively bright.

The emotional impact of color is often underestimated, belittled, and underemployed. I still remember what the senior architect (female) at the City of Richmond said to me about color during my work-study days in graduate school: "Every color is good if it is used appropriately." Appropriateness may be relative, but she put forth a great challenge.

The *maisonette* layout accentuated the house's flexibility and neutrality—any room could be a bed-holder. I've always thought it funny how bedrooms in the United States often have only enough space for a bed and a closet. During my travels, I noticed that sleeping took place next to clay fire pits for cooking, low tables for entertaining, cribs for childcare, stools for repairing tools, and nooks for musical instruments or materials for crafts, like baskets, quilts, or brooms. In this country, most bedrooms are decreasing in size, while one bedroom grows, replete with a private bath and the rudely ringing title of "master bedroom," at a time when there are no masters or slaves in most houses. None of the eight definitions for the word *master* in my dictionary makes sense when applied to a bedroom. I use the adjective *main* or *largest* whenever the word *master* comes up next to *bedroom*. Much could be done to increase the usefulness and aesthetics of bedrooms, beyond their traditional fate as nighttime caves and empty daytime chambers. The Murphy bed, a bed that lifted up into the wall to free up space during the day, was a good example of maximizing a room's daytime floor space.

My vision was to design in more variety. For example, I wanted to try small changes that would encourage more day use of the bedrooms. Add a little built-in workbench in one corner, increase the flexibility of natural and electric lighting, and provide a small balcony/patio with space for a table and chair. Create an office nook or add a sink with a mirror. Design more than one door to a room, as well as to its closet, so that their use might change with cultural and/or family needs and desires. I was thinking that the two "bedrooms" in my *maisonette* could be changed to enrich an active daily life rather than just hold beds, and that did come with time.

I'd taken ownership of my eccentric gem knowing it needed attention, but for the first few months, no specific visions of an enchanting architectural remake surfaced. I was too busy getting used to or fixing what was already here. My architectural friends politely didn't comment on my problem property, but later they admitted I had definitely seen more in it than they had.

Mother flew up from San Diego to see my purchase, which made it a special house celebration, as she didn't come to visit very often. The enduring rustic cottage certainly did need attention and care, but it was livable once I unblocked the sewer, replaced the condemned gas heater, and installed a new water heater in the lower unfinished level (getting the water heater out of the kitchen). After the critical repairs were made, I felt ready to become acquainted with other facets of the cottage. I slowly engaged in a tenderly curious acquaintance with my living space, exploring the limitations and opportunities. I began with do-it-yourself-sized mending gestures—like changing door and window hardware, repairing 30-year-old hanging light fixtures, washing walls, sanding floors, and painting shelves—which helped introduce me to the circulation flow, the charm of corners, and the sunnier spots. House preening and nesting became an integral part of my new San Francisco homeowner's lifestyle.

An administrator at the French-American Bilingual School linked me up with another parent, Leslie, who lived down the hill in the next block. Leslie drove her son Erick to the school on her way to work and gave Shanette a ride both ways. What a gift! Erick would stay with us sometimes on weekends or evenings, but Leslie buttressed more of my childcare needs than I did hers. I was delighted to observe Shanette and Erick interact. One time, we were shopping together and I overheard Erick say, "Why are you picking out that toilet paper?" To which my artistic offspring replied, "Because it is the prettiest." "That's funny," Erick replied, "I would pick the cheapest."

Some of my work projects required that I visit sites in out-of-the-way places, such as when I was assigned to recommend repairs to the Naval Reserve Center in Idaho or when a central Californian Air Force base needed to make space for additional equipment in a parachute-drying tower. My travel increased to about once every four months, and each time I arranged for Shanette's care in a different way: a neighbor, a babysitter, Leslie, an overnight with a friend. I was grateful for the support of my immediate community as I once again faced the need for affordable and reliable childcare. I knew from reading that only 15 percent of American families could be considered the so-called "traditional nuclear family," where the mother was at home all day while the father worked. Our culture's denial of the need for childcare has impacted workingwomen, who are still automatically and singularly held responsible for childcare tasks. If men thought they needed childcare, I reckon, super childcare services would be as common as hardware stores.

Tom and I broke up after less than a year, shortly after tax time because that was when he said he was going to clear up the paperwork for his divorce and he didn't. Five months later, a few weeks before my move to San Francisco, I met a new man at the WesDiv Toastmasters meeting. DS was an attractive engineer 12 years younger—I was now reaching 35. He believed a smile could take you a long way in the work world, which, ultimately, for him, it did. He was living in the East Bay and joined our Oakland carpool while looking for another place to live.

Upon hearing stories of my new house project, DS offered to help me with a bathroom-sink plumbing problem. The first weekend after I moved in, we were both on our backs with wrenches in our hands, wrestling with a tight, rusty P-trap. The moment we succeeded in replacing it with a shiny silver one, our lips automatically touched, as if it were the obvious next step in the repair job.

DS moved to Valley Street, just two blocks away—a good sign, I thought, for our budding relationship. In San Francisco, we took the same carpool to the office, but his desk was in a different building from mine, and our work never interfaced. His gentle, kind, and attentive manner enlivened my heart, as well as my daughter's. The relationship unfolded so delightfully that after a few months, DS moved in with us. We adored his optimistic, supportive presence, and he proved to be very helpful on house projects. On weekends, the three of us nailed cedar shingles in rows to cover the ruddy, paint-chipping siding. Only

With DS in San Francisco

a few people at work guessed that DS and I were a couple. Sometimes after work, the minute we entered the house, he would sit me down in the kitchen, take off each high heel, and massage my feet. Ecstasy.

Our first Easter in the new house, I organized a party for parents and children to hunt for decorated eggs and munch an elaborate picnic lunch in the yard, which was twice as long as *la maisonette*. Before the others arrived, I suggested to Shanette that she look under a basket out in the yard. She rushed down the wooden stairs, giggling with anticipation.

"Oh Mommy, I always wanted a rabbit," she gasped as she lifted the silent fur ball to her chest. Maternal emotions swirled with endearment.

"Is it a boy rabbit or a girl?" she asked, rubbing her nose into the rabbit's coat.

"I don't know, but it doesn't matter for the name, does it?"

"We can call it Zibi," Shanette announced. "Because it is black and white like a zebra." Zibi went into a cage but also had daily jaunts in our ample backyard. Shanette became an attentive animal owner.

As the months rolled on, architectural concepts percolated in my mind: How could I hold on to the house's century-old character while still making the place contemporary? What could be done to catch the country feel in the city—with modesty and elegance? How best to narrow the gap between garden and house? And how should I frame the distant and intimate views; should I make one big house with two floors or a duplex with two flats?

I was anxious to get my hands moving on paper, but some creative instinct allowed me to wait and let these questions generate their own natural forces. Soon enough, I would engage in the design process that would lead to the rejuvenation and enlivenment of my home sweet home in San Francisco.

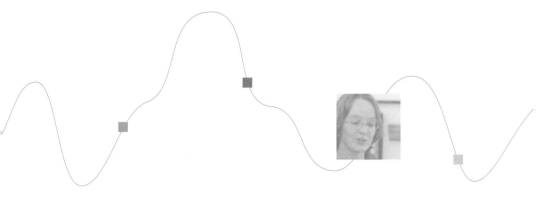

Swimming Swiftly

1976 to 1977: San Francisco

The previous year's celebration of International Women's Year, organized by WestDiv's Womens' Coordinator, had set the pace with events organized around the theme of "communication." The cover folder for the week's activities featured pictures of workingwomen throughout the organization, and included a photo of me leaning over a blueprint (my triangle earrings dangling), measuring a foundation detail with an architectural scale. On the one hand, this made me—and the few recently hired female architects, engineers, and contract specialists—feel welcome. On the other hand, it felt funny to have our femaleness celebrated at the office (or anywhere).

Other educational and cultural events also took place during these socially more progressive years, including celebrating the history of African-Americans, Hispanics, and Asian Americans—even a Pacific Islander feast with dancing. These events underlined the federal government's stated goal of being a "model employer," which sounded super. As awareness levels rose, I watched and hoped to see significant hiring and promotional increases within these groups.

The navy's objective of being inclusive extended to its hiring of A/E firms. Again, the stated policy was to distribute the design contracts widely among a broad spectrum of A/E firms, but once I began sitting on preselection and selection panels, I noticed a definite trend of rehiring firms who had performed well in the past. In fact, EICs seemed to have their favorite A/E firms. When my close friend Paul from the Project Management Branch became head of the A/E Services Branch, I quizzed him as to how the number of minority-owned and women-owned firms were tracked and reported. Was the navy really spreading the work around? He told me, "Some statistics are being kept for minority-owned firms, but none for women-owned firms." Until Paul took over the position, no one with authority seemed to be paying attention; no one followed up, reviewed the record, or proposed adjustments to organizational behavior.

Paul at my WestDiv desk

Paul often stopped by my desk, even though in his new position he didn't have much time to go to coffee. He respectfully chuckled at my audacity and assured me that he had begun keeping records to determine if women-owned and minority-owned firms were being included in preselection slates and selection panels. But progress remained clogged. In one instance, when a woman-owned firm was not selected (by an all-male panel) for a design contract I thought that this firm was extremely well qualified for, I asked one of the panelists how he came to his decision. "I have never worked with a woman-owned firm" was his honest reply!

During panel interviews, some A/E firms wedged slides of sexy women in bathing suits reclining by the pool between slides of their previous projects—male comic relief? After one such presentation, the principal of the firm hurried up to me. "I apologize for some of those slides," he mumbled, slightly rattled.

"They didn't add to your qualifications on this project," I kept my response as professional as possible without stepping back or losing my cool.

"It won't happen again," he assured me. His tan expression was strong, masculine, and all business.

"I hope not," I replied, smiling as I offered him a firm feminine handshake.

He acted as if he hadn't expected to see a female face on the selection panel, especially not one with full voting power. The three of us voted in writing, rating the firms' qualifications with a number from one to five and using the same criteria for each firm. For example, we ranked "Firm's experience with similar work" and "Firm's record meeting deadlines and budgets." A discussion was only necessary when the scores of the two top-rated firms were very close. The EIC's concerns held considerable weight, as she or he would be the liaison with the firm for the duration of the contract. Contrary to common hearsay, no points were given for being a minority-owned or woman-owned firm. It was only during the preselection phase that an effort was eventually made to include qualified minority-owned and women-owned firms on the short lists because Paul, a sensitive black man who was aware of the meaning of discrimination, was now the head of A/E Services.

The summer of 1976, I took Shanette to France. While she visited her father and grandmother, I visited the friends I'd kept up with by letter. One quick jaunt was to see my architectural schoolmate Alain J., who had arranged for me to stay with his family, still living in Montpellier. He invited the other ten classmates from our 1964 architectural class for a fancy luncheon prepared by his exceedingly attentive mother. One fellow had gone to Germany for his education, several worked together in Montpellier, and I was the only one working for government. The camaraderie that comes from being together in school is a strong tie for the French, a close bond much like best friends growing up together. My classmates were happy about my success and flattered that I had come to visit them. Their unexpected recognition validated my growth from student to professional. They had walked by my side during my first steps, and their opinion warmed my sense of self.

Feeling wonderfully comfortable in France, I submerged myself into the language and culture with the intimate and guiltless pleasure of sinking into a warm scented bath at the end of a long workday. Not surprisingly, while delving into a bit of family genealogy in 2001, I learned that my father's grandfather had been a merchant marine, married a French woman, and lived in France for three years. I reckon those few dominant French genes have fueled my lifelong fascination for everything French. I continue to feed my Francophile fetish with French books, foods, friends, clothes, fabrics, yarns, and cars.

When one of the senior architects in my office retired, I inherited the contract for alterations to Bachelor Enlisted Quarters (BEQs) at Travis Air Force Base, prepared by architects Braccia, Joe & Woodbridge. Mr. Andy Braccia was a retired admiral, a well-respected architect, and an active member of the Society of American Military Engineers (SAME). During our first encounter, he recruited me to join the younger members (under 35) of SAME for one of the lunchtime meetings he routinely held in his delightful brick North Beach office.

The San Francisco SAME chapter was touted as the largest (800 members) in the country. Monthly dinner meetings at the historic Presidio Officers' Club near the Golden Gate Bridge featured a general engineering program; exhibited two member firms' work; and allowed social time for the military officers, government employees, and principals of A/E firms to mix. I decided that since I worked for the navy, SAME would be a good professional group for me to join. I'd continued to shy away from the American Institute of Architects (AIA) because of its rigidly conservative, monopolist clutch on the profession. OWA was the rare parallel organization, working to dissipate some of the soggy sexist behaviors of the AIA's "Old Boys' Club."

Unfortunately, the AIA had established a reputation with the public for being the architects' *only game in town*. To this day, you may write "AIA" after your name only if you are a registered architect and a member of the AIA organization. However, the public still considers the letters "AIA" to be an indication that one is a professional architect, much like the initials "MD" indicate that one is a medical doctor. Meanwhile, the states—not the AIA—govern licensing, as well as the registration title *architect*. Another large group calls itself the Society of Registered Architects and puts RA after member names. A few architects in OWA also belong to the AIA and write *AIA* and *OWA* after their names. The AIA organization is very good at contractual matters and frequently offers excellent workshops and interesting programs. But from a feminist perspective, the AIA carries the fatty burden of traditional sexism on its bones, and the group's efforts to improve the public's understanding of architecture remain too thin to measure. The AIA's few attempts toward inclusiveness of nonwhite males continue to fall feebly short. Recently published books have documented that shortfall: Kathryn H. Anthony's *Discrimination by Design: Gender, Race, and Ethnicity in the*

Architectural Profession (University of Illinois Press, 2001) and Victoria Kaplan's *Structural Inequality: Black Architects in the United States* (The Rowman & Littlefield Publishing Group, Inc., 2006).

More than a hundred people in conservative business attire regularly attended the outwardly friendly, yet inwardly formal, SAME dinner meetings. A fair number of women were there, too, but only because the male members brought their spouses. I made it a point to talk to these women, as part of my personal feminist commitment. When we sat down at the long tables to eat, I would introduce myself to the man sitting next to me, "My name is Wendy Bertrand, and I'm an architect with the navy."

"Oh hello, I'm Steve from Bechtel Engineering," one would say, then turn his torso without a pause and say, "This is Nancy, my wife." He'd turn to the tired-looking woman beside him about to swallow a gulp of red wine—her mind apparently trekking somewhere in Nepal—his demeanor making it clear to both his wife and me that he wasn't an available man.

"Nice to meet you, Nancy," I'd respond, reaching across him to shake his surprised wife's hand. The women were often interesting in their own right and glad to have a conversation about something other than engineering.

Although the officers considered these meetings worthwhile, I was often the only architect and the only woman from WestDiv; few other civilians from our office attended. I breathed easily at the meetings, and appreciated them because I learned things about the military construction program that I might not hear at work. It was also a good opportunity to talk with the military officers, who were approachable at these meetings but less so on work time. Our commanding officer, Captain Paul D. Olson, became president of SAME when the position rotated to the navy (as it did every four years). Captain Q. Lewis, our executive officer, with whom I later worked on a project, also attended regularly. I found him uniquely worldly and inclusive in his interactions with staff and members.

Andy Braccia introduced me to several other long-time SAME members who had a special interest in young people carrying on the organizational torch (the average member's age was well over 50). Wes, a 60-something widower with white hair and a ruddy stern face, was a retired Army Corps of Engineers manager. He liked my enthusiasm and became a SAME ally, introducing me to important people and offering valuable suggestions—and surprising me with a twinkle in his crooked left eye.

Unlike many architects, who typically work in small offices with six to eight people, I liked working in a large organization for a variety of reasons, but mostly because there was so much room for innovation. For example, when I learned about the artistic hobbies of my colleagues, I was able to set up a revolving art gallery in the front hallway of the Architectural Branch. As curator, I collected art and craft and hung it carefully, always on my own time either at lunchtime or before work. Like any curator, I searched for talent, and once the exhibition became better known, co-workers told me about items they were willing to show. I made sure the exhibitions were inclusive in terms of department, discipline, age, gender, race, and the type of artwork—watercolor,

Architecture Branch Gallery

oil painting, pottery, bonsai, sculpture, or photography. No one questioned the pieces I selected from what they offered. Each two-week show was announced in *WESTWORD*, the in-house WestDiv newsletter. For more than a year, my in-house gallery added what I considered a missing human dimension to the workplace. It was a means for people to get to know each other, the art delighted and amazed my co-workers, and the whole experience was undeniably fun and rewarding.

Surprise. During the final luncheon of the 1976 Federal Women's Week, my OWA architect friend from the planning department and I shared public recognition for our "respective contributions as involved and conscientious women." Tellingly, the organization dealt with change by putting the focus on us, the new arrivals, rather than spotlighting positive shifts within the agency. We felt like new fish being introduced into a stagnant pond.

At OWA meetings, we were still discussing juicy topics, including how to stay healthy under stress, how to understand the benefits of the law, and how to choose our work attire. One meeting included a discussion of *The Woman's Dress for Success Book* (1977), in which author John T. Molloy's main point (summed up in a review by Michael C. Gray) was, "Women could improve credibility and authority in the workplace by establishing guidelines for a women's executive dress uniform." The book raised the question, *what kind of an image are we projecting?* A silk blouse and a suit were considered appropriate, but not a gray blouse, which was perceived as indecisive and mousy. Some members didn't think dress important, but in an effort to be both feminine and professional, I searched out suits in subtle tweeds of turquoise and deep purple. Precision haircuts and elegant Italian and French shoes became my trademarks. The belief surfaced that we were technically competent but that all sorts of side issues related to gender and communication effectiveness were more critical to success than we'd ever imagined. We needed to pay attention to how we looked, spoke, handled situations, interfaced with our male colleagues and female staff, related to our bosses, networked in professional events, and negotiated—many multifarious subjects we hadn't learned in architecture school.

I volunteered to prepare a program for the SAME National Meeting, slated for April 1977 in San Francisco, and chose *Priorities Ahead* as the theme of our younger members' program. My idea was to ask the younger members nationwide to present their engineering priorities for the future. I was given total control and full financial backing by the SAME leadership, which opened the waterways for me to continue swimming swiftly. Six young members received paid trips to San Francisco. I matched each young speaker with a senior professional from our chapter, with the intent of underscoring the importance of junior-senior teamwork. We gave every attendee a red-covered book of the speeches—which was very well received. An article in *The Military Engineer* (March–April 1978) covered the event. A few years later, one of the officers I'd worked with mentioned he had been to this SAME program. It was nice to know he remembered it.

Some women thought of professional organizations as minor side streets, but I saw them as shortcuts for learning professional and organizational skills. I leaned heavily on, and was rewarded by, OWA and SAME. Soon after my success at the SAME San Francisco Convention, I was tapped to be a board member at-large of our SAME chapter. This was my first board membership outside the OWA steering committee. I attended all the SAME board meetings and, with Wes's encouragement, took on a number of projects, including the creation of an elegant brochure for the chapter, for which I received a service award.

After I'd served on the SAME board for a year, the future civilian president of SAME drove his jazzy red Porsche from San Francisco to my office to take me to lunch. Gordon M. was a married mechanical engineer, in his golden years. Since this was my turf, he suggested I select the restaurant, so we went to a popular Chinese restaurant near my office in San Bruno. Well into the rice and stir-fry, Gordon M. said, "Wendy, I have come in person to invite you to be the SAME secretary."

I set down my chopsticks and looked up. "Gordon, I am flattered, but the secretary position has no future." As far as I knew, I was the first woman SAME had ever invited to serve as an officer, but this didn't influence my decision.

"What do you mean?" Gordon M. asked, picking up his cup of tea and trying not to appear chagrined.

"The vice president is in line for president, while the secretary never becomes vice president." I focused my gaze beyond his eyeglasses, alert for his reaction.

"That is true," he returned in his gentlemanly voice. "But I couldn't make you vice president." He stated his position with certainty and lowered his head, showing his bald spot.

"I'm sorry to disappoint you, Gordon, but I'm not interested in the secretary position." I lifted the white cloth napkin to my lips, closing the topic while quietly thinking how many men had also turned down the secretary position and probably for the same reasons—the job involved lots of work and held no future. The crisp sound of my fortune cookie breaking open filled the silence as I read to myself, *Stick to your druthers and life will be golden*, or some such pertinent proverb.

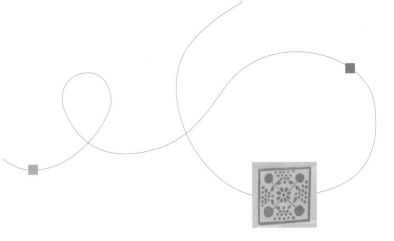

Hanging In There

1977 to 1978: San Francisco to Geneva

As if it were part of the normal work climate, a corporate breeze pushed us all to climb the organizational ladder. I was optimistic, even though moving to journeyman level and then into management required competing with my colleagues. However, because men held the tangible advantage of being the norm, I felt compelled to complement my skills with as much strategy as I could rally. How-to books on negotiating and time management became my bedtime pleasure reading, as did management articles from the Harvard Business School. I learned from one study that men took substantially less time interviewing women than they took with men because they didn't know how to keep the conversation going with women as easily as with men. I interpreted this to mean that it was up to me to keep the conversation going and make the interviewer feel comfortable. Books about corporate life, such as *The Managerial Woman* (Henning & Jardim, 1978), a source still used today by international researchers interested in feminine leadership, fueled my hope for success.

Because of an increase in work, the Architectural Branch staff had recently expanded to include several new female and young male architects, as well as a number of male and female interior designers. This was a welcome relief; I was fed up with fielding the constant drip of mini-comments from the old guard about being female. The expansion also ushered in a new political willingness to improve the quality of shore facilities for navy personnel. I now thrived during my days on the job, and people accepted my unusually direct yet female approach, in spite of its creative strangeness.

Right around this time, life at home was dimming toward an unsettling loneliness. I was losing DS, who had decided to move to San Diego for a promotion to another navy job. We wrote love letters and tried to see each other a few times, but our differences pried us apart. "You're very sure of what you want in a relationship," he wrote, "but I'm still in limbo." The sunny relationship had lasted a total of two years—a good test period for any romance, a length of time I still recommend to friends whenever the topic of lasting romance comes up in conversation.

As was my pattern whenever I felt my emotions melting into sizable puddles, I reached for a new project like a safety jacket. The house shingling had been completed before DS moved away, so I began to think about transforming the hollow lower level of my *maisonette*.

Looking back with a wider perspective, I can now see that I was following two currents that seemed to flow in opposite directions. On the one hand, I wanted to move up in the hierarchy at my job; during 1977, I applied, was rated highly, and was not selected for my first possible promotion at the journeyman level. (I thought then that moving to the GS-12 level would be a sign of growth—an acknowledgment of my skill level in the office hierarchy—but opportunities were few.) On the other hand, in OWA, we were trying to avoid hierarchy and rotated duties in a collegial style. I didn't need a specific position in OWA in order to participate or gain recognition, but OWA was much smaller than the navy.

Later in my career, I became aware of other feminist organizations running businesses without hierarchy, like Sixteen Rivers Press, a shared-work, nonprofit poetry collective founded by seven women in the San Francisco Bay Area in 1999. This nonhierarchical approach has not yet materialized in the field of architecture (as far as I know), although I have heard that some female architects in England have grouped together in nontraditional ways to create a cooperative structure. Nina

Boyd Krebs in *Changing Woman Changing Work* (MacMurray & Beck, 1993) explains why this is not such an easy thing to do:

> The traditional patriarchal approach to work is to maintain a clear chain of command … [while] feminine connectedness and creativity flow more freely when women can work in collaborative ways…. These approaches, of course, are diametrically opposed.

But I was influenced by the prevailing climate, and when three more GS-12 architectural positions opened in January 1978, I once again applied for a promotion. Notification arrived by mail that not three but four *men* had been selected. Devastated, that weekend I called several of my OWA friends to cry and express my ire.

"Wendy, go to Personnel and find out what happened; you can't let this pass," said a woman from another department. Her encouragement took the edge off my outrage.

Calmed somewhat, I decided to take Shanette out for dinner, a rare event for us. As we walked down to 24th Street, the pin-dropping silence alerted me to the fact that she knew I was upset, and my feelings rolled out.

"My job is not going too well," I choked, and then tried to explain as simply as I could. "Some men architects at work were promoted, and I think women should get promotions, too."

"Women are just as good as men." Shanette's voice bounced back with such sincerity that I immediately felt better. We soon sat face to face at a small table in a lovely Italian restaurant, dipping petals of fresh artichokes into the lemony-scented mustard sauce.

Nevertheless, when I arrived at work the next day, I was still shaken. My desk-neighbor, Dixson, had been selected for one of the positions. He turned to me first thing and said, "Wendy, you are more qualified than all of us put together." That was an exaggeration. We both knew all the people involved, but I appreciated the point he was making.

I made an informal complaint to the EEO Office. I wanted to see evidence of the rating process that had left me out. Fortunately, the EEO counselor assigned to my case a female whom I knew was fair-minded. After rigorous review, she concluded, "It appears that the aggrieved was not given proper consideration in the ranking." She ended her report with, "I request that a new panel be convened to re-rank all the applicants."

She had taken affidavits of several people, including my branch head, Mr. Scamell, who wrote, "I was surprised that Wendy was not on the list and also surprised that the list was so short. Only six names were sent forward, and I had four positions to fill because one more became available during the rating period."

Of the 16 people who had applied, I was the only female. These males probably didn't even know what the word *discrimination* meant, except that it was bad, and if they did know, they didn't want to recognize their actions. I don't know who came up with the term *glass ceiling*, or when they came up with it, but I sure felt that I was separated from my goals by an invisible and impervious barrier.

Just the other day, I spoke with an artist who had chosen to leave architectural school in the 1960s to study art history. "It was horrible," she told me.

"You mean the discrimination?" I responded.

She shook her head, "We didn't call it that then."

The same narrow thinking lingered in the navy. It was more than belittlement, as anyone who has been discriminated against knows. I felt as if I'd been knocked flat, my professional standing suffocated by a pillow stuffed with prejudice and sexism. The distress was similar to how one must feel when caught in a preventable landslide, going through a divorce because of awkward misunderstandings, or losing a child to the drunkenness of a driver.

One reason I was so disappointed was that a system of steps had been set up to resolve these issues, making it look like justice was desired for the individual and for the organization. An August 1977 assessment report on the status of women at WestDiv listed 212 employees in GS-12 positions, 8 of whom were women, with a goal to increase the number by 24 positions. This sounded as if someone was counting, but numbers on paper can fool readers who don't follow the action trail. While the reigning executive officer, Captain Aubau, openly ignored rule breaking, I was learning about what is commonly called "lip service," even on paper.

Shanette was in France for the summer, so I had the time and drive to *go formal*, which meant making a detailed explanation of my case in writing, after which the personnel staff prepared a two-inch-thick file of all related documents—an arduous task. A fiery and dogged determination energized my resolve not to let the navy's unspoken yet institutionalized discrimination slide into the unknown. That would have been submissive and would not have moved fairness forward. With full self-righteousness, I called a spade a spade—hoping for a re-deal—but the cards didn't move.

When Mr. Scamell retired, Ray became the Architectural Branch head and John D. became my next supervisor. Getting along with supervisors was no problem. I paid attention to their directions, responded to their concerns, and aimed to please. In turn, they rated me highly and appreciated my independence and ability to get things done.

Work continued, while my discrimination case dragged on for months. Finally, at what I thought was a good moment, I entered my supervisor's cubicle and said with pluck, "John, I noticed that everybody else has received an annual rating, but I haven't." I didn't expect to see the contours of his lips twist as if biting into a hot pepper.

"I know, Wendy." He tried to rearrange his mouth into a smile while reaching for the phone as if he was busy.

I felt comfortable enough with John D. to speak my mind. After all, he had rated me very highly after the first six months. Seeing things at face value, I naïvely pressed, "Why are you waiting?"

He set the phone down in its cradle. "I was hoping this discrimination complaint would be settled," he admitted, and stood up, not sure how to dodge my concern or plead for more time.

I figured out that he didn't want to give me another good evaluation if the promotional rating panel was saying I wasn't qualified. So this was how reprisal worked. Since I had called the cards on management's actions, I was considered a hot potato, a misfit, someone who was perhaps on the edge of a downward career spiral. Yikes.

Moral support came from people in nonpowerful places—from the women's coordinator, other females, and some male colleagues who knew my qualities and qualifications. I was churning in a sick organization, and there was no combination of pills the organization could take to get well. My unwavering ambition to participate kept me from withering; meanwhile, the A/E firms I worked with were remarkably respectful and fully engaged in creating excellent architecture. They knew nothing of this in-house cancer.

Months later, the National EEO office found no discrimination in my formal complaint. I appealed and sent copies to President Carter,

Mary Spencer of the National Organization for Women, and US Congressman Phillip Burton. I assumed this was the appropriate next step, but it turned out to be empty arm-waving, as no one responded.

Vanity in the lower unit

At home, I held together the pieces of my sanity by playing with the idea of making the downstairs area in my house more useable and possibly joining it to the first floor, but I couldn't find anywhere to squeeze in a staircase. So, I concentrated on making the space into a big room connected to a day-lit dressing area with a sink and vanity, adjacent to a tiny room with shower and toilet. Two tile-setters installed the hand-painted Mexican tiles I'd selected for the one-person shower. I spent a long day with them making decisions of tile location and joint lines. Some tiles had blue paintbrush-stroked designs, while others were a solid flour tortilla color. I wanted the shower experience to be poetic, imagining that anyone stepping into the shower's decorative embrace would relish the visual touches while washing and singing. I was *flowing* in the sense that I was wonderfully engrossed in conducting my design into the physical. Time passed seamlessly; it never occurred to me to look at my watch.

Shower detail, lower unit

Shanette was due back from France within the week. Her father had written that she would return on the first Friday in September, later than I had wanted. Unexpectedly, on that Monday, I received a letter from Arnaud, in English. He wrote:

> Shanette will not be returning to California, after some reflection I think she would have a better education with me in France, and it is my turn to have her live with me.

The letter went on and on with his reasons and demands, including how much child support he wanted me to send to him. By Tuesday, after many calls to France, I reached Linette, still living in Chamonix, and learned that Arnaud had taken Shanette (just 12 years old) to stay with her in the Alps. Linette understood this was wrong and against the law. She told me that Shanette was suffering from an angry red rash running down the length of her back. I was frantic and reared into action.

Since Arnaud had kept her passport and no relative could verify her identity, I needed to go myself to pick up Shanette. I had spoken with the American Embassy before leaving San Francisco and knew what I needed to do. Linette agreed by phone to deliver Shanette to Geneva, Switzerland, the closest airport and American embassy. I requested leave from work, and on Wednesday, I headed to SFO to buy a ticket on the first plane to Geneva. I didn't carry much more than traveler's checks worth $5,000, an inheritance I'd just received from my grandmother Lydia. Friday night, Linette drove her van across the French-Swiss border, with her two boys and Shanette sleeping in the back. Since it was the American Labor Day weekend, we had to wait until Tuesday morning to get a passport for Shanette before leaving Geneva and before Arnaud found out that Shanette was on her way home.

"He kept asking me to stay; I didn't know what to do," she recounted, looking past my worried gaze. I was emotionally drained and exhausted from the effects of jet lag. "I'm so sorry he did this," I said, pulling her into my arms and feeling greatly relieved that we were together. Our bodies breathed in unison; my hand stroked her worried head.

After a needed rest, but still somewhat stunned, we strolled through the picturesque Swiss village where we were staying with friends of friends. On Sunday, we rode the local bus into Geneva. We walked there for more than an hour, perusing posted menus, all very expensive. Finally, we sat down at an outside table on a sidewalk lined with fragrant hanging flower baskets. As we waited, Shanette said, "My clothes and things, even my clarinet, is in Paris."

"We will write to your father and ask him to send your things home," I replied, lifting my glass of water casually. I took a swallow, trying not to sound or look as bruised as I felt.

"So much trouble," she said, her confused eyes looking up into mine.

By midday Tuesday, we were on an Air India flight to London. I phoned Linette the moment we arrived in San Francisco. She told me that when Arnaud heard the situation, he announced he was going to have all French borders shut; he thought we were still in France. I couldn't believe his audacity. But as one of my friends said, "He obviously underestimated you."

At breakfast, Shanette said she wanted to leave the French-American school because it was too small and "cliquish." She transferred to Everett Middle School, a public school on Church Street, only a ten-minute ride away on the J streetcar. The new school worked out well; Shanette met interesting new girlfriends, and I attended the teacher/parent meetings regularly. Arnaud never returned her things, so I bought her a used flute to replace the clarinet. She easily adjusted to the new instrument and soon began to compose original music for flute. Her father continued to yell and scream on paper, but his letters had no effect on me, as his actions had worn away the last threads of trust between us.

When his family heard of the events, emotional letters poured into my mailbox. Moucha, who in 1971 thought he was wrong for taking a mistress, had turned her opinion 180 degrees. She wrote with rage:

> I am profoundly traumatized and disappointed by you—you are not a fair girl. Only an American could do such a thing and I had hoped your marriage would mend. Everybody is upset, you have ruined everything, nothing but bad, so sad.

Only my sister-in-law, Chantal, understood my concerns for Shanette's well-being and wrote me of her attempts to get her mother to understand the consequences of her son's behavior.

The French newspapers named similar cases *stunts in kidnapping*. A bill on "child snatching" came before President Carter because hundreds of thousands of children were snatched every year, in most cases taken by the father to another state. With international marriages and divorces on the rise, child-stealing incidents began to occur internationally, but no international laws were in place to deal with the problem. I learned that parents abducted their own children much more often than I'd ever imagined; even the French writer George Sand had to retrieve her daughter from her ex-husband at his country house, and that was more than a century earlier.

After an intense week of drama and trauma, I was glad to learn that one of my architectural projects in the Yuma Desert had just been advertised and would soon be under construction. Evenings, I studied and finally passed all the written parts of the architectural license, leaving only the oral exam.

On the scheduled date, I entered the oral interview without fear or hesitation, carrying the Recruit-in-Processing Facility drawings and specifications under my arm. I passed as easily as blowing out a candle flame. I could now call myself an *architect* per the State of California, and the fireworks of personal achievement exploded deep inside me, with satisfying bang, sparkle, and color. Years later, I would sit on the evaluators' side

Recruit-in-Processing Facility,
by Mathew Lapota and Associates

of the table in my quest to make women architects more visible, but it wasn't long before the oral exam was eliminated as a relic.

Finally, when two more architectural GS–12 positions in our branch were advertised, I and another female were promoted. I didn't even check if any men had applied. I didn't hold grudges, but I felt in my stomach and soul that the brass didn't want any more challenges—plus, we were highly qualified.

After waltzing from GS-09 to GS-11 so easily three years before, my advancement from GS-11 to GS-12 (journeyman) had taken cliff-hanging skills—more muscle, endurance, and determination. As a lipstick-and-mascara-wearing architect, I had stayed on lower ground longer than my male peers. Gender seemed to be the only mysterious difference in my ability to traverse the promotional slopes toward management, even though I had armed myself with extra skills, state-of-the-art strategy, and high ratings, and had proven myself on all sorts of professional terrain. It didn't help much to know I wasn't alone. As far away as France, a friend sent me an article about female architects, 2 percent of French architects, who were having trouble penetrating the profession. Reaching this second plateau felt right. Hanging in there had helped. Even so, I didn't put my mountain-climbing gear in the closet.

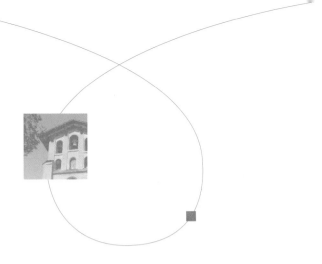

Social Gravity

1979 to 1981: San Francisco

I've never had much patience with the content of traditional newspapers; so-called news stories are usually covered in a way that seems vast, distant, thin—and often alarming. But I always looked forward to the arrival of my monthly OWA newsletter, partly because of the pertinent content and partly to see how the product changed. The content slant, color of ink and paper, graphics, and length, were all adjusted according to each new editor's personality.

During the 1970s, our newsletter reviewed two important new books, both written by women architects: *From Tipi to Skyscraper,* by Doris Cole (i press incorporated, 1973), and *Women in American Architecture: An Historic and Contemporary Perspective,* by Susana Torre (Architectural League Archive, 1977). Until I'd read these books, if someone had asked me to name any of the pioneer female architects, I could have come up with only one—Julia Morgan. But Julia Morgan, whose half-century career spanned the early 1900s to 1957, was far from being the only woman in her time. Long-time OWA member Inge Horton tells us about many amazing early women practicing architecture in her book, *Early Women Architects of the San Francisco Bay Area: The Lives and Work of Fifty Professionals,* 1890–1951 (McFarland, 2010).

The prolific and talented Julia Morgan designed about 800 buildings, but in 1979 few people were acquainted with her work, including most of our OWA members. Sara Holmes Boutelle, an architectural historian, brought Morgan's work into better focus at one of our OWA meetings, when she shared her lengthy research in preparation for her book, *Julia Morgan: The Architect* (Abbeville Press, 1988).

El Campanil, by Julia Morgan

I was pleased and curious when our newsletter announced that the 1979 annual OWA photo would be taken at El Campanil, a bell tower designed by Morgan for Mills College in Oakland. Founded in 1852, Mills College was the first women's college west of the Rockies. According to its website, college president Susan Mills hired Morgan in 1903 to design a half dozen buildings—with the specific intent of furthering Morgan's career. After the 1906 earthquake, Morgan began attracting commissions because her concrete bell tower stood unscathed. To this day, the momentum of Morgan's well-earned reputation continues to inspire those interested in women, history, and architecture.

On the designated Saturday of the photo shoot, Shanette and I sat on the wide steps at the foot of the bell tower, along with the other OWA members gathered for the picture. Although we were small in the image—

OWA Membership Directory
cover photo, 1979

the photographer (unknown) had to shoot from a distance in order to fit enough of the town for it to be recognizable—it was important to us that our membership be recorded in front of a distinctive and historic building, preferably one designed by a woman architect.

Along with book reviews and articles, our newsletter announced related local events that I would have otherwise missed. One such event was the exhibition of *The Dinner Party* by feminist artist Judy Chicago at the Museum of Modern Art in San Francisco.

After work one evening, I joined the line of museumgoers waiting to view the exhibition. *The Dinner Party* was controversial for its time; it featured a triangular table laid out with unique place settings, each plate individually hand-painted with erotic symbolism by Chicago. The line moved swiftly through the dramatically lit room, giving us a meager moment to stare at each of the exotic, colorful place settings, as well as the room's hand-painted floor tiles featuring the signatures of 100 great women. The intense feminist atmosphere enveloped my awareness with the luxurious fit of a hand-knit sock. Almost no one in the line spoke as we moved along the edge of the table dressed with handmade textiles, every molecule of our attention dedicated to looking. Chicago's daring penetrated my pores. The experience influenced my life the way people say a particular book has or the way a homegrown tomato can raise the bar of a fruit's taste potential. Chicago blended feminism and artistry into a physical reality that sent me away feeling inspired and confident that I could do the same in everyday architecture. Uplifted, I bought her book and read with admiration the story of the exhibition's development—in particular, how she had rallied and coordinated the dozens of mostly female artists who made the furniture, textiles, tiles, and banners.

Arnaud's letters continued to be angry. "You suffered one month of September, but my heart has been hemorrhaging for 12 years." In another letter he wrote, "All I want is to be free, to be with Shanette whenever I want, then there will be no more plotting or secrets." I started copying his letters and my responses because I felt his tactics were eerie and inappropriate. He also cried to the French Consul in San Francisco, who then wrote to me of Arnaud's concerns. I explained the gory details; fortunately, the Consul understood and let the issue drop.

Shanette was now old enough to correspond independently with her father. Sometimes she showed me her letters to him:

You said if I left France I would ruin the life for you and your mother and you would never do anything again for my mother or me and forget us. But you do just the opposite, you are making a big drama, you would be better to do what you said about forgetting us, you say you love me but you won't help pay for my food. It is as if I am your entertainment. I understand you are so very sad, but you bring it upon yourself.

She was going on 13. One minute she was mature and clear; the next minute she was confused and pained from being pulled between two determined parents with opposing views.

Arnaud responded:

> Family, and all the friends who follow the family drama, say I have been deprived of my daughter, rendering Shanette an orphan of her father. She suffers, and no human can pardon this. If Shanette had stayed in France and spent a school year with me, then we could have voted on where she lived after that. Wendy has done a terrible thing.

The emotional shaking triggered a hunger for self-improvement, and I dove into classes related to shore facilities planning and design: energy conservation, earthquake design, and architectural plywood design. One Saturday, I attended Janet Stone's workshop, "Speaking Up," arranged by OWA. I learned not to rush my words as if they were less important than other people's words.

That summer of 1979, Shanette wanted to go somewhere exciting—since France was out. I arranged for her to visit Sandra, my college roommate and close girlfriend in Vancouver, Canada. Arnaud went to Hong Kong, but the verbally abusive letters kept coming. I tried to ignore their gist, but I was also afraid that if I didn't read them, I would miss being alerted to his plans. Although I wanted to protect my daughter from his demanding behavior, filtering it out was almost impossible—there was just so much of it. Shanette ultimately chose not to open many of the letters, explaining, "They just keep saying the same thing."

At work, the organizational mechanics interested me, and I felt capable of influencing the machinery. For example, when I received yet another memo from my boss informing me who would be acting supervisor in his absence, I casually mentioned, "I notice that you *always* assign the same person to be acting supervisor when you are out of the office."

"Yes, I usually do," said John D., curious as to my concern.

"I, and perhaps others interested in eventually becoming supervisors, might also like a chance," I ventured. I'd read that Frank Lloyd Wright once played his students a record of music over and over—and over and over—with the intent of teaching them that the music would not stop if you didn't speak up.

As if it were just a new idea, John D. agreed to rotate his appointment for acting supervisor. I was included, and this was important to me because his memo could be enclosed with an application for promotion, thus showing that I had carried the responsibility of acting supervisor. I held on tightly to the mid-span of the promotional ladder, determined to continue my upward climb.

However, at home, I felt forced to take a big step backward. I was served with legal papers from Arnaud on June 3, 1980—Shanette's 14th birthday. I used vacation time to attend the hearing. Although angry, I was not too worried. It seemed obvious to me that the history of Arnaud's behavior—his child-stealing and his contempt of court—would result in the case going in my favor. I sat in the courtroom, stunned when Arnaud didn't show. Instead, an attorney presented Arnaud's desire to change the terms of the divorce: he wanted custody. Boy, was I naïve! I drastically underestimated the Superior Court's ability to understand the facts. Soon I had to pay out big bucks to hire my own attorney—robbing my daughter and me of peace of mind.

Court orders required that Arnaud pay child support, past debts, and attorney fees, and that he refrain from making derogatory remarks. He was further to stop—directly and indirectly—exerting pressure on Shanette regarding visitation and which parent she should reside with. Yet, none of these actions influenced Arnaud's behavior. I began missing work because of the monster headaches that put me to bed for hours—even days.

Unbalanced, I became more aware of the unevenness of social gravity. Individuals described the pull differently—in terms of poverty, family dynamics, gender, class, race, or immigration status—depending on their social situation. While *all* humans are subject to the exact same gravitational force of the earth, it seemed to me there were other social downward forces. I didn't compare my situation to those of others experiencing greater social burdens; rather, I felt tryingly unsteadied by the pull of the government's systemic discrimination against me as a workingwoman, and I felt pained by the relentless battering and tugging from my daughter's father.

A few weeks after the school year ended, Shanette and I sat on our deck enjoying a delicious Sunday lunch. "Mom," she said, turning to me during a lull, "Can I go to France *this* summer?"

"No, not yet." I kept it short.

"I will tell him to send me back," Shanette promised. "I don't want to live there."

"No, that didn't work in the past. You know that. I am responsible. You can go when you are 18 years old if you still want to." I looked as sternly as I could into her questioning face, wondering at what age she would understand my motherly reasoning.

"Then what will I do for the summer?"

"You can attend a music camp on the Russian River." I got up from the kitchen table, fetched the flyer, and handed it to her.

"This looks fun," she said, reading the description of the weeklong camp. Then her eyes clouded. "Dad will be mad at me."

"I know, but it's not your fault. With all he has done, he has brought it upon himself. You were going before; now he has to come here or wait until you are 18 and finished with high school."

Her expression toggled between happiness and disappointment.

A few weeks later, we drove to the music camp, a two-hour drive north of San Francisco. I sensed a tinge of apprehension as my daughter shifted in her seat, sighed, and looked out the window. "I wonder what kind of kids will be there," she mumbled. She had told me several times about the cattiness of young girls at previous camps. In this case, I thought music was a broad enough subject for her to explore at her own pace—unlike horse camp one spring break, where each activity was timed and controlled and the horses were lined up for every rider to take on the same tour.

When we arrived at the shady site, the atmosphere seemed calm. Many of the male and female students appeared to be older than Shanette, and I drove away feeling comfortable that she would enjoy herself.

While Shanette attended music camp, I traveled to Yuma, Arizona, for one of my more unusual projects. The housing officer drove Mr. Earl Kai Chann, the architect, and me to the site, where blocks of four homes, built back-to-back, beautifully blended into the desert. We spoke with a number of tenants living in the semi-underground prototype housing. Unlike much of navy housing, which was generally shoulder-

Meso prototype, by Earl Kai Chann Associates Ltd.

to-shoulder rows of exactly the same house, these *mesoquad-raplex buildings* (as they were named) were half submerged into the earth to reduce the summer heat and conserve the land. Even though I had been assigned the project late in its development, my concern for the users' needs made me particularly interested in this kind of visit, where I could see first-hand how residents were using the buildings.

We walked down the concrete steps into one of the individual semiprivate courtyards, the coolness refreshing us as we waited for the occupant to answer our knock. I noticed a few outdoor toys.

"There are windows in every room, so we don't feel like we are underground," she told us, keep-ing one eye on her smallest child. "We really like living here."

Meso plan by Earl Kai Chann Associates Ltd.

I wanted to know more. "Because it is new?"

"Yes … but also because it is different; we have lived in so much boring navy housing."

My architectural soul warmed.

Even though we'd been apart for only a week, I was excited about going to pick up Shanette at the music camp. Wes, my widower friend from SAME, took the drive with me. Twenty-five years my senior, he had become a good family friend, but we were not lovers because I didn't feel that way about him. When we arrived, Wes sat down on a bench by the river so that I could be alone with Shanette. All smiles, she promptly showed me around. I was enthralled with her passionate description of dancing and playing music in a rustic setting. There was a lovely performance for the parents before we left the camp. We sat in a grove of tan oaks, listening as Shanette performed with a small group of fellow campers on the stage of the camp's tiny amphitheater. Each rhythmic note resonated with the gratification in my heart.

Many architects and engineers prefer the technical aspects of project design to the management aspects of organizational effectiveness. But I was different. Leadership suited my temperament, and I particularly liked organizational design. I believed that the work environment could be stretched and shaped in all sorts of new ways to be more inclusive, flexible, and democratic. Most of the managers were engineers, but my maxim was that *an architect could manage just as well as an engineer.* Further, I was convinced that good architecture would be better appreciated if architects in high places were lobbying for quality.

Advancement has become the commonly acknowledged sign of growth within most organizations. Perhaps the professional peaks are more visible in government than in private industry, because positions are advertised, salaries are published, and opportunities appear greater. However, my climb, along with others' (women and nonwhite males), was proving to be unusually rigorous and unpredictable, so I wanted to get started on the next rung. At the first possible opportunity, in early 1980, I applied for a supervisory architect position.

A white male architect was selected. "Oh well," I thought. "There goes another lost chance to meet the Command EEO goal of adding seven more supervisory-level females." Only one female held the title of Supervisory (GS-13) in the entire engineering command (254 people). Clearly, so-called affirmative action was not automatic. But I wasn't too upset, since this was only my first attempt, although I did decide to improve my résumé in terms of supervisory skills. I signed up for Basic Supervision, a Saturday class at Skyline College. The assistant design division director observed my interest in management and told me he was impressed with my initiative. Evidently, he thought I might become the first female supervisory architect, and he wanted me well prepared, because soon after the class ended, he sent me to a class called Women in Supervision. When the next supervisory architect position vacated, he announced that he would rotate all eligible architects into the position for a month, and I was to be the first. I jumped right in and was well received.

In September of 1980, the court ordered child counseling for Shanette. I was reassured when the counselor said not to worry, that the relationship between Shanette and me had a solid foundation. She gave the example of the special Sunday lunches, which we made together, as evidence of our strong bond.

Although slowed, I made a presentation at the statewide "Design Forum '81: Women Up Front," a three-day conference in San Luis Obispo. I liked to keep up with what others were doing and to share my ideas. Architects were interested in learning how to obtain work with the navy, so I focused my talk on interviewing and negotiating with the navy as a client.

In July 1981, Shanette, Wes, and I rented a two-bedroom apartment on the island of Kauai for one month to celebrate my 40th birthday. Shanette and I swam under waterfalls and made fantastic meals with exotic-smelling fruits. We all walked the cliffs, beaches, and bamboo forests. On the way home from Hawaii, Shanette unexpectedly asked to spell her name with a "C" (as it was spelled in French), instead of an "S." It took me time to change the spelling of my daughter's name from "Shanette" to "Chanette." She hadn't said *why* she wanted to change it; I let it be.

Chanette attended Lowell High School, touted as the best public school in San Francisco. Her grades were good, but she stayed away from after-school activities, and her interest in judo practice and flute playing slowed.

Now 15 years old, Chanette was spending most of her time with her teenage friends. She belly-danced at a nearby dance studio, where I saw her perform and met her friends. Periodically, she linked up with an older boy who had lived across the street from us in Oakland. She also made friends with Amy, the daughter of a doctor and nurse (the mother) who were happily married and whom Chanette admired. Amy was rebelling big time: missing school and failing classes. I became worried, as did Amy's parents; we called each other if our girls didn't come home. Later, I learned that both girls were experimenting with drugs, but I was so naïve at the time that I didn't know. Reading about teenage issues influenced me to take a "tough love" approach. After one of her not-coming-home stunts, I said, "Chanette, I want you home by midnight."

"I want to stay out as long as the others do," she argued.

"This isn't about others," I continued. My mind was made up, but that night about 2 a.m. she yelled, "Mom, let me in," and pounded on the locked back door. I tensed in my bed—it was hard to hold to my statement. She soon went to Wes's house for the rest of the night, and he drove her home the next morning.

My daughter told me again that she didn't want any limits. My wits shriveled. Rebellion was considered normal by the people I talked to but, I wondered, to just what degree? I was surprised at how much turmoil teachers and parents were willing to accept. My teenage experience had been so different from my teenage daughter's reality. I had never expected my role as mother to become so formidable, but it had, due to a virulent divorce, an unreasonably behaving ex-husband, and a rebellious child. I only wanted to see my daughter happy, and yet she was so troubled. My headaches continued.

At my WestDiv desk

At work, however, I thrived. My performance evaluations were highly satisfactory and outstanding. Engaging assignments continued to arrive with my name on them, but I never worked more than 40 hours a week; I'd learned to adjust my effort to the time allowed. Meanwhile, projects were growing in size and complexity. I was assigned to be the EIC for a compound at the Marine Corps Recruit Depot (MCRD) in San Diego. The project consisted of three buildings with three different A/E firms. Two of the projects were for Unaccompanied Personnel Quarters for 800 recruits, and the third was a dining facility sited between them. Fortunately, experienced and talented A/E firms were selected. We worked together to ensure that the projects linked in flow and character, using paths, parking, and design elements for a campus-like feel. MCRD, located next to the San Diego airport, had already established an early California Mission architectural style, which the staff civil engineer and I wanted to respect and continue. However, normal funding guidelines would not allow for the cost of red tile roofs, so I included the cost of the roof tiles under a special line item called "historic character."

Another noteworthy design aspect of this complex was that the ground level was lowered to reduce mass and avoid the airspace needed near the airport, and to use the land efficiently. Bradt Ackerman & Associates, the first A/E firm, proposed plazas surrounded by two levels of sleeping units, connected by a continuous arched walkway echoing the character of other arches at MCRD. I made sure that the other firms (Wheeler/Wimer Architects and Richard Lareau & Associates) followed this theme. Unlike family housing, the units had no kitchens; unaccompanied personnel would take their meals in the dining facility.

Dining facility
by Richard Lareau & Associates

The term *unaccompanied personnel* began to replace *enlisted men*, reflecting the navy's move to use fewer sex-linked and possibly sexist terms. Nice move by whoever made that happen.

At home, I fussed with paint, sheetrock, concrete, copper pipes, electrical boxes, and wires as I remodeled my *maisonette*'s downstairs space. Chanette helped, especially with the painting, but she preferred to be with friends.

One fall night in 1981, after an OWA meeting on Russian Hill, I found a carefully printed note on my car windshield—"I broke your headlight, please call me at this number"—signed "Jules." When I called, he asked where I lived, saying he wanted to come and to replace the broken headlight.

"Just bring a new headlight. I can replace it myself," I answered and gave him the two cross streets but not my address. The next day, there was Jules with the headlight—Warren Beatty handsome, with a big smiling mouth.

"How did you know where I live?" I asked, opening the door.

"Oh, I just asked the fellow at the corner house."

I reached to take the light.

"I will put it in for you," said Jules. "Really, I want to."

"Okay." I shrugged, feeling a shift in the mood, and followed him out to the street where my Peugeot was parked.

Jules cheerily unleashed a stream of unrelated stories to hold my attention. It worked. I stood by, watching him, and finally realized this guy was flirting. What was he about? He said he repaired refrigeration on ships. He lived in Bernal Heights, and he appeared to be single, with lots of wavy hair framing a darling freckled face.

The headlight installed, Jules came in to wash his hands and noticed that the kitchen light bulb cover, high on the ceiling, was missing. "I have one of those—I could bring it over another time and put it up for you," he offered, as casually as a neighbor might have.

"Fine," I said, because he was attractive and I was longing for romantic attention. Jules, with his bulging grin and plaid shirt, drove an old baby-blue panel truck and liked to fix things. The more I got to know him, the more I understood that his Boy Scout enthusiasm to please people was a keystone of his personality and often detracted from our relationship because he was *helping* so many people.

My compelling—seemingly innate—desire to participate at higher levels in government continued. Not because the promotions included a significant increase in pay, but because they were a sign of growth, recognition, and influence. In November 1981, I responded to another supervisory architect announcement for two openings in our Architectural Branch. These opportunities within my organization gave me hope. However, once again, both positions went to men. Disillusioned, I began considering other work options, including opportunities outside of architecture. During this time, one of my French architecture schoolmates wrote me about a friend who was looking for help getting their gourmet preserved mushrooms and snails into the US market; I was interested and wrote back to learn more.

Without warning, Arnaud arrived back in the country for skiing season. After a hearing on December 23, 1981, the court said:

> The court finds, beyond a reasonable doubt, that respondent Mr. A. Bertrand willfully failed to provide child support for two months, despite his ability to make such payments … (and is) sentenced to ten days in San Francisco county jail. Execution of said sentence is stayed until January 8, 1982 at 6:00 PM.

Not surprisingly, Arnaud did not show up for the hearing; he had left the country. The court finally realized that we were dealing with a social criminal. But my fears persisted. I had read that a tug-of-war between parents was potentially harmful for children of divorce. The child feels a need to choose one, but he has to reject the other that he needs and loves. The resulting conflict is profound and terribly destructive for the child.

When I realized that Arnaud's behaviors appeared to match symptoms of an antisocial personality disorder, I felt better, thinking I now understood the problem. But my new understanding didn't make dealing with it any simpler. I just wanted the things most mothers want for their children: peace, love, health, and happiness. The custody court battle reopened the kidnapping scar, and I feared that my protective abilities would be less and less effective in shielding my daughter from the fallout of her parents' legal entanglement.

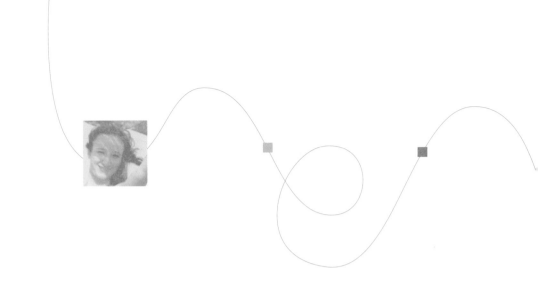

Crater in My Heart

1982 to 1984: San Francisco

Jules radiated a cheerful, romantic mood; I hungered for this. He was willing and able to help do all sorts of construction work on the house out of genuine fondness. He was only 31, never married, and lived at home with his mother. My parenting and divorce problems were far outside his personal experience; yet he sympathized and smiled. His optimistic help and playfulness offset my burgeoning anxiety—but we never delved into philosophical or literary discussions or plunged toward the emotional depths of a husband and wife. The needs of his mother and two sisters filled his heart, while my heart swelled with worry about how my daughter's outlook might be damaged from this miserable aftermath of divorce. Worst of all, I blamed myself for not being able to get off the string that Arnaud Bertrand was pulling on my emotions.

To lessen my domestic distress, I concentrated on designing the remodel of my house into two units, with the idea of eventually renting the lower unit. I extended the house 14 feet at the north end to the full width of the existing house. Simply by turning the floor plan of the house inside out, I was able to maximize my home's distant downtown views. I relocated the front door to the side of the house facing the rear of the lot, so that as you entered, you looked out over the tapestry of San Francisco rooftops and back lot gardens scrolling down

My SF house during construction

Kitchen with new skylight

Looking at the new entrance

Living room from kitchen

to the bay. My upstairs flat stood four feet above the garden level, so I designed three steps up to a large deck that spanned over a low spot in the garden and then up three more steps to a porch at the entrance to the new living room. Out of respect for the hundred-year-old rustic cottage character, I selected elements for the new living room that kept, echoed, or complemented the cottage's period features and quirkiness, like the curved wall in the kitchen that was the back of a bedroom closet. And I designed new wood windows to match the detailing of the existing windows, used the original antique light fixtures with glass shades, and installed high thick Victorian baseboards instead of the narrower, thinner contemporary baseboards that were popular and cheap.

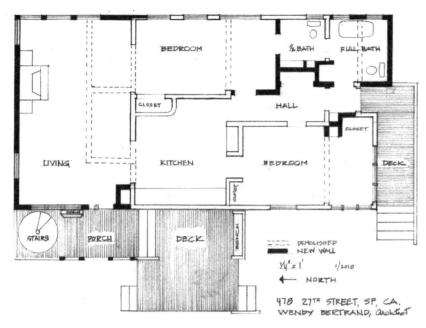

BEDROOM

½ BATH   FULL BATH

CLOSET

HALL

CLOSET

LIVING   KITCHEN   BEDROOM   DECK

CLOSET

STAIRS   PORCH   DECK

BENCH

- - - - - DEMOLISHED
▬▬▬ NEW WALL

¼" = 1'   1/2010

◀— NORTH

478 27TH STREET, SF, CA.
WENDY BERTRAND, architect

Upper flat after remodel

My architect's heart still flutters when guests enter the new living room and I tell them it was added, whereupon they say, "But it looks like part of the old house."

My old front door, perennially in the shadow of the adjacent three-story apartment building, became the back door. Upstairs, Chanette's library became part of the new bathroom. The old living room was divided up (and extended) to make more space in both bedrooms for closets, built-in shelves, and desks and tables with chairs so that these rooms could be used for more than sleeping. I eliminated some doors and carved out others. Every room enjoyed two doors; no room would be a dead end, not even the bathrooms.

The new upstairs living room became the biggest room, taking up the entire 20-foot width of the house; the view west looked out onto the Mirabelle plum tree, the view east onto the neighborhood, city, and bay. A set of double doors opened from the living room into the original kitchen, while a set of glass doors allowed one to see the fireplace from one of the bedrooms. When the doors were opened, this bedroom could be used as an extension of the living room.

Tile floor and fireplace   Lower flat living room windows

Downstairs, I added on to each end of the basement and introduced interior walls to make a not-so-traditional floor plan with two possible front doors. Tenants use the kitchen door as their main door.

In the lower unit, under the new upstairs living room, I designed a small living room with a fireplace and a darling kitchen. Earth-colored floor tiles, similar to tiled floors I had seen in southern France, provided the French accent I love. An existing glass door was adapted to be a pocket door (one that slides into the wall out of sight) to let in light between the kitchen and living room when the door needed to be closed. The morning rays shine into the new kitchen, while the tenant can peer into my neighbor's garden several feet lower on the hill. When the city building permit arrived, Jules and I demolished the upstairs bathroom, porch, and backstairs. In the meantime, I asked my OWA friends about contractors.

I was relieved when we finally started the work. It had taken me more than a year to get a variance permit from the city because the house was nearer the rear-yard property line than allowed by the planning code. The permit was further delayed during the hearings when my front neighbor spoke out against leaving the existing joint sewer intact. Little did I know that this neighbor had a friend in the Planning Department; thus, even though my preference to keep the existing

Crater in My Heart

Lower flat after remodel

sewer was reasonable and legal, my neighbor was able to block my request. I ended up installing a pump system in a pump house for a new sewer line, at great expense. But even with all the surprises, I loved arriving home after work to see my vision come to life, and I relished making the myriad decisions needed to keep construction moving forward. Being an architect helped!

Early in June 1982, Jules drove me to the Naval Air Station in Merced for an overnight business trip. Chanette had turned 16 years old the week before and she stayed alone that night, as she had done in the past from time to time. In spite of her periodic rebellious nature, I trusted her completely. But when Jules and I returned the next afternoon, we found her room cleared out. She had taken what she needed or wanted in a hurry. The room had been pillaged, and there was no note. I was beside myself. Stunned numb, I waited for news. Jules stayed, although he hadn't expected to. He held me close to his chest all night while I sobbed, thinking of how I had prepared for Chanette's birth, how her lips nursed at my breast and her body floated in my arms before she could walk. Mothering her, feeding her, washing her, reading to her, loving her into my life day after day for 16 years flashed before my eyes like a slide show of memories.

Jules rose at four in the morning to go home and take his sister to work at the stock exchange, as he often did. Hours passed. No news. I couldn't do much, so in the afternoon I went into the garden with my gloves and hand clippers, and began hacking off the ivy runners coming over a rickety fence from my neighbor's yard.

"How are you?" asked Ellen from the other side of our fence.

"Miserable. Chanette has left without a note, I have no idea where she is."

"She left for France," Ellen said from a face that could have been pretty except for the bug eyes and pebbly skin.

"What do you mean?"

Ellen explained softly, "That boyfriend of hers came with a truck and they loaded all her stuff."

"You didn't say anything to her?" I lashed out, my hand frozen on the clipper handles in mid-air.

"No, I thought it was okay."

"What do you mean, 'okay'?"

"Well, she asked me about going, and I guess I didn't think about you."

Ellen was married without children and she was a psychologist of some kind. I couldn't believe her actions. She didn't know much about me, or my situation, but we had been friendly neighbors until then.

Lifting off one last ivy runner, I squeezed the clipper handles with all my might—maybe to release tension, maybe to cut my frustration, maybe to snip the neck of my relationship with Ellen.

She called the next day. "I'm sorry, Wendy, I didn't think about you or the consequences. I was wrong." We never spoke again, and when she had her first child, they moved back to New York.

A few days later, a letter addressed to Chanette Bertrand arrived and I ripped it open. The return address said Steve Eli, Attorney, our roommate in 1962 when Arnaud and I lived in Monterey. I unfolded a letter from Arnaud, who wrote to Chanette in English:

Many children find the courage to live with the other parent between 14 and 16 years old. You must at 16. If it is not now, there will be no more tomorrows between daughter and father, now or never.

There were two more pages of pleas. My throat pinched as if in siege; I had never imagined that my daughter would go for this. In that moment, I felt the enormity of what it is to be an unloved and unappreciated mother. Red-hot and unmanageable explosions erupted in my heart, my soul fired, and my mind faltered as I tried to comprehend the turn of events.

I recently reread a letter Arnaud wrote to Chanette dated June 1, 1981, three pages typed in French promoting the same arguments: "You must come now, or you will never have a father. Wendy was not raised by a father and you must not suffer the same thing. Your grandmother is ill ..." He even included the name of a person from her school to contact if she wanted to go to France. His final argument was that if she would just say she wanted to live with him, the judge would agree.

It must have been a difficult decision for her. Chanette finally wrote to me, three months later, in August: "I feel like if I leave you now... others won't suffer and I'll feel better too, cause then I don't have to feel guilt." I felt there was nothing I could do, so I simply waited to hear from her while I grieved in her absence. The spew of letters from Arnaud and Moucha, his mother, stopped—that part was a relief.

Since my house was under construction, I threw myself into the project every free moment. I noticed that the head carpenter's work was much more thorough and thoughtful than that of the contractor he worked for. Toward the end of construction, when the contractor was out of sight, I asked Tada, "Do you ever work on your own?"

Tada

"Yes," he said, beaming sincerely. When the exterior envelope of the house was completed, I telephoned to Tada to do the interior finish carpentry, which started a lifelong relationship between architect and builder. Tada, originally from Kyoto, eased conversations with a jovial giggling gesture and rarely said no.

By September 1982, the downstairs one-bedroom apartment was ready to rent. Jules and I spent our weekends tying up loose ends in the yard. I made meals for Jules, who could only broil a couple of hot dogs if no other food appeared. Nevertheless, my life's routine had radically changed without the continuing responsibility, loving, and caring of Chanette.

Nothing in my past life had reached this present peak of suffering: not sickness, broken bones, disappointments, divorce, discrimination, or child snatching. An irrevocable pain filled the crater in my heart. To relieve accumulating stresses, I began jogging at lunchtime with some of my coffee break buddies. Soon I was running a race every month, even the Bay to Breakers—always slowly but completely.

After one year, my heart still hurt, but at least Chanette's letters arrived more often. Her letters didn't say much about her departure, except that she thought it was the best thing for her and me. She never referred to the pull of her father. I always wrote back and sometimes asked her about her leaving. But even though she wrote, "With time we will be able to have a good relationship," and that she loved me and knew I loved her, the letters were strained. I later learned of her Cinderella-like life—that she was being used to do the cleaning and take care of her new half-brother, the son from Arnaud's marriage to his new wife. I knit and sent Chanette a mohair sweater. She wrote back how cold she had been and how happy she was to receive a warm sweater.

In August 1984, the *San Diego Tribune* ran an article with three photos in its Home section, titled, "Navy Takes a Good and Hard Look at Itself." Herb Lawrence interviewed me for the article, which featured one of my projects. He explained my approach and quoted several of my comments:

> The Navy doesn't want its bases to be a hodgepodge of design that doesn't hold together architecturally and doesn't fit in with the surrounding area. Aesthetics are important, not just for the exterior, but for the interior.

This quote appeared above the rendering by Bradt Ackerman & Associates, designers for the Unaccompanied Personnel's Quarters at MCRD in San Diego. None of my old high school mates from La Jolla ever mentioned seeing the article, but that was to be expected. I hadn't stayed in contact with anyone but Jeannie, my European travel partner, whom I visited when in San Diego on business. She was married to her second husband and had a second child. We stayed in contact because of our common childhood and our landmark trip together, not because of similar life paths.

When I found out, through a mutual friend, that my daughter had returned to San Francisco in the fall of 1984 and was working in a flower shop, I called the shop and asked her if I could come by and say hello. That broke the ice, but relations didn't warm as quickly as I had hoped. She was now an adult, and at 18 years old, she was trying to make a living, apparently staying away from both mother and father.

Suddenly, after a few months and without much notice, Chanette returned to France to study movie-making at the Sorbonne. Letters were rare. These were tough years for her, and she depended on her own abilities to survive—earning

Chanette belly dancing in the 1980s

money by belly dancing, she told me later. Our relationship remained estranged, although I felt more patient, understanding that she had to find herself by herself.

I thought I was doing well, but then I started to lose blood, especially when I was running. I ended up having a hysterectomy that slowed me down for a year.

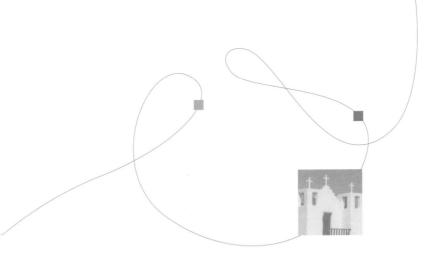

The Perfect Venue

1985: San Francsico

As my body healed, my ambition hollered. After watching all three of the supervisory architect positions I'd applied for go to others, I was so concerned about my future that I seriously began surveying potential architectural positions outside of WestDiv—but still in federal service. I sold Francy Gourmet products for a while, and that was fun because people at the food shows were so upbeat. Selling did help to keep my mind occupied for several years after Chanette's departure, but my sales got ahead of the products arriving from France. I couldn't deliver, and then I had too much and had to sell it at a loss. I realized that sales wouldn't work as a substitute for architecture. Understandably, when I read that the Design Division of the San Francisco Navy Public Works Center (PWC) was recruiting applicants to build an Architectural Branch, I moved quickly.

Up to this point, the centers held less prestige than the field divisions. This was mainly because we, at WestDiv, managed larger projects within the nine western states, while the projects handled by the centers were primarily small alterations and repairs within the San Francisco Bay Area. Some of that changed, however, in the early part of 1985, when "special projects" (those over $400,000) were transferred from the Field Divisions to the Public Works Centers, worldwide. For this reason, PWC San Francisco needed to add an Architectural Branch to their Engineering Division—an anomaly because all the other PWC Engineering Divisions already had Architectural Branches.

Even with the addition of these larger projects, working for the centers rated low in desirability—it was much like transferring from a position in a country's capital to one in the provinces, where intensity and sophistication wane in the eyes of movers and shakers, especially those who like to feel the organizational heartbeat near the neck. Knowing this, I reasoned I'd have better odds competing for this position closer to the organization's pulse, but mostly the idea of setting up an Architectural Branch intrigued me. I applied, made the short list, and was called for an interview—all within a few weeks.

The PWC office, 12 miles east of San Francisco, was located at the Naval Supply Center in Oakland, adjacent to the first exit from the Bay Bridge—the exact distance from my house to WestDiv—so my commute time would not increase. Passing through the security gate, my Peugeot seemed out of place in the bulky industrial zone, where imposing, unremarkable buildings poked up out of a sea of calm asphalt, and concrete loading docks, instead of landscaping, lined the paved roads. I parked in front of a massive, foam green metal warehouse of a building, and entered.

Feeling wide-minded and hopeful—in spite of the blocks of drabness I'd driven through to get here—I moved up the somber, carpeted staircase toward daylight. Skylights spotted the magnificently high (20-foot), open, metal-trussed ceiling. Boldly naked of decoration and freshly remodeled with clean, white walls, the enormous space enveloped me with the productive feel of an artist's studio. A checkered pattern of low, soft gray and green partitions came into view from the stair's top landing. I took a few more steps, pausing to admire the rich, tight grain of the varnished floor at the lobby's entrance; my best Italian high heels reflected back at me. *Could I work here?*

Bert Peck, the Design Division director and a mechanical engineer, interviewed me in his solid but windowless office. "Your experience with the Engineering Field Division would be good for us," Bert told me. He was younger and taller than I, athletically tanned, and his V-neck, long-sleeved jersey matched his informal demeanor. Two tennis rackets leaned against his otherwise ordinary desk. "We'll be getting much larger projects, and architectural services will be more in demand."

"Tell me about the kind of Architectural Branch you would like to have," I said. I kept my tone inquisitive and even, in spite of my mouth-watering desire to be the authority in charge of creating this new branch.

"In a word, quality would sum it up." He leaned back in his swivel chair. "I've never met anyone who has been part of starting a new professional organization." He was referring to OWA.

Basking in the pleasure of being recognized for a topic so close to my heart, I missed the link Bert was making. He was saying that I had what it took to create something new, like a *new branch of the organization*. Instead, my thoughts flashed back to six years earlier, when the same activity wasn't deemed worthy of receiving any points from the three men who had rated me during my repeated quests for promotions. Yet, here was a manager who considered my OWA experience a unique benefit and a noteworthy demonstration of unusual capability. I now realize that Bert had probably already made up his mind when he called me for the interview, and his comments were just a confirmation of his decision. He was emphasizing that this position would suit me, while I went in thinking I was going to have to convince him that I was the best applicant.

Our conversation glided along comfortably, but I noticed he didn't elaborate or launch into long discussions. Soon, he took me on a quick walk through the plenary space, where conservatively dressed men, and a few women, worked without radios in fabric cubicles. It was nice and quiet.

As I drove away from the PWC, my thoughts rambled. Creating an Architectural Branch from scratch would be the perfect venue for practicing fine architecture and progressive management. For example, I wanted to acknowledge the individual's participation, perhaps put an expression on the navy's faceless approach to individual contribution. Architectural drawings had the tiny signature or initials of the designer and drafter in the lower right corner, but this seemed too small compared with the time and effort it took to create these drawings. Reports, studies, and booklets didn't name the author at all. Generally, the names of authors, designers, and administrators remained invisible behind the credit to WestDiv, a practice common to most large architectural firms. If there was any positive reason for this practice, I certainly didn't see it; why not identify individual contributors to a project, as well as the agency or office? By not doing so, management was missing a valuable opportunity to show its appreciation, and individuals were not enjoying their deserved credit—a valuable ingredient of job satisfaction. Maybe that was something I could do at PWC.

I mused on my own attempt to secure this type of recognition. Four years before, when the drawings and specifications for the dining facility at MCRD were completed and ready to advertise, I'd asked the architect, Mr. Lareau, to include my name as EIC on the photo rendering—and he did. Some of my colleagues snubbed me for my audacity, but their opinions didn't sway me. Years after I left WestDiv, a colleague found an extra photo of the rendering and sent it to me since my name was on it.

The PWC grounds were isolated and ugly, but if I stayed at WestDiv, it would take two promotional leaps to become Architectural Branch head. On the other hand, if I got this job at the center, I would have full responsibility and set the standards for the architectural design quality of all projects, albeit in a smaller area of influence. The job was equivalent to being principal of your own medium-sized architectural firm in private industry, but without the financial burdens, the heavy marketing tasks—or the profits.

I liked the navy system of rank because rank carried authority. You were allowed and expected to take on the role of your title, so there was no doubt in my mind that I would have full control of the Architectural Branch. Making money was not my goal. However, doing a good job to support the fleet with quality shore facilities was the ever-repeated mission, spurring me on.

The pleasure of being selected to be an Architectural Branch head was more satisfying than college graduation and a much sweeter revenge than any I could have imagined; it was acknowledgment of my success in the high jump from worker to leader. Within days and on my daughter's nineteenth birthday, my 24 WestDiv projects, all at different stages of design and construction—which included the Youth Center, Twenty-Nine Palms; Repair Supply Administration Building, Miramar; Child Care Facility, Fallon, Nevada; Family Service Center, Moffett Field; and the three MCRD projects in San Diego—were reassigned.

The traditional farewell party photo appeared in the July 1985 issue of *WESTWORD*. I was touched and slightly amazed by the number of people who came to the party to wish me well. At that event, 25 years ago, I said, in my unprepared comments, "Someday I will write a book about all this." A young architectural intern came up to me afterward and said, "I never thought of that—good idea," as if he hadn't heard of anything new since he arrived. His comment stuck with me as one of those bursts of energy, small but encouraging, that we all need to fuel our intent.

Photography opportunity with Pueblos in Arizona

Before reporting to PWC, I took another trip with my college roommate and traveling friend, Sandra. This time we drove around New Mexico, looking in trading posts for native crafts and knitting yarns. The adobe architecture of Taos, Santa Fe, and Albuquerque wowed my sense of space and color. I perceived such places—held together by buildings of the same material and shape—to be like beautiful languages: strong with cultural history, music, and character. I took some photos.

It was years later that I realized the type of uniformity I saw in New Mexico could feel restrictive to a community's inhabitants. At a dinner party one evening, a Frenchman mentioned to me that he was tired of living in a building that had stood for centuries among similar ones. "You can't live in a modern house here, a glass house, or a wooden house. It's not like in San Francisco, where there is so much variety on the same block." His remark reminded me that if you've grown up in an area where a certain type of building has been duplicated over a wide region—even for good reasons, such as climate or the technology of an era—you may come to feel forced to fit into the local vernacular, in spite of the fact that it may have outlived its original *raison d'être*.

We found the structures in the Southwest so charming, perhaps, in part, because the thick-walled, rounded adobe shapes were new and different and carried no historical or emotional baggage—for us. Coming from San Francisco, I could understand that too much homogeneity might clash with an individual's choice and could even be at odds with the visual benefits and needs of the community. This new contradiction shook my thinking about harmony and place.

Returning to San Francisco, I found myself still very excited about my work promotion and especially relieved that I didn't have to move to a new location, as so many of my colleagues had done. I approached my new position with the enthusiasm of a chef entering a new kitchen.

My Architectural Branch

1985 to 1986: San Francisco and Oakland

Now to sculpt my Architectural Branch! Before I arrived at the San Francisco Public Works Center (PWC), all the architects reported directly to the Civil/Structural Branch head. Since branch staff meetings weren't part of the PWC office culture, I spent time that first week with each architect at his or her desk. By the second week, I had initiated a routine of weekly Architectural Branch meetings. There were no meeting rooms in our department, so I signed us up for the conference room—windowless and rarely used—in an adjacent department.

When it came to reshaping organizations, I dared to believe that meetings were to management what chisels were to sculpture. At our first meeting, I asked my staff to write down (without identifying themselves) any matters of concern they had about working at PWC. I instructed them to include items they didn't like, as well as things they did or would like. My idea was to focus on what the group deemed important.

Near the end of our next meeting, I passed out a sheet listing all their items, which I had compiled into two columns.

"There are some duplicates," said Ann, an experienced architect recently hired from private industry. Ten years my junior, Ann was well trained, licensed, and closely watching the gestures of her first female boss.

I stood and responded. "You are right, I wanted you to see all the items."

No one looked up; they were all busy surveying the 46 *like/would like* items and 40 *dislike* items.

"Please read this at your desk," I said, ending the meeting. "Mark your top ten priorities, and return the sheet to my inbox by Friday."

Because the organization was changing so dramatically, the majority of *dislikes* included very basic things, such as not having a phone for each person, not having enough office supplies, and not having a fair distribution of awards. *Like* or *would like* items included having an international character of the workforce, being busy, seeing growth potential, getting helpful technical support, having flexible hours, and going to on-site visits.

I opened one meeting by stating, "I want the Architectural Branch to be a recognizable entity." Up to this point, newly hired employees were assigned to whatever desks happened to be left vacant by departing employees—*anywhere* in the Engineering Division. My thought was to reorganize the pattern of cubicles so that each branch sat together and was recognizable as a group.

"We will need a sign that says who we are," said Ann, grasping my concept and building on it immediately.

"I want to sit next to Connie," Alfredo said, so earnestly that we all laughed. If Alfredo wasn't rushed, his warm middle-aged smile could melt butter.

"Maybe the Civil/Structural Branch can fit into the smaller side room," Li suggested, gesturing confidently with his drawing pencil. "And all the other branches can be in the main space."

Mei, a talented fine art painter as well as an architect, had concerns for our health. "The ventilation is so bad, smokers should smoke outside."

Encouraged by the interest, I asked for a new layout in two weeks and left the completion of the plan to those who volunteered.

About the fourth meeting, I waited until everyone had settled into his or her seat, before casually saying, "It may be a little different working for a woman instead of a man."

The three women dipped lower in their chairs as if ready to slide under the table, while the men seemed to sit taller and welcome the discussion.

"I wonder how many of you have worked for a woman before."

Fred, an older Filipino-American, carried himself with a stern demeanor that demanded respect. He was the first to speak up. "I worked for a woman once," he said, "and she didn't seem to realize that men have feelings, too." His voice trembled—you could have heard a paperclip drop. "She would get angry and start yelling—" he stopped mid-sentence, apparently remembering something personal he'd rather not share.

"Thanks, Fred." I had wanted to get the subject of women out for discussion, and now Fred had opened the conversation with emotion. "It would be good to hear from each person," I continued, compelled to release some of the anxiety about the changing roles of women by pressing for the unspoken to be verbalized. Listening intently, I sat at the head of the long conference table while people shared their perspectives and experiences. A few people passed. But I felt that going around the table was necessary to dissipate any hidden awkwardness in our common new reality.

Getting people to speak up was part of my style, and my staff eventually became comfortable with my expectation that they participate at every meeting. Over time, we began acting like a group: defining policies, procedures, and our own group identity, rather than deferring to the one-on-one, top-down, supervisor-to-employee operating behavior used in the military chain of command.

To help us transition into this group thinking, as well as to showcase each individual's interests and talents, I posted a meeting schedule and asked employees to fill in their name and a five-minute topic of their choice. Two people were scheduled to speak at each meeting, so by the end of six meetings, all 11 people had spoken once. The topic could be about one of their projects, a design issue (such as how to choose a roofing material), a communication issue in construction management, or a procedural problem, such as how to reschedule work. I sometimes helped people choose a topic, as I did for Alfredo, the butter-melting drafter, who had worked for PWC a long time and for whom this was a bizarre idea.

We continued having our staff present mini-speeches for the next several years, although Fred complained that we were having too many meetings. He liked to work independently and probably felt he had nothing to learn from me, his junior. Occasionally, I played an educational tape, followed by discussion, on topics such as the difference between assertiveness and aggressiveness, but most of the 60 minutes addressed ongoing work. Meetings get a bad name because they are too often unplanned and uninteresting, like mass transit when it doesn't work. I saw my meetings more as a purposeful conversation mixed with the lively learning of a thoughtful seminar—we were all learners and teachers. Of course, I was the instigator, so I had my bias, but if the group hadn't been engaged, our meetings wouldn't have been so much fun.

Connie told me that Marc, an engineer from one of the mechanical branches, admitted, "I wish our branch had meetings, I feel so isolated."

Actually, none of the other branches held staff meetings. But once my meetings were operating smoothly, I invited the Electrical Branch to join us. Although the Architectural Branch depended on all the other branches to support our projects, we had the most trouble getting the electrical portion of our projects on time. Meeting with the Electrical Branch proved to be helpful, and after a while, most of the other branches began holding their own meetings—by employee request.

Like most large organizations, the navy had jillions of procedures to follow, and it was easy to miss steps. Although the navy is known for its good manuals, and WestDiv had an EIC manual, there was no PWC manual. We needed one for the new special projects and A/E contracts. Without a manual, each Architectural Branch member had no choice but to guess, ask, or advance until blocked. Sharing our experience at meetings helped us to learn quickly and be consistent.

Ann, the most organized of the group, often took the lead. "Whenever I get a new project, I set up a site visit with the customer and meet him at the site."

"I just go to the site and look around," offered Bob, a graduate architect usually hesitant to speak up.

"Do we have to go to the site?" challenged Ernie, a handsome fellow, obviously secure in his working style.

"Well," Ann bounced back, "when do the rest of you go over the scope of work with the customer?"

"I call the Staff Civil on the phone," answered Li.

"It would be better if we were consistent so the customer would know what to expect," I interjected, wanting to come to a consensus.

And so, week by week, month by month, we discussed our way toward consistency. Increasing my staff's interactions felt like sculpting a responsive material. It was an unprecedented time for the Design Division; our project sizes were growing, many employees were new, and I had just arrived. I facilitated mutual support among my staff in a democratic style that may be considered an example of feminine management; I certainly hadn't experienced this kind of dialogue with my male bosses.

Managers—to their peril—commonly neglect the relationships among employees. I read recently on the Web that in 2007, women in England were leaving the profession of architecture because of "lack of encouragement and support from co-workers," among other reasons. Female architects have been dropping out of the profession in numbers large enough to trigger the more enlightened to wonder why. This trend began surfacing in 2000, but no one wants to admit that it may be due to a component of sexism, the side effects of discrimination, and the fallout of a profession in duress.

As focused as my work life was, my love life was flaking away like the old paint on my house before its make-over. Jules and I would have so much fun, and then he would have no time, come late, and break dates. The major construction on my duplex was complete, so I was already seeing him much less. I wrote often in my journal about my interest in one attractive man at the Saturday farmers' market. More than once, I told Jules I was not satisfied with our relationship, and we would agree to break up but then get back together. In between, other men were beginning to tempt me at work, in the neighborhood, and at the Sierra Club singles.

Jules and me

Designing architectural projects for PWC involved inventing something original each time; discretion, analysis, and creative thought were required to find solutions, even if the administration of projects followed the same procedures. In fact, since no two designs were exactly alike, each architect's experience contributed to his or her unique portfolio or profile. Each architect on my staff was at a different stage in the development of his or her work life and had more or less sophistication and confidence. As a manager assigning projects, I needed to get to know each of them individually, and meetings helped me to do so quickly.

There were many times I wanted to talk one-on-one to other managers about my management ideas, somewhat in the same way that mathematicians test their findings and theories on peer mathematicians. But I never felt it was appropriate to call a male co-manager after work—married or single—to discuss the ideas I was turning over in my mind. This was one case where gender was a major factor in my managerial behavior; talking with male managers at work was fine, but after hours, it had to be a sister manager. It was in OWA that I found these sister managers to discuss pressing issues, like the use of English in the workplace.

I started getting complaints from the neighbors of two of the Taiwanese architects on my staff, because of their long talking sprees. Finally, I went over to them when they were talking; Eddy's cubicle was not far from mine. "I notice you two have been conversing a lot in Chinese."

Ming answered quickly, "We like to speak in our native tongue."

"I understand, but others may feel left out."

"We are not trying to exclude anybody. We are just talking," she rebutted. Eddy didn't say anything. Ming continued, "We are talking about work."

There were other Chinese speakers in the office, but this had never happened before. Not sure how to respond, I simply said, "That may be so, but I would prefer if you two spoke Chinese during lunch." I left it at that, but I still didn't feel good about it. Bert, my immediate boss, believed we should stick to English at work. But he was an English-only speaker, and I knew how automatically people tended to speak in their native tongue. I explained my concern and self-doubt to an OWA sister, a manager, who also recommended that English be the rule. Still, I was troubled, remembering stories of Mexican children forbidden to speak Spanish in elementary school and how they suffered from it. Of course, my employees were adults, but I felt that Ming thought I was denying her part of her rightful identity, and I didn't want to do that. Even so, I had a gut feeling that she was socializing more than working.

We discussed the language issue at the next staff meeting. The Philippine-born architects thought English at work was the way to go, and the English-only people wanted English to be the rule. In the end, the final consensus was to use English, as the Chinese speakers decided they could live with the majority. But I never really felt comfortable about it. Fuzzy shadows lingered.

When my staff was satisfied with the new seating layout for the Engineering Division, organized by branch, I took it to Joe's management meeting. Joe was the Design Department head, a civilian who reported to a navy commander whom we didn't see too often. A true Virginian gentleman, Joe had earned himself a reputation for being reasonable and easygoing; I liked him very much. The Design Department he headed included our Design Division, as well as a group called the Planners & Estimators (P&Es), who planned the in-house construction projects Joe, who had retired three years earlier as an Air Force colonel, ran his meetings in the style of a military officer telling his

At my PWC desk

troops the things he thought we should know—there was rarely any dialogue. Happily, Joe accepted our plan, and a moving date was scheduled.

All supervisors' cubicles, including mine, were slightly bigger than those of the other architects. Hoping to make my office feel less institutional, I brought a low coffee table and a standing lamp from home to offset the large simulated-wood desk. From the two chairs facing my desk, one could see my credentials and awards, hung traditionally on the wall behind me, but I easily left the desk to sit informally with visitors next to the low coffee table.

At one of Joe's Monday morning meetings, when the moment seemed right, I held up our narrow white cardboard sign with the word

ARCHITECTURE in bold capital letters. "I will have my staff make a sign for each branch if you want," I offered, moving the sign high over my head so that everyone in the semicircle could see it.

"Yes, I would like one for my Mechanical Branch," an engineering supervisor quickly put in his order.

"I think it would be good for all the branches to have a sign," said Bert.

Pleased with my boss's can-do attitude, I felt that things were starting to take shape. These minor changes to our business-as-usual practices were encouraging and only inspired me to push for more. Joe was one of four upper-level managers whose office allowed him to enjoy the building's few exterior walls with windows. His weekly meetings were held in his well-lit office, and this got me to thinking. Views, like the abundance of resources, have come to mean status in our culture. All humans need light and air, but the higher-ups usually get more of it, not because they biologically need more light and air to function, but to emphasize their social status. Secretaries, usually female, often sit in areas *without* windows, just outside the offices *with* windows. And here I was, along with all the engineers and architects, working in a space without windows. I did, however, use my design authority to insist on windows for all the design projects under my jurisdiction. My personal goal was that anything designed by my Architectural Branch would continue to be useful and valuable even if the military left the Bay Area and the buildings became private facilities. And even if they remained part of the public trust, they deserved to have windows.

PWC architectural staff (I am at right)

At PWC, employee amenities were few. There wasn't even an outside picnic table. The truck selling lunch items came twice a day so that the people could buy a ready-made breakfast or burrito lunch to take back to their desks. The kitchen had a refrigerator, two microwaves, and a sink, but everyone was supposed to take lunch during the same half hour, so it was crowded. We could eat in the Construction Department lunchroom, a long walk from the kitchen—another reason most people ate at their desk. After a year of this, I planned for once-a-month staff meetings to be held in a restaurant or park, to add some variety to the workday routine and to celebrate our professional achievements, like when Bob passed part of the architectural registration exam. The following year, I added the option of an employee going out to lunch with me, one-on-one, which I found extremely enjoyable and many looked forward to. "I told my wife I was having lunch with the boss today," Eddy confided as we sipped hot tea in the sunny courtyard of an Oakland restaurant.

Chanette returned to San Francisco with a new boyfriend, whom she said had no money. That seemed strange, and I felt somewhat uncomfortable. They became roommates with others in an apartment on Grand View below Twin Peaks. Jules and I didn't know how to deal with the situation when they moved out of that apartment unexpectedly. I seem to have deleted the details in my mind about this trying period. I prefer to remember her job upholstering furniture. She found time to cover pieces for me and some of my friends after hours. Chanette presented me with lovely brocade and quality cotton fabrics to select for re-covering my six dining room bentwood chairs, a small fauteuil, and two ottomans. I was thrilled with the finished work and the rewarding emotional experience, feeling a little closer to my dear daughter.

Joe was using the lobby space for his monthly stand-up safety meetings and for award presentations, but I felt that my department needed a private sit-down space for staff meetings and for our meetings with customers and A/E firms. When I suggested that we renovate the unfinished long, narrow room behind the computer and technical support section to become our Design Division conference room, Joe immediately approved, allowing us to fix the room with in-house supplies bought on his budget. I stayed late one night while Ray, one of the unmarried P&Es I'd made friends with, showed me how to texture the walls. For the first and only time in my career, I worked on a

Saturday, along with several others, to paint the walls with the off-white color provided.

In the meantime, when not focusing on my career, I cultivated my friendships, worked on my house, jogged in short races, joined the Bay Area Knitting and Crochet Guild, and continued to be active in OWA.

Not long after our Saturday workday, I was delighted to find that our in-house construction crew had installed heat and ventilation. The head secretary ordered a long conference table and cushioned swivel chairs, adding a plush touch to the four basic walls. There actually was a window in this room, but since it was an inside space, the window looked down into the construction workers' staging bay below. Soon after completion of the new conference room, all the branch heads and Joe began using it. This felt fantastic, not only for me as a manager, but for everyone to be part of an office community so willing to define, paint, and improve our work environment, both organizationally and physically.

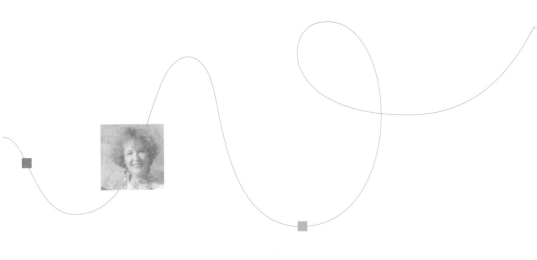

Management Climate

1986 to 1987: San Francisco and Oakland

While my staff sculpted our Architectural Branch, the projects continued to pour in. Unlike private industry, where clients select their preferred architectural firm, government agencies have only one designated internal design office. We serviced the US Navy, Air Force, and Marine Corps bases in the San Francisco Bay Area. These military bases were the size of small towns, complete with their own credit unions, hobby shops, childcare centers, nightclubs, warehouses, office buildings, housing, gas stations, and so forth. Much like facility managers in private industry, our government customers were responsible for any physical changes to the buildings. In other words, the housing officer was our customer for housing, not the tenants temporarily living in the residences. When the Naval Hospital at Oak Knoll wanted to make alterations for C-section birth procedures, or the Treasure Island staff civil engineer wanted to serve more personnel in the dining facility, those projects came to the PWC Design Division, and the "customers" paid us from their budgets.

We always negotiated a feasibility study as the initial task or the design phase of these types of projects. Sometimes the customer invited the users to attend the scope-of-work meetings. Feasibility studies looked at questions like these: How will the utilities be impacted? Is this project feasible? How will the neighborhood be affected by traffic, noise, or character? What is the intent? How much might the changes cost to build?

Before my arrival at PWC, the role of architecture was less prominent and projects were smaller, so whenever customers wanted to change walls and paint rooms, they merely had to fill out a form. Then the Planners and Estimators (P&Es) would prepare cost estimates and schedule the work to be done by in-house trades. *Just build it.* Although a discussion with an architect about feasibility is a natural first step in any design process, it was unexpected by some of the military staff who were are customers; they were accustomed to giving orders, rather than opening a dialogue they had to pay for.

Customers came and went, but buildings *lasted.* Architects are always confronted with the dual responsibility of providing optimum short-term satisfaction along with long-term investment. Because I was a government architect, the clamoring to build appropriate buildings was an aspect of my job I both liked and felt good about doing. Buildings are prominent components of place; they impact appearance, character, circulation, vistas, environmental health, resource use, and future options. But perhaps even more intriguing to me is the way buildings form the social stamp of their time. Like judges setting precedents with their decisions from the bench, we architects mark the land with our structures.

The private sector has some of the same pressures, of course, but with their own twist. Recently, a local city planner for Arcata, California, shared with me her disappointment about the ongoing debate she found herself in with developers and politicians about the proposed construction of two high-rise luxury hotels. Sadly, the movers and shakers in Arcata were all too willing to exchange the quality and character of their quaint town for the tax revenue they hoped to gain.

Our culture needs more architectural writers like Jane Jacobs, author of *The Death and Life of Great American Cities* (Random House and Vintage Books, 1961). Jacobs wrote about, among many things, urban planning. Her perspective was that of an informed citizen. She was not trained as a planner, yet because of her engaging essays and love of lively cities, she became a household name. Critics of the built world, like Jacobs, point out the disadvantages of pursuing the short-term financial interests of a few, who willingly burden our urban fabric with an unfortunate lack of aesthetics, quality, diversity, and delight—elements we truly need. Jacobs advocated more attention to the built world, stating, "Cities have the capability of providing something for everybody, only because, and only when, they are created by everybody." In a way, she was promoting a citizenship of place, not just of country.

During one of our together periods, Jules and I planned a trip to Grass Valley, where we walked the acres his family inherited from an Italian grandmother. He talked of his dreams of building on the knoll. Even with that wonderful long October weekend in a rustic cabin, I realized that Jules was not going to leave his mother. I came to understand that this man was a classic Peter Pan—and here I was, his Wendy. I'd read both books by Dan Kiley: *The Peter Pan Syndrome* (Dodd, Mead, 1983) and *The Wendy Dilemma* (Avon Books, 1985).

On a Tuesday evening, not long after gaining this insight, I sat with Jules on the couch in my dawn-colored living room, talking about nothing in particular. "Jules," I squeezed in between kisses, "our relationship is not growing."

"What do you mean?" he replied, looking shocked.

"You don't seem to want to be on your own."

"I come whenever I can," he objected, and pulled away slightly from our embrace.

"I don't feel you are really available the way I want." Tears flowed.

He looked with puppy sadness at my wet cheeks. "Don't cry, Wendy. I do my best."

"Jules," I whispered, leaning on the softness of his well-worn plaid flannel shirt, "I have to find someone else."

I knew he didn't want me to be sad, but he wasn't available either, and I couldn't accept the situation the way it was. Jules gave me an extra long kiss before leaving, suspending the prickly subject of our relationship.

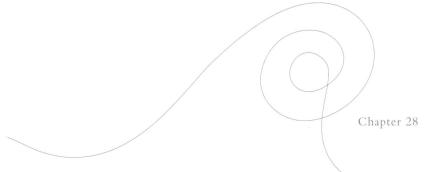

Chanette and me in
Grand Canyon, 1987

On the happier side, in the spring, Chanette and I took the train to visit my sister in Flagstaff, Arizona. We visited some of the buildings designed by architect Mary Colter. In 1902, Colter began a 50-year architectural career for the Fred Harvey Company, which developed resort facilities for the Santa Fe Railway in the Grand Canyon. I bought Virginia L. Grattan's book, *Mary Colter: Builder Upon the Red Earth* (Northland Press, 1980). According to Grattan, Colter loved the Spanish heritage of the Southwest, ignored the European focus of many architects in vogue, and created simpler, indigenous structures that have endured with pride.

I hand over OWA newsletters to the
Environmental Design assistant librarian

The year 1987 marked OWA's fifteenth year, and I wanted to make sure that our *herstory* was not lost. I proposed to the group that we have our OWA newsletters microfilmed and made available at the University of California, Berkeley Environmental Design Library and at other schools around the country. After collecting all the issues of the OWA newsletter, I began thinking it would be useful to have them indexed and found a professional indexer. On weekends, I took it upon myself to compile a table of contents by year. When all was completed, I ceremoniously delivered our newsletters to one of the College of Environmental Design librarians.

After the publication of our April 1987 OWA newsletter, we decided to make the monthly newsletters bi-monthly. The editors still rotated, and I was the editor for the May–June 1987 issue. I saw this as an opportunity to summarize Marilyn Loden's book, *Feminine Leadership, or How to Succeed at Business without Being One of the Boys* (1985). Loden made the case that women's leadership style would add valuable dimensions to the workplace. We needed both male and female management styles, as she described them:

Management style	Male	Female
Operating style	competitive	cooperative
Organizational structure	hierarchy	team
Basic objective	winning	quality output
Problem-solving style	rational	intuitive/rational
Key characteristics	high control	lower control
	strategic	empathetic
	unemotional	collaborative
	analytical	high performance

Her premise rang true, and I noticed that some of my own behaviors fit the model. Loden argued that being yourself was a good thing. Being female was okay, and using your female values was even beneficial. You didn't need to try to copy men, as I had in bizarre ways—like attempting to smoke a pipe early on in my career, when I sat next to Gary, who wielded his favorite pipe like a wand of superiority. However, Loden's call was not the current canon. Many women at that time felt required to wear pants, downplay their femininity, use "old boy" behaviors, and work obsessively to fit in and outperform others. But we were a new generation of women architects.

Gender wagged tongues. *The Daily Pacific Builder* (November 30, 1984) included an article by C.B. Crump: "Women Architect Group Is an Entity in Transition." And in the October 21, 1987, issue, I was interviewed for an article titled, "Woman Heads Bay Naval Architectural Operation." It included a photo of me, dressed in a well-cut suit, my hair in all the curls I was wearing during those years. Many questions were about gender, such as, "What advice do you have for other women?" They ended the piece with my response:

Learn how to negotiate. Know the five ways to resolve conflicts—not just one: competition, escape, compromise, collaboration, and accommodation. If one doesn't help you to cope, another will. Often, men don't feel comfortable communicating professionally with women—we women have to keep them talking. Accept the fact that women are different from men, but can be equally effective. Be creative. Take reasonable risks.

This advice may still be useful to individuals today, but I'm now more aware of the systemic social pressures on the individual, including social gravity (a force on us constantly), cultural structure, and institutional habits. Some scholars of racism, enjoying Barack Obama as the US president, want to go beyond a conversation about race. They assume that the playing field will never be level and want to deal with the issues of poverty, prisons, and education—issues that clearly impact some races more than others. I would follow their lead and apply the same thinking to women's issues. It is not only a case of women catching up and men being more fair (which was my primary thinking 20 years ago); the issues of gender are also biological, emotional, social, and organically complex. Women's styles and priorities are continually being explored and encouraged by both scholars and writers. Women have their own qualities and need not be considered inferior, nor should these qualities be altered to conform to a "man's world."

The world is evolving. Slowly, the reality of women's issues is being addressed: the need for childcare, the continued low earning power for more than 40 years ($.77 to $1), the discomfort of a rigid work structure and a long work day. And communication styles between men and women are finally getting attention from the linguistic community (*You Just Don't Understand*, Deborah Tannen, Morrow, 1990), from the male/female relationship community (*Men Are from Mars, Women Are from Venus,* John Gray, HarperCollins, 1992), and online by the world of management (*Gender in Management: An International Journal* (Emerald Group Publishing, UK).

The unevenness of general shifts added hope and uncertainty to my work climate. But one had to be alert to the work at hand and not be blown off course by the unnerving social gusts. So, like most architects who love the creative process, no matter the storm, I tried to stay concentrated on the work and gladly delved into problem after problem related to good architecture and creative management. Even during construction, there were design decisions to be made. Some changes came from customers changing their minds, others from unforeseen conditions or design and construction errors. I lobbied for construction managers and customers to respect our design role. Without our intervention, construction managers would sometimes opt for the easiest or cheapest fix. They eroded the quality of projects when they allowed the builder to substitute materials, like using particleboard in cabinets when wood was specified, or installing windows that didn't open when opening windows was necessary, or allowing the painter to paint one color instead of the three colors specified. Dimensions were important, too; building a room two inches shorter might mean the bathtub wouldn't fit or the door would not meet wheelchair access regulations. Architects are constantly shifting their attention from the overall concept, use, and feel of the building to the details, making sure that every decision adds to the theme and quality of the design. This requires constant attention and alertness, and my staff was good at it. I rewarded them by highlighting their skills in staff meetings, writing articles about the projects in the PWC newsletter, and giving cash bonus awards.

Ironically, the civilian employees had to hold on to the quality rudder at PWC because the military officers changed so often, and each new officer had his or her own focus. On the other side of the coin, the changing military guard brought benefits. Captain Dames arrived at a time when the Department of Defense was considering eliminating some of the services at PWC. He presented his new direction with the slogan, "We want to be the provider of choice," which triggered a higher awareness of quality and professional services throughout PWC. His slogan inspired me to develop what I called an *Architectural Branch Annual Report*. Some private architectural firms publish annual reports, and I felt producing one for our branch would give pride and visibility to our design services, which otherwise would have been obscured by the "hide button" so common to government agencies.

In spite of our excellent design operation, many military bases were on the chopping block. And, although Captain Dames's and our effort may have prolonged PWC's design and construction services, PWC eventually lost its design authority in the San Francisco Bay Area.

My annual report listed by name and position all 17 of the employees who worked in my branch during the year. By the end of 1987, that list included architects, landscape architects, and several intern architects from WestDiv who came to my branch for a training rotation. I collected Polaroid photos of staff members with their customers at the job sites: Bob, always sharp and neat, with the housing officer at the Department of Defense Housing Facility, Novato; Eddy, in his everyday black vest, with the PWC transportation director; and Ann, in her hardhat, holding drawings next to the head of the PWC Utilities Department. Of the annual reports printed (always at my own expense), some went to customers, a few to my bosses, others to A/E firms, and many to my employees, who could now share their work with friends and family.

I continued to see that I could push the organization into graceful action. Much like the coach of a baseball team or the artistic director of a ballet company, I came to understand that the range of productivity in a person could be aroused, stimulated, and facilitated in great part by the management climate. Granted, the Earth's climate is not that predictable, but we managers, coaches, and artistic directors like to think we help, encourage, and provoke a healthy working climate by our planning and behaviors. Unfortunately, bad management is quickly identified, while good management is enjoyed like an easy sunny day.

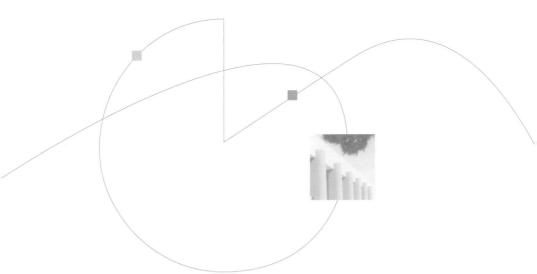

Ideal Timing

1987 to 1990: San Francisco, Denver, and Oakland

After more than a year of winding between the same softly colored cubicles to my office, the routine began to feel slightly too predictable. My body and mind yearned for more variation, accent, and surprise, so some Monday mornings I'd bring a bouquet of daisies or daffodils to counter the sameness. The atmosphere with high ceilings was pleasant enough for concentration—sedate and professional. Fortunately, my co-workers refrained from cluttering their cubicles with posters of favorite rock stars or wild animals, but living plants were rare, as there were no windowsills or direct sunlight. Eventually, the day-in, day-out lack of variety throughout the enormous converted warehouse wore on me, and it didn't help that there was no attractive place outside to wander. A longing grew within me for a fresh breeze, a few active sounds, and a visual urbanity with leafy plants and tall trees.

Social interaction was scarce as well. Without fail, around 9:30 each morning, I felt an internal tug on my thoughts, wishing I had a nice place to meet colleagues and socialize as I had done at WestDiv. However, there was no cafeteria at PWC, and the only people who stopped by to discuss business were members of A/E firms or PWC employees. My work life was edging toward loneliness. Occasionally, I would sit and knit at my desk.

My colleagues and I worked well together, but we didn't visit one another's desks to chat. I guess I was longing for other architects at my level, female supervisors, or women with common interests to join for coffee or lunch. During one of these 9:30 lulls, I sat at my desk and opened a current issue of *Navy Engineer Magazine.*

My eyes fell on an article about the Engineering Executive Management Development Program (EMDP), a Naval Facilities Program to preselect and train management talent while they continued working at their full-time jobs. Successful completion of the program would pre-qualify graduates for specific high-level positions within the Naval Facilities Engineering Command worldwide. Engrossed to the last sentence, I applied.

On the second try and after a grueling panel interview, I was accepted. The *Executive Management Bulletin* (March 1988) announced that 31 new cadres had been selected from more than 100 nominees worldwide. Three of us were female, and four of us were from engineering—I was the only architect. The other 26 were from finance, personnel, contracting, planning, environmental engineering, or other functions. My unique experience in both the Design Field Division (WestDiv) and the San Francisco Public Works Center (PWC) led me to hope that I would have a fair chance at obtaining a high-level management position once I graduated from the program.

Less than two years after I discovered that career-changing article, an open letter expressing full support of my involvement in the program, written by our executive director, Commander Tyler, was published by the PWC newsletter, the *BayGram*. Ideal timing too, because my capable, effective, and trustworthy staff stood ready to back me up, assuring that our work would move smoothly forward in my periodic absences during training.

My staff was stable but not static. New employees were hired when others left—and the mix of professional skills and experience shifted. One of my best ideas was to divide my branch into subgroups. Each subgroup included one senior architect, as I believed teaching was part of everyone's job. At first, some of the senior architects saw their seniority being acknowledged and thought they should get a promotion based on this new approach—they even persuaded many of the junior members to support their request. But eventually my plan fell into place the way I'd envisioned it, as an organizational tack to share expertise rather than a restructuring to increase the hierarchy of the organization. After we reorganized the seating layout for the subgroups, the personalities clicked and produced excellent work, so I decided to feature their successes in my *1988 Architectural Branch Annual Report*.

The fruit of my decision to form subgroups ripened quickly. Soon after the change, a project to remodel a large dining facility at the Naval Air Station in Alameda landed in our office, and we were prepared. The lieutenant commander above the Air Station's staff civil engineer came in person to express the project's goals.

"My captain wants something worthy of a design award," Lieutenant Commander Steimer said as we sat at the round table in front of my office.

Taken by surprise, I paused, and breathed deeply to consider the prospect of this unusual and welcome challenge. "Wonderful," I said.

The lieutenant commander described the existing dining operation, serving hundreds of sailors, three times a day, in the historic building he wanted upgraded. I paused and suggested, "What do you think about my staff coming up with three different designs?"

"That does sound interesting," the lieutenant commander responded, an edge of confusion in his educated voice; competitions in government were rare. "But," he emphasized, "we must have the project built on this captain's watch."

I assured him the project would be designed in a timely manner once he'd selected the winning design. We set a day

Dining facility, Naval Air Station, Alameda

for the three groups to visit the existing dining facility so they could listen to the suggestions and concerns of the dining facility manager and employees.

My staff immediately embraced the competition because it meant more design in their day. The ratio of design to project completion is always too low for architects, who love the design process—no

I explain the three designs for the
dining facility at NAS Alameda

matter where we work. All three groups were eager to prove themselves, and we outlined the rules together; for example, they wanted to be sure they didn't have to do other work during the concept development. I agreed to clear other responsibilities for two days so each team could devote itself to the initial design phase. One of the important and unusual aspects of this event was that the entire winning team would be assigned the project, rather than only one person—a real paradigm shift for PWC.

The groups produced three fantastic design solutions, and I proudly hung the presentation boards on the wall of our conference room so the lieutenant commander and his staff could select their favorite. I used this opportunity to take a photo of the customers looking over the boards. If everything worked out well, I wanted to submit an article to the *BayGram* about the competition, highlighting customer participation and quality design.

The designers remained anonymous at this stage, and I alone presented the three solutions. However, instead of making an immediate selection as I had envisioned, the lieutenant commander asked to take the boards out of the office to show his captain. A couple of days later, he reappeared.

"Wendy, I liked this one with the 1940s look and the booths, but the sailors picked this other one. My captain has also approved it." He pointed to the design that resembled a quiet, elegant restaurant with low solid dividers and a central entrance dividing the large space into two areas.

The lieutenant commander had gone to the dining facility, shown the boards to the users, and solicited their design preferences. I was impressed with his decision to let the sailors choose the design, and told him so. As I leaned the boards against my office partition, I couldn't help but feel relieved that it hadn't been left up to me to select the winner; all three solutions were well thought out and aesthetically pleasing, each with its own distinct character and appropriate atmosphere.

Within minutes of the lieutenant commander's departure, I called a meeting to announce the competition results. The groups were invested, were excited, and felt the suspense. The winning team had named itself the Montserrat Group (the other two groups were named the Annex Group and the Torpedoes). Moonyeen, an intern architect preparing for her license, was new to PWC, but that didn't make any difference; the Montserrat Group had put her in charge of the design. Everybody was a good sport about the event, and I was pleased that I had taken the risk of roughcasting the groups. Within a day, the staff civil engineer received the call that we were ready to begin work on the dining facility remodel.

My first rotation of executive training (November 1988) was with the PWC Planning Department, and this turned out to be pivotal. Not only because my temporary boss, John P., had graduated from the same Executive Management Development Program that I was now beginning, but also because when PWC's top managers scheduled a two-day site-level management planning session, John P. leaned on the organizer to let me fully participate; I had been denied attendance when I asked on my own. My major contribution to the session was to introduce and hold above water—at each attempt to dunk it—the goal of *valuing people* as one of the Command's Business Plan goals for fiscal year 1990.

Steve, a quality control supervisor at my level, was one of the supporters of this goal. After the two-day session, the business manager assigned Steve and me to co-chair the valuing people committee.

"I don't think the committee should be co-chaired," Steve quickly told the business manager as the three of us stood in the hall near his office.

"You and Wendy both seemed interested," rallied the business manager, visibly taken aback.

Tension appeared on both their faces. I watched and remained silent.

"I don't care who the chair is," Steve replied curtly. "It doesn't matter to me." He was a clean-cut fellow, not many inches taller than I, and relatively new to PWC.

"Okay, then, Wendy will be the chair and you will be vice chair," the business manager said firmly.

"Right," Steve chirped, turning and heading straight toward his office.

But apparently, Steve wasn't exactly happy with that answer, because he dropped out of the committee soon afterward. This was one of the few times when management acted on an apparent power grab, and I took full charge of the committee without Steve.

As chair, I requested that representatives from each department be assigned to our valuing people committee. I held each of our several meetings in a different building, always allowing a 15-minute period for anyone in the building to drop in; but not many came. We produced the *Quality of Work Life Plan: People*, to be included in the Corporate Improvement Plan. I made sure it was completed ahead of schedule, to be ready before the 1989 Commanding Officers' Conference, a world-wide meeting for Naval Facilities Engineering Command top officers, because I hoped our Captain Crane would take it with him to the conference in Hawaii.

On the home front, my neighbor Greg lived down the block in a light blue stucco house. One Sunday morning, as Greg was looking out his bay window, he saw me descending the steep block toward the neighborhood bakery (What's For Dessert?) and decided he needed a coffee, too. (He later said it was because I was wearing cute short shorts.)

When he entered the bakery, I spoke to him right away: "Hi, I remember you from our street tree-planting. How is your wife?"

"We broke up about six months ago." He sat down at my table. Greg's clean, straight hair hung just below his ears; his pearl gray eyes plunged into mine. "Divorce will be final soon."

I was surprised but relaxed.

The next day, sweet Jules was actually out in the yard, digging a hole for a fence-post foundation near the baby fig tree, when Greg—as tall as Jules but more reserved and with less of a suntan—arrived. I happened to look out the window when he bounced down the garden stairs, unannounced. I invited him into the living room.

Greg, who usually sees all, didn't even notice Jules. Standing beside me, only a few steps inside the front door, Greg pulled out the black-and-white photo of an alligator he'd just had enlarged from a trip to the Everglades. Admiring the photo, I was pleasantly dazzled by this turn of events—yet together enough to agree to go for a walk with Greg the next day.

By the end of the walk, I'd decided Greg was not for me. I don't remember why; maybe it was his shy, short sentences. But then he asked me to come over for a homemade dinner the next night, and I couldn't refuse that. Having a meal prepared by a man was such a special event, I had promised my single self never to refuse such an offer. The only other time I'd had such an invitation was from a Russian PhD economics student who'd made me a wonderful lunch with a grape and radish salad in a creamy dressing, laid out on a small tablecloth on the floor next to a dish of black olives and a delicious roasted chicken. We sat on cushions.

So, there I was, comfortably seated at the tiny table in Greg's kitchen next to the refrigerator. He set out all the fixings of an Indian dal dinner and dimmed the lights. Each topic that surfaced seemed to increasingly attract us to each other's voices and views, until my heart flipped, softly out of control. We ended the evening by kissing on his indigo tie-dyed futon couch, and I floated home that night—the first negative impressions had withered.

Greg worked at home, as a computer games program design developer. His hobbies included not only photography, but also growing vegetables and building furniture—when he was not procrastinating (we called it the "BIG P"). Maybe that was why he and his wife finally split up. He said she just left because of too much TV watching.

Much later, Greg told me he was depressed at times, but when I was around, his depressions were gradual, not debilitating enough for me to recognize the symptoms until too late. Greg's bushy dark eyebrows accented his light-colored eyes. He had a distinctive distaste for men's business attire and wore long-sleeved, colorful T-shirts, silk-screened with endangered animals or logos from the Chicago Art Institute.

The next day, I called Jules and asked him to take a walk with me after work.

"Jules, I met a new guy," I said, holding his hand as we strolled. We both knew that Jules wasn't the man for me. In fact, I actually felt Jules wanted me to find someone else; he wanted to see me happy in a relationship.

"Really?" Jules asked, looking attentively down at me with that gorgeous wide smile. "Who is he?"

"His name is Greg. He lives down the block. Remember that guy you saw come into the garden?"

"Oh yes, how old is he?" I could tell Jules was expecting Greg would be more my age.

"He is 33," I said, enjoying the warm March night, the scent of the flowering vines as we passed by, and the fresh swirl of new romantic feelings. I was 46.

"Wow, he is younger than me," spouted Jules, who was 37. "I'm happy for you, Wendy." He leaned toward me and gave me a gentle peck. "I would like to meet him."

"Thanks, Jules." I squeezed his hand, smiling at his cheerful acceptance. Even then, I believed Jules was relieved he'd no longer have to carry the responsibility that relationships need to thrive.

But Greg never wanted to meet Jules, so I had coffee with Jules by myself a few times.

Within two weeks after meeting and falling for the new boyfriend, I flew to Denver for a required Federal Executive Development Seminar. I called Greg every evening about sunset and even wrote him love letters from Denver, and he wrote back. The training was excellent; I particularly liked the part on ethics because the lecture showed how gray political issues could be. The example given in the lecture was smoking, which was bad for your health but good for the economy of tobacco farmers. We watched an old film documenting how politicians involved in this issue had allowed journalists to follow their discussions as they prepared legislation. The details have faded, but I remember that my tendency toward absolutism was shaken because the film covered so many different points of view.

About the fourth day, Susan—our fair-haired instructor who answered most questions with "Why not?" in keeping with her philosophy to try new things—gave us the Myers-Briggs test. I had never heard of this personality test before, but others in our class were already using it in their agencies to improve communication. I learned that I was an ENTJ personality type on the Myers-Briggs scale: "E" for extrovert, "N" for intuition, "T" for thinking, and "J" for judgment. According to the handout, "ENTJs are logical, organized, structured, objective, and decisive about what they view as conceptually valid." Potential pitfalls included, "May appear impatient and domineering, may ignore and suppress their own feelings." Sounded like me, all right. ENTJ-type people are called *Field Marshals.* Meaning that I was part of the 5 percent of the population who liked to rally the troops; meaning also that since I was female, it would be difficult for me to find a life partner—scary news, especially when I had just found Greg.

A color photo of my Federal Executive Class shows that racial and gender diversity was still merely tokenism, which in 1989 was considered any number below 15 percent. (By 2007 that number was much higher in some corners of the world: I heard that Norway enacted a law requiring equal representation of men and women in government—and in Chile, the new female president has quietly set up her cabinet with equal numbers of women and men.) My class members—3 females (one black, two white), 2 black males, and 31 white males—came from a wide range of federal agencies, including the Department of Labor, Army Material Command, Office of Management and Budget, Food and Drug Administration, and Soils Conservation Service. It was here that I began hearing about the ingrained personalities of government agency cultures. Compared with what I had heard about other agencies, the Naval Facilities Engineering Command seemed enlightened. "We don't get much training at GSA [the General Services Administration]," said one fellow. "Hard to be creative," admitted someone from the Department of Commerce.

Meanwhile, in the spring of 1989, back at PWC, our department head, Joe, retired. My fine boss Bert—subordinate to Joe—suddenly transferred into the utilities department, rather than being promoted to Joe's position. Word came that John P., the PWC planning department head, would move to our building to head the engineering and planning departments. This was fine with me, as John P. had given me exceptional support during my executive training. I liked John P., who seemed consistently calm at work. His arrival was like the canary in the coal mine, an indicator of the new trend of federal organizational downsizing; but I didn't recognize the canary's song until much later.

The Friction of Change

1989 to 1990: San Francisco, Gasquet, and Oakland

Not everything was smooth. Working in a *Titanic*-sized organization required nimbleness, hip boots, and a navy can-do attitude. In spite of my branch's successful record of accomplishment, the surface of our work pond radiated ripples from certain swamplike activities.

Employees were bogged down in the mangrove thickets of procedures, the mugginess of scheduling, and the stickiness of time pressures. As one employee wrote in his departure letter, "This place wears you down." Conflicting direction, lack of resources, and wasteful procedures were on his mind. He rightly pointed out the disconnect between upper management and workers' concerns. For the most part, I was able to negotiate the countercurrents when the military wielded its power with the autocratic croaking that caused employees unwittingly to jump. I like to imagine that my managerial style demonstrated a blend of positional authority, feminist professionalism, and personal power. But after ten years of taking risks and successfully navigating my way across what author Marilyn Loden (*Feminine Leadership,* 1985) might have called the navy's masculine work pond, I still often waded through unexpected muck.

I'll never forget the time when Lee—a program analyst who had been promoted from typing pool supervisor after the typing pool was dissolved—handed out reports in a top management meeting indicating that my staff was working negative hours. Fortunately, upper management understood the impossibility of the accusations and ignored them. I was fairly sure that Lee had accurately transferred the hours from everybody's timecards, but his computer program had serious holes in it. I learned then that people who feel powerless could become gate closers for those on the move. Lee clearly disliked my successes and openly resented my involvement in the Executive Development Management Program (EMDP). He annoyed many of us, but in the pond of PWC, he was like a water snake that could only be ignored. Upper management continued to let his inaccuracies slide.

Otherwise, whenever I found myself approaching muddy puddles, I facilitated, negotiated, and designed ways to go around, above, or below them. Daily, I sought to convince management of the consequences of its actions: inefficient employee behavior resulting from the organization's uneven awarding of rewards and the tendency to avoid correcting misconduct. At the same time, when employees were not performing, I confronted them. And sometimes they confronted me.

Sharon, an attractive, 30-something filing clerk from downstairs, didn't like one of my notes requesting a change in routing. She marched into my office, hands on her full hips. "Now, I'm going to tell you woman to woman," she announced. I had introduced myself to Sharon months before, and we'd had a few friendly encounters, so she knew me.

"Okay," I responded, standing quickly and feeling tickled that she'd changed our relationship to "woman to woman" from "filing clerk to architectural branch head."

"I need to know what the system is before I can route the folder correctly," she said, sincerely bothered.

"I agree, Sharon, and I appreciate your coming and talking to me directly. I like the way you are getting this straight," I answered calmly. "Now I know what you need." I put my white hand out to her black one. "I should have consulted you first."

She shook my hand with vigor, pivoted, and headed downstairs.

Curiosity about the working conditions in other agencies fired my search to find a non-Department of Defense (DOD) agency for a short management residency. This was not the norm for EMDP cadres in executive rotation; most stayed within the navy. I discovered Diane C., a senior executive at the Office of the Secretary of the Treasury, in an article titled, "Managing for Excellence in the Federal Government." Without introduction, I wrote to her, and she invited me to be a resident. Diane C. assigned me to a planning unit at the Treasury, but she didn't mentor me, which I had hoped for. Nevertheless, it was a great experience to be in a nonmilitary government culture working on long-range planning and research.

The Treasury workforce, even at high levels, was more than 30 percent female. Gender friction diminished dramatically—it was like being in a lake without currents to swim against. When my friend Paul moved from WestDiv to the Environmental Protection Agency in Oakland, he, too, noticed that women and nonwhite men held many of the high-level positions—even the top slot. These agencies appeared to value diversity at the top in a way I hadn't experienced, but I was just an observer wishing discrimination would melt away around me. I don't really know how their work cultures operated in the long term.

Meanwhile, I concentrated on my executive training. It turned out that the trickiest requirement I faced was to find, be accepted to, and attend a two-week university executive management session. Fortunately, I found the March 1990 session at the Jesse H. Jones Graduate School of Administration, Rice University, in Houston, Texas. However, Commander Tyler, who had been steadfastly committed to my success, no longer worked at PWC, and the new boss above my direct supervisor said they wouldn't pay for the executive management training. Stunned, I argued passionately that the training was mandatory and that I had searched for closer executive sessions without success. I also offered to take two weeks of my own vacation time to go. That sacrifice must have helped because, at the last minute, the top brass agreed to pay for travel and tuition.

My first day at Rice, a hostile, competitive atmosphere permeated the class of 29 men and me; the only other woman in the class had decided to drop the session after the first morning. Most of the men were local oil executives who spent the two-week seminar strutting their vice-president titles, like male elephant seals vying for their spot in the sun as they tried to determine who outranked whom. Now that I've seen the film *There Will Be Blood*, about the early oil days in Texas, I understand the legacy behind my classmates' distaste when I announced that I didn't work for a profit. They could not begin to imagine what planet I'd landed from. Money was their only bottom line. These executives absolutely did not understand my values of job satisfaction, quality architecture, common good, fairness, and quality in one's work life.

For the last assignment, the class randomly divided into six groups by going around the room and numbering off: 1, 2, 3 ... 6. In my group, the elephant seals made gestures that made me think they felt encumbered by my presence. Within minutes, one short seal with red suspenders suggested that I be the group's leader, but when he realized I wouldn't be his surrogate, he bullied me off the team by dismissing my comments and dominating the conversation—cleverly jockeying and posturing to get me out of his way. Traumatized by rejection, I circled the building several times to collect my wits and dry my tears.

After I painfully recounted the details to the director, Mr. Kohoe, he suggested I do the assignment by myself and asked me to be the first presenter on the final day of class. This I did. However, when I gave my presentation about the importance of respecting individuality and using it to gain cooperation and motivation within the organization, the other program attendees seemed confused. Even so, Mr. Kehoe kicked off a polite applause. The next year, he sent me a photo of the class with a kind note: "We have four women in this year's class, what happened to you last year won't happen again."

About this time, PWC received an unusual request for the design of a new Family Housing Office to be located on the Naval Air Station

Alameda, serving the entire San Francisco Bay Area and replacing the rundown temporary office on the Oakland Army Base. WestDiv, the designated design office for all new buildings, had reported that it could not meet the deadline for the year's construction funding cycle, so PWC took on the housing officer's anxious request. My big boss, the design director, John P., assigned me to make it happen. Connie, a diminutive

New Housing Office designed by PWC
(my staff to right)

and soft-mannered architect in my department, cheerfully designed the new building, and Bob drew the architectural construction drawings by hand since we still didn't have reliable computer drafting equipment. I made sure the architectural design team, landscape architect, and engineers attended the building's festive ribbon-cutting ceremony. We approached the new Family Housing Office on a wide sidewalk covered by a trellis where false grape and sweet honeysuckle vines would soon bloom. Housing Office staff carried refreshments to the central conference room, designed with a ceiling several feet higher than the adjacent rooms to let in daylight through the clear story. We toured the circular corridor with beaming pride. A week later, Commander Bill Lewis wrote me a note:

> I just had the opportunity to visit our new Bay Area Family Housing Office. It is a great facility that will serve as the focal point for the most important service we provide the Fleet—family housing. It's hard to imagine that you and your team designed this facility in only fifty-four days—it is comparable and even better than designs from the best A/E firms.

My staff genuinely appreciated this ultimate compliment.

I had been seeing my neighbor, Greg, for more than a year. He usually considered thinking about what could happen the next day, week, or month a strange and unreachable activity. Yet he surprised me by making reservations at inns along Oregon's Rogue River to celebrate my 48th birthday in July. Wanting to get an early start, we got up at dawn and made our way to the trailhead's discreet low brown sign: *Rogue River Trail.*

"Kind of intimidating," said Greg, veering away from the grazing cows at the trail's edges. Photo-perfect red apples dangled from gnarled limbs.

"Picturesque start," I responded, but I kept my eyes to the ground, watching for cow pies.

Once we were among the conifers, the pasture fragrances faded. I smiled, and Greg looked happy, too. Our eyes adjusted to nature's greening, browning, and blending. A film of reddish dust covered our hiking boots as we ambled down the dry path paralleling the river below.

"This is fantastic!" Greg said, and I agreed, stopping for gulps from a shared canteen.

The heat pounded in despite the sylvan shading. I breathed fully, the forest scent soothing my urban lungs. "One of my architects wrote a long letter when he quit this week," I said, untying the blue bandanna that I wet often to cool my neck.

"About you?" Greg asked the question without looking back over his shoulder.

"About how the office wears one down—the conflicting direction, the lack of resources, and the wasteful procedures, mostly caused by Lee, nicknamed the Water Snake. I have to agree with his concerns."

Greg nodded. His camera hung ready, and perspiration spotted his hat and his long-sleeved T-shirt. At a dip in the trail, I stripped to my bathing suit and slipped into streaming coolness.

"Maybe I need a new job?" I said, quickly out of the water and back on the path, feeling refreshed.

Greg surveyed the horizon, as was his habit. "Maybe." (This was one of his keystone words.)

The trees thickened. We banged a stick against a tin plate when we thought of it, but smelled no bears nor saw any humans. The pine needles cushioned our slow rhythm. I scanned the sky. "Not much wildlife, not even birds' songs."

"Too hot," agreed Greg, clearly disappointed.

"Soon I will be certified for a top management position, but the navy is downsizing."

"Would you leave government?"

I wasn't sure of my answer and was surprised that Greg was staying on topic. Although I didn't expect him to say anything about how my changes might impact him, I was still thinking about it. Greg's hands-off decision-making style usually kept our discussions short. He treated my issues as mine; I felt he didn't want to be held accountable for them and didn't want to hold me back. In these moments, our relationship resembled two advancing bicycles rather than a couple dancing.

The bushes rustled as if a deer had jumped, but we couldn't see anything. We sighed, and Greg stepped back to let me walk in front for a while, a move I appreciated. After six forest hours, we came upon an A-frame house with a real horse tied to an old tree stump—the first inn.

No other guests arrived. Two fellows in shorts cooked us a special down-home dinner, served at dusk with cake and candlelight. Alone in the empty dining room but very much together, we watched the Rogue's current flowing west into the blushing gold sunset.

"Wow! Champagne. They *are* prepared," I said, caressing Greg's arm.

"I hauled it in my backpack." He looked at me for appreciation and got it. Greg had gone out of his way to fill this day with surprise, pleasure, and fun—and expected the same for his birthday.

Because of our lusty infatuation with the wild and scenic Northwest, we accepted an invitation from my architect friend Nan, who lived in San Francisco but had lived with a friend for six years in a little place called Gasquet. Since her friend was visiting her in San Francisco for the summer, she suggested we stay in his empty cabin on the Smith River.

After two hours of driving and wowing at sculptural sea stacks, we left the Oregon coast to wind up the Smith River Canyon, home of the only non-dammed river in California, rated as one of the pristine rivers of the world and designated "wild and scenic" by Congress.

"I think I am going to see what other federal jobs are out there," I said.

"Why not?" Greg replied and sank back into the silence of driving.

The bluish water splashed and whitened against the sharp granite boulders of the riverbed. I breathed easy, the scenic magic of this lively setting relaxing me to an unusual level of openness. At the green road sign—"Gasquet, Population 489"—we turned left from Highway 199, and within minutes, the van rolled into the empty cabin's driveway.

From the cabin's deck, we could smell the riparian fragrance of ferns, orchids, wild grasses, yellow wildflowers, and columbines drifting up the rugged riverbank. A pool in the torrent dominated our view and beckoned us down the one-person-wide path, shouldered with high vegetation. Hand over foot, holding point to holding point, we climbed down boulders to flatter rocks where we could dangle our feet in wet splendor. Upstream, the bubbling river spit and sparked over the stones with giggling sounds, while the still water below our feet magnified the finger-long fish twitting above a mosaic of pebbles. Greg went for his camera; I pushed into the chattering current. Work issues swirled away in the eddy.

After lunch, I glided my hand around Greg's arm (too hot to hold hands) as we crossed the cabin's front wild grass, browned by heat. No sidewalks here; instead, tree needles formed a textured carpet beneath our sandals. Cars were few on the paved one-lane road. Cedars, pines, and firs rooted along the edge, reminding me of animals drinking from a stream. We walked down the middle of the road (not our figurative political position). This was country—the way San Francisco was city.

The wall of trees jogged for three white cottages set back from the lane. A small sign hung from one of the porch roofs: "The Gasquet Getaway, Since 1935." We paralleled the river, but dense vegetation, including poison oak vines we knew to avoid, blocked views of it. Mellowed with the romance of this simple place dominated by self-seeded tall trees, we ambled past a couple of tiny houses next to several undeveloped wooded lots.

For sale in Gasquet

"Look," I whispered, "For Sale." The real estate sign leaned in the front of an overgrown lot inhabited by unpretentious fruit trees. We flattened the drying tall grass, not noticing the driveway we had passed. My eyes steadied on the tin-roofed, unpainted building.

"It's falling down," Greg remarked.

"Abandoned and neglected for a long time," I guessed, smelling musty wood and mildew and mentally analyzing what could be saved.

"I like how it is just across the lane from the river," Greg said.

Even without his camera, nature was Greg's enchantment, preserve, and sanctuary.

"Let's look at the back side."

Greg and I had been together ample time, according to my instinct, to shift a gear up on our relationship—but not by having children or getting married. "What do you think about having a place together?" I asked nonchalantly as we reached the plateau above and behind the first floor of the boarded-up, two-story shack.

"But this is so far to drive," Greg countered, following me up the short rise of the bank.

"It is, but areas close to San Francisco are being invaded by suburban sprawl." I had looked around in Sonoma County on and off for years.

Later that evening, we had the neighbor of Nan's friend over for dinner. As I set a plate of sliced tomatoes topped with fresh basil confetti onto the table for a meal, we learned she was a real estate agent. "We were just looking at the property down the lane," I said.

"The owners are friends of mine."

Greg refilled our wine glasses. "I see," he said. "How much are they asking?"

The Smith River in Gasquet

Both Greg and I sat up much straighter when we heard the reachable price. She talked about her job. Greg ate. My nose lingered at the rim above my wine, contemplating the red bouquet.

Completely seduced by the idea of summer rural living, I drove to the county seat, about 20 miles down the canyon, to research zoning and get the parcel map of the property. Five days later, before leaving Gasquet, we made an offer on the one-acre lot in California's northernmost coastal county—Del Norte.

Chanette had returned to France to continue her studies in filmmaking at the Sorbonne. Although she didn't talk about her studies much, I wasn't surprised at her departure, since she didn't seem to be putting down any roots here. I was sad to see her go but felt that continuing her education was positive and natural.

When I returned to work, my boss John P.—just one year into his new position—presented a dramatic organizational change. He envisioned linking our services to geographical zones and customers rather than to branches and engineering disciplines. His reasoning, which I favored, was to have the same designers serve the same customers and to have an entire design team of engineers and architects under one supervisor. However, the employees were horrified by the idea of changing a system they were comfortable with (all architects together, electrical engineers together, etc.). It was as if we were asking alligators to ride across town on bicycles!

John P. requested input from the supervisors. My approach emphasized decision-making transparency. I proposed a series of group dialogues to reduce the friction of change for the employees and the supervisors; John P. gave me three months.

Within two days, I posted Dialogue #1, announcing two optional meetings: a morning meeting for the engineers and an afternoon meeting for the planners. John P. asked a somewhat passive male supervisory planner to be part of what I called the "Dialogue Committee." I think John P. wanted to shield me from any resistance I might get by acting alone, and the planning supervisor just went along with me, not saying much. Both meetings were packed.

"Why will the zone concept be better for the customers?" challenged one senior engineer.

"How will people be assigned to zones?"

The questions flowed. I noted all 20 or so in my second posting, Dialogue #2, and summarized the main concerns. A few days later, I posted my detailed diagram of the new organization, with three engineering circles and one planning circle. The following week, John P. addressed the questions about motive and reaffirmed his commitment to the reorganization. However, the question of exactly who was going to fill which slots was still undecided.

One by one, all the supervisors were called into John P's office. The six engineering supervisors were grouped into three zones based on seniority, and I was one of the top three. An obvious suggestion was to use performance evaluations and longevity to select which employees would work with which supervisors. However, I had determined from the dialogue sessions that "personal preference" was the overriding priority for both supervisors and employees. So with the help of Ben, a math whiz on my staff (who later became a cartographer), I devised a mathematical model for supervisors to rank their choice of employees and employees to rank their choice of supervisor. Where the highest score of supervisor and employee matched, they were automatically so assigned. The mathematical model gave equal value to employee and supervisor choice.

I posted Dialogue #3 to propose what I called a "50/50 Preference System." It was accepted unanimously.

Dialogue #4 listed the events to follow. A September memo announced the opportunity for employees to hear each supervisor's pitch about how they supervised. This would help employees to determine their preference. Everyone returned his or her preference questionnaire in a sealed envelope.

When I got home from work that day, Greg phoned, "I received the final sale papers for the cabin." Excited and amorous, we dined out, within walking distance, to celebrate our together spot in the forest—the new centerpiece of our relationship.

Dialogue #5 posted the preference results, and John P. finalized the realignment. I calculated that 75 percent of the 105 employees got their first preference. About 25 people were less happy, but 15 accepted the situation. Of the 10 very unhappy people, half began looking for another job and the other half appealed to John P. I felt good that such a high percentage (90 percent) were ready to pedal into their new place on the organizational diagram; when the restructuring was first announced, 95 percent had been opposed to it. My title went from Architectural Branch head to engineering director. I had a full staff, including a secretary, technical quality assistant, and landscape architect, along with nine architects and four engineers (civil, structural, mechanical, and electrical).

And yet, in December, organizational anxiety set in when John P. accepted a job in Washington DC. He had been a great boss, especially because whenever he asked an employee to perform an assignment, he knew exactly what the job required and cleared the way for success—as he had for me in the case of the Family Housing Office and the reorganization. This was unlike other bosses, who often gave their employees assignment after assignment with the expectation that they'd automatically absorb the increased workload into their schedules—as if they had infinite capacity, rather than just eight hours a day! (Overtime was discouraged.)

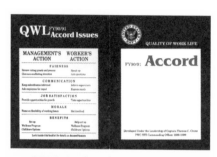

PWC *Quality of Work Life Accord*

As part of my EMDP training, and with input from my in-house "people" committee, I designed and had published the *Quality of Work Life Accord*, a blue-and-gold booklet that fit into a PWC information packet and was distributed to all PWC departments. The accord elements included suggestions about fairness, communication, job satisfaction, morale, and benefits. I was stunned (and thrilled) when the executive officer and top managers agreed to include 90 percent of our committee's suggestions. Fifty percent would have been great; we had been prepared to settle for 30 percent! (One should always aim high.) The biggest change instituted was to allow flexible work hours for PWC employees; I got the most credit and thanks for that item. Our commanding officer, Captain Crane, was an amazing advocate for the *Quality of Work Life Accord*; he even held it up (fresh off the press) in front of hundreds of people at his farewell ceremony. Surprised and vindicated, I thought, "This is good management and I am part of it." I'm sure Captain Crane took it forward because, soon after, NavFac Headquarters added *People* to their business plan, with the stated intent of improving quality of work life for all 22,000 employees worldwide.

A Horizontal Direction

Spring 1991: San Francsico

My job satisfaction crested just before the lieutenant commander replaced John P., my greatest boss. In the federal civil service ladder, the rank of lieutenant commander is equivalent to a GS-13, so the department head position was losing clout—one notch down from the GS-14 grade held by the engineering department head for as long as I'd been there. This meant that just when, as a recent graduate of the Executive Management Development Program, I was qualified to hold a GS-14 position, one less civilian high-level position was available. Was the crown of my head nearing my feared glass ceiling?

On the other hand, the top brass decided that the engineering department should move to the Oakland Army Base, where the officers could keep a closer eye on our operations. We rejoiced at the idea of moving the five miles outside the Navy Supply Center security gate, mainly because the offices had windows and the grounds were landscaped with picnic tables.

Since my staff was so busy with projects, I managed the entire move. Along with deciding where people would sit, I directed all the repairs and changes, including new electrical outlets, some bathroom alterations, and an added touch of the exotic with two colors of paint cutting our office doors into two triangles.

Once we were installed in our new day-lit location, my staff hosted a festive open house at coffee-break time—complete with balloons and refreshments—right under management's noses. We sent invitations to our customers, colleagues, and top managers, as well as to the construction workers who had helped with the renovation. My employees were jovial about their new offices but not at all happy with the talk of base closings and continued downsizing. As for me, I was increasingly seeing the possibility of my upward climb becoming unlikely—even farfetched.

Greg and I relished our togetherness, but we each lived in our own house, only a half block apart. On Sundays, we'd cook a fancy new recipe together or go out to eat; during the other six days, we divided the cooking duties between us; each one cooked three consecutive dinners. All possessions stayed in our respective homes, except for my tools, which migrated to his basement workshop because he had more room there and because we often repaired things at his house.

As we were cooking Jerusalem artichokes one Sunday, I said, thinking aloud, "There must be some federal agencies in San Francisco. I'd like to experience the city—including public transit."

"Do you mean you would change jobs without a promotion?" Greg asked.

"Having an interesting place to work is part of the package," I responded, feeling confident I could handle whatever came my way.

Greg took the finely chopped garlic and threw it in the pot. "San Francisco is closer too," he said. "What about green onions?"

"I love our cooking sessions," I gushed, and stood up for a much-needed hug, taking all work concerns off the table, for the moment.

No high-level management positions in San Francisco were being advertised, so I applied for a position at my existing level—GS-13—even though in the navy I was now qualified for a GS-14/15. The position was supervisory engineer in the engineering department of the US Forest Service in downtown San Francisco.

At PWC, projects were moving well. The Naval Air Station of Alameda hired us to select the furnishings for their soon-to-be-completed dining facility. Public works designers and managers, both civilian and military, were invited to the splashy opening, which boasted an ice sculpture and all the trimmings of a navy celebration. Everyone was so pleased with the renovation results that I decided to enter the dining facility into the annual Naval Facilities Engineering Command Design Competition, in the "remodeled projects" category. Although I had never entered the competition before, I requested and received special authority to have the base photographer take professional photos of two projects—the dining facility and the Oakland Supply Center's captain's office, which was also recently completed by one of my teams with Kriss at the helm.

Only two months later, out of all the submittals from around the (NavFac) world, the dining facility was selected as Best Remodel of the Year. The award arrived at an ironic moment, because we were now a design award–winning center in a declining market. This was the first time the PWC had won a design award; usually A/E firms working for the field divisions were the recipients. The PWC military brass was amazed and reawakened to the fine talent they had at the center. The head of design at NavFac headquarters called our PWC commanding officer to say that NavFac designers were surprised and extremely proud when they opened the envelope and found that the designers were the in-house staff of the SF PWC. I was elated for my staff, and pleased that the designers would now have professional photos of their work for their portfolios.

I could have been selected to fill my lieutenant commander boss's position when he transferred to another position; however, a more senior (and male) EMDP graduate, an architect I knew from my years at WestDiv, was handed the job. I was relieved when the Forest Service offered me a position as the supervisory engineer in charge of planning the Engineering Out-Year Funding Program, yet I tensed slightly at how quickly I had to report for work—in two weeks.

When I announced my departure to the commanding officer, he was visibly taken aback, "Why, just a week ago you brought us a design award, and now you are leaving?"

I didn't say much more than "Yes," but I was thinking, "Hey, I'm not going down with this ship." Since Congress had passed the 1990 Base Closure Act, it seemed obvious to us at PWC that our services would not be in great demand.

Greg and I began to visit our country property in the hamlet of Gasquet. Nestled in the Six Rivers National Forest, it was an eight-hour drive north to what would become our cherished summerhouse.

The long-neglected structure stood in the center of an acre lot. On one winter trip, I measured the building carefully. Generally, I wanted to retain as much as possible of the rustic character, historic spirit, and

Wendy measuring summerhouse

original materials of the structure, inside and out. However, the house was not well attached to the earth, so my design ideas included lifting the house two feet and replacing the river stones it was balanced on with a two-foot-high concrete block foundation. The winter channel that went around the house—a dirt moat about waist high—filled with water during heavy winter rains, dictating that the entrance porch be eight feet wide, a good width for a table and chairs and with space to circulate. I have always thought that oversized decks create an emptiness that people don't connect with. We used a few planks in two locations to get over the channel; building real bridges is still on the to-do-list.

Transformation by design is gloriously engaging. It is definitely one of the most alluring attractions to the architectural profession.

For my sixtieth birthday in 2001, I visited Finland, homeland of my maternal grandmother, and discovered the roots of my drive for a summer place. The publisher's description of the book *Finnish Summer Houses* (Jari Jetsonsen, Princeton Architectural Press, 2008) best describes my feelings about the Gasquet summerhouse:

> Summer is when Finland is at its spellbinding best. Emerging from a seven-month long winter, Finns head outdoors to savor the magical light of the all-too-brief Scandinavian summer. Cityscapes give way to pristine lakes, endless forests, and idyllic seaside vistas. The Finnish summer house offers a unique opportunity for their owners to relax, get back in touch with nature, and enjoy outdoor activities such as boating, swimming, and hiking. Not surprisingly, the architecture of the Finnish summer house occupies an almost mythic, even mystical, place in the hearts of their inhabitants as well as their architects. Indeed, many Finnish architects regard the design of their own summer residence or weekend studio as one of their most important works. For them, the summer house is not only a place to spend leisure time, but also a chance to study specific technical details and experiment with new spatial concepts.

Of course, summers in California are much longer than in Finland, but the pull of nature and love of summerhouses seems to be part of my core DNA.

Ranko, my delightful tenacious secretary, organized the best going-away party of my life at the Hong Kong East Ocean Seafood Restaurant in Berkeley. As was her style, she cajoled all the top brass to attend and even charmed my boyfriend to bring me. He wore the only sweater I had ever knit for him—no suit and tie for Greg!

When Ranko first applied for the job, I reviewed her application and was most interested in the fact that she translated Japanese film titles into English. Her boss had also given her raving recommendations. Once she arrived, I learned that the recommendations were not for her technical secretarial skills, as her English was uneven, but rather for her outstanding social skills. Ranko could smooth over any situation with her doggedly kind determination. Her habit of bringing in flowers from her garden rubbed off on others, and they began doing the same, while her grandmotherly gift for dealing with people balanced my tendency for efficient seriousness.

Somehow, my fight for survival in the work world had suffocated my teenage cheerfulness. Even in college, I'd been a playful prankster; perhaps my sense of humor had been quieted from my battles for inclusion. So much of my energy had been fixed on dodging discrimination that I just didn't have the wit or wherewithal to incorporate a joke, pun, or funny insult into my reaction to being pushed out of the way. Often I yearned for a bit of Southern belle diplomacy, the feminine finesse that some women from the South are able to swing out so cleverly. But no Southern belles appeared to teach me their skills.

Thanks in great part to Ranko, even shy loner Bob, who usually avoided parties, joined the celebration. And my first boss, Bert, came sporting a new moustache. Over a hundred people poured in, and many stood at the front of the room to tell stories of our working together. But for me, the most profound moment came when I astonished my staff by presenting each member with a framed photo, and stating one word that reminded me of him or her: Ranko the "facilitator," Alex the "reliable," Singh the "dependable," Connie the "delightful," and so on for everyone. We had developed mutual respect and affection, built a reputation, and accomplished excellent work together. The satisfaction of acknowledging being a part of a group effort is too often taken for granted. Is that because corporations focus on the dollar, or because our American culture is infatuated with celebrity?

Before leaving on my last day, I opened the log I'd kept during my six years at PWC and tallied up my statistics to see how well I'd done in terms of living the talk on diversity. Several times, I had stretched to persuade a Hispanic architect to move to San Francisco to work for me, or reached to transfer an African-American woman to my team from another department. Of the 50 people who worked on my staff over the six years I was at PWC, 32 were men (21 were nonwhite men) and 18 were women (half of them nonwhite). There was age diversity, too. I was proud of my record, although I had tried unsuccessfully to hire a wheelchair user and a person with hearing loss. Whenever people asked me about my experience working at PWC, what I bragged about most was the satisfaction of designing successful projects with such a diverse staff, where half the staff spoke English as their second language. Working well together productively is one of the true and universal pleasures of living; of this, I am sure.

After 18 years of reaching for vertical growth within the navy, the time had come to crab walk, in a horizontal direction, to the new organizational territory of the Forest Service, in San Francisco not far from the docks of the bay.

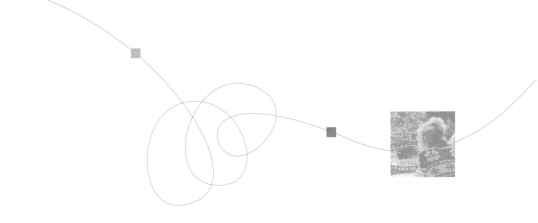

Getting to Know the Forests

1991 to 1992: San Francisco and Gasquet

Striding into the bright and busy San Francisco morning, I headed toward the administrative body of our public woods—the Forest Service. It was several blocks from the BART station on Sansome Street to my new offices. Moving with the momentum set by the other early workers, I reveled in the sophisticated urban detail of a lively city in action: the rich, inviting aroma of coffee cubbies, the colorful allure of flower stands, and the elegant marble lobbies of high-rises.

Located in the epicenter of San Francisco's Financial District, the agency's offices took up three floors of a 16-floor building—without a tree to tend. From a distance, the entrance to my building looked as if it were the box office to a popular movie theater; people lined up along the sidewalk, waiting to process their immigration papers at the offices on the building's ground floor. Cars stormed into the street from a nearby Embarcadero Freeway exit, filling the air with the noisy rush of traffic that forest dwellers dislike about cities but I missed at PWC.

In my position at the Forest Service, I oversaw the budget for future projects of the Pacific Southwest Regional Office (RO). The RO, also called Region Five, administered the 18 national forests and 21 centers in California (and a few offices in the Pacific Islands). During my tenure, engineering was the third largest department, after forestry and fire protection. My title—supervisor for engineering program development—would soon appear below my name on the unusually well-designed and friendly, coral-and-green Forest Service business card, printed on recycled paper.

But the real and legal reason I was asked to sign in as an employee on that first Monday in May—May 6, 1991, to be exact—was so that my female name could be included in the list of female employees working in the engineering department, published in compliance with Region Five's *Consent Decree Quarterly Report*.

After 18 years of fighting for and enjoying improved conditions for women in the Engineering Command of the navy, little did I fathom that my new agency was drowning in deep legal straits because of its discrimination against females and was dangerously close to a "contempt of court" ruling for decades of uncorrected discriminatory practices. In 1973, Ms. Bernardi, a Forest Service employee, had finally called foul. As one of the few professional women in the agency, she filed a class action lawsuit for gender inequality titled Civil Action No. C-73-1110 SC, *Bernardi v. Yeutter, Secretary of Agriculture*. (The Forest Service is part of the Department of Agriculture.) Twenty years later, the Forest Service was still unable to demonstrate sufficiently to the court that it had changed its ways as required by law.

A "consent decree" is a judicial decree that sanctions a voluntary agreement between parties in dispute. This was a new term for me, but I quickly learned it, since being female was the issue at hand. At first, I thought I would be treated well because of the urgent call for female inclusion. However, Forest Service managers had been ignoring, resisting, and deliberately avoiding the women's movement mantra for social, political, and work equity—so consistently and for so long that the court dictated the concrete requirements it thought would end sex discrimination. Although many of the requirements sounded as strong as steel—"hire and promote more women ... include women in leadership meetings"—from my vantage point, the court had greatly underestimated the Forest Service managers' bullying mind-set.

Patriarchy and loyalty truncated compliance and performance. Those who "grew up" in the Forest Service felt unable to criticize their organizational kin, ignoring poor performance as if it were a personality trait rather than a behavior. Worst of all, the reigning fathers demonstrated deep denial of the hostile work environment they'd created, while the consent decree shifted the balance of organizational components into a downward spiral of discontent. Women at the lower grades wanted to be promoted, and they were darned mad seeing women from outside the Forest Service hired into management positions, in spite of the fact that they didn't have the required professional education. The men were angry because they had followed a system of ticket-punching, and now women without tickets were taking the slots they wanted. We, the new professional women from outside the agency, were upset because the born-in-the-Forest-Service employees—including top managers—shunned us.

All this while the Forest Service's mission, vision, and guiding principles—"Caring for the Land and Serving People"—sounded worthy, convincing, and doable. Even the 13 guiding principles were compelling in print; I could hear the theme music, but I soon realized that few followed the beat.

Of the 135 engineers and 6 architects, only 20 were women. I was the most senior female in time and grade for all of Region Five (California) during my three years on the payroll. The eleventh *Consent Decree Quarterly Report* listed 212 employees at my level (GS-13 in Region Five), and only 37 of these were females. Of these women, 21 had been hired in the last two years. This was because the Forest Service hadn't raised enough qualified women; they had no choice but to hire women for high-level positions from other agencies.

The new director of minerals area management (GS-15) told me that her staff had removed her desk chair so that when she arrived to work on her first day, she would have nowhere to sit. And she wasn't the only female getting the negative we-don't-want-you-to-sit-here treatment. The Forest Service culture used behaviors I hadn't even heard of to discourage and upstage women: undermining positional authority, assigning women to special out-of-the-way projects, paying women *not* to come to work, and giving women unimportant jobs or no work at all—then claiming they were incompetent.

Set up over 100 years ago to protect our nation's wild, vast, and beautiful lands from poachers, the Forest Service owes its beginnings to the admirable intentions of Gifford Pinchot. In 1898, while studying forestry in France, Pinchot witnessed the destruction of France's forests and wanted to prevent the same thing from happening in the United States. Gifford Pinchot is often considered the Father of American Forestry, not just for his careful use and conservation ideas as the first chief forester of the US Forest Service, but also because under his leadership, the number of national forests increased from 32 in 1898 to 149 by 1910.

One afternoon, as I quietly walked through National Forest lands not far from Greg's and my new property, I found myself reflecting on the disparity between the organization I now worked for and the forest it was dedicated to caring for and preserving. The tall trees, soft forest floor, and wildlife revealed a seamless diversity of ecological health—something the Forest Service was sorely lacking. The ecology of the organization had been stressed out of balance—particularly during the last quarter of the twentieth century—by tradition, poor decisions, and misguided self-interest.

Nevertheless, there were pockets of attractiveness. The ranger station in Gasquet was only a mile from our cabin. Built in the 1930s during the active California Conservation Corps (CCC) years, it retained CCC's white cottage feel and was identified as *Forest Service* by the Christmas-tree-shaped cutout in its decorative shutters. According to history, a past district ranger's wife had been inspired by simple building plans, common even in the 1930s Sears catalogs; remarkably, she has been credited for influencing the arrangement and character of the picturesque compound. Sixty years later, the grounds are still inviting. The grouping of structures, integrated with sloping earth and stands of tan oaks, exudes a sense of welcome and deliberate planning. I had seen other ranger district offices on my forest visits, and this was definitely one of the more attractive. It remains one of the better "woman inspired, manmade" features in Gasquet.

My informal tour around the half-dozen roads in Gasquet was part of a casual visual survey I was making in search of local features to echo in the design of my summerhouse. Although most Gasquet residences demonstrated variety, they lacked regional character or architectural integrity. Even so, the extraordinary beauty of the natural setting overrode anything that may have been lacking in the settlement's manmade features. Pristine tributaries of the Smith River accented the forest's steep vegetation, and rare spots of endangered insect-eating *Darlingtonia* plants grew near a favorite swimming hole on the North Fork. Greg and I dunked into nature's wet splendor every day. Being in Gasquet helped to refill my contentment reservoir for when I went back to work on Sansome Street, where the heat of frustration made contentment evaporate quickly.

For the first six months of my new position, I was sent to all sorts of meetings, but always as an observer accompanying another staff member. According to the higher-ups, this was so I could "get to know the organization." At best, I was given trivial assignments. I thought this strange, but I utilized my abundance of extra time to investigate aspects of the organization that were different from what I'd experienced in the navy.

I made a deck of cards, the size of playing cards, to help me remember the 36 funding codes that engineering employees were supposed to use on our timecards. The card design was either blue or yellow, depending on the construction category: blue for reconstruction and yellow for new construction. Each card also showed funding code letters and included an image for the type of work: for example a bridge, road, or culvert.

Forest Service funding
code card

A few months later, when I was sent to spend a week (as all GS-13s were) at the Forest Service Headquarters in Washington DC, I showed my funding cards to the engineering director. Our conversation started out cordially. My deck was only for engineering tasks, but everybody had timecard codes. Quickly the director seemed to understand how complexity could jeopardize accuracy throughout the Forest Service. In spite of the engineering director's enthusiasm, my approach to timecard codes was not adopted by the agency; evidently, my deck was too radical a concept, much as a new scientific theory takes time to prove the existing theory invalid. Still, the engineering director and I had a gratifying talk. We touched on other issues, too, such as the lack of women in engineering. After our meeting, I became hopeful that my skills would be engaged rather than remain on stand-by.

The fellow who had hired me retired shortly after my arrival. It was during my eye-opening visit to the Washington office that I learned from my headquarters' counterpart some interesting news: my assistant (one of the angry, untrained, but fiercely loyal females who had grown up in the agency) and my male engineering colleague were quietly undermining my job—by keeping my arrival quiet. The two of them had simply continued doing my work that they'd been doing since my predecessor left almost a year before. This was unsettling. Yet, they had underestimated my ability and determination to find out what *my job* was supposed to be. After my return from Washington, I continued investigating by meeting with professionals in other departments. A kind Chinese-American fellow in the budget department, several floors below, explained that it was my job—not my subordinate's—to interface with their office.

Hostility glared from the faces of long-time employees, while newer employees smiled at one another in the wings of orientation meetings, hoping to find friendly co-workers. One positive result of the back-stage networking was the launching of a program we called "Friendly Brown Bag Lunches." I started the get-togethers with two other new managers: Molly, a pretty Hispanic fireball in the finance department, and Leslie, the assistant public affairs officer, who had awards on her wall from the Air Force. The weekly event was conceived as a forum, not as an exclusive group but as a lunch hour where any Forest Service employee could meet with others from the different floors and departments to socialize, as well as to soften the existing and unnatural hard-edged fragmentation. Conversation topics were planned, but the guiding principle was for dialogue rather than presentation. The atmosphere was casual; managers and workers voluntarily sat together democratically—there was no director, no star, and no audience. We called the group "Professional Friends."

Our stated goal was to promote working well together. So much was going on, but no one was talking about it. We invited senior and top managers, one at a time, and they came. During these lunches, better working relationships were seeding, nourishing, and flourishing. The lunches percolated with enthusiasm and grew in popularity. Our group was documented in the *Pacific Southwest Newslog* (September 1992:29), and we met for more than a year. However, some top managers became suspicious of our growing influence and finally undermined our existence. This went against the Forest Service Vision, "Employees work in a caring and nurturing environment where leadership is shared. All employees are respected, accepted, and appreciated for their unique and important contribution to the mission."

The Forest Service's mission and guiding principles stated concerns I believed in, like the sentence in the mission statement "Listening to people and responding to their diverse needs in making decisions." As an employee, I was trying to apply them, unlike many old-timers, who outwardly claimed them unreachable and unnecessary. Now that I was getting to know the forests, I was keen to learn how our RO administrative actions played out *on the ground*—a new term to me, meaning "at the scene of action," which in this case was the forests. But the more I found out, the more I became disillusioned. I met a few open-minded employees who genuinely wanted to follow the new direction. Some didn't want to authorize the clear-cutting of trees without concern for ecological ramifications—but did it anyway. I've since learned of the behavioral syndrome in which "good people" do "bad things" when entrenched in certain strongly structured situations, such as guards in prisons, doctors in Nazi Germany—and, I now add, some employees in the Forest Service.

In 1989, an open letter on the internal computer system (DG Network) to the head of the Forest Service, sent by a concerned timber planner on the Willamette National Forest, addressed the issue of preserving old-growth trees. The planner's concern was heard, and soon an unusual thing happened: The Forest Service Employees for Environmental Ethics (FSEEE) was formed. Several employees working in California forests were members, but I didn't personally know anyone in FSEEE. The group became a nonprofit corporation and eventually (in 2001) began publishing *Forest Magazine*, a bi-monthly full-color magazine with the mission of "conserving our natural heritage."

I tried getting our forest engineers to offically return roads to the forests, as required by law, but old practices were against it. "We might need the roads for a timber harvest," was the given rationale. I eventually came to understand from my engineering budget position that the Forest Service was funded according to the levels of income it generated by selling timber. Thus, it was against the Forest Service's financial interest to exchange its timber-industry sleeping partner for any of the available partners who actually cared for the long-term health of the land. Wildlife biologists, insect specialists, fisheries experts, hydrologists, cultural anthropologists, and ecologists sustained the forests' watersheds, where half the water in California lands as rain or snow, but these people didn't bring in direct dollars for their (or the Forest Service's) livelihood.

New framing added where old
needed replacement

I answer questions for workers
who lifted summerhouse

Sitting at the future kitchen nook

Kitchen table nook in use

Because trees attract and hold moisture, cutting trees actually lowers the amount of rainfall. Trees also keep the land cooler. I am hopeful that policies are changing as water becomes scarcer and the Earth warms. Who said, "There were forests, there was man, and then there were deserts"? If more Forest Service managers read *Forest Magazine*, perhaps things could get better.

Greg and I started working on our summerhouse in the summer of 1991 Once the drawings for the remodel were completed that spring, I'd made arrangements from San Francisco to have the building lifted so a block foundation could be installed below it. I'd also worked with the window manufacturer in Sacramento on the design of the windows and two glass doors so they'd be ready for us to haul to Gasquet on our drive north.

My first task was to obtain approval from the Del Norte County Community Development Office. Fortunately, the permit process went smoothly. Once the new foundation walls and piers were constructed, the house lifters returned from Eureka and lowered the house. When

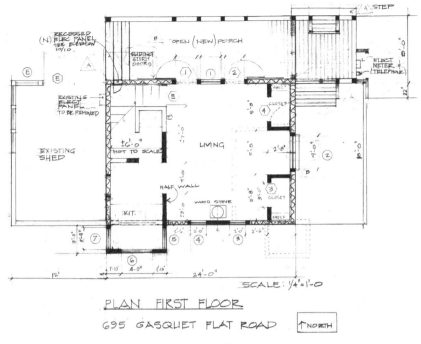

RECESSED (N) ELEC PANEL SEE ELEVATION 10/10.

RECESSED (N) ELEC PANEL SEE ELEVATION 10/10.

OPEN (NEW) PORCH

SLIDING STORM DOORS

STEP

ELECT METER & (TELEPHONE)

E   E

EXISTING ELECT PANEL TO BE REMOVED

EXISTING SHED

±6'-0" NOT TO SCALE

LIVING

CLOSET

HALF WALL

WOOD STOVE

KIT.

CLOSET

SHELF

SCALE: 1/4"=1'-0

PLAN FIRST FLOOR

695 GASQUET FLAT ROAD   ↑ NORTH

Summerhouse floor plan

one of my neighbors saw that I intended to renovate the fallen-down building, he donated a big drafting table he wasn't using. I set it up outside, and the table came in very handy for showing my design to workers and to Tada, my San Francisco carpenter, who came to Gasquet. Tada had pitched a tent under one of the walnut trees near the winter channel, while his young helper slept in his truck. Greg and I slept in Greg's Nissan van.

For 26 days, we walked down the lane to a friend's place until a toilet and sink were installed in the new bathroom. The claw-footed bathtub, now painted brick red, stood in the bedroom so I could enjoy taking my bath in the big space.

I didn't change the original footprint of the ground floor much. Once the foundation was in place and the structure lowered and attached, we began checking each piece of wood to determine if it would stay or be replaced; I wanted to save all the good wood, either by keeping it in place or for future use in a woodpile.

We made an outside kitchen in the makeshift horse corral, cooking our meals on a propane burner and eating them on an old ping-pong table.

This was wonderful because of the long days and warm temperatures. By the end of summer, the building was watertight for another winter.

It turns out that Gasquet and the surrounding area receive more rainfall than any other spot in California—more than 100 inches a year—but not during the summer. The wild and scenic Smith River provides most of Del Norte County with its drinking water. In winter, the high wild waters roar, while in summer, the river is very low and water conservation is essential. Any time we went swimming, we knew we were looking our water source right in the eye. Our drinking water came directly from the river; it was treated and piped straight to our house. Greg and I purposefully adapted to living with nature by conserving water in summer, accepting the black bears' eating our apples, and choosing not to let exotic, nonnative plants spread. At dusk, we'd often go to the river and observe the playfulness of river otters—indicators of a healthy river. We didn't want this forest to become a desert because of our overuse.

Each summer, we worked on another phase of our precious property. Tada often came from San Francisco with a helper. One summer we worked on the front porch; another summer we lifted the roof to add dormers.

"Tada, I want all the space I can get here; tell me what thickness you need for the roof." I pointed to my drawing of a second-floor sleeping nook over the kitchen alcove, one of Greg's best suggestions.

"Remember, Wendy," Tada counseled, "we need enough slope for the roof to drain."

"Yes, but inside I want headroom."

"Well," he said patiently, "I'll need two-by-fours here at the header."

"How about turning one two-by-four or both of them flat," I gently pressed. "Just at this area, so I get an inch more headroom at the door?" I reached my hand to the location of my concern.

"Okay," Tada smiled with friendly appreciation. There was a synergy and respect between us. Ultimately, my design got better because of his concerns, and his construction tightened because of my designer's eye. Tada envisioned my concepts and knew how to achieve my intent with elegance. He also knew how to read people—Tada knew when to say things without hurting my feelings.

The cabin became Greg's and my spoiled wooden offspring. We gave it our full energy and loved it with parental pride. Over the years, our diligent minding and rearranging resulted in an artful practical homestead, delighting and engaging us summer after summer.

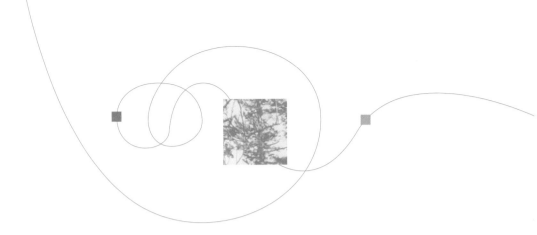

Forest Stewardship

1992 to 1994: San Francisco and Gasquet

Greg took great pleasure in using a scythe to cut the tall grass that was waiting for us each summer around our cabin. Gasquet's locals thought it strange, but we thought it appropriate, preferring the quiet of manual labor to the disruptive noise of power tools. We picked our own delicious grapes, and I patiently hand-weeded the numerous nonnative plants invading the property—English ivy, Scotch broom, and French broom—to protect the natives from being overrun.

Gasquet summerhouse
with tall grass

Countrified by our surroundings, we wanted to practice the stewardship we were learning from our readings and from our knowledgeable environmentalist friends.

Meanwhile, the deeper I moved into the Forest Service, the more I realized how quickly the organizational ecology was decaying—as quickly as a forest is ravished by insects when its trees are weakened by drought. One day, an urgent request came from the budget department

Greg and me with grapes

to reduce the engineering budget before two o'clock. Being the only senior staff member present, I analyzed the documents and took the entire amount out of one category in the geo-technical laboratory budget, thus ensuring that no *person* would be impacted. The next day, the longtime engineering director, a pulpy patriarch from Alturas, telephoned my boss, Tom, who passed the call on to me and stood by listening.

"Why did you do this on your own?" the engineering director demanded, so loud that even Tom could hear.

"I was the only one here," I confidently responded.

"Why didn't you call one of my assistants at home?"

"That never crossed my mind. I took responsibility. That's the way we would do it in the navy." I looked over to Tom for some direction, but his face was impassive.

"Well, you should have called someone," the director was decidedly upset.

"But how would I know?" I couldn't understand what his problem was.

"Everybody here just knows," he sputtered—and hung up.

Tom's face eased into an amused amiable expression as I looked at him wondering, *What do I do now?*

The following Monday morning—in front of all the engineering group leaders and assistant engineering directors—the engineering director announced, "Wendy made the best possible decision on the budget." And then he quickly changed the meeting subject.

I wasn't used to having my actions justified to a group. Why would he have made such an announcement? I later realized that, unlike me, the engineering director understood just how fast word traveled about such things; others would already know I'd made the call on my own. He wasn't complimenting me on my can-do action; on the contrary, he wanted to make sure it didn't happen again.

Rebuffs like this effectively clipped my joy for work.

Events in my personal life helped to dilute my professional discontentment. My daughter wrote from Paris that she and a new man friend would be leaving France to live in San Francisco; this sounded serious. I bought a big bouquet of blue irises for their room before picking them up at the airport. Chanette had met Pascal on a movie set where they were both working. They stayed with me for a month until they found their own apartment, within walking distance from me, one little hill away in Bernal Heights.

Having my happy adult daughter so close by brought me much joy. We attended artists' openings, made fine meals for each other, and enjoyed many conversations about the successes of both Chanette and her boyfriend—successes that included photo contracts for the cover of the *Guardian* newspaper and graphics in the debut issue of *Wired* magazine.

Day after day on Sansome Street, I continued searching for ways to participate while avoiding organizational malice. At Region Five's annual engineering workshop in Reno, I distributed my funding code decks to the architects and engineers from forests throughout California. I'd had the card decks reproduced by the printing office and then packed them in hand-sized plastic envelopes.

"Did you receive a monetary award for your funding cards?" asked a female forest engineer, intrigued after seeing how the cards could be organized by color or code.

"No," I answered, touched by the recognition from my co-worker, but again reminded that upper management seemed to hope I would soon shrivel up and be carried off by a gust of opportunity. The oppressive situation at work did irk me, but when the national in-house magazine, *Engineering Field Notes*, published my article about the funding cards, I felt validated.

Since the consent decree advocated promoting women, and since I was well qualified, I was optimistic that at some point I might have a fair chance to take on a leadership role. However, 15 months after my arrival, the regional office announced its intent to downsize. The news unleashed even more hostility, underhandedness, and sabotage from some of my co-workers, while others simply melted into the woodwork. "Hunkering down," they called it. I first heard this expression at one of the Friendly Brown Bag Lunches, and I soon heard it so often that I finally looked it up in the dictionary—*to squat: crouch*. Wow, this was a 180-degree rotation from the navy's can-do approach. I found myself bobbing about in the status quo, only attempting occasionally to move up in the organization.

At one point, I applied for an engineering assistant director position, and another time I attempted to move sideways into a district ranger position. As usual, both positions went to good Forest Service ticket-punching white males. Looking back, I think I must have been slightly stunned by my predicament. Idealistically, though, I held fast to my belief in the organization's ability to carry out its mission of caring for the land and serving people—if only the organization would heal. My abused state of mind can be compared to that of a battered wife, so invested in hoping for change that she blocks her need to move on.

Since then, I have come to accept that the Forest Service's DNA makes change unlikely. On March 20, 2009, 15 years after my difficult tenure, Stephen Losey reported "Morale Problems Plague Forest Service." In the article, published on FederalTimes.com, Losey stated that according to the Office of Personnel Management's 2008 Federal Human Capital Survey, job satisfaction in the Forest Service had decreased.

My suggestion would be to take the Forest Service out of the Department of Agriculture and put it with the National Park Service under the Department of the Interior. That would shift the tree-farming/lumber-harvesting focus to one of beautification, recreational use, and caring for the land. Perhaps the merger would raise the bar of stewardship and organizational integrity, bringing healthier land-use practices, along with increased satisfaction to employees and to the public.

I would have gladly considered taking a position with another agency, but the reality in the early 1990s was that most government agencies were trying to shrink—which only added to my quandary. While I tensed and cringed at what was going on around me, other top-level female managers were already showing signs of physical and emotional illnesses. My personal stress peaked when the engineering department director took steps to challenge my competence and fire me, a move I managed to dodge by a hair. After trying organizational channels, as I would have done in the navy, I finally made an appointment to see the psychologist contracted by the Forest Service.

That one visit was pivotal, as it confirmed my assessment: I wasn't the only woman suffering from the toxic anti-female dynamics. The psychologist (a woman) suggested that I relieve the stress with exercise. I hired a personal trainer to come to my house and teach me how to lift weights (I lift them to this day), probably saving me from the cancer, comas, and other grave health problems my female colleagues experienced. Tragically, one of my good female friends, a top manager, died quickly of stomach problems.

Finally, the organization was so infected that the top managers hired a consultant to eliminate the symptoms and pain. Ernie Long, from the US Office of Personnel Management, called his assignment the "Positive Work Environment Project" (August 24, 1992). I got to know him and tried to pass on my experience, but it took him time to believe what was going on, and the solutions were complicated and too radical for him to suggest.

My personal short-term solution was to use the agency like a university—a place where I could learn something. I got myself assigned to several committees that others in the engineering department did not want to serve on because they viewed the topic as too new, sure to fail, or not a good ticket-punch for advancement. By serving on these committees, I learned about forest ecology, land management, and strategic planning—information that has served me well to this day.

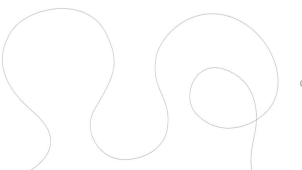

Chanette and Pascal marry
in San Francisco

Late in the summer of 1992, Greg and I attended Chanette's civil marriage service in the renovated and gilded San Francisco City Hall. My daughter looked gorgeous in a light-blue silk dress, her blonde hair pinned in an elegant upsweep. Pascal, her groom, covered his head with a bandanna, Spanish style (Pascal's father was Spanish and his mother was French). I surprised her with a bouquet of white freesias and golden bud roses. The only other witness was a friend of theirs, a professional photographer who snapped photos of the simple, quick ceremony. Chanette's few sweet tears evaporated before we reached an Italian restaurant close by.

The Organization of Women Architects (OWA) was gearing up to celebrate its twentieth anniversary in Tilden Park, in the hills above Berkeley. When asked to be on the program, I suggested that my topic be OWA strategic planning. I was disappointed with the cartoon scribbles I received after I'd asked the attendees to note their strategic planning ideas on white paper placemats I'd laid out on picnic tables before the meeting began. Clearly, the current membership had little interest in strategic planning for OWA.

Chanette and Pascal were hired to take the OWA anniversary photo. This was an exceptional moment for me, as my daughter had grown up knowing the group and had been in several of the previous OWA photos; now she was a professional behind the camera.

OWA 20-year celebration in Tilden Park
(I am standing at back left), October 17, 1993

After the photo session, I overheard one of the younger members of the OWA steering committee say that she felt her hands were
tied because longtime members were always overriding her ideas. Her
words evoked in me the mental image of a mother controlling an adult
child. After reflecting on her comment for several weeks, it occurred
to me that I didn't want to be one of those controlling OWA mothers,
so I decided to cut the umbilical cord attaching me to OWA's navel. It
wasn't easy for me to let go of this grown kid, this nurturing source, this
symbol of equality in architecture, but OWA was mature enough to be
on its own. Of course, I still had friends in the group, and I continued
to follow the organization's activities. Ten years later, when I rejoined
to participate in OWA's 30-year anniversary, I learned that some of the
other OWA founding mothers had interpreted my decision as aban-
doning the cause; in fact, I was acting from my conviction that the time
had come to recognize our grown child as her own person.

At the two-decade mark, well over half of the 150 OWA members
had served as steering committee members; some, including myself,
had served several times. As I write this now—with 35 years of hindsight—I can appreciate how brilliantly our original 1972–73 organizational design had built a culture of participation. Regrettably, for the
past 15 years, OWA general meetings have been held only every other

month and business discussed only once a year. A few members have held on to certain tasks, while the larger group has been left to coast on the strength of earlier days. Slowly, both newer and longtime members have begun to review the operations and by-laws because of signs of cronyism, loss of democratic opportunities, and poor administration. In private, I have mentioned the need for transparency to several steering committee members because the organizational drift has been causing uncertainty for too long.

Our original design of the organization did not include means for evolution or self-correction, other than the democratic method of voting on policy and spending. My initial introduction to organizational design came from conceptualizing and being active in OWA. The resulting synergy was fantastic, and working together in a collegial fashion—as we did for many years—was a profound and premium experience. In reviewing our newsletters, I am awed by how much we did, mostly due to the many active and creative members working together. It was a glorious experience because we were caring, energetic, and ambitious, and we democratically decided on our action. We rode a general wave of feminism, and we built the organization slowly enough to recognize, welcome, and quickly include new members in activities.

Even at the Forest Service, my love of architecture never wavered. In 1993, I was assigned to work with the landscape architect in the recreation department on a scenario for implementation of Nondiscrimination on the Basis of Disability in Forest Service facilities. Mike, the engineering assistant director for facilities, became my sixth boss in two-and-a-half years. Mike was about my age and a fine architect. I genuinely liked him. He was one of the few supervisors who recognized that competent female professionals in the Forest Service were being rejected out of hand. Mike assigned me meaningful work. He appreciated my ability to grasp abstract ideas and put them into concrete practical proposals.

On one elevator ride, I noticed a younger woman using a wheelchair. "Hi," I ventured. "I've seen you around. Where do you work?"

"In the legal section of the Immigration Department," she openly said, adroitly turning her chair to face the door.

From behind her I said, "Could I come see where you work?" I didn't want to lose her.

"Sure."

She rolled out onto the eighth floor, and I followed. Kathy was an attorney. Born without legs, she'd brought in the special equipment she needed for a private bathroom, and her boss had had it installed.

"One solution doesn't fit everybody," Kathy emphasized. She and her disabled husband knew well the limits of the manmade world, especially when they traveled.

It is mind-boggling how narrow our general criteria for design have been. After meeting Kathy, I noticed so many more people for whom walking was a challenge. Immediately I understood that more thought and a few design changes could make moving around so much easier for so many people. Too often, architects and building owners have let ignorance or economics drive decisions that could instead have been driven by concerns that were both socially inclusive and user-friendly. At the same time, what is good for people using crutches may not work for the limbless. Add sight and hearing to mobility needs, and you will understand why universal design has become a popular architectural specialty.

Chanette found a job working at a blueprint company downtown. Every week or two, we would meet for a picnic in Yerba Buena Park during her lunch break.

In November 1993, Chanette and Pascal made the long drive north for their first visit to the Gasquet summerhouse. They loved our place, and the four of us spent a heartwarming Thanksgiving together hiking in the mushroom-blooming forest.

In March 1994, I heard about a Forest Service plan to reduce the rolls by 2,000 people nationwide. Word soon came about incentives for retirement. To take the deal, I had to sign up by April 1, 1994, and be ready to leave in 30 days. The offer was on a first-come, first-served basis; you could just give personnel your name—and I did.

Greg and I had talked it over. I figured that between my retirement money and my rental income I could be financially independent. Several days later, the list of buyout takers circulated. Mike, my tall, sensitive boss, visited me in my office. "I had no idea you would take this," he said, lowering his slim bones into the stiff chair across from my desk.

"Mike, I am not happy here."

"But I can help you go where you want to go," he said half-heartedly.

"I like working with you, but the overall organization remains too hostile for me. There is life outside the Forest Service, and I don't have the years to wait for this organization to right itself."

April whizzed by, thanks to knowing the end was in sight. A week before my departure date, Mike took me to lunch at a deli on Washington Street. I suggested he also consider leaving the Forest Service, but he declined; perhaps the tumult in the Forest Service seemed mild compared with the Vietnam War, in which Mike had served with great chagrin.

After trying a variety of ways to fit in, I was leaving the troubled Forest Service the same way many women and people of color quit their architectural jobs "because of unfair treatment," according to author Kathryn H. Anthony in her book *Discrimination by Design* (University of Illinois Press, 2001). The gender issue for architects goes beyond our borders. In England and Canada, researchers have started to compare the number of female architecture students graduating with the numbers staying in the profession. The low retention rate was confirmed by a research paper (available online) titled "Why do women leave architecture?" by Ann de Graft-Johson, Sandra Manley, and Clara Greed, from the University of the West of England in Bristol (funded by the Royal Institute of British Architects and University of the West of England, May 2003). Eva Matsuzaki and Patricia Gibb identified concerns for retention in their report *Consultations & Roundtables on Women in Architecture in Canada* (the Royal Architectural Institute of Canada, December 19, 2003). Other studies have compared architecture with medicine and law, where women fare much better.

I left the Forest Service a decade before this growing awareness of gender-based institutional ills surfaced. But I had observed that the top female regional office managers who were there when I arrived had dropped away due to health problems, death, being transferred to other forests, or moving to other agencies, or because they had retired prematurely—as I was doing. The organization was hemorrhaging its female blood from the subtle steady pressure of sexism.

On my last day at the Forest Service, Friday, April 29, 1994, I signed a few papers in personnel, turned in my desk items, and said good-bye to several "Professional Friends." The halls of government seemed tired, dim, worn—and I was ready for something else. When I walked out of the building, my spirits were refreshed by the blue sky of spring. I smiled at the splashing sounds of fountains and admired the sky walkways that made San Francisco such a vibrant and artful city.

I had crab-walked to the Forest Service three years before with a dream of working in the heart of San Francisco to get to know the city; I felt satisfied that I'd achieved this. Still, I would miss sharing the sidewalks filled with a range of fashionable people, miss seeing the sophisticated holiday decorations in office building lobbies and fancy window displays of lavish furnishings, and miss shopping for pork buns and spicy teas in nearby Chinatown.

Moving with the gait of freedom, I thought about the number of hours that work takes in each day. Now I would have time to do something else—not go to a government office, not swim against the current cultural conflicts. Optimistic uncertainty quivered somewhere between my heart and soul. Pleased and relieved, I strode away from a working environment I thought inappropriate for this *everyday* short-skirted architect who had enjoyed a creative and rewarding career until she tried the Forest Service.

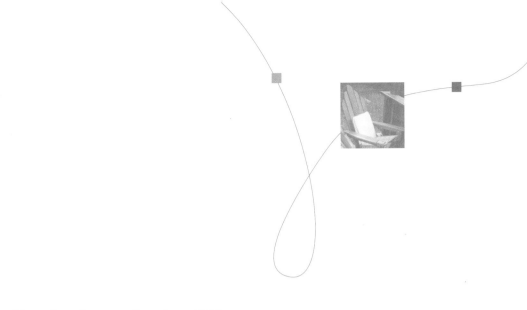

Delving into Place

1994 to 1995: Gasquet

I tapped on the weathered screen door. "Hello?"

"Come *on* in," hollered back Patti and Lynn, both busty grandmothers.

Yellow jackets buzzed above my head as I stepped onto the Adams Station wavy kitchen floor, sagging from long use and an ancient foundation. The kitchen's built-in antique sideboards supported gallon-sized china pitchers, used nearly a century before for water in the guest-rooms. Adams Station was a testament to the homesteading roots in Gasquet's narrow valley, and the old arbor is still clad with grapes that Mr. Gasquet brought from France and gave to Mary Adams for the station. Since 1898, the compact two-story, bark-brown house with a leafy green roof had remained uncontaminated by so-called upgrades—other than a pink tile bathroom, a porch for laundry equipment and refrigerators, and an adjacent carport.

"How was San Francisco?" Patti asked.

"Come and sit in the living room," said Lynn, leading the way.

My feet automatically followed the faux-brick linoleum, worn thin by the shoe soles of stagecoach travelers heading to the warmth of the stone fireplace. "Well, I left my job … Greg and I are up for the summer."

I slipped into the Mission-style chair, resting my eyes on the multi-colored, braided oval rag rug in the center of the room. If I ignored the TV, I could imagine myself being carried back by the aged wallpaper to a life of days gone by, captured in the historical photos hanging on the walls. The pictures were mostly of Mary Adams, who ran the stagecoach stop for Horace Gasquet, the Frenchman after whom the hamlet is named. In 1886, Horace Gasquet had Chinese-American and other workers build the toll road to provide access over the mountains between O'Brien, Oregon, and Gasquet. A side door, rarely used today, opened for guests traveling the toll road so they could enjoy a well-advertised Adams (Stagecoach) Station chicken dinner in this very room.

"Wendy, have you heard about the new gas station?" asked Lynn.

"You are the first people I've seen since we arrived." I sank into the comfort of my chair, letting the restfulness of the room envelope me.

Patti filled me in, "A Pelican Bay Prison guard wants to add another gas station in Gasquet." Built in the late 1980s, Pelican Bay Prison was 20 miles west of Gasquet. Like many of the prison guards, the aspiring gas station owner lived in Gasquet. From the gist of what Lynn told me, this ambitious fellow's intentions had rocked many longtime residents out of their *minding-their-own-property-ostrich-head-in-the-sand* position. Riled by this "unnecessary intrusion," the community's live-and-let-live attitude appeared to be shifting to include the wider well-being of place. New neighbors and old-timers had swelled into a somewhat united swarm.

"I'm part of the group." Lynn flipped up the footrest on her super-sized recliner to unload her troubled hips.

"I don't see the purpose," I added. "Gasquet already has a working gas station and several abandoned ones."

"It would be too close to Mary's Creek and the Smith River," Patti topped off the argument from her regular spot on the vintage couch. "Who knows what kind of fluids would go into the river from a gas station?"

My two friends rattled off other recent threats. A paint truck's missed turn had resulted in toxic paint spilling into the river; rumors were circulating that the nearby Idyllwild Caltrans work center, where several people worked, might soon be closing; and the increasing speed of cars on Highway 199 was regularly causing accidents. Lynn was part of the group of seven who had placed an announcement in the local paper about a town hall meeting to form the Gasquet Community Council. Everyone was welcome. The forum was to be held in the Veterans' Hall, a low-key beige building, centrally located to the 400

Gasquet residents—close enough for them to walk, even though most drove their trucks. I rode my bike.

Gasquet residents weren't the only ones who hadn't been particularly community-minded. I guess Greg and I weren't, either, especially during the first years when we were busy building our summerhouse, not reading the local paper or socializing. I told Greg about the news from Adams Station during our usual late-afternoon porch chat. Dusty, my affectionate tabby cat, who traveled each summer with us from San Francisco, curled up on the wide redwood railing, since he couldn't find an available lap to crawl into. Greg held his binoculars searching for hummingbirds, his favorite photography subject, and I was knitting. He listened as I rambled on about Gasquet's qualities and how easily they could slip away with the helter-skelter building sprawl that hid under the overused label of *development*, a term that was often more speculative than appropriate. The tendency here was to replace nature with manmade, enclosed ugly spaces. Although the owners claimed they had them built to stay in, these eyesores generally ended up on the market within months of construction, then waiting years to be used.

Greg and I often sat in the Adirondack chairs we'd built with the best redwood boards left over from our house, facing slightly west so we didn't have to look at our neighbor's clutter. Our neighbor Jud loved animals, and his dogs were friendly—when they weren't barking. He'd fed feral cats for many years, and his pet pigs were constantly getting out of their pen and running erratically into the road, trampling my flowers and squirming under our porch. Jud loved to play midwife and was slow to get

The Adirondack chairs
Greg and I made

his animals neutered, especially the cats. To this day, the scenery at Jud's remains uncannily cluttered with nonworking cars, furniture parts, tires, gas cans, and scatterings of odds and ends around his driveway in full view. However, his vegetable garden looks well tended. Jud, my not-so-bad-keep-to-himself neighbor, is still the main storekeeper in Gasquet, on Highway 199. He never attended any of the community meetings back in 1994 and 1995; instead, he dispensed his opinions to his shoppers, one by one.

Our western neighbor's house wasn't visible from our porch, but John and Marn let us use a brushy path on their property to get down to the river, and we did so discreetly. Slipping into the wide pristine water of the Smith was magical because we were usually the only ones there. We would swim up close to the west bank and float down the east edge. Greg wore his mask and snorkel, but I liked to keep my head above the icy clear water so I could enjoy the bright green shore grasses filling the spaces between sculptured boulders and the blue dragonflies hovering near the fingertip orchid ladders. Built before Fish & Game declared riparian zones essential, the houses along this stretch of the river's still water were small and regressed into lush vegetation. "Here is another good community topic," I thought, swimming upstream against the gentle current.

Sadly, people continue to build as close to the river's edge as they can, ignoring the fact that they are destroying what they say they love and not following Fish & Game guidelines. Years later, I wrote a letter to the editor of the *Triplicate*, our local paper, explaining how the bank of the river is like the skin of a person. A river cannot thrive without its riparian zones—its breathing skin—for river vegetation, wildlife, and long-lasting stability.

Greg always brought work with him and wasn't much inclined toward community organizing, but I definitely was. The surge of concern in the community felt like something I wanted to join. I envisioned a more sympathetic fit between the buildings and the natural forest landscape. The newer houses looked out of place to me; newly arrived homeowners tended to cut down the tall trees and then transplant their house designs from Sacramento and Los Angeles. On August 31, 1994, as I rode my bike through the warm afternoon to the first Gasquet Community Council meeting, I wondered, could leadership and planning influence the visual impact of development?

Forty-three residents signed in on the attendance sheet I posted to record and measure community participation each month. (If you came once, the next time you just had to check your name.) Attendees elected officers, and soon two committees were launched: one to prepare by-laws and one to develop strategic planning. I was selected to be the leader of the strategic planning committee because I had proposed it.

Oddly, one of the first people I'd met in Gasquet was the only person to speak out against the idea of applying for a grant to help with strategic planning. Nan, my architect friend who had introduced Greg and me to Gasquet, had also introduced us to a cheerful couple living on our road in the tiny house they'd designed themselves. It stunned my expectations when my otherwise friendly neighbor strongly protested the idea of obtaining funding. This move seemed incongruent with our past interactions, so I invited her over for a *tête-à-tête*.

"I'm concerned as to why you objected to going after a grant," I began, leaning forward on the low stool I used to build fires in our wood-burning stove. The room's dark natural-wood ceiling contrasted with the bright midday light outside.

How strange, I thought. Here was a smart woman who joked, laughed fully, and planned games for other couples she entertained. For three years, we had invited each other to meals, marveling at the compatibility of our social views. When she and her husband came to our house for dinner, we often played ping-pong, but they never wanted to keep score; it was just for fun. Her husband once told me, "Everything is about people," and she smiled most of the time—but not now.

"Money always corrupts." With a stern glare, she let the meaning of her words sink in. Apparently, grant money was going to spoil all the good stuff in the community, like a drop of oil in water.

"It doesn't have to." My self-esteem stuttered. What was she telling me?

"You shouldn't do it." Her voiced tightened and I sensed her fear, as though she were trying to warn me about something dangerous that she couldn't describe.

In the slice of silence between her sentences, the scent of peaches ripened—and my patience waned. "We can use all the money for the project expenses and not for people's time," I said, spontaneously molding my response to her apparent concern.

"People get nasty when money is involved." She suddenly stood, lips pinched and arms straightened alongside her pastel Bermuda shorts. "I just think you should stay away from it."

Up to this point, I had registered her politics as being compatible with mine, but now she seemed concerned about an aspect of small-town dynamics that I somehow couldn't picture. I knew she wanted the hamlet to organize and have a voice because she had volunteered for the by-laws committee. She couldn't have known about my skills as an organizer and manager, but even so, this plea not to go after funds struck me as sharply odd. Perhaps a painful past event petrified her position. But I never found out, because she and I never talked about how I planned to handle and account for money.

When I picked up my knitting that evening, my fingers fluttered for a few easy rows as I tried to imagine what my friend was warning me about. She radiated social fear, but I'd need a pithy reason or two to alter my course. After several sets of knits and purls of weighing the risks, I decided I should still apply for the grant.

As far as I knew, this was the first grant that the citizens of Gasquet, an unincorporated part of Del Norte County, had applied for. The Forest Service was encouraging small forest communities to strengthen their ability for self-determination, and a $10,000 grant for Gasquet on May 23, 1995, was an amendment to the Del Norte County Strategic Planning budget of $34,000.

Because of my concerned friend's comments, I persuaded members of our committee not to pay themselves in the first two of our eight working principles:

(a.) Do as much of the work as we possibly can to preserve grant monies for meeting facilitator, professional photos, maps and other expenses.

(b.) Document carefully the "in-kind" time and expense using a standard value system, in dollars, for different levels of work and equipment used.

The by-laws moved slowly, as President Rick Bennett didn't want to spend much time on them during each meeting. The strategic planning committee looked lively in comparison, because the Forest Service representative from Eureka was willing to facilitate a planning session with the newly aroused residents.

The Forest Service called it *capacity building*, which meant increasing the community's ability to take care of itself, not as individuals but as a group. A rickety "for-or-against" operating procedure had been the standard way to approach any problems brought up in the newspaper or in groups like the PTA and volunteer fire department. Group conversations, cooperation, envisioning, respecting roles, and focusing on community concepts were all behaviors I had taken for granted from a career in large, highly structured organizations, but they seemed to be missing in Gasquet. Other dynamics popped up that I was equally unprepared for; for instance, people who lived in Gasquet but worked in large businesses in other parts of the county suddenly appeared at our town hall talks and began undermining opinions they didn't like without really becoming involved. It was soon obvious that some "old families" wanted to take care of "self" and willingly snubbed any talk about taking care of "place." Their American fixation on seeing property as something so *private* that it was isolated from the earth seemed to deafen our call for community dialogue about our *common* and beautiful place.

Greg and I often discussed the dynamics of our rural surroundings over a stir-fry dinner at our ping-pong (and dinner) table. We sat, comfortably cool beneath the bay leaf canopy near our outside kitchen, with whiffs of soy sauce, garlic, and fresh ginger punctuating our paragraphs of discovery. The more we learned about nature, the more we were in awe of its order and beauty. Delving into place became my passion; yet, the more I interacted with the people living in Gasquet, the more I felt bewildered and amazed at the lack of interest in cooperation, beneficial actions, or reasonable rules. One of my examples of the value of cooperation was placing traffic lights at road intersections; traffic would move better and it was safer for everybody. It didn't occur to me then that I might have appeared to be a know-it-all city slicker coming to the country with foreign ideas, or that what worked in organizations might not work in rural communities. Greg thought Gasquet residents were probably not used to my style of leadership, and I lacked the reputation I had built up in OWA and in my navy job. However, when I saw the way people treated the president of the Gasquet Community Council at meetings, I came to think that rural people resisted leadership in general. Respecting role was not the norm.

Our committee of four—including my bold entomologist farmer friend, another articulate woman who worked for her less articulate accountant husband, and a sheetrock contractor from Los Angeles now trying real estate—went to work on a strategic plan, anyway.

More and more people came to the meetings, and community interest soared. On March 29, 1995, we were asked by the Forest Service facilitator to write, anonymously on 3-by-5-inch cards, our image of Gasquet in five years. Within minutes, the facilitator read all 31 cards aloud. The circle of casually dressed residents smiled at each other, openly surprised by the positive words they heard. The room's mood had noticeably bounced upward from the guarded tone at the start of the meeting.

Encouraged by the outcome, our strategic planning committee wanted residents who had not been present for the March meeting to know what was going on. We endeavored to provoke discussion within households and among neighbors, hoping that more residents would turn out for the June town hall meeting, when we planned to develop a Gasquet Vision. To this end, I assembled the 97 vision items we'd written on small white cards into themes: Beauty, Community Character, Community Services, Protection of Nature, Recreation, Safety, and School. Topics ranged from "building moratorium" to "more public facilities," and from "post office and school to remain where they are" to—of course—"NO new gas stations." I titled our booklet, *Your Gorgeous Gasquet.* We used some of our grant money to publish it and sent it to every Gasquet post office box one week before the Gasquet Community Council meeting on June 28, 1995.

This sort of community activism was new territory for me, and, I must admit, I enjoyed the motive and the momentum. I gladly spent time each week preparing for our committee meetings and thinking about how to keep people interested in Gasquet as a unique place deserving of our conscious attention.

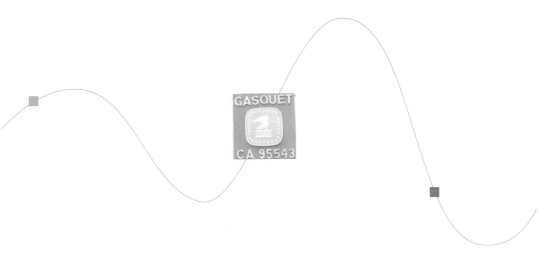

The Gasquet Vision

1995 to 2000: Gasquet

After the Gasquet community council strategic planning committee published *Your Glorious Gasquet*, we prepared a survey of 30 questions on a wide range of topics and sent it to all 400 Gasquet post office box holders. I made sure that several questions related to architectural character and most responded favorably to the idea of design guidelines, which greatly surprised me in the county with no architect on staff.

Natural features—like the river, mountains, and trees—were mentioned in the survey results for their aesthetic values but without much attention given to their ecological health, value, and vulnerability. However, the love of the Smith River was so dominant in discussions that finding ways to take care of these natural treasures piqued my curiosity.

I became alarmed when longtime river-dwellers, hearing of my concerns, started to ask me how to be good stewards of the river. Coming from the city, I wrongly assumed that people living in nature would know what was needed to keep nature healthy. It would take a few years before I understood the interface between man and the natural elements of the watershed well enough to make specific suggestions. At the time, my main concern was how to identify natural and man-made features for the community to steward, but I was still thinking in terms of planning, zoning, and building—elements from my world of architecture.

Longtime and large landholding residents in other parts of the county claimed they knew the place better than anyone. The anti-environmentalists barked offensively, and many residents didn't link their individual actions to the cumulative effect on their river or on nature in general. Their narrow perspectives seemed to have derived from a combination of habits and livelihoods that hindered their ability to grasp a picture of the planet as our common and only place to live.

Public dialogue was difficult. Beliefs were buried and tangled. A biologist working for a timber company shed new light on my approach when he said in a public speech, "I am careful not to threaten someone's livelihood." Here I was, retired, not depending on my money from an employer, while people in this community were dependent on very few jobs. In this small county, finding out where someone worked was easy, and fear traveled faster than praise. The people of Del Norte were prey to a culture of realistic worry that they could lose their jobs if powerful people didn't like their point of view.

One person told me that when he spoke up against highway expansion for super trucks, he saw his business take a dive and close. A Park Service friend told me that in the 1960s they always wore jackets to cover their uniforms because of local hostility. Thirty years later, attitudes had tapered down to common lip service; I overheard derogatory slurs about environmentalists in the hardware store, the cell phone outlet, and supermarkets. Now, after 20 more years, slurs in public places, including chamber of commerce meetings, continue to ring out against those concerned about the environmental issues brought up by environmentalist and local authors.

Had I been employed in Del Norte, I'm sure my job would have been in jeopardy after I advocated that citizens prepare a set of design guidelines to take ecological concerns into account when developing property. I wanted local landowners to consider positive actions toward stewardship: disturbing the ground as little as possible, keeping the trees and vegetation along the river's edge wild, minimizing pavement and the size of houses. After searching the planning literature, I found Randall Arendt's book *Rural by Design: Maintaining Small Town Character* (Planners Press, 1994), which suggested physical elements to stay away from in rural planning, such as grid streets and cul-de-sacs. *Ecological Design*, a book by Sim Van der Ryn and Stuart Cowan (Island Press, 1996), advocated looking to natural systems for design decisions.

I used the word *rural* as if everyone understood my meaning. At that time, I didn't fathom how much the word *rural* depends on context. In literature, the words *pastoral, rustic,* and *rural* have been used to suggest serenity, quiet, sparsely populated areas, and verdant landscapes; but these words also can connote a lack of sophistication, elegance, and education in an area's people. The term *rural* can apply to specific numbers of people for school busing or grant eligibility. In December 2004, Washington State's Clallam County put measures in its Comprehensive Plan to preserve "rural character" as defined by nine measures. Even though I was from San Francisco, I had high apprecia-

Stoney Creek

tion for the attributes of the countryside and the forests in Gasquet. I would have loved nothing better than to see people in our county work together on valuing the idea of rural character—where manmade features complement and highlight rather than upstage the natural surroundings.

At a Smith River Advisory Council meeting, I stood to make my pitch for stewardship guidelines for development along the river. A head table of solemn male board members faced the attendees, many of whom were dressed in government uniforms and the nondescript sports garb of commercial anglers and local fishing guides. Ted and Jack, whom I knew as avid anglers and active members of the local environmental group, sat next to me. I shifted my head left and right, speaking in the long room so people at both ends could hear my proposal. There were a few questions, and then a scruffy, gray-haired dairy farmer stood and simply stated, "We don't want that."

"Why not?" I asked, wondering what he could possibly say.

Smith River (North Fork)

"We don't want to educate the public," shouted one of the few female fishing guides from the back end of the barren room.

I was stunned, but remained standing. Then I recognized, sitting across the table, the best-known and most cantankerous, long-time anti-environmentalist in the county. He stood, confirmed the previous statement, and aimed to close the discussion.

Again, I asked, "Why? The guidelines would be voluntary and good for the Smith River. We are not making regulations." I was unaware that I had used a red-flag word, *regulations*.

"It just wouldn't be good," said a voice several seats away.

"Next agenda item," ordered the spokesman from the head table.

Disappointed, I lowered myself into the hard stiffness of my chair.

As we left the meeting, the two environmentalists said I did well to stand up for my convictions. and I was glad I hadn't embarrassed them with my naiveté of local politics. That meeting was enough for me to understand that those with commercial interests in the Smith River dominated the Smith River Advisory Council. Their love of the river didn't appear to include a concern for preserving its health or treasuring its natural beauty as a community asset; it was about their personal livelihood and, as such, was not on the table for any type of guidelines.

The next day, I visited one of the county supervisors so he would understand the reasoning behind my guidelines when I brought the idea up at the next County Board of Supervisors meeting.

"I have already heard about your guidelines," the round-bellied, balding supervisor said, "and am not interested in knowing more."

Obviously, the behind-the-scenes power structure had already moved, effectively blocking my push to have the community sit down, talk about, and prepare a list of what was good and bad for the ecological health of the land and the river. The local supervisors seemed accessible in this small town, but clearly a few rich old families held their strings because of their business clout. An atmosphere of social fear developed because of their ability to hurt others financially, a sad situation that is difficult to cure.

I dropped the guidelines idea and decided to try other ways to help the community better get to know the value of place. Our committee used part of our grant funds to hire a local photographer to document the physical features. I felt it important to have a benchmark of the existing development—the contemporary kit-log houses with generous front porches, the unstoppable mobile homes, the revived cabins, the few historic houses, and Adam's Station. Our committee paid to enlarge nine of the color photos to display at the following County Board of Supervisors meeting in Crescent City. By this time, we had the full support of Barbara Clausen, the new county supervisor from our district, who began attending our Gasquet Community Council meetings.

Fifty-three people attending the June 28, 1995, town hall meeting came to a consensus (with the help of a paid out-of-town consultant) for our vision of Gasquet. I was particularly pleased that the Forest Service ranger and the National Park Service superintendent (players usually doing their own thing as directed from Washington) were sitting with us in the audience during this local authoring. The residents were not for or against. It was just the opposite; they worked carefully to find words that everyone in the room could live with. This was remarkable and rewarding. I rejoiced.

We printed our vision of Gasquet on calling cards to give out to meeting attendees, government offices, and to post outside the Gasquet Post Office.

Gasquet Vision

Gasquet will be a small, quiet rural community with attractive basic services clustered for residents and visitors. The village will be known for its friendly, self-reliant nature, unique quality of life, sound infrastructure, support of education and pride in its community, as well as its clean river and beautiful forest.

Gasquet Market and Post Office

The idea was to provoke pride in place and to alert those who could impact our settlement— Caltrans, the County Planning Department, public utility companies, developers, and new homebuilders—that we cared about the future of our community.

At that meeting, we also decided to work as a group on four priorities: having a gymnasium for the school; protecting the health and beauty of the Smith River; enhancing the beauty of Gasquet; and improving traffic safety measures. Small groups formed.

The Gasquet Beautiful group was one I joined, and we talked about appearance issues. One issue we discussed was whether commercial zoning should be reduced to a few blocks along the highway instead of stretching through the whole town. Most of the commercial zoning was already being used as residential. Unfortunately, when the county land use plan was reviewed, only minor changes were made, perhaps because of our suggestions. The County Planning Office was shy about making dramatic changes. The common belief among some was that property values lowered when zoning changed from commercial to residential, but I never saw any real numbers used to back that claim.

When a Gasquet property owner made a bid to expand the Gasquet Post Office by moving it from its historic location next to the only grocery store, I contacted the Regional Post Office's project manager in Sacramento via letters and phone calls to request that she come to Gasquet and hear the community's concerns. Many wanted a larger post office, but not by moving it to a new location off the highway. Three postal employees and more than 30 community members attended a meeting about the post office. Many in the group had strong feelings and were willing to speak up about where the post office should be. No one person dominated the discussion; it felt like democracy. I was happy to experience this sign of increased community capacity. In the end, the Gasquet Post Office didn't move.

In spite of some negative gossip by a few about the council's doings, our committee published the *1995 Strategic Planning for Gasquet: A Del Norte County Community in California* (February 1996), which stood alone and also became part of the official Del Norte County Strategic Plan. More than 30 people were credited on the last page for working on the plan, along with two sets of Gasquet Community Council officers.

Since Greg was a freelance computer design developer, he could work anywhere; so I was surprised when, years later, he resentfully confessed, "You just announced one day that we'd be staying in Gasquet during the summers." Maybe that shift was the first invisible crack in our relationship. Greg and I had traveled to Hawaii several times and to Australia in 1995. We'd had wonderful adventures snorkeling and even decided to get married.

This all changed in 1996 because of a historical Japanese love story that I'd randomly picked out at a used bookstore on Main Street in Hood River. Greg and I had driven up in late fall for a week's vacation in northern Oregon, taking advantage of one of Greg's time-share apartments. As I read how the husband and wife communicated about their feelings, it hit me that I was unhappy with the lack of intimate depth in my communication with Greg. Back in San Francisco, other cracks occurred. Finally, I broke off the relationship, but the feeling seemed mutual. We didn't fight over the Gasquet cabin. I bought out Greg's share by renting out my two apartments in San Francisco and living a full year in Gasquet.

By the year 2000, the Gasquet Community Council had succumbed to negative forces and fizzled. People shrugged it off with, "You need a crisis to keep people's interest." I decided to limit my activism to voicing my concerns as an individual. The will of the community wasn't there, so I spoke up on my own against billboards, excessive highway signs, and truck network expansion on the scenic byway. I wrote comments to the Border Coast Regional Airport Authority against oversized airport expansion into our valuable wetlands. I also wrote several letters to the editor of our local paper, including a letter exposing the details of the litter I picked up in Gasquet one day on my walk to the post office. I wrote to Fish & Game about the need for stronger riparian guideline enforcement and attended local water district meetings asking for administrative transparency. All issues, in my mind, related to caring for the quality of a unique geographical place, but addressing them didn't bring me long-term satisfaction, as my efforts seemed to be about as effective as spitting on a volcano.

The Gasquet Community Council had lobbied for a new school gymnasium, but it was not built until some school kids burned down the school for fun or by accident late one summer night. I know that our strategic plan was being read all over the county because Hiouchi, the hamlet six miles west of Gasquet, later used our argument to keep their commercial district clustered. Another time, the administrative officer of Crescent City told me he knew how hard it was to write a vision statement and he admired our success.

But, ultimately, I couldn't help but conclude that the collective DNA of rural communities makes it close to impossible for individual citizens to influence the personality traits of place. I was disappointed to find out that our local, state, and federal politicians only saw big development as the solution for community well-being. None of the politicians I talked to were concerned about stalwart stewardship; faceless expansion seemed to be their major goal.

Two architects now practice in Del Norte County; perhaps they will foster the value of place as unique and irreplaceable. Maybe some places learn faster than others. Maybe some places are healthier than others. Maybe there are keyholes to places. In Gasquet, we tried to form a "key" out of clear intentions, but it didn't fit well enough to turn our future toward recognizable and deliberate stewardship of Gasquet's natural assets. Perhaps our plan, photo survey, and vision will be helpful in a future community surge to care for the natural and historical features of Gasquet.

Until then, our Gasquet Vision is still alive in our strategic plan and a copy of it was submitted to the College of Environmental Design Library at the University of California, Berkeley. Because of the Forest Service grant, Gasquet was able to produce this excellent plan and it remains as a good example of a community attempting to better understand the elements of place that are so treasured by the residents. But I am disappointed that the Gasquet Community Council is no longer, leaving Gasquet without a friendly forum to help build community capacity. Happily, I remain friends with many I worked with during those six years. I certainly fell in love with Gasquet, enjoyed it, and learned many things about a rural place by experiencing it over 20 years. I know that others made friendships too. However, even when the individuals tell you they love the place, taking care of the natural and human-made features is a mighty difficult thing to do.

Seasons

2000 to 2009: Gasquet and San Francisco

The splitting of my routine into seasonal cycles settled in so naturally that after several years I began describing my activities according to the season: "I write in the winter … I weave in the summer."

Write is a verb that means to scratch, draw, or inscribe on a surface to make text. *Weave* is a verb that means to interlace, or make textile on a loom. I advance in each activity row by row, with linear determination, discipline, and creativity.

In summer, the Gasquet sun arrives at the end of my porch just in time for an early breakfast. I use morning's prime time to step into my garage-sized studio, accented with the faint fragrance of linen from the loom's warp threads. The barn-like door stays propped open for light and for viewing my fig tree, ripening in the distance. Butt to bench, I keep track of the quantity, color, and order of my yarns in a spiral notebook close at hand, by my right hip. Invented patterns are coded like a fancy formula: 4 X ABACD, or 2 X A B AC, with letters (A or A') representing colored pieces of yarn that I tape into the notebook, the numbers representing how many times I repeat each set. Writing down what I am doing is essential because you can't read the yarns on the surface of the textile the way one can read words on a page; you must weave several rows before you have the equivalent of a sentence, and many hours for an inch of a paragraph.

When I was younger, I fell in love with fiber and fabric. I first held sport-weight wool yarn while knitting a mauve cardigan in high school. Until then, I'd search the San Diego department stores for twin sweater sets made of 100 percent lamb's wool. The fineness of lamb's wool lends itself to machine knitting, while the sport weight works well for hand knitting. Forty years later, my passion for fiber fashions endures. My preferred knitting material these days is mohair, abundant in La Drôme, France, where women like to knit and wear long mohair scarves—so much so that raising Angora goats continues as a cottage industry.

In the early 1990s, I became a faithful member of the Crescent City Friday group of knitters, spinners, and weavers who call themselves Windy Weavers and Spinners. After three seasons of knitting, the spin-

Spinning yarn

ners decided I should learn to spin, a calming activity that turned out to suit my love of making fiber and introduced me to its strange lingo. I learned about the various wool-producing breeds; alpaca from the Andes is often a brown sugar color, soft and very costly, while the Navajo raise Churro sheep, a primitive breed with a layer of longer fibers used for making rugs. Mohair is a glossy fiber from Turkish goats, referred to as the "diamond of yarns" by the east Texas ranchers who claim to pro-duce more mohair than anyone else in the world.

The difference between com-mercially spun and hand-spun yarn is as dramatic as the tasted difference between an inexpensive frozen pie from the store and a homemade pie crafted by a loved one. Hand-spun yarn, rich with grain, character, and texture, is rare—producing the yarn takes so much time that spinners usually want to keep it for themselves! As in any language, individu-als often vary in their use of words, expressions, and arguments; this is also true for hand spinners, for whom the individuality of yarns speaks volumes. You are not likely to see hand-spun yarn at your local yarn store unless you live in a region of productive spinners, close to where sheep graze. The craft of spinning is showcased at the "Black Sheep" gathering, held annually in Eugene, Oregon, a six-hour drive northeast of Gasquet. There are conferences and a magazine dedicated to spinning yarn, as well, for anyone who wants to try this ancient meditative art form.

After three seasons of spinning, I bought my first loom from a weaver in need of funds. Her Fireside Jack loom was solid enough to make small rugs with my tightly spun, two-plied yarns. Over the years, I have spun and bought yarns for their intrinsic appeal, not knowing when I would use them—almost like collecting dishes I had no specific use for. Cupboards bulging with yarns are common to fiber artists; we collect faster than we can weave or knit. But it doesn't matter. We love being surrounded by our long-living materials (thank goodness they don't require refrigeration). Using up one's stash is a challenge; while making two of my rugs, I used 32 pounds of my collection; yet I still had enough for at least five more weaving seasons.

There are those who say, "Why not just buy a sweater or a rug?" It may be difficult to imagine for someone who has never tried it, but the act of creating with fiber offers an extremely joyful experience, and the resulting handcrafted creation holds up well over time in its unique wearability, value, and beauty.

Howard Risatti reminds us (*American Craft* magazine, February/March 2008 issue) that in Italy before the Renaissance, the act of making things was not consciously separated from the mental activity of thinking about what to make. When practicing architecture, I primarily use my mind—designing for builders to construct the building—while in the fiber arts I use my "thinking hands" (Risatti's lovely phrase). What some may forget about craft is that much of

My hand-spun, natural dyed yarns

the maker's pleasure is in striving to improve her technique, to master a skill.

Of course, the same striving holds true for writing. Ten years ago, I joined the Wednesday Writers of Harwood Press for a couple of writing seasons, writing a thousand words every day and showing up to participate in the circle on Wednesdays. Although the number of colors I use in my rugs comes close to the number of letters in the alphabet, the complexity of meaning from words greatly challenges the verbal side of my brain, while the visual vocabulary of yarns differently indulges the artistic side. Settling on my vision for a rug design comes quickly, and I feel as if I am pushing the design forward with my thinking hands as I work on the loom. But when I write, where I stew and stir, and question the clarity of my ideas, I am less sure of myself. Nevertheless, the hours I have spent writing in winter probably match my weaving time in summer.

Rug weaving studio
built by Leonard

When I weave, I am entirely engrossed. No music or radio is playing; the sounds I hear are the beat of the loom's reed on the fell of my thick rug. Silence is dear when blue jays don't screech, weed whackers don't buzz, and neighbors don't ride their lawn mowers. I concentrate on the foot pedals that control the order of different colored yarns as they cover the warp threads. One hand throws the shuttle full of yarn; the other has to catch it at the other side of my weaving, or the shuttle may crash to the floor and I'll have to get off the bench to fetch it. Each row incorporates many tiny hand movements. Since I use yarns with varying thicknesses and colors, I have more to think about than if I used only one type of yarn throughout.

After a set or two of my design, I run my right hand over the taut surface to relish the feel of fibers. If a finger feels a dry piece of stiff grass stuck in the handspun yarn, I pick it out to be sure the rug will be soft underfoot. When a shuttle runs out of yarn, I move to the alcove to wind more onto it from the skeins hanging on poles, or from the cones or balls I have stacked by color in baskets. The yarn slides through one hand, dispersing a woolly smell as it fills the shuttle. Before climbing back onto the bench, I often bend down to see what the backside of my work looks like. The shaft-switching technique I use makes my rug usable on both sides, so I think of both the front and the back design as I weave.

Now and then, I review the design that began as a vision, evolved into a small diagram, and is still open to design accent and opportunity. Back on the bench, I ad-lib details, not as a painter would move the brush anywhere on the canvas, not by going back to a previous page like a writer, but only row after row, by pedal and thread-color order.

From time to time, my hand tests the linen warp threads to make sure their tension is as tight as it can be. During weaving, my hands and eyes check the two selvages for evenness, in a routine similar to placing a period at the end of a sentence. If the yarns twist too much, my foot pedaling gets out of order. If I pick up the wrong shuttle, I know I have lost my train of thought. Then it is time to get off the bench and go into my orchard to see if anything is ripe for a snack: a few sensuous bites of a green-skinned fig or a handful of shiny plump blackberries.

After three to five hours of weaving, I'm drained and I stop for the day.

For the last ten summer seasons, rug-making—designing, spinning, dying yarns, and weaving—has been my Gasquet focus. My secondary activity has been the completion of several construction projects. Leonard, an excellent Crescent City carpenter, often comes with the sun on Saturday mornings for a full day of construction: transforming a lean-to shed into my weaving studio, strengthening my outside kitchen, and building an elegant carport where I display my rugs for photographing.

The 2008 weaving season culminated in an exhibition in Bandon, Oregon, featuring 23 of my rugs. The show inspired me to publish a book—*Rug Retrospective: Eight Weaving Seasons 1999–2008*, which became both the exhibition catalogue and my rug portfolio.

One of my all-hand-spun rugs

Oregon guild sisters from the Humbug Mountain Weavers and Spinners had arranged the show with the gallery curator, Victoria

Tierney. They believed the time was right for me to step back and see my rugs hanging together in one place, a fantastic artist experience I had not anticipated as I wove. Wonderful fiber guilds exist in American cities and rural counties, continuing the tradition of teaching and mentoring. The weaving community asserts great appreciation for making and sharing; our common love of fibers links us by an exceptional enthusiasm for practicing our craft.

Elizabeth Wayland Barber dug down to the deepest roots of the fiber arts in *Women's Work: The First 20,000 Years: Women, Cloth, and Society in Early Times* (W. W. Norton, 1995):

> Four thousand years ago in ancient Mesopotamia ... respectable women were in business for themselves, weaving textiles at home to be sold abroad for gold and silver. Look back even further to 20,000 years ago, women began making and wearing the first clothing created from spun fibers. Until the Industrial Revolution, the fiber arts were an enormous economic force, belonging primarily to women.

Like many modern women, I didn't associate textiles with feminine history. Women around the world have been creating textiles for everyday life and special occasions for a long time; however, for centuries in the art world, it was considered a *domestic* art and not worthy of public viewing. Estelle B. Freedman, author of *No Turning Back* (Ballantine Books, 2002), claims that only 5 percent of the artists represented at New York's Whitney Museum were female in 1970, a remnant of the long separation of private and public themes in politics, culture, and art—themes challenged by the women's movement and feminism. I wonder if that percentage has grown.

In September of 2008, I cut my twenty-fourth rug—*Political Fireworks*—from the loom's front beam, where it had been rolling around itself out of sight. Only then could I see my creation—the reds and blues, the curves and slants, the double "O" for Obama, the stars, and the explosions—as a full rug. I have shown every one of my 24 rugs to my two summer guilds, as if it were a necessary step before calling a rug complete.

Rugs make an immediate impression, like the cover of a book, the handshake of a person, or the profile of a building. And, as with architecture, books, and people, the more your eyes explore my rugs, the more you notice the playful parts, the unexpected beats, shapes, or colors—the interconnected yarns that dance but don't move.

2008 *Political Fireworks* "O" detail on loom

I close my Gasquet cabin in late fall because the long days of summer shorten quickly, and it isn't as pleasant to weave or be outside. Leaving friends is one of the disadvantages with changing places seasonally. For example, there is my friend Hope, whom I worked with on the Gasquet Community Council. Hope grew up in Del Norte County, teaching, gardening, and tending her family. We used to walk together before my breakfast, until her husband became ill and could no longer stay at home. Missing our social exchanges on foot, I took up the habit of stopping by her house on my way back from the Gasquet Post Office.

Hope also had a welcoming way of opening her door and inviting me in, her lapdog trailing her steps.

"She's my pal!" Hope leaned down to rub Brandy's short trunk with five fingers, all accented with her fancy rings.

"Yes," was all I could muster from the floral fabric sofa on the other side of an overly wide space.

"She's getting so fat," Hope mused, sinking into the recliner she always landed in upon my arrival. "But I hate to put her on a diet."

Hope's husband was already sick when, against her will, he bought the eight pounds of pup for Hope.

"How is he doing?" I asked.

Hope sighed. "Some days it seems he doesn't know me." She put her feet up and Brandy settled on her lap. "Yesterday was better—he was moving his hand as if to write, so I got out a notebook from my purse and gave him a pen. And, you know, in perfect letters, he wrote, 'get gas and change the oil.'" Nervous laughter followed. "I was hoping he would have written 'I love you' or 'thanks,' because he doesn't talk much. But that was a caring phrase. After all, he used to take care of those things," she mumbled.

"That's a good idea—having him write," I said softly, thinking how she must have felt undervalued for her devotion, kindled by the love of a 50-year marriage.

Shifting her attention, Hope asked, "Are those your new shoes?"

My feet automatically began twirling my new short boots above her wood floor.

"Are you taking them to France?" she quizzed before I could answer her first question. Hope loved France, and our visit took her mind off her self-scheduled daily visits to the nursing home. "I like the red color."

"You must miss your travels," I said.

"Yes. Change is good," she said, without a thread of conviction.

"That is part of the reason I bought these new shoes for my old feet," I chirped, trying to lighten the mood.

"I've thought of changing the furniture, but it never worked out." Her voice had the tone of a defeated debater.

I stood. "Let's try a few things just for fun."

"Okay," Hope said with the joy of playing a game. Her beloved Brandy bounced off her lap as she stood.

I approached the recliner and pulled it out about two feet from the dark corner so she could sit in it and see her blooming potted plants on the porch and her prized garden beyond. The sofa was easy to swing 90 degrees to face the fireplace, making a tighter relationship between the two biggest chairs and the sofa. Then I pulled the coffee table to the center of the group, slightly closing the distance to increase intimacy among people conversing. "I like it," I said, dropping onto the comfortable sofa cushions and gesturing for Hope to sit with me in the new arrangement.

Her face registered careful caution.

"It's not perfect, as the TV is now behind the sofa," I said, thinking I had at least demonstrated the value of moving furniture—a bit like trying on shoes.

The night before a dawn departure, I packed my car with rolls of rugs, fig jams, jars of pickles, and boxes of golden apples. At dawn's threshold,

I stuffed the last items into my Citroën and buttoned up my summerhouse for the season, turning off the electrical main, closing the water lever at the lane, and sliding solid storm doors over the glass front doors, the final gesture indicating that I had left Gasquet for the season.

The shorter days triggered my migration from the evergreens of the Smith River watershed to my city home planted on San Francisco bedrock, among a dense population of painted ladies.

San Francisco's winter days are mainly for writing, and my friends have learned to respect my morning writing hours,

New fences and handrail
at my San Francisco house

wondering if this dedication will bear juicy Wendy-like fruit. In the afternoons my time goes to working with Tada on house maintenance projects. We have repaired settling foundation walls, leaking windows, and crumbling plaster. I designed, shopped for materials, and supervised new fences, flowerboxes, benches, decks, and handrails that Tada crafted. This constant care of home takes a parenting-like dedication that I enjoy.

In general, I stay away from designing for others; however, we worked together on two projects for client-friends: a kitchen/hallway/ stair remodel in San Francisco that needed unusually careful calculations to accomplish the client's goals, and a house entry with garden fences

in El Granada—major concrete and wooden fences to create outdoor rooms. I have had no intention of opening a private office; I only got involved because the owners were willing for Tada to be the builder, which I value because of his skills and our mutual respect.

For the El Granada project, I suggested that a community bench be designed into the wooden fence on the corner of Avenue Granda and Solono Avenue. That bench may be the icon of my style to

Tada

El Granada public corner bench in fence

design for public and private dimensions at the same time. My architect's heart warmed hearing the neighbors comment on it, use it, and marvel at the gift to their street.

My sister hired me to explore design possibilities on her entry and carport in Flagstaff, Arizona —but, in principle, I continue to resist taking on architectural design work for others, preferring at this stage of my life to write, weave, and spend more time with my daughter in France.

I started my writer's life by attending writers' groups on Wednesdays or Fridays with author Elizabeth Fishel in Oakland. My first short piece, "Book Building," appeared in *Wednesday Writers: 10 Years of Writing Women's Lives* (Hardwood Press, 2003). I shared that book and announced my goal to write a memoir at the 2003 OWA September Retreat. My colleagues appeared surprised. Nevertheless, determination to highlight women architects' experiences has held in check my self-doubt and my wonder at their silence as I lock-stepped into a schedule of pushing and pulling words, puzzle-like, on and off the page six days out of seven—from 9 to 12.

In spite of thousands of hours writing, my verbal skills on paper still feel like the weaker flank of my creativity, the visual arts the stronger.

El Granada residence, before

El Granada residence, after

Architecture has so many visual traits, as does weaving, but I have grown to understand the impact of writing and how important it is to work with words in support of visual meaning and quality. So, with feminine vigor, I have returned to my San Francisco workers' Victorian for another writing season, compelled to crystallize my trekking footprints and thoughts as a woman + as an architect.

Epilogue

If I Knew Then What I Know Now…

When I was first starting out in architecture, the reality of being female in a male-dominated profession didn't appear to be that big a problem. Despite discouraging literature on the subject, I somehow felt I had the ability to overcome any obstacle. Perhaps my optimism was a carryover from the days of my youth, when I played tennis with the men at the La Jolla Community Center and joined the all-male Model A Car Club. Powered by this optimism throughout most of my career, I pushed confidently forward, never quite grasping how tenacious the roots of sexism were in my chosen field or how deeply entrenched they were in society as a whole. It would be years before I realized the degree to which these thickly networked roots hinder women architects from looking at "place" with the concerns of women in mind.

I suppose I believed architecture was inherently neutral; it just currently happened to be filled with men, and we women merely had to prove ourselves before our presence would be widely accepted—even appreciated. In the meantime, I learned, researched, and persisted.

I'd read that male interviewers tended to give male candidates an hourlong interview while giving women candidates only 20 minutes because men often ran out of things to say to women. My approach was to keep the conversation going, reasoning that equal time would give me a much better chance of being hired.

As I advanced in federal service, my reading focused on how to succeed as a woman in a man's world—in other words, how to copy the skills, qualities, and mannerisms that effective men demonstrated, such as spreading my arms to take up more space (and claim more status) when sitting down at a meeting, pushing myself to stand and speak up, dressing as smartly as my budget would allow, and trying not to let foul play discourage me. I even tried smoking a pipe to appear confident, strong, and able to do what I saw male co-workers do. (Some of the bold gestures were helpful, but the pipe smoking didn't last.) I went to coffee with the men, invited myself out to lunch with the boys, and played tennis with my male colleagues. All of this was done to combat the fact that the men tended to share information with one another when they were in social groups, and I didn't want to be left out. At the same time, I defended my status as a woman whenever I felt slighted and encouraged the women around me to be all they could be. These strategies felt reasonable to me at the time, and I enthusiastically applied myself to my work tasks, trusting that my efforts eventually would pay off.

But I didn't know then what I know now.

While I was busy holding off the discrimination I perceived above the waterline, the full masculinity of architecture lay out of sight, hidden like the underwater depths of an iceberg. It did strike me as unreasonably strange that my female colleagues and I were referred to as *women architects*; I didn't understand why the word *woman* was added, since our femaleness was obvious. Due to recent research,[1] my understanding now includes why being female *and* an architect is still considered an oxymoron.

For centuries, women were often the crafters of dwellings, structures, teepees, yurts, and grass huts. Thus, it seems perfectly reasonable that as the practice of making buildings developed into a profession, women would have taken an active interest in architecture. But, from the profession's inception, male architects have unfortunately defined the institution in terms of a male point of view, male history,

---

1. This essay is intended to share my reflections on my career, almost like a case study, rather than being a scholarly paper. I use footnotes when I feel they might be useful to readers who would like to know more of the details behind general statements. I also use footnotes for sources of ideas I recently learned from others. In each case, I give the author and title of the source. Please check the selected bibliography for more information.

male social privilege, and male social norms. In other words, the profession of architecture doesn't just lack women; the profession *was born masculine.*

As a result, the profession of architecture has developed conservatively, its male founders instilling their chauvinistic values into architecture's educational programs, tests, apprenticeships, and work-culture taboos. While I find it perfectly natural that men would have instilled some of their own values into the profession they populated, their outright resistance to the presence of women defies worldly wisdom. Nevertheless, over the years, men have given all sorts of strange and funny reasons as to why women should not practice architecture:

- Architecture is damaging to the female reproductive function, the prime responsibility of women.
- Men need to concentrate in school and remain undistracted by women.
- Women don't have the ability to practice architecture.
- Men don't want to take orders from a woman.
- Women aren't willing to commit to architecture as a total lifestyle.
- Women don't want to commit to the travel required by international projects.
- Women can make it through school (half the students in my class were women), but then the competition, especially in math and engineering, knocks them out of the profession.

This list may appear out of date, even ridiculous, but its spirit lives on in the thriving undercurrent of opposition to the success of women in the profession—even after more than 100 years of women practicing as professional architects. True enough, the percentage of women architects in the United States has steadily and slowly increased in fuzzy[2] numbers, but those numbers are not accurate and they don't tell enough of the story. Although the impact of being female in a male-dominated profession has changed somewhat over

---

2. I say fuzzy because the numbers are not kept systematically on a national scale. Also, the numbers for students are better, at 40 to 50 percent, and quoted more often than for working architects. Since many who study architecture don't get registered, that group is estimated at about 7 percent but hard to know. Fuzzy then because some people use 20 percent; others use 13 percent or a combination. I estimate that there are about 140,000 people practicing architecture in the United States today.

time,[3] the day-to-day reality is distressing and unnecessarily negative, both for society and for the individuals who are impacted. Admitting this sad fact only intensifies my determination to understand women's long struggle to be free of the sex-linked roles that have been male defined and controlled. I have especially wanted to understand why this basic limitation continues to be so significant, to the point where traditional architects have all but lost sight of including gender concerns and important social issues in design decisions that affect the making of place.

Like many professionals, I lost touch with what new scholars were writing and teaching about the status of women in architecture. Catching up has been very rewarding because the new literature digs deeply into how we architects are educated, how we practice, how the current design priorities usually ignore gender, how the lack of equity in design impacts society, and how there is a strong tendency to take for granted long-accepted practices without question when we should instead be exploring appropriate goals for our time in history.

The more reading I did, the more I worried about a growing trend within the Organization of Women Architects and Design Professionals (OWA) to avoid feminist issues. Since many books are now available about women and architecture, I decided to see if a few OWA members would like to join me in reading and discussing books that linked women and architecture. I made an official proposal for the first OWA Book Circle at the annual business meeting in 2010 and was delighted that the circle filled up quickly. We began with longtime OWA member Inge Horton's freshly published book, *Early Women Architects in the San Francisco Bay Area: The Lives and Works of Fifty Professionals 1890–1951*, not only for the content but because I wanted to highlight and celebrate

---

3. Marguerite Wykoff, "The Outlook for Women in Architecture and Engineering." Wykoff reports that 477 women, or 2.3 percent, out of 20,000 total architects practiced in 1939. Also of interest is that all 34 schools of architecture reported they had at least one woman student, and the total added up to 21 percent of undergraduates and 15 graduate students being female, or 914 women, twice that employed in 1940 (page 146). The author suggests that the independence of architecture makes it advantageous to women, who could work from home and still have a family. The article ends with the claim that architecture is demanding and satisfying. (This claim comes right after the article says that there was a civil service exam in 1940 that two women passed for assistant architect positions in federal service. Sixteen positions were filled but none by women.)

her contribution to women's history. Horton's rigorous research uncovered many contemporaries of California's best-known pioneer woman architect, Julia Morgan. We agreed that becoming aware that Morgan wasn't alone was relevant to our understanding of women's history in architecture. More than 50 women were practicing architecture during her lifetime; although they were less famous, they pursued parallel paths that were equally interesting and commonly rockier, and they occasionally moved beyond private practice into public housing, planning, or teaching.

The OWA Book Circle went on to read Professor Leslie Weisman's *Discrimination by Design*, which was an exposé written from a serious feminist perspective, documenting the ways in which social issues in building design are presently being addressed, as well as those that still need attention. We then read *Women and the Making of the Modern House,* by historian Alice T. Friedman, a delightful look at the unique architectural programs resulting from design requests made by several extraordinary female clients whose modern houses were designed by famous architects. Public awareness of how these women influenced architecture has been eclipsed until now, even though their homes have been well covered and well visited.

Gender is one element of a person's identity—yet this fact is often overshadowed by the multitude of pressures for women in architecture. Architectural theorist, professor, and author Catherine Ingraham (1998) has suggested that sexual identity is part of the original primal sexual/spatial equation that humans formed for property, originally owned by men and shared with women in exchange for sex. This has resulted in an automatic linking of male identity and architecture to property and to the men who own, develop, and protect it. Although I had not thought of this specific connection, I am aware that American women were not allowed to own land or buildings until relatively recently and that, globally, women still rarely do. As a result, I would say, our identity is not tied to property in the same way that male identity is.

From its Renaissance beginnings, Western architecture has primarily concentrated on the public, civic, and political role of buildings and traditionally been commissioned by powerful patriarchs and institutions. This *public* aspect of architecture—historically not a place for women—is another reason why men in the early years of French architectural education[4] determined that architecture was unsuitable for

4.   Meredith L. Clausen, "The École des Beaux-Arts: Toward a Gendered History."

women. Sadly, this unwarranted paradigm was adopted in many regions of the world and continues to exert its stifling influence.

For those who think that women have been incorporated into the workplace without a hiccup, problem, or struggle, let me mention playwright Theresa Rebeck's *What We're Up Against* (the world premier play produced by Magic Theatre San Francisco, 2011), a play bringing home some of the "self-worth drama" faced today by women working in architectural offices. At first, I thought her title was from the female perspective, but it works both ways. The key line of the title is actually spoken by the senior "old boy" who is trying to hold the traditional system of power in place. This older fellow loudly complains about "what we're up against," venting his frustration about the way young women in the office want to get right to work, take responsibility, and see results, without paying their dues to the established order of seniority or playing the power games so well understood by men. Rebeck shows a newly hired woman "up against" the common tactic of being assigned insignificant work, which frustrates her. This happened to me in 1991, and it was home-hitting to see it onstage in 2011.

What is going on here? Shulamith Firestone (1970) wrote about how the reproduction of the species cost women dearly because the division of labor was institutionalized by men to free them up to do the business of the world. She welcomed the technology available for women to take control of their bodies to free themselves from the tyranny of the traditional division of labor based on a sexual class system. This year, 2011, is the 163rd anniversary of the first Women's Rights Conference, which was held in Seneca Falls, New York, in 1848. While today we can see observable progress toward what is often called social justice, Firestone reminds us—and we seem to need to be reminded often—that any privileged group with power over another group will not give up that power without a struggle.

Although holding on to power is the most obvious reason why women still don't have the kind of equality we want, I think Leonard Schlain (2003), a medical doctor and humanist thinker, offers another interesting take on the current lopsided condition of the sexes. He questions the widespread and almost unconscious misogyny lingering in our species. His theory is that women have evolved differently from men in their sexuality. Men are still very much driven by their sexual instincts and urges, while women have evolved to reflect on the consequences of sexual behavior because we have died from childbirth, have had fewer resources, and have become burdened with too many off-spring and limited earning power. According to Schlain, this gap builds resentment in many men, who take out their frustrations on women through abuse, discrimination, and domination, in spite of widespread modern lip service to the value of gender equity.

This theory doesn't sit right with my editor, Lisa Zuré, because men seem to look down on and disrespect (and persecute) women who are sexually accessible or who enjoy sexual freedom. She thinks there is a deeper misogyny based on self-loathing and a general disdain for and fear of women, stemming from the "world view" of "Western Civilization." Lisa mentioned to me that in ancient Greece, the rule was that you should never have sex with an equal—only with a subordinate, which a wife was at the time!

This is all so messy and tangled. Yet both men and women freely admit that architecture is a male-dominated profession, as if everyone automatically understands what that entails—much in the same way we assume that everyone knows what *global warming* means. Some feminist theorists point out that the profession of architecture is so masculine that women architects feel an ongoing anxiety yet are unaware of the reasons for their discomfort. This anxiety shows up in different ways. One way is to try not to stand out as female.

> "When I decided upon architecture, I resolved that, because there were so few women in the profession, my efforts should bear no sign of the touch of a woman's hand: I was not hoping for that kind of distinction."
> —Marcia Mead (1931)[5]

> "Subtle qualities such as graciousness, livability and charm, harmony, rest-fulness, peace, and homelikeness … are often forgotten in the so-called perfect garden … because they are feminine qualities, and unimportant …"
> —Mary Lou Drosten (1938)[6]

5. Marcia Mead, "Women's Versatility in Arts Enriches Field of Architecture" in the *Christian Science Monitor,* November 27, 1931. Note that her name as author was fol-lowed by: "Member of American Institute of Architects and National Housing Associa-tion." Despite this cautious approach, Mead constructively spoke out for women to be active members of the profession.

6. Mary Lou Drosten, "The Keystone National Fraternity of Women Architects (March 1938)," in Inge Schaefer Horton's *Early Women Architects of the San Francisco Bay Area: The Lives and Works of Fifty Professionals 1890–1951,* p. 44.

"The gender issues surrounding architecture are extraordinarily complex and frequently highly emotionally charged. Even the title of this book generated controversy: The original title, *The Female Architect*, was rejected because it highlighted the fact that the architects whose work is featured here are women, when most want to be considered just as architects."

—Maggie Toy (2001)[7]

"In an atmosphere that was the opposite of Hollywood, we were there *teaching at the University of California* [italics added] for our brains and God forbid we should use any womanly wiles to succeed in our careers. I sacrificed my femininity and never let people see the full person that I am."

—Clare Cooper Marcus (2010)[8]

Paradoxically, although many women architects feel compelled to downplay their femaleness, I dare to speak for many when I say that women as a rule don't rely on their work to validate their femaleness in the same way that men use work to validate their maleness. Just the opposite—most workingwomen don't want their gender getting more attention than their work. This dilemma of being female and a working professional is complicated but worth contemplating. During an excellent interview with Marcia Feuerstein (2002), Susana Torre, an admirable architect, educator, and writer, discussed attempts to sidetrack her interest in women in architecture: "Many male colleagues and former professors had warned me that the exhibition ("Women in American Architecture," 1977) would 'brand' me: I would no longer be seen as a real designer." Feuerstein clarified with, "You were warned that if you were identified as a 'woman architect,' the 'woman' would obscure your work as a serious 'architect.'" "Yes" answered Torre, continuing, "In the late 70s, such an exhibition *and book* [italics added] was disturbing to many people. Those who wished me well thought that all my aspirations as an architectural designer and practitioner would be diminished because of my association with this project."

In the introduction to *Women in American Architecture* (1977), Torre writes about prevailing issues related to being a woman architect. For example, one common comment from men was that there were no

7. Maggie Toy, ed., *The Architect: Women in Contemporary Architecture*.
8. Clare Cooper Marcus, *Iona Dreaming: The Healing Power of Place*, p. 217. Professor Marcus taught for 30 years at the College of Environmental Design, University of California, Berkeley.

great[9] women architects, insinuating that women were not recognized and so not up to the task. I am glad to know that no one can use that excuse anymore. Along with many other awards to women architects since 1977, two women have received the top architectural prize. Even many architects don't know that in 2004 Zaha Hadid (an Iraqi-born British architect) became the first woman laureate to win the Pritzker Architecture Prize—$100,000 and a bronze medallion from the Hyatt Foundation—known as the highest honor in architecture. National Public Radio's Edward Lifson didn't make a big deal of Hadid's gender when he reported the news; he just noted she was the first woman and the 25th architect to win the annual prize since its creation. However, when Hadid won, Clay Risin of the *New Republic* loudly criticized her win, calling it more politically correct than deserving, on the grounds that she hadn't built enough. I read some of this volley and backlash on the Internet.

With these kinds of reactions to highly accomplished females, not to mention all the everyday jabs, setbacks, and missed opportunities experienced by everyday architects, it is not surprising that discussions of gender are often perceived negatively by women—who feel put on the spot, overly scrutinized, or totally dismissed—while men neutrally and naturally continue to see themselves as the norm, the default. I understand that most women would prefer to drop the "woman" in "woman architect" and not dwell on gender; otherwise, they would start calling architects who are male "men architects." But whenever I hear a woman say, "I have never been discriminated against," I think she either is unaware of what discrimination is or feels too embarrassed to admit it. Maybe she has done nothing in architecture to make her stand out as a woman, or perhaps she has stayed within the pseudo-neutral boundaries of the discipline. This is not to say that women don't want

~

9. "Great" is defined by mainstream traditional values, usually based on original-ity, and art-as-object and image-making criteria, rather than on a community's social well-being. It is not widely known, but the California Women in Environmental De-sign (CWED), a short-lived organization (1990–1994) seeded from the Organization of Women Architects, the Association of Women Architects in Los Angeles, and the Women in Architecture of San Diego, used a custom nomography to come up with an innovative evaluation graph to judge architectural values much differently than is typi-cally done. Karen Van Dorn published the evaluation nomography in February 1991 after it was presented at the CWED 1991 conference, which I attended. It is listed at the International Archive of Women Architects as record MS-1990-059.

to be appreciated and acknowledged for what they do at work. Take the renowned architect Denise Scott Brown, who felt rightly slighted at not being recognized for work done in partnership with her husband, Robert Venturi. Apparently, even after her husband wrote to the media, insisting that they highlight her full contribution, writers continued to underscore the firm's work as his. And so did the Pritzer Architecture Prize committee in 1991, when they awarded their prize only to Robert Venturi, although Denise Scott Brown had been his architectural partner since 1968.[10]

Try as they may to downplay the fact that they are female, women architects continue to encounter professional hindrances in a variety of direct and indirect ways. For instance, a woman architect is often asked to play a subordinate role, designing only the kitchen or calling-out colors, rather than designing entire projects. I personally didn't use the strategy of deflecting my femaleness, femininity, or feminist concerns during my career. Although I will never know how much my authentic overt behavior helped or slowed my success, I do believe I lived my values as I saw them. I didn't see my female identity in conflict with my way of acknowledging the importance of equity for women; yet the friction of discrimination definitely impaired my professional growth and satisfaction. As much as I wanted to progress up the career ladder and enjoy recognition for my achievements, I also wanted to improve things for women in general, retain my feminine self, and be a good single parent. My mother was aware of these issues and lived her life as independently as possible, but she was also quiet about sexism, so I had little guidance for accomplishing these goals. Creative trial and error worked some of the time. Thirty years ago, when I felt that I was making satisfactory headway, I purposely shared my struggles and triumphs openly with my daughter, in the hope that my road map could serve as a reference for her own journey.

Not long ago, Rachel, a younger architect and OWA member, said to me, "Wendy, you were a trailblazer!" I was genuinely taken aback. It had never occurred to me to use that phrase. I never thought of myself as a trailblazer, since I was among other colleagues in the Organization of Women Architects and Design Professionals who also were keen on making it in a man's world by supporting one another, filtering out what we felt was sexism, and working together

10. Alice T. Friedman, *Women and the Making of the Modern House: A Social and Architectural History,* p. 207.

on whatever we could improve. In looking back, I now realize we were on the right trail. We were enthusiastically trimming away at the obstacles and clipping blatant barriers, without paying much attention to our path's direction or how much wider the path needed to be enlarged.

Today we know more about that trail because of dedicated researchers (usually female) scouting latent sources, drilling for details, and investigating the early history of women architects. They have provided us with books from the United States (1977,[11] 2008,[12] 2010[13]), Finland (1983),[14] Germany and beyond (1987),[15] New Zealand and Australia (2002),[16] Canada (2000[17] and 2008[18]), the United Kingdom (2003),[19] and France (2010).[20] Note that these newly published histories provide a solid and permanent foundation for current students who want to understand the past, strengthening them as they prepare to continue the struggle. The bulk of this noteworthy and supportive history was unfortunately not available during my education, but I enjoy reading about it, even at this relatively senior point in my career. The international range of these historical facts helps us to realize that despite so much blazing, remarkable women still have to cope with many of the same social obstacles, as well as newly understood systemic hurdles, on the trail today.

Perhaps we need a shortcut, as the existing trail resists clearing.

History helps, but gender difference is much more than women standing on a broad historical foundation, mimicking masculine savvy or overriding anxiety rooted in ancient cultural structure. There is more.

11. Susana Torre, ed., *Women in American Architecture: A Historic and Contemporary Perspective*.

12. Sarah Allaback, *The First American Women Architects*.

13. Inge Schaefer Horton, *Early Women Architects of the San Francisco Bay Area: The Lives and Work of Fifty Professionals 1890–1951*.

14. Museum of Finnish Architecture, *Profiles: Pioneering Women Architects from Finland*.

15. Union Internationale de Femmes Architects, German Chapter, *The History of Women Architects Catalogue: A First Survey Starting in the 20th Century* (1987).

16. Julie Willis and Bronwyn Hanna, *Women Architects in Australia: 1900–1950*.

17. Annmarie Adams and Peta Tancred, *Designing Women: Gender and the Architectural Profession*.

18. Joan Grierson, *For the Record: The First Women in Canadian Architecture*.

19. Brenda Martin and Penny Sparke, eds., *Women's Places: Architecture and Design, 1860–1960*.

20. Meredith L. Clausen, "The École des Beaux-Arts," pp. 153–161.

What I want to make clear is that the feminine gender difference does not mean women are *inferior*; however, it might mean we *all* need to work fewer hours and redefine childrearing norms and sex roles in the family. It might also mean increasing social dimensions and underlining values within the profession and the built environment.

In particular, the issue of "long" and "inflexible or family unfriendly working hours" may be a specific roadblock for women, especially in an age when nuclear families (the man works and the woman is a homemaker) make up only 15 percent of current American families; the others are nontraditional households (two working parents or single working parents, for example). The US Census Bureau in November 2009 noted that in 2007 there were approximately 13.7 million single parents in the United States, and those parents were responsible for raising 21.8 million children (approximately 26 percent of children under 21 in the United States today). Also of note is that almost 80 percent of single parents work part time or full time and that in 2011, the number of workingwomen outnumbered workingmen.

There is evidence that architecture enjoys a special place in this area of discrimination. Consider that *two out of five architects* work more than 40 hours a week, while *only one out of four of all other working males and females* work more than 40 hours a week.[21] Other professions also work long hours; however, this statistic is alarming, as it compares the tiny profession of architecture with *all* other types of workers. The excessively long hours that architects work, whether out of habit or peer pressure, strike me as unhealthy. Is this a distribution problem? Two senior women architects working for Kaiser Permanente told me separately that they each worked 50 hours a week. When I asked why, they both said they "need to." I don't think they were getting double pay for overtime. Maybe this is a cultural trait of that particular corporation, but I don't see why—the work is constant and there should be limits. I see this as a problem with management assuming that employees should absorb any overload rather than management taking responsibility for workload scheduling. Students, interns, and young architects say online in their blogs that 70-hour workweeks are too long. Where will work compulsiveness stop? There needs to be a differentiation between being committed to and being submerged in architecture. As Chinese medicine reminds us, balance requires constant attention and adjustment.

~

21. Blythe Camenson, *Career in Architecture*.

At the time of this writing, I estimate that 28,000 American women practice architecture. This number includes both registered architects and those who have graduated from architectural school and are not registered. Yet, the structure of work has not changed much since when I started working in 1973, even in progressive San Francisco, where there is a high percentage of both male and female architects. Childcare is still difficult; discrimination against young women who might have children exists; employment interviewers still ask young women if they are married (even though the question is illegal); women architects earn less than men; and senior women consistently experience a lack of rewarding projects, high positions, and recognition for their contributions.

It is rewarding for me to see, and I loudly applaud, the increasing yet still thin body of publications from professors, feminist critics, and architectural theorists looking to better understand the modern role of gender in architecture. A number of anthologies come to mind: in 1989, *Architecture: A Place for Woman*;[22] in the 1990s: *The Sex of Architecture*[23] (1996), *Architecture and Feminism*[24] (1996), *Reconstructing Architecture: Critical Discourses and Social Practices*[25] (1996), *The Architect: Reconstructing Her Practice*[26] (1998), and *Design and Feminism: Re-vision Spaces, Places, and Everyday Things*[27] (1999). Some of the accounts in these books are deemed classics, such as the one by architect Denise Scott Brown, who admitted in 1989 that, for her, "the discrimination continues at the rate of about one incident a day." She also wrote, in her contribution to *Architecture: A Place for Women* that she had written an article in 1975 but decided against publishing it because she feared that exposing "the strong sentiments on feminism in the world of architecture would bring a hostile reception, which could hurt my career and the prospects of my firm."[28] I look forward to reading a new

~

22. Ellen Perry Berkeley ed., and McQuaid, Matilda assoc. ed., *Architecture: A Place for Women*.

23. Diana Agrest, Patricia Conway, and Leslie Weisman, *The Sex of Architecture*.

24. Debra Coleman, Ann Danze, and Carol Henderson, eds., *Architecture and Feminism*.

25. Thomas A. Dutton and Lian Hurst Mann, eds., *Reconstructing Architecture: Critical Discourses and Social Practices*.

26. Francesca Hughes, ed., *The Architect: Reconstructing Her Practice*.

27. Joan Rothschild, ed., *Design and Feminism: Re-visioning Spaces, Places, and Everyday Things*.

28. Denise Scott Brown, "Room at the Top? Sexism and the Star System in Architecture," in *Architecture: A Place for Women*, pp. 237–46.

collection, boldly titled, *Architecture: A Woman's Profession*. According to editor Tanja Kullack, "This is a reference book, a 'tool' for the everyday application of young architects; inspiring, optimistic, and sometimes subversive."[29]

Of course, architecture isn't the only profession missing the intrinsic and full contribution of women; patriarchy in the family and sexism in the workplace grip the cultural substrata of most societies. I checked online under science, engineering, business, accounting, medicine, and law; every category expressed substantive claims by women of mistreatment, discrimination, and frustration. One woman in broadcasting reminds us that the men consistently get more money than the women, even when two newscasters anchor the same program. I had no idea; they looked equally important on the screen.

But now that the statistics in architecture have finally been collected, there is clear evidence of the seriousness of existing professional impediments for committed women and other groups.[30] Scholars have sorted through statistics reflecting the tangles of discrimination, amazing the establishment with concrete facts about the inequity that previously was noted by a few journalists but otherwise whispered about among women in break rooms and within private feminist gatherings. Women and nonwhite males have suggested changes, but actual change is rare. Traditional organizations like the American Institute of Architects (AIA) in the United States, the Royal Institute of British Architects (RIBA) in the United Kingdom, and more recently the Royal Architectural Institute of Canada have been challenged about their structural and behavioral discrepancies, but they don't appear to consider addressing these issues as a priority. The most famous study to expose the seriousness of the problem (2003) documented the alarming number of women architects leaving the profession in the United Kingdom.[31] The reasons given for these professional departures tended to be a combination of a number of factors and/or a "final straw" moment. Some of the key complaints:

---

29. Tanja Kullack, ed., *Architecture: A Woman's Profession*.

30. Kathryn Anthony, *Designing for Diversity: Gender, Race, and Ethnicity in the Architectural Profession*.

31. Ann De Graft-Johnson, Sandra Manley, and Clara Greed, *Why do women leave architecture? Research into the retention of women in architectural practice*.

- Low pay
- Unequal pay
- Long working hours
- Inflexible and/or family-unfriendly working hours
- Sidelining
- Limited areas of work
- Glass ceiling
- Stressful working conditions
- Protective paternalism preventing development of experience
- More job satisfaction elsewhere

There was little evidence that women left because they were incompetent designers or because they no longer wanted to be architects.[32] This gap between the number of women educated in architecture and the number happily employed in architecture continues to be significant. What a heartbreaker for women!

Women's issues are considered part of the larger category of social issues whose cultural force has been dramatically declining for the last 30 years. Social architecture, as compared with art-as-object architecture and science architecture, also suffers from this general political turn away from addressing social ills and from incorporating democracy into the making of place. Now the focus is on capitalistic concerns, such as speculative office buildings for renting space, the corporate image making of skyscrapers, and the warehouse mentality of box stores—all showing little concern for the character, well-being, and livability of place for observers and users. Add to the downturn in social concern the stigma that *anything* having to do with women is considered by men (and women) as *women's work* and therefore less valuable, and you have a trend influencing many women to focus their efforts on new technology, green buildings, teaching, or high-end residential—areas of architecture where gender is less likely to surface as a stumbling block for them.

Henry Frost, teacher at the Cambridge School of Architecture and Landscape Architecture from 1917 to 1942, indicated that women's concerns for the social values in architecture have been evident for a long time. In 1941, he wrote in a letter to a friend about his female students:

---

32. Miragestudio7 March 2010 online summary of above study shows that this study is still being summarized and referenced.

She thinks clearly, reasons well, and is interested in housing rather than houses; in community centers for the masses rather than in neighborhood clubs for the elect; in regional planning more than in estate planning; in social aspects of the profession more than private commissions.... Her interest in her profession embraces its social and human implications.[33]

It appears that women students of 1941 held some of the same concerns I dwell on in 2011.

Unyieldingly, I hang on to the hope that groups like the Organization of Women Architects will play a relevant role in working out solutions to concerns for women in the designed world. In spite of my experience that women are often shunned as complainers if we bring up concerns and problems with the status quo of gender and architecture, I believe that many women (and some men) architects today sympathize with these issues, but too often social values and concerns have been repressed.

I am convinced that from the inception of architecture to current times, everyday women architects (like myself) have been forced to practice their chosen profession with only one hand, while their other hand holds the barrage of discriminating behaviors at bay. This is my premise as I review the dust of my career path, wondering, how do we free up that hand—kept so busy shielding us from sexist swats—for more productive concerns, like expressing cultural issues in the built world?

Since women scholars are now writing more and more about the inherent mutual influence of cultural values (including gender) and the built world, I feel the time is right to launch a call addressing these cultural issues in our practice without the fear of being belittled, ignored, or made invisible by discrimination. As I observe and analyze how the architectural profession has limited others and me, I am emboldened to reflect on and expose unnecessary flaws. With adequate hindsight, I feel quite sure that had I been free of the major constraints of sexism (and *had I known then what I know now*), I would have focused my work, from an evolving feminist perspective, on building design and

___

33. Doris Cole, *From Tipi to Skyscraper: A History of Women in Architecture,* p. 97. Note that all of chapter 4 is devoted to the Cambridge School, where Frost was a great mentor and advocate of women learning architecture and going on to practice. Cole bemoans the loss of such a champion of women architects, still missing 30 years after the school was forced to merge into Harvard's architecture program in 1942. Now, another 40 years later, I would add that we still lack our champions in 2011.

dialogue, concentrating on instilling progressive cultural values, including women's issues, in our workplaces and livable spaces. I believe that many others might also want to incorporate more deliberately the new scholarly findings about how social equity can be better understood and expressed in our design of both everyday and landmark spaces and places.

Therefore, combining my career experience with my values of social justice and dignity, I envision a new approach to making place. I can imagine a practice that respects the essence and quality of architecture, yet at the same time is slightly removed from the discipline, tradition, and discrimination of the profession—a practice, guild, or association, constructed outside the institutionalism of the profession as we know it. I call it *placitecture*.

I envision a more democratic workplace with structural elements, managerial policies, and a working atmosphere without the injustice and anxiety because of physical differences. I think of a more gender-sensitive and socially aware workplace, in tune with one's whole life—not structured as if everyone had lots of money, a wife, or servants, and not structured around the power of privilege or based on the privilege of concentrated power.

In *The Architect: Reconstructing Her Practice*, Francesca Hughes extols the virtues of women architects' dual position in the profession, both on the inside, as architects, and on the outside, as women. She has no problem asserting that women could make a special and particular contribution to architecture while at the same time being capable of fully practicing architecture as men do. "It is precisely this diversity, this ability to be central and marginal *simultaneously* that will allow women to expand the territory of architecture."[34]

I remember hearing in management classes that innovation comes from the fringes; from my own experience, I know this to be true, and I still feel hopeful about the possibilities that those on the "outside" will fire up enough energy to spin open opportunities for the changes I can imagine.

In placitecture, I suggest not that we replace masculinity with femininity; my intent is to explore, integrate, and value both critically and contextually. I think that facing sex-role issues in society will help individuals to better craft their whole lives. Of course, rearranging the twisting threads of pressures and practices concerning culture, gender,

34. Francesca Hughes, ed., *The Architect: Reconstructing Her Practice*, p. xv.

and architecture is an incredible design problem of its own. But this is a task certainly worthy of our problem-solving skills and creative talents. The work of placitects would be a cocktail of evaluation, planning, social science, ethics, design, and research—all mixed carefully to make culturally radiant places. Our defini-tion of culture can include many variables, such as how we respect nature and beauty,[35] as well as how we deal with the density and inequity of earning power or status connected to the making of place.

The binding, container, or framework holding together the dimensions of placitecture is still open for discussion, definition, and development. My idea is to find some way to bring together the scattered existing efforts to preserve character of place, nature of place, history of place, vitality of place, democracy of place, and even size sensibility of place, while at the same time inserting new ways of expressing fairness and inclusion into humankind's drive to cover the natural world with our made places.

Could women architects, clients, and users enamored with place be ripe to create a new influential force? Why keep butting heads against a wall that doesn't give? I now believe we must investigate beyond the initial attraction of the word *architect* to clearly define what architectural activities we want to spend our time on. Making computer details for big-box stores or finding an image for speculative office space doesn't seem that interesting to me, but many architects are doing just that for not much money.

Upon meeting architectural PhD student Alexander Ja Yeun Lee at the "Death + Life of Social Factors" conference this year,[36] I was struck by the realization that she was redefining what her role as architect might be through her exploration of emergency housing, especially timely in her homeland of New Zealand as it recovers from earthquakes. She spoke to the social dimension of memories that crumbled

35. In *Architecture and Beauty: Conversations with Architects about a Troubled Relationship*, Yael Reisner includes the following in her class abstract at the AA School of Architecture in London: "Personal expression is a reflection of one's culture and, architecturally, a visual discrimination that comments on a broader, collective cultural spectrum. It is through culture that architectural poetics are evolving. The aesthetic capacity of architecture is charged by visual qualities that might evoke emotions in people. This is when beauty comes into the conversation." (On Line, July 2011).

36. "The Death + Life of Social Factors," conference at the College of Environmental Design, University of California, Berkeley, May 2011.

with the physical structures in the city of Christchurch, and also, she took a critical look at the transition housing provided to the earthquake victims. There is much to be done around the world that placitects can put their mind to, whether they are working with the United Nations, nonprofit organizations, or governments at all levels interested in including the richness of their culture in their built places.[37]

We live in a time when social values could be a part of professional conversations with the same abundant flair that fashion designers use to tag clothing. I can imagine devising a means of measurement to ensure transparency in building design and land use—a transparency similar to what we see for coffee growers, with the use of fair trade stickers, building products with sustainability ratings, and financial investments with social criteria.

In ten years, placitecture may be a vibrant and rewarding new stream of study and practice. This year may be the right year for those swimming so hard against the existing current—and using so much energy to stay in the mainstream—to consider a move to less-traveled waters, to the innovative shores of social awareness and responsibility. We need thinkers, writers, and placitects to blaze the path of placitecture so that the making of place will include contemporary and complex values of *more* social justice, planet peacefulness, respect for nature, diversity in history, ethical distribution of resources, and land conservation stewardship—at all levels—from the corner of a city block to the patterns of buildings claiming our natural geography.

Since I know much more now than I could have known then, if I were starting out today, placitecture would certainly be my focus because I remain enamored with place … and place-making needs plenty of attention.

37. Anthony Ward, "The Suppression of the Social in Design: Architecture as War" in Thomas A. Dutton and Lian Hurst Mann, eds., *Reconstructing Architecture*, pp. 59–65.

Selected Bibliography

Adam, Peter. *Eileen Gray: Architect/Designer.* New York: Abrams, 1987.

Adams, Annmarie, and Peta Tancred. *Designing Women: Gender and the Architectural Profession.* Toronto: University of Toronto Press, 2000.

Agrest, Diana, Patricia Conway, and Leslie Kanes Weisman, eds. *The Sex of Architecture.* New York: Harry N. Abrams, Inc., 1996.

Ahrentzez, Sherry. "The F Word in Architecture: Feminist Analysis in/of/for Architecture." In *Reconstructing Architecture: Critical Discourses and Social Practices.* Edited by Thomas A. Dutton and Lian Hurst Mann, Minneapolis, MN: University of Minnesota Press, 1996.

Allaback, Sarah. *The First American Women Architects.* Urbana, IL: University of Illinois Press, 2008.

American Institute of Architects. "That Exceptional One: Women in American Architecture 1888–1988." Exhibition, 1988.

Anthony, Kathryn H. *Designing for Diversity: Gender, Race, and Ethnicity in the Architectural Profession.* Urbana, IL: University of Illinois Press, 2001.

Barber, Elizabeth Wayland. *Women's Work: The First 20,000 Years: Women, Cloth, and Society in Early Times.* New York: W. W. Norton & Company, 1995.

Berkeley, Ellen Perry. "Women in Architecture." *Architectural Forum* (September 1972): 46–53.

Berkeley, Ellen Perry, ed., and Matilda McQuaid, assoc. ed. *Architecture: A Place for Women.* Washington DC: Smithsonian Institution Press, 1989.

Betsky, Aaron. *Building Sex: Men, Women, Architecture, and the Construction of Sexuality.* New York: William Morrow and Co., 1995.

Boutelle, Sara Holmes. *Julia Morgan, Architect.* New York: Abbeville Press, 1988.

Bullock, Susan. *Women and Work.* London: Zed Books, 1994.

Camenson, Blythe. *Career in Architecture.* London: McGraw Hill, 2008.

Carter, Morris. *Isabella Stewart Gardner and Fenway Court.* Boston: Trustees of the Isabella Stewart Gardner Museum, 1971.

Clausen, Meredith L. "The École des Beaux-Arts: Toward a Gendered History." Society of Architectural Historians, *Journal of the Society of Architectural Historians* 69:2 (June 2010): 153–161.

Cole, Doris. *Candid Reflections: Letters from Women Architects*, 1970 & 2000. New York: Midmarch Art Press, 2007.

———. *Eleanor Raymond, Architect.* Philadelphia: Art Alliance Press, 1981.

———. *From Tipi to Skyscraper: A History of Women in Architecture.* Boston: i press, 1973.

Coleman, Debra, Ann Danze, and Carol Henderson, eds. *Architecture and Feminism.* New York, N.Y.: Princeton Architectural Press, 1996.

De Graft-Johnson, Ann, Sandra Manley, and Clara Greed. *Why do women leave architecture? Research into the retention of women in architectural practice.* Bristol, England: Royal Institute of British Architects, University of West of England, 2003.

Doumato, Lamia. *Architecture and Women: A Bibliography.* New York: Garland Publishing, 1988.

Drinkwater, Sheryl, and Kristina Raupach, eds. *Women's Work: Architecture + Design.* San Francisco: Organization of Women Architects and Design Professionals, 1991.

Dutton, Thomas A., and Lian Hurst Mann, eds. *Reconstructing Architecture: Critical Discourses and Social Practices.* Minneapolis, MN: University of Minnesota Press, 1996.

Feuerstein, Marcia Fae, assisted by Dawn Bushnaq. "An Interview with Susana Torre." In *The Reflective Practitioner.* Edited by Paul Knox. Blacksburg, VA: University of Virginia, Spring 2002.

Firestone, Shulamith. *The Dialectic of Sex: The Case for Feminist Revolution.* New York: Bantam, 1970.

Friedman, Alice T. *Women and the Making of the Modern House: A Social and Architectural History.* New York: Harry N. Abrams, 1998.

Grattan, Virginia L. *Mary Colter: Builder Upon the Red Earth*. Flagstaff, AZ: Northland Press, 1980.

Grierson, Joan. *For the Record: The First Women in Canadian Architecture*. 2008. Kindle edition.

Griffin, Marion Mahony. *The Magic of America: Electronic Edition*. The Art Institute of Chicago, 2007. http://artic.edu/magicofamerica.

Gruskin, Nancy. *Designing Woman: Writing about Eleanor Raymond*. PhD dissertation, Boston University Department of Art History, 1998. http://escholarship.org, 146–162.

Hanna, Bronwyn. "Australia's Early Women Architects: Milestones and Achievements." *Fabrications* 12:1 (June 2002): 27–57.

Hayden, Dolores. *The Power of Place: Urban Landscapes as Public History*. Cambridge, MA: MIT Press, 1997.

Heilbrun, Carolyn G. *Writing a Woman's Life*. New York: W. W. Norton & Co., 2008.

Hesse–Biber, Sharlene, and Gregg Lee Carter. *Working Women in America: Split Dreams*. 2nd ed. New York: Oxford University Press, 2004.

Horton, Inge. "Young Ladies with T-Squares—Early Women in Architecture at the University of California at Berkeley." In *Design on the Edge: A Century of Teaching Architecture at the University of California, Berkeley, 1903–2003*. Berkeley: College of Environmental Design, University of California, February 2010.

Horton, Inge Schaefer. *Early Women Architects of the San Francisco Bay Area: The Lives and Work of Fifty Professionals, 1890–1951*, Jefferson, NC: McFarland & Co., 2010.

Hughes, Francesca, ed. *The Architect: Reconstructing Her Practice*. Cambridge, MA: MIT Press, 1998.

Ingraham, Catherine. *Architecture and the Burdens of Linearity*. New Haven, CT: Yale University Press, 1998.

Kaplan, Victoria. *Structural Inequality: Black Architects in the United States*. Landham, MD: Rowman & Littlefield Publishing Group, 2006.

Kilbourn, J. P. *One Woman's Unique Architectural Journey: The Life and Times of Mary Alice Hutchins*. Portland, OR: J. P. Kilbourn, 1999.

Krebs, Nina Boyd. *Changing Woman: Changing Work*. Denver, CO: Macmurray & Beck Communication, 1993.

Kullack, Tanja, ed. *Architecture: A Woman's Profession*. Berlin: JOVIS Publishing, 2011.

Leach, Neil, ed. *Rethinking Architecture: A Reader in Cultural Theory*. New York: Routledge, 1997.

Lin, Maya Ying. *Boundaries*. New York: Simon & Schuster, 2000.

Loden, Marilyn. *Feminine Leadership, or How to Succeed in Business Without Being One of the Boys.* New York: Times Books, 1985.

Lorenz, Clare. *Women in Architecture: A Contemporary Perspective.* London: Trefoil Books Ltd., 1990.

Lunneborg, Patricia. *Women Changing Work.* New York: Bergin & Garvey, 1990.

Marcus, Clare Cooper, *Iona Dreaming: The Healing Power of Place.* Berkeley: University of California College of Environmental Design, 2010.

Martin, Brenda, and Penny Sparke, eds. *Women's Places: Architecture and Design, 1860–1960.* London: Routledge, 2003.

Martin, Rochelle. *The Difficult Path: Women in the Architecture Profession.* PhD dissertation, University of Michigan. Information Service, University Microfilms International, 1–24, 121–45, 1986.

Matsuzaki, Eva. PP/FRAIC, Royal Architectural Institute of Canada, Consultations & Roundtables on Women in Architecture in Canada, December 2003.

Metz, Don. *Confessions of a Country Architect.* Piermont, NH: Bunker Hill Publishing, 2007.

Mitchell, Melvin L. *The Crisis of the African-American Architect: Conflicting Cultures of Architecture and (Black) Power.* San Jose, CA: Writer's Club Press, 2001; 2nd ed., New York: Writers' Advantage, 2003.

Museum of Finnish Architecture. *Profiles: Pioneering Women Architects from Finland.* Helsinki, 1983.

Nye, Joseph S. Jr. *The Powers to Lead.* London: Oxford University Press, 2008.

Perriand, Charlotte. *Un Art de Vivre: Charlotte Perriand* (for a Paris Musée des Arts Decoratifs exhibition of Perriand's work, February 5 to April 1, 1985).

Pinet, Celine, and Kimberly Devlin, eds. *THREADS: Insights by Women Architects.* Milwaukee, WI: Center for Architecture and Urban Planning Research, University of Wisconsin, 1991.

Pregliasco, Janice. "The Life and Work of Marion Mahony Griffin." *Museum Studies*, the Art Institute of Chicago 21:2 (1995): 164–181. http://www.jstor.org/pss/4102823.

Reisner, Yael. *Architecture and Beauty: Conversations with Architects about a Troubled Relationship.* Hoboken, NJ: Wiley, 2010.

Rothschild, Joan, ed. *Design and Feminism: Re-visioning Spaces, Places, and Everyday Things.* New Brunswick, NJ: Rutgers University Press, 1999.

Schlain, Leonard. *Sex, Time, and Power: How Women's Sexuality Shaped Human Evolution.* New York: Viking Adult, 2003.

Seabrook, John. "The Abstractionist: Zaha Hadid's unfettered inventions." *The New Yorker* (December 21, 2009): 112–24.

Searing, Helen. *Equal Partners: Men and Women Principals in Contemporary Architectural Practice.* Samuel P. Harn Museum of Art, Smith College, January 1998.

Stevens, Garry. "How the Invisible Stays That Way: Sociology on Architects Thresholds." (1998): 54–6. http://www.archsoc.com.

Thornton, Sally Bullard. *Daring to Dream: The Life of Hazel Wood Waterman (1865–1948).* San Diego: San Diego Historical Society, 1987.

Torre, Susana, ed. *Women in American Architecture: A Historic and Contemporary Perspective* (publication and exhibition organized by the Architectural League of New York through its Archive of Women in Architecture), 1977.

Toy, Maggie, ed. *The Architect: Women in Contemporary Architecture.* New York: Watson-Guptill, 2001.

Van Slyck, Abigail A. "Women in Architecture and the Problems of Biography." *Design Book Review* 25 (1992): 18–20.

Ward, Anthony. "The Suppression of the Social in Design: Architecture as War." In *Reconstructing Architecture: Critical Discourses and Social Practices.* Edited by Thomas A. Dutton and Lian Hurst Mann. Minneapolis, MN: University of Minnesota Press, 1996.

Weisman, Leslie Kanes. *Discrimination by Design: A Feminist Critique of the Man-made Environment.* Urbana, IL: University of Illinois Press, 1992.

Welch, Diane Y. *Lilian J. Rice: Architect of Rancho Santa Fe, California.* Atglen, PA: Schiffer Publishing, 2010.

Weltge-Wortmann, Sigrid. *Bauhaus Textiles: Women Artists and Weaving Workshop.* London: Thames & Hudson, April 1998.

Williamson, Roxanne Kuter. *American Architects and the Mechanics of Fame.* Austin: University of Texas Press, 1991.

Willis, Beverley. *Invisible Image: The Silent Language of Architecture.* Washington DC: National Building Museum, 1997.

Willis, Julie, and Bronwyn Hanna. *Women Architects in Australia: 1900–1950.* Canberra: Royal Australian Institute of Architects, 2001.

Wykoff, Marguerite. "The Outlook for Women in Architecture and Engineering." *Zapoleon Bulletin of the Women's Bureau* (1948): 223–5.

Acknowledgments

Thanks to Inge Schaefer Horton, author of *Early Women Architects of the San Francisco Bay Area: The Lives and Work of Fifty Professionals, 1890–1951*, who shared with me her enthusiasm for research and her unswerving drive to see her topic in print, better understood, and discussed widely. Her generous mentoring was instrumental in my long writing journey. Also, she instilled in me an appreciation for history and herstory, something I ignored in my younger years when the future seemed like the only horizon.

Thanks to the late Milka Bliznakov, founder of the International Archive of Women in Architecture (IAWA), who, since our meeting in 1988, encouraged me and other women in architecture to write down our history for the world to know about our concerns and contributions.

Thanks to Lisa Zuré, singer/songwriter and my developmental editor and principal line editor over many drafts. Her wise, womanly, and worldly manner kept me working hard and enjoying the rewards and fruits of profound collaboration.

Thanks to Ellen Perry Berkeley, architectural journalist, writer, and editor, who read my manuscript thoroughly and gifted me with expert professional advice and friendly support over many years.

Thanks to Lorri Ungaretti, my copy editor, for her prompt responses, helpful changes, and excellent suggestions.

Thanks to Elissa Rabellino, my proof reading editor, who skillfully tucked into the fiber of my text the wildest of loose ends.

Thanks to Elizabeth Fishel, longtime author and leader of the Wednesday Writers' Workshops in Oakland, California, where this project started to bud.

Thanks to the early members of the Organization of Women Architects and Design Professionals for the joy we shared integrating our first feminist ideas with our organizational structure, behavior, and ideals.

Thanks to longtime friends Casimir Lesiak, Robin Slovak, Ase Marstrander, Anne Foreman, Dory Bruce, Lynn Morris, and Patty Adams, as well as to Lee and Linc Taiz, who supported my goals, motives, and efforts during many writing seasons.

Thanks to casual acquaintances for saying, "That's interesting" or "I would like to read your book."

Thanks to Irene Rietschel, my book designer, who gave me the privilege of experiencing the unique partnership between authors and book designers. Her bold, artistic, and conscientious approach to work delighted me from cover to cover.

And

Thanks to you, my readers, for giving me the benefit of the doubt—page after page—for what may have fallen between the lines of my narrative.

Photo Courtesies and Credits

Chanette Manso (cover photo, page 4)

Curt Holder (photos on pages 72, 74, 80, 90)
David A. Friedman (photo at top of page 166)
Jeremiah Bragstad (photo on page 167)
Mathew Lapota and Associates (photos on pages 201, 227)
Inge Horton (photo at top of page 230)
Earl Kai Chann Associates Ltd. (photos on pages 234, 235)
Dean Freedman (photos on pages 277, 278)
Greg Hospelhorn (photos on pages 292, 293, 300, 315, 339)
Michael O'Callaghan (photo on page 320)
Manso-Manso (photo on page 321)
Dory Bruce (photo on page 347)
Bryant Anderson (author photos)

About the Author

Wendy Bertrand has been a mother since 1966 and a registered California architect since 1978. She graduated from the University of California, Berkeley with a bachelor of architecture (1971), and with a master of architecture (1972) after study in France at the École des Beaux Arts in Aix-en-Provence (1964) and in Montpellier (1965). She divides her time between her city house in San Francisco and her country cabin in Del Norte County, and frequently visits southern France, where her daughter, Chanette Manso, is one of the top internationally recognized light painters.

HONG KONG
JAPAN
HAWAII
LA JOLLA
SANTA BARBARA
MONTEREY
PARIS
VENCE
LES CONTAMINES
NICE
PARIS
AIX-EN-PROVENCE
MONTPELLIER
PEKING
CHAMONIX
BERKELEY
SAN FRANCISCO
GASQUET
SAN FRANCISCO
GASQUET
SAN FRANCISCO